André Mastmeyer

Patientenspezifische
Virtual-Reality-Simulationen

Ultraschallgestützte Nadelpunktionen
in atmungsbewegten virtuellen Patienten

Patient-Specific
Virtual Reality Simulations

Ultrasound-Guided Needle Punctures
in Breathing Virtual Patients

© 2018 Infinite Science Publishing
         University Press and
         Academic Printing

Imprint of Infinite Science GmbH
Technikzentrum | MFC 1
Maria-Goeppert-Straße 1
23562 Lübeck, Germany

Cover Design and Illustration: Uli Schmidts, metonym
Editorial and Copy Editing:
Institute of Medical Informatics, University of Lübeck and Infinite Science Publishing
Publisher: Infinite Science GmbH, Lübeck, www.infinite-science.de
Printed in Germany, BoD, Norderstedt

1. Auflage 2018
ISBN: 978-3-945954-40-9

Bibliografische Information der Deutschen Nationalbibliothek:
Die Deutsche Nationalbibliothek verzeichnet diese Publikation in der Deutschen Nationalbibliografie; detaillierte bibliografische Daten sind im Internet über http://dnb.d-nb.de abrufbar.

Author

PD Dr. André Mastmeyer
Institute of Medical Informatics
University of Lübeck
E-mail: mastmeyer@imi.uni-luebeck.de

Series Editor

Heinz Handels
Institute of Medical Informatics
University of Lübeck

**Research Series of the
Institute of Medical Informatics
University of Lübeck**

The book series includes research foci of the Institute of Medical Informatics at the University of Lübeck, Germany, which is working on Medical Image Computing, Virtual Reality Simulations for Medical Training and Planning, Medical Data Science and eHealth.

André Mastmeyer

Patientenspezifische Virtual-Reality-Simulationen

Ultraschallgestützte Nadelpunktionen
in atmungsbewegten virtuellen Patienten

Forschungsberichte aus dem
Institut für Medizinische Informatik – Band 1

Reihenherausgeber: Heinz Handels

Infinite Science
Publishing

Vorwort

Es ist mir eine besondere Freude, mit dem vorliegenden Buch eine neue Buchreihe aus dem Institut für Medizinische Informatik der Universität zu Lübeck (Direktor: Prof. Dr. rer. nat. habil. Heinz Handels) eröffnen zu können. Der vorliegende erste Band der neuen Buchreihe beinhaltet die Habilitationsschrift von PD Dr. André Mastmeyer, mit der er sich kürzlich für das Fach Medizinische Informatik an der Universität zu Lübeck habilitiert hat.

In seiner Habilitationsarbeit hat sich Herr Mastmeyer mit der personalisierten Virtual-Reality-Simulation von ultraschallgestützten Punktionseingriffen in atembewegten virtuellen Patientenkörpern beschäftigt. Hierbei werden Methoden der Medizinischen Bildverarbeitung, der Medizinischen Visualisierung sowie der Echtzeitsimulation in Kombination eingesetzt, um eine verbesserte, zeitnahe personalisierte Planung und das visuo-haptisch unterstützte Training komplizierter Punktionseingriffe zu ermöglichen. Ausgehend von 3D-Bildfolgen der Patienten, die in der Computertomographie routinemäßig generiert werden, wird zunächst eine weitgehend automatisierte Modellierung der patientenspezifischen Anatomie, krankhafter Gewebeveränderungen und Atembewegungen vorgenommen. Mithilfe neuartiger Methoden des direkten Volumenrenderings für die 4D-Visualisierung und haptische 4D-Interaktion wird danach die realitätsnahe Echtzeitinteraktion in virtuell atmenden Patientenkörpern möglich. Hierzu werden aus 4D-Bilddaten extrahierte, individuelle Bewegungsfelder modelliert und zur realitätsnahen Simulation auch von unregelmäßigen Atembewegungen verwendet. Um die hohen Echtzeitanforderungen erfüllen zu können, wurden optimierte, visuell-haptische Algorithmen entwickelt und hochgradig parallelisiert auf Grafikkarten mittels CUDA-Programmierung umgesetzt. Der Simulator wurde von medizinischen Experten und Studierenden begleitet und positiv evaluiert.

Das vorliegende Buch eröffnet interessante Einblicke in den Stand der Wissenschaft und die entwickelten Methoden in dem hochinnovativen und sich schnell entwickelnden Forschungsbereich der Virtual-Reality-Simulation in der Medizin. Am Ende findet sich darüber hinaus eine Zusammenstellung von ausgewählten, englischsprachigen Publikationen von PD Dr. André Mastmeyer aus renommierten internationalen Fachjournalen und Tagungs-Proceedings. Diese geben den interessierten Lesern detaillierte Informationen und Erläuterungen zu den vielseitigen methodischen Entwicklungen und Erweiterungen, die in den letzten Jahren am Institut für Medizinische Informatik im Bereich der visuell-haptischen Virtual-Reality-Simulation entwickelt wurden.

Lübeck im Dezember 2017
Prof. Dr. rer. nat. habil. Heinz Handels

Kurzzusammenfassung

Ziel der referierten Arbeiten war, das patientenindividuelle, visuo-haptisch immersive Virtual Reality (VR) Training und die personalisierte, pre-operative räumlich-mentale Planung von ultraschallgestützten Punktionseingriffen GPU-basiert zu ermöglichen. Hierbei galt es den Einfluss realistisch simulierter Atembewegung zu berücksichtigen. Daher wurden einerseits Verfahren zur weitgehend automatischen Segmentierung der punktionsrelevanten Organe und Strukturen in einem neuartigen atlasbasierten Konzept entwickelt [1]. Andererseits wurden innovative, effiziente Algorithmen zur volumenbasierten haptischen und visuellen Simulation und dem direkten Rendering dynamischer Prozesse in partiell segmentierten CT-Daten vorgeschlagen [2]. Ein generischer Patientenatlas wurde zunächst definiert und mittels eines Atlaspersonalisierungsverfahrens [1] zur Segmentierung neuer patientenspezifischer 3D-CT-Bilddaten genutzt. Neben adaptierbaren Organmasken und Formmodellen für Teilbereiche des Bildvolumens stellten die Atlanten lückenfüllende Segmentierungsschätzer basierend auf Transferfunktionen für das visuo-haptische Volumen-Rendering bereit [6, 8]. Die während des patientenindividuellen Virtual Reality Trainings instrumentenbedingt auftretenden Weichteildeformationen wurden mithilfe eines regularisierenden Diffusionsverfahrens für Verschiebungsfelder simuliert, in welches Divergenzen zwischen realen und virtuellen Instrumentkontaktpunkten als Randbedingungen eingingen [2]. Außerdem wurden im Rahmen der publizierten Arbeiten Methoden für die realitätsnahe visuo-haptische VR-Simulation von Atembewegungen in virtuellen Körpermodellen entwickelt [3]. Statische 3D-CT-Bilddatensätze des Patienten wurden dazu mit individuellen 4D-Bewegungsmodellen animiert, die aus 4D-CT-Bildphasen mittels nicht-linearer Registrierungsverfahren sowie auf Basis von linearer Regression gebildet wurden und zur Voxel-bezogenen Beschreibung realistischer Atembewegungen dienten. Die 4D-Bewegungsmodelle wurden erstmals in ein visuo-haptisches VR-Simulations-Framework integriert. Dieses ermöglichte schließlich die benutzergesteuerte Interaktion einer Ultraschallsonde und Punktionsnadel mit dem atmenden virtuellen Körper [5]. Für die effiziente visuelle Darstellung wurden neuartige volumenbasierte 4D-Rendering-Techniken mit atembedingt gekrümmter Strahlverfolgung entwickelt. Durch die Umsetzung der rechenintensiven Algorithmen auf moderner Grafikhardware wurde die Echtzeitfähigkeit der Simulationsalgorithmen gewährleistet. Im Rahmen der Arbeit wurde schließlich ein VR-Simulator für die Beispielanwendung der perkutanen transhepatischen Cholangiodrainage (PTCD) realisiert. Weitere mögliche Anwendungsbereiche sind die patientenindividuelle Planung und das Training von Punktionen für Radiofrequenzablationen unter Atembewegung. Die Methoden wurden in Kooperation mit klinischen Partnern entwickelt und von Medizinstudierenden in einer Benutzerstudie erfolgreich eingesetzt und evaluiert [2]. Potenziell reduziert das pre-operative und personalisierte Training die Anzahl der Nadelrepositionierungen deutlich.
Ergebnisse: Es wurde ein neues effizientes und für die Leberpunktionssimulation optimiertes Modellierungskonzept mit transferfunktionsbasierten und organspezifisch opti-

mierten Methoden für virtuelle Patientenkörper entwickelt [1, 4, 7, 8]. Insgesamt konnte für die notwendige plausible Vollvolumensegmentierung erstmals ein signifikant attraktiverer Modellierungszeitrahmen von zwei bis drei Stunden [1] im Vergleich zu 32 bis 63 Stunden aus [18, 19] erreicht wurden.

Die transferfunktionsbasierte Segmentierung der Füllstrukturen Haut, Weichteile und Knochen ergab vollautomatisch mittlere DICE-Überdeckungskoeffizienten [20] (max. 1,0) von 0,79, 0,97 und 0,83 [1]. Im Methodenkanon der organspezifisch optimierten Methoden für Schlüsselstrukturen wurde zur Multi-Atlassegmentierung (MAS) der Leber eine vollautomatische, verbesserte Methode mit neuer, deutlich beschleunigter Label-Fusion vorgeschlagen [7]. Diese wurde anschließend mit Atlasselektions- und Postprocessing-Schritten optimiert und Cloud-basiert berechenbar formuliert [1]. Sie wurde schließlich anhand von 10 Testpatienten unter Verwendung einer Atlasdatenbank mit 59 Atlanten evaluiert. Es ergab sich eine genaue, sehr präzise und kompetitive [21] Segmentierung der Leber mit einem DICE-Koeffizienten von 0,93±0,01. Die intrahepatischen Strukturen der Blutgefäße wurden in [1] mit DICE-Koeffizienten von 0,51 und die Gallengänge mit 0,48 plausibel und kompetitiv [22] segmentiert.

Im Vergleich zur Benutzung vollsegmentierter [18, 19] Referenzdaten wurde die Kraftausgabe mit kaum wahrnehmbaren mittleren quadratischen Fehlern von 0,07 N sehr gut bewertet. Statistisch bedeutende Fehler ($p <0,05$) wurden bei nur 0,8 % vorher automatisch geplanter Testtrajektorien gefunden. Die mit dem neuartigen Evaluations-Framework [4] ermittelten Resultate wurden erstmals publiziert.

Die visuelle Plausibilität und Echtzeitfähigkeit des Renderings für die stereoskopische Ansicht und die Kontrollbildgebung wurde qualitativ in einer Benutzerstudie und quantitativ mit Bildratenmessungen (Hz) bestätigt. Alle für die ultraschallgestützte Punktion relevanten Visualisierungsmodule lieferten auch im Zusammenspiel Bildraten deutlich oberhalb von 25 Hz auf einer Nvidia GTX 680 GPU-Grafikkarte [2].

Zur Bewertung der Trainingsqualität des Simulators wurde eine Benutzerstudie mit 16 Medizinstudierenden des 10. Semesters durchgeführt. Es wurde hinsichtlich der technischen Umsetzung gutes bis sehr gutes Feedback erreicht. Das Selbstvertrauen der Studienteilnehmer, eine Leberpunktion nach einer einstündigen standardisierten Trainingssitzung durchzuführen, stieg signifikant an ($p <0,01$), was ein sehr positives Licht auf einen möglichen Trainingseffekt wirft [2].

Das vorgestellte VR-Trainings- und Planungssystemkonzept zeigt neue Perspektiven des risikolosen, haptischen und räumlichen Trainings von ultraschallgestützten Nadeleingriffen für Ausbildungszwecke sowie der personalisierten Planung und Interventionsvorbereitung (Case-Preview) auf. Das vorgeschlagene Modellierungskonzept für virtuelle Patientenkörper lässt sich auch auf andere Anwendungsfälle übertragen, indem für neue Zielstrukturen organspezifisch optimierte Methodenbausteine ergänzt werden. Das Simulationskonzept kann in Zukunft auch für therapeutische Nadelinterventionen wie bspw. Ablationen erweitert werden. Der vorgestellte 4D-VR-Simulator hat das Potenzial, aus dem Prototypstadium hinaus in die Ausbildung von Medizinstudierenden sinnvoll einzugehen. Zudem könnte er den interventionellen Mediziner bei der räumlich-mentalen Vorbereitung und Planung für konkret anstehende Eingriffe unterstützen.

Abstract

The aim of the peer reviewed works was to enable GPU based patient-specific, visuo-haptically immersive Virtual Reality (VR) training and the personalized, pre-operative spatial-mental planning of ultrasound-guided needle puncture procedures. Additionally, the influence of realistically simulated respiratory motion was considered. On the one hand, a new atlas-based approach for the mainly automatic segmentation of puncture relevant organs and structures was developed [1]. On the other hand, innovative and efficient algorithms for volume based visuo-haptic simulation and direct rendering of dynamic processes in the partially segmented CT data were proposed [2].

First, a generic patient atlas was defined and used by an atlas personalization method [1] to segment new patient-specific 3D CT image data. Besides adaptable organ masks and shape models for parts of the image volume, gap filling transfer function based segmentation estimators enabled the full volume visuo-haptic rendering [6, 8]. The soft tissue deformations occurring during the patient-specific virtual reality training by instruments were simulated using a diffusion regularization method for displacement fields, in which differences between real and virtual instrument contact points were introduced as boundary conditions [2]. In addition, methods for realistic visuo-haptic VR simulation of respiratory movements in virtual body models were developed [3]. Individual 4D motion models were used to animate static 3D CT patient image data sets. The motion models were built from 4D CT image phases by a nonlinear registration and linear regression process and served as a voxel based description of realistic breathing movements. The 4D motion models were integrated into a visuo-haptic VR simulation framework for the first time. Finally, this allowed for the visuo-haptically controlled interaction of an ultrasonic probe and a puncture needle with the breathing virtual body [5]. For the efficient visual 4D rendering of the animated 3D image data, new volume based 4D image synthesis techniques were developed by casting curved rays bent by the motion field.

By the implementation of computationally intensive algorithms on modern graphics hardware, real-time capability of the simulation algorithms was ensured. This works final outcome is a VR simulator for the sample application of percutaneous transhepatic biliary drainage (PTCD). Other possible applications are patient-specific planning and the training of punctures for radiofrequency ablations under respiratory motion. The methods were developed in cooperation with clinical partners and successfully evaluated by medical students in a user study [2]. Potentially, by the pre-operative and patient-specific training the number of needle repositionings is reduced significantly.

Results: A new efficient and optimized virtual patient modeling concept for liver puncture simulations with transfer function based and organ-specifically optimized methods was developed [1, 4, 7, 8]. Overall, for the necessary and sufficiently plausible full volume segmentation a significantly more attractive modeling time frame of two to three hours [1] compared to 32 to 63 hours [18, 19] was realized.

The transfer function based automatic segmentation of the large volume structures skin, soft tissues and bones revealed mean DICE coefficients [20] (max. 1.0) of 0.79, 0.97 and 0.83 [1]. In the organ-specifically optimized methodology for key structures, a fully automatic multi-atlas segmentation (MAS) was first suggested for the liver. The method was enhanced by a significantly accelerated and favorable label fusion technique [7]. This work was then optimized with atlas selection and postprocessing steps and transferred to a cloud based setup [1]. The method steps were evaluated on 10 test patients using an atlas database with 59 atlases. The results showed a very precise, accurate and competitive [21] segmentation of the liver with a DICE coefficient of 0.93 ± 0.01. The intrahepatic structures were plausibly and competitively [22] segmented with DICE coefficients of 0.51 for blood vessels and the bile ducts with 0.48 [1].

Compared to the use of fully segmented [18, 19] reference data, the force output yielded a hardly noticeable very low mean square error of 0.07 N. Statistically significant errors ($p < 0.05$) were found in 0.8 % of the previously automatically planned test paths, only. The results from the newly proposed evaluation framework [4] were published for the first time.

The visual plausibility and real-time capability of the visualization methods for the stereoscopic view and imaging control were proven in a user study and quantitatively confirmed using frame rate (Hz) measurements. All combined rendering modules for the ultrasound-guided puncture showed frame rates well above 25 Hz on Nvidia GTX 680 GPU hardware [2].

To evaluate the quality of real life user training with the simulator, a study with 16 medical students in their 10th semester term was conducted. The feedback ranged from good to very good in terms of technical implementation. The self-confidence of the participants to perform a real liver biopsy after a one-hour standardized training session, increased significantly ($p < 0.01$), which gives a very positive outlook towards possible training effects [2].

The presented VR training and planning system concept shows new perspectives of risk free, visuo-haptic and spatio-mental training of ultrasound-guided needle interventions as well as the personalized planning and intervention preparation (case preview). The proposed modeling approach for virtual patient bodies can also be applied to other applications. First, new organ-specific optimized methods could be added for new target structures. Second, the simulation concept can be extended for therapeutic interventions such as needle ablations. The presented 4D VR simulator has the potential to help in the training of medical students. It could also assist the physician in the spatio-mental preparation and planning of upcoming real life interventions.

Inhaltsverzeichnis

1 Einleitung und Fragestellung

Im Bereich der Flugpilotenausbildung ist die computergestützte Simulation virtueller Trainingsszenarien bereits etabliert. Die visuo-haptische Simulation chirurgischer Eingriffe im Rahmen von Virtual Reality (VR) Trainings- und Planungssystemen hat in der Medizin in den nächsten Jahren das Potenzial, ein wichtiges kosten- und risikosenkendes Standardwerkzeug in der Ausbildung medizinischer Studierender zu werden [23]. Zudem könnten VR-Trainer den Chirurgen bei der räumlich-mentalen Planung realer Eingriffe mit personalisierten virtuellen Körpermodellen unterstützen.

Das in dieser Arbeit zusammengefasste patientenspezifische VR-Trainingssystemkonzept umfasst als Schwerpunkt erstens Methoden zur patientenindividuellen Patientenkörpermodellierung. Zweitens werden visuo-haptische Darstellungsmethoden für das Feedback an den Bediener unter Berücksichtigung der Weichteildeformation z. B. durch Atmung behandelt. Besonders zwerchfellnahe Punktionen der oberen Leber oder unteren Lunge können stark durch atembedingte Verschiebungen bis zu 5 cm [24] beeinflusst werden und die Nadelnavigation erschweren.

1.1 Motivation

Als medizinisches Anwendungsgebiet wird hier die Nadelpunktion pathologischer Leberveränderungen betrachtet. Der Schwerpunkt liegt dabei auf cholestatisch aufgestauten Gallengängen durch den endoskopischen Zugang behindernde Gallensteine, Tumoren oder Narbenbildung [25]. Die Cholestase wird als Leitsymptom von einer Gelbsucht sowie weiterhin von blassem Stuhl, Anzeichen wie Appetitlosigkeit, Müdigkeit, Juckreiz und Übelkeit begleitet [26]. Fluoroskopisch kann die Krankheit minimal-invasiv durch intravas-

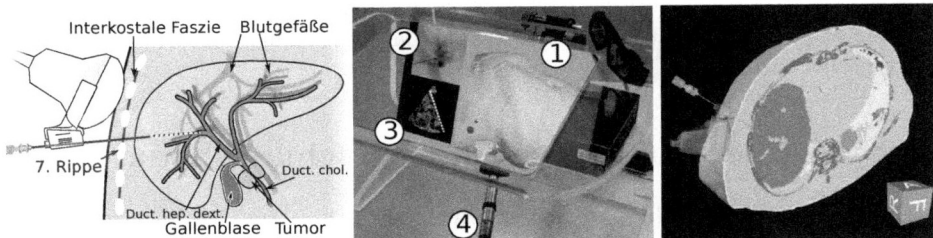

Abbildung 1.1: Simulierte Ultraschall(US)-gestützte Nadelpunktion eines cholestatischen Gallengangs: Links: US-gestützte Nadelpunktion eines cholestatischen Gallengangs. Mitte: Hardwareausstattung mit Stereobrille und halb durchlässigem Spiegel für verbesserte Hand-Auge-Koordination und Benutzerschnittstelle: (1) 3D-Hauptansicht, (2) Fluoroskopiesimulation, (3) Ultraschallansicht mit Ziellinie (gelb) und (4) Nadelsteuerungs- und Kraftausgabegerät. Rechts: 3D-Hauptansicht (1) des Simulators mit Schnitt entlang der US-Ebene und Zielstruktur (grün). Aus [1].

kuläre Kontrastmittelinjektion mit der „Perkutanen Transhepatischen Cholangiografie"
(PTC) dargestellt und durch eine zusätzliche Katheterdrainage („Perkutane Transhepa-
tische Cholangiodrainage", PTCD) des punktierten Gallengefäßes [27, 28] therapiert werden. Beide Eingriffe werden im Folgenden mit PTC/D abgekürzt. Sie sind hauptsächlich
durch die schwierige minimal-invasive Nadelnavigation oftmals zwischen der sechsten und
siebten Rippe zu den aufgestauten Gallengängen definiert. Aktuell werden diese Punktionen häufig durch Ultraschallbildgebung (US) als Navigationshilfe unterstützt (Abb. 1.1,
links) [29, 28].

Ziel der Arbeiten war ein Patientenmodellierungs- und VR-System-Konzept für das patientenspezifische virtuelle Training der Nadelnavigation zu einer ggf. atembewegten Zielstruktur, Methodenbausteine dafür und die prototypische Implementierung und Evaluation wichtiger Teilaspekte des Systems. Hardware, Visualisierungs- und Bedienele-
mente eines adäquaten PTC/D-VR-Trainingssystems sind in Abb. 1.1 (Mitte) dargestellt.

Der Erfolg der Punktion eines Gallengefäßes mit Navigationsunterstützung durch Fluoros-
kopiekontrollbilder (Abb. 1.1, Mitte (2)) wird durch die Ausbreitung des in dem Nadel-
katheters unter Druck vorgehaltenen Kontrastmittels angezeigt. Die mit dieser Kontrollbildgebung schwierige Navigation birgt die Nachteile der zusätzlichen Strahlenbelastung
durch Röntgenkontrollaufnahmen, erhöhter Navigationspräzisionsfehler und Anzahl der
Nadelrepositionierungen [23, 30].

Aus diesem Grund setzen sich in der Nadelnavigation zunehmend US-gestützte Methoden durch. Diese bieten eine erhöhte Genauigkeit und Präzision, die durchschnittliche Anzahl der Nadelrepositionierungen wird vermindert und dienen somit der schnel-
leren Genesung des Patienten [29, 28]. Dabei ist häufig an der Seite des US-Kopfes eine Nadelführungsschiene angebracht (Abb. 1.1, links), deren Verlängerung auf dem US-
Bildmonitor einer Nadelpfadprojektionsline als Zielhilfe entspricht (Abb. 1.1, Mitte (3)).

Die in dieser Arbeit vorgestellten Methoden ermöglichen die visuo-haptische VR-Simulation der Nadeleingriffe unter Fluoroskopiekontrolle und der US-gestützten Navigation bei
atmenden virtuellen Patienten. Die mit dem System erzielbaren Trainingsfortschritte und
Planungseinsichten könnten sowohl dem Studierenden als auch dem chirurgischen Arzt
nutzen. Sie erstrecken sich auf die Darstellung der Anatomie in der Röntgen- und US-
Bildgebung, die Positionierung des US-Kopfes zur optimalen Navigation und das Durchführen der Punktion. Im Rahmen der verfügbaren Hardwareausstattung wird auf eine
möglichst realitätsnahe bzw. plausible visuo-haptische Immersion geachtet [31]. Mit zeiteffizient patientenspezifisch aufbereiteten, atmenden virtuellen Körpermodellen könnte der
Arzt die Effizienz und Effektivität seiner Behandlung zum Wohl des Patienten im Vorfeld
eines Eingriffs optimieren.

1.2 Stand der Forschung und Forschungsbedarf

Systeme der virtuellen Realität werden heutzutage in Lehre, Training und Unterhaltung
eingesetzt [32]. Auch die medizinische Ausbildung und Praxis [33] profitiert von dieser
Entwicklung. Die zunehmende Menge hochauflösender 3D- und 4D-Bilddaten für Diagno-
stik, Therapie- und Operationsplanung sowie neuartige VR-Methoden gestatten zukünftig
den regelmäßigen Einsatz von VR-Systemen im medizinischen Ausbildungsalltag und der
klinischen Praxis. Neuartige hoch immersive visuo-haptische Darstellungstechniken erlau-

ben genauere und präzisere 3D-Interaktionen in virtuellen Körpern mit immer geringeren Ermüdungserscheinungen beim Benutzer [34].

Bisher finden patientenindividuelle VR-Trainingssysteme in der Medizin noch selten praktischen Einsatz. Dies ist unter anderem im aktuell noch erheblichen Zeitaufwand der Datenaufbereitung begründet. Insbesondere die patientenspezifische Segmentierung anatomischer Organe und Strukturen bildet den Hauptzeitanteil in der Vorverarbeitungsprozesskette. Bisher wurde lediglich in ersten prototypischen Studien die Unterstützung der Ausbildung von Medizinern durch VR-Systeme ohne patientenspezifische Körpermodelle untersucht [35, 36, 37, 38].

Die Grundlage der patientenspezifischen VR-Simulation wird durch aktuell aufgenommene 3D- bzw. 4D-CT-Bilddaten des Patienten gebildet. Im Allgemeinen sollte im klinischen Alltag mit geringem Zeitaufwand die semi-automatische Segmentierung der Bilddaten möglich sein. Konventionelle Methoden können ca. 32 bis 63 Stunden Zeitaufwand pro 3D-Bild erfordern [18, 19, 39]. Aus diesem Grund bieten viele aktuelle VR-Systeme oftmals keine Interventionssimulation auf gerade neu akquirierten Patientendaten an. Neben der effizienten Patientenmodellierung ist die visuelle und haptische Darstellung (visuohaptisches Rendering) in dieser Arbeit ein wichtiges Thema.

Keines der aktuell existierenden Systeme bietet bisher Vereinfachungen des notwendigen und sehr zeitaufwendigen Prozesses zur semi-automatischen Segmentierung der Patientenbilddaten an. Die adressierten Strukturen wurden in dieser Arbeit in großvolumige Füllstrukturen, die von der Nadel auf dem Weg zum Ziel passiert werden, oder relevante Schlüssel- oder Risikostrukturen aufgeteilt. Letztere sollen entweder erreicht oder nicht punktiert werden. Für die Füllstrukturen wurden schnelle Echtzeitklassifikatoren vorgestellt, für die akkurat zu segmentierenden Zielstrukturen wurden organspezifisch optimierte Methoden verwendet, die in Organsegmentierungsmasken resultierten, welche den Bildraum partiell ausfüllten.

Im Zwischenraum wurden großvolumige Füllstrukturen wie Luft, Haut, Weichteilgewebe und Knochen in dieser Arbeit durch Transferfunktionsheuristiken in Echtzeit segmentiert. Hochpräzise semiautomatische Methoden für knöcherne Strukturen wurden in [10, 11, 40] vorgestellt. Leider gibt es nur wenig Literatur zu effizienten, automatischen Segmentierung dieser Hintergrundstrukturen, da sie nicht im Zentrum des Interesses der Forschungsgemeinde stehen und oft mit Standardmethoden [41, 39] bearbeitet werden.

Ein Zielorgan, das weitere Zielstrukturen enthält, war in dieser Arbeit die Leber. Es existieren zwei nennenswerte fortlaufende Wettbewerbe zur ihrer Segmentierung. Aktuelle Ergebnisse zur Lebersegmentierung wurden in [42, 21, 43] veröffentlicht, aktuell können abhängig von der jeweils verwendeten Datenbasis DICE-Koeffizienten [20] klar über 0,9 semi-automatisch erzielt werden. Aktuell werden im VISCERAL-Challenge laufend neue Segmentierungsmethoden getestet, aktuelle Bestwerte für die Lebersegmentierung mit vollautomatischen Methoden liegen hier maximal bei einem DICE-Koeffizient von 0,93[1]. Aufgrund ihrer Robustheit bietet sich im Kontext des VR-basierten Trainings von Eingriffen u. a. der multi-atlasbasierte Segmentierungsansatz [44] für die Organgruppe Leber, Milz, Pankreas und Nieren an [42, 21, 45, 46, 47, 48, 49, 50]. Dieser hat durch die robuste Mittelung vieler Segmentierungsschätzungen das Potenzial, unterschiedliche wichtige

---

[1]`http://visceral.eu:8080/register/Leaderboard.xhtml` besucht am 14.5.16 (CT, Liver)

Organe des abdominalen Zielbereichs gleichzeitig robust zu segmentieren und bietet sich auch in dieser Arbeit an.

Die Segmentierung von Gefäßstrukturen allgemein wurde von verschiedenen Autoren untersucht. Meist handelt es sich methodisch gesehen um auf der Analyse lokaler 3D Hessematrizen [51, 52] beruhender Verfahren. Der zum größten Eigenwert gehörende Eigenvektor zeigt die vermutete Verlaufsrichtung des aktuell betrachteten Gefäßasts an und geht in eine Wahrscheinlichkeitskarte ein [53, 54, 51, 52]. Leider stehen für diese schwierig zu segmentierenden Gefäßbaumstrukturen keine laufenden Wettbewerbe zur Verfügung. Realistische DICE-Koeffizienten aus der Literatur liegen im Bereich von 0,5, welche für diese Baumstrukturen mit dünnen Gefäßästen bereits gut sind [22]. In einer für klinische Bilddaten nicht relevanten Phantomstudie wurden DICE-Koeffizienten von über 0,9 erreicht [55].

Die verschiedenen Einsatzmöglichkeiten von VR-Systemen in der Medizin werden in [56] dargelegt. Hardwareseitig wird die Immersion des Benutzers in die virtuelle Realität durch stereoskopische und haptische Ein- und Ausgabegeräte unterstützt [57]. Besonders die Auge-Hand-Koordination bei der Behandlung in anatomisch komplexen Körperbereichen ist ein wichtiges Trainingsfeld [35, 36, 37, 38]. Verschiedene Autoren [58, 57, 59, 60] fassen die Entwicklungen zu VR-Systemen mit patientenbezogenem Ansatz zusammen. VR-Systeme für die virtuelle Endoskopie sind am weitesten fortgeschritten. Bei den virtuellen Körpermodellen dominieren vollmanuell erstellte Segmentierungen einzelner Organe und Strukturen und daraus triangulierte Oberflächen- oder Volumenelementmodelle sowie FEM-Simulationsmethoden [61]. Die Einsatzmöglichkeiten vermarkteter VR-Trainingssysteme [62] decken endoskopische [63, 64, 65, 66, 67, 68, 69, 70] und chirurgische Eingriffe [71, 72, 73, 74, 75, 76] ab.

Erste und aktuellere VR-Simulatoren für nadelbasierte Eingriffe wurden von diversen Forschungsgruppen für verschiedene Anwendungsgebiete vorgeschlagen: (1) Lumbalpunktion [77, 78, 79, 80, 81, 82, 83, 84, 85]; (2) Biopsien [86, 87, 88, 89, 60, 90, 91, 92]; (3) Blutabnahmen [93, 94, 95, 96, 97]; (4) Injektionen [98, 99, 100, 101]; (5) Brachytherapie [102, 103] und (6) Radiofrequenzablationen [104, 105, 106]. Atembewegungssimulation findet bisher nur rudimentär auf Oberflächenmodellen durch simple Atembewegungsmodelle mit sinusförmiger Amplitudenmodulation und dem Chainmail-Deformationsalgorithmus Berücksichtigung [86, 107, 108, 109]. Die Visualisierung dynamischer Effekte wie der Verformung des Gewebes durch verwendete Instrumente und durch realistische Atembewegungen war dort nicht verfügbar. Surrogatgesteuerte Atemmodelle aus der Analyse von 4D-CT-Bildphasen, wie sie in [110, 111] vorgestellt wurden, waren bisher noch nicht Bestandteil aktueller Simulatoren.

Derzeit ist die Simulation minimal-invasiver Nadelpunktionseingriffe mit echtzeitfähiger und erhöhter, qualitativ hochwertiger Immersion in die virtuelle Realität ein aktuelles Forschungsgebiet [86, 102, 93, 94, 87]. Diese Entwicklung wird durch den Fortschritt der Hardware mit schnellen Mehrkernprozessoren und GPGPU-Computing getrieben. Methodisch gesehen wurden durch die hier vorgestellten Arbeiten für das direkte haptische Volumen-Rendering dem spärlichen Stand der Forschung hierzu [112, 113, 114, 115] neue Impulse beigesteuert. Dies ist u. a. durch die Verwendung von partiell segmentierten und simuliert atembewegten Patientenbilddaten begründet. Für die neuen Haptikalgorithmen wurde ein entsprechend neuer Evaluationsansatz vorgeschlagen. In diesem speziellen Simulationskontext sind auch für die benötigten visuellen Rendering-Methoden die entwickelte haptisch-visuelle Kopplung und die Berücksichtigung der realistisch simulierten Atmung in einem gemeinsamen, effizienten Deformations-Framework neu. Die vorgestellten Methoden sind eine Innovation im Themengebiet des GPU-basierten direkten 4D-Volumen-Renderings [116, 117, 118, 119, 120, 121].

1.3 Fragestellung, Ziel- und Schwerpunktsetzung

Die zu untersuchende Fragestellung dieser Arbeit ist, eine hinreichend plausible, patientenspezifische Leberpunktionstrainingssimulation mit reduziertem Patientenmodellierungsaufwand anzubieten, die von repräsentativen Benutzern akzeptiert wird und ein motivierendes Trainingserlebnis bietet.

Im Fokus dieser Arbeit liegen wichtige innovative Schlüsselmethoden des vorgestellten VR-basierten, patientenspezifischen Nadelpunktionstrainingssimulators: (1) effiziente Methoden zur Modellierung virtueller Patienten, (2) Algorithmen zur effizienten Berechnung von visuo-haptischen Darstellungen, (3) neue haptische Evaluationsmethoden und (4) quantitative Methodenbewertungen und eine Benutzerstudie zur qualitativen Bewertung des Systems in einem medizinischen Anwendungsfall mit einer komplizierten Zielstruktur (cholestatische Gallengänge):

(1) Erster Schwerpunkt ist die Erstellung generischer und daraus abgeleiteter patientenspezifischer virtueller Patientenatlanten mittels ausgewählter, unterschiedlich genauer, strukturspezifisch optimierter Teilsegmentierungsmethoden bei auf wenige Stunden verringertem Zeitaufwand. Ein solches Konzept [1, 6, 7] wurde bisher noch nicht in der Literatur vorgestellt.

(2) Die hier vorgestellten echtzeitfähigen z. T. GPU-gestützten und Voxel-gitterbasierten Methoden des visuo-haptischen Volumen-Renderings der Bilddaten [2] unterstützen die zielführende Navigation der Nadel in ggf. atembewegten Bilddaten [5, 3]. Ein spezielles US-Fenster des Simulators ermöglicht das Training dieser präzisen Navigationsmethode. Dieser Themenbereich umfasst auch die Vorstellung eines neuen plausibleren Kraftausgabeverfahrens an Organgrenzen [2]. Die zielgerichtete Nadelpunktion mittels einer Führungsschiene an der Seite der US-Sonde wird dabei ebenfalls unterstützt. Bisher wurden Deformationen der Patientenkörper eher mit FEM-basierten Methoden simuliert [61].

(3) Um die Kraftausgabe quantitativ bewerten zu können, wird eine neue *in silico*-Evaluationsmethodik für Kraftausgabealgorithmen vorgestellt [4]. Ziel ist, über geeignete Gütemaße die auf partiell segmentierten virtuellen Patienten basierende Kraftausgabe [8] im Vergleich zu einem manuell vollsegmentierten und bereits positiv evaluierten virtuellen Patienten zu vergleichen. Die Kraftausgabe des vollsegmentierten Patienten wurde in Vorarbeiten mit punktionserfahrenen Medizinern auf Plausibilität überprüft und in dieser Arbeit für die PTC/D verfeinert [2, 19].

(4) Medizinisches Anwendungsbeispiel der VR-Simulation ist die Gallengangspunktion mit der röntgengestützten und vor allem der US-kontrollierten bzw. -zielgeführten PTC/D. Qualitativ wird durch eine Benutzerstudie mit Medizinstudierenden die Plausibilität der VR-Simulation bewertet. Quantitativ wird das System unter verschiedenen Einzelaspekten wie Segmentierungsgüte, -geschwindigkeit [1, 7] und zeitliche Performanz der Rendering-Module [2] bewertet.

2 Material und Methoden

Wünschenswert für eine möglichst hohe Immersion in die virtuelle Realität ist eine genaue Simulation der relevanten visuo-haptischen Phänomene. Dazu wäre idealisiert ein Modell nötig, das alle Aspekte der Realität exakt abbildet und echtzeitfähig simuliert werden könnte [122]. Da dies offensichtlich unmöglich ist, wird als Kompromiss zwischen Rechenaufwand, Echtzeitanforderungen und realitätsgetreuer Darstellung das Konzept der „hinreichenden Plausibilität" als Zielkriterium definiert [123, 124, 125]. Es soll jeweils zu einem Stand der technischen Entwicklung eine möglichst genaue Echtzeitsimulation für die menschlichen Sinne erreicht werden. An der Grenze einer finanziell-technischen Machbarkeit sind Vereinfachungen in Modellbildung und Simulationsmethoden erlaubt, wenn gleichwohl ein erfahrbarer Nutzen der Anwendung gegeben ist.

In dieser Arbeit wird die Modellbildung und Simulation von hepatischen Punktionseingriffen thematisiert. Das Modell, der virtuelle Patientenkörper, wurde mit einem hinreichenden Detailgrad modelliert und diente als Eingabe für eine Simulation, die eine plausible Abbildung der Realität lieferte.

Zur zeiteffizienten Segmentierung der benötigten Strukturen wurde ein integriertes Gesamtkonzept entwickelt [1], in dem organspezifische, rechenlastige automatische Prozesse im Hintergrund (Lebersegmentierung) laufen und mit Benutzereingaben an anderen Strukturen (Faszienmodellierung) parallel einhergehen (Abb. 2.1).

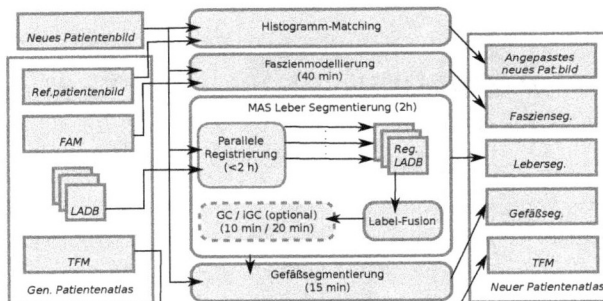

Abbildung 2.1: Datenobjekte (eckig) und Prozessabläufe (rund) zur Modellierung virtueller PTC/D-Patientenatlanten: Ein generischer Patientenatlas (GPA) wird durch z. T. parallele Rechenprozessschritte (Mitte) zu einem neuen Patientenatlas (NPA) spezialisiert (LADB=Leberatlantendatenbank, TFM=Transferfunktionenmodell, FAM=Faszienmodell, GC=GraphCut-Methode, iGC=interaktiver GraphCut). Aus [1].

Ein PC-Cluster mit 24 Rechenknoten dient z. B. zur Erstellung der benötigten zeitaufwendigen Multi-Atlas-Segmentierungen der Leber (Abb. 2.1, weißer Kasten, Mitte). Der Prozess ausgehend von einem generischen (Abb. 2.1, links) zu neuen, spezifischen Patientenatlanten (Abb. 2.1, rechts) wird in den folgenden Abschnitten (§) zusammengefasst. § 2.1 stellt das Datenstrukturkonzept der Atlanten vor. § 2.1.1 fokussiert die effiziente Segmen-

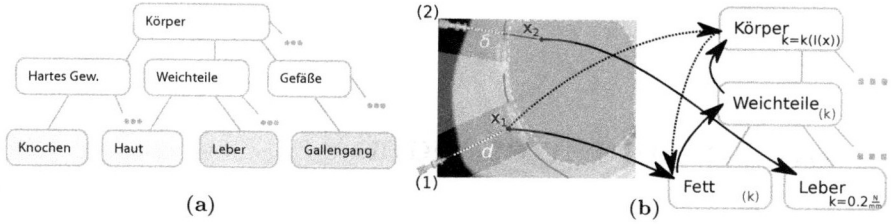

Abbildung 2.2: Sinnvolles Baumstrukturschema des Patientenatlas: (a) Eigenschaften werden in einer begrifflichen Hierarchie vom jeweiligen Elternknoten vererbt. (b) Parameterbestimmung per Wurzelknotenabfrage und Vererbung (x_1) oder knotenspezifischer Hinterlegung des Wertes (x_2) in einer partiellen Segmentierung. Faszienhaut zur Trennung von peripherem und viszeralem Kompartiment in Magenta. Nadelweglängen (1: Periphere Lage) d bis zur Nadelspitze und (2: Viszerale Lage) δ bis zur Faszienhaut. Knochen wird von der Nadel nicht durchdrungen. Modifiziert aus [2].

tierung von großräumigen Füllstrukturen (Haut, Weichteile, Knochen). Es schließt sich die Beschreibung der organspezifischen Modellierung von Schlüsselstrukturen in § 2.1.2 an (Faszien, Leberstrukturen). Dabei wird zwischen Ziel- (Gallengänge) und Risikostrukturen (z. B. Blutgefäße) unterschieden.

Im zweiten Methodenteil (§ 2.2, § 2.3) werden ausgewählte Themen des direkten visuo-haptischen Volumen-Rendering vorgestellt. § 2.2 erläutert die Multi-Proxy-basierte haptische Kraftausgabe und die nicht-lineare Kraftausgabemethode an Organgrenzen zur Erhöhung der Plausibilität. In § 2.3 werden entwickelte Ansätze der simulierten optischen Bildgebung und zur bildgestützten Positionskontrolle (Fluoroskopie, US) der in atembewegten Patienten eingebrachten Nadel zusammengefasst. Schließlich wird in § 2.4 die Methodik zur qualitativen und quantitativen Evaluierung wichtiger Aspekte des Simulatorkonzepts präsentiert.

2.1 Modellierung patientenspezifischer Atlanten

Ein Patientenatlas ist im Kontext dieser Arbeit ein attributierter Baum mit simulationsrelevanten visuo-haptischen Eigenschaften für die vorgestellten Rendering-Methoden (Abb. 2.2a). Ein generischer Patientenatlas (GPA) [1, 2, 8] besteht aus einer monohierarchischen Ordnung anatomischer Begriffe, die zueinander in einer begrifflichen Beinhaltungsbeziehung stehen, Bild-, Segmentierungs- und Hilfsdaten. Allgemeinere anatomische Begriffe stehen generell weiter oben in der Baumhierarchie. Ein GPA mit Intensitätsdaten und einem Multi-Label-Datensatz mit passenden Organsegmentierungen kann analog zu Mannequins zum allgemeinen Training von Interventionen in der medizinischen Ausbildung verwendet werden. Der GPA als Grundform kann zu patientenspezifischen neuen Patientenatlanten (NPA) adaptiert werden, die als personalisiertes Modell für Patientenkörper dienen. In einem Adaptionsprozess (Abb. 2.1, links) wurde der GPA inklusive der Eigenschaften an individuelle neue Patientenbilddaten angepasst und bildete den neuen Patientenatlas (Abb. 2.1, rechts) [1].

Abb. 2.2a stellt die verwendete Baumstruktur schematisch dar. Das Wurzelelement des Baumes hat die besondere Rolle, Standardeigenschaften rudimentär jedoch hinreichend

über den Vererbungsmechanismus zur Verfügung zu stellen. Die visuo-haptischen Gewebeparameter wurden weitestgehend aus den Vorarbeiten von Färber [78, 19] zur Lumbalpunktion übernommen. Für neue PTC/D-relevante Strukturen wie Leber, Lebergefäße
und Faszien wurden diese mit in der Leberpunktion erfahrenen Ärzten in Einstellungs-
sitzungen bestimmt [2]. Die Abfrage visuo-haptischer Parameter während der Simulation
und des Renderings wird in Abb. 2.2b für einen Nadelspitzen-Voxel in (1) peripherer ($\mathbf{x}_1$)
und (2) viszeraler ($\mathbf{x}_2$) Lage vereinfacht dargestellt.

Befindet sich an einer Voxel-Position keine Segmentierung, wird die Segmentierungsschätz-
funktion h des Wurzelknotens befragt, die abhängig auch von der Eindringtiefe d von der
Haut (Abb. 2.2b(1)) intensitätsintervallbasiert auf den zu verwendenden Materialblatt-
knoten mit den Labeln l_{risk}, l_{skin}, l_{soft}, l_{bone} oder l_{air} verweist:

$$l(\mathbf{x}, d) = \begin{cases} L(\mathbf{x}), & L(\mathbf{x}) \in \left\{ l_{fascia}, l_{liver}, l_{blood}, l_{bile} \right\} \text{ aus Multi} - \text{Label} - \text{Datensatz} \\ h(\mathbf{x}, d), & \text{sonst} \end{cases}$$

$$(2.1)$$

In Gl. (2.1) ist wird das Konzept der Verwendung partieller Segmentierungen deutlich.
Segmentierungslücken werden durch eine heuristische Label-Schätzfunktion h gefüllt. Das
lokal gültige Transferfunktionstupel (Ordinatenwerte) kann im Fall stückweise konstanter
visuo-haptischer Parameter äquivalent zur Bildintensitätsdomäne $I(\mathbf{x})$ auch einfach kom-
pakt über der geschätzten Segmentierung $l(\mathbf{x}, d)$ angegeben werden:

$$(r, g, b, a; \ k, R, T_N)(I(\mathbf{x}), d) \Leftrightarrow (r, g, b, a; \ k, R, T_N)(l(\mathbf{x}, d)). \qquad (2.2)$$

Es beinhaltet visuelle Parameter für Farbe und Opazität (r, g, b, a) und haptische Parameter wie Federsteifigkeit k [N/mm], Reibungskraft R [N] und Durchstoßkraft der Ober-
flächenhaut des Materials T_N [N]. Transferfunktionen über dem Definitionsgebiet der In-
tensitäten $I(\mathbf{x})$ mit stückweise linear geneigten Ordinatenstücken wurden in [8] für die
Lumbalpunktion für die haptischen Parameter Federsteifigkeit und Reibungskraft verwendet und sind ggf. für unsichere Gewebeübergänge nützlich [126].

Die Methoden zur Bestimmung der heuristischen Label-Transferfunktionen h und der
priorisierten Segmentierungen in $L(\mathbf{x})$ mit organspezifisch optimierten Methoden werden
im folgenden § 2.1.1 und § 2.1.2 zusammengefasst.

2.1.1 Transferfunktionsbasierte Segmentierung

In diesem Abschnitt geht es um die Definition der effizienten heuristischen Segmentie-
rungsschätzfunktion h aus Gl. (2.1) mit zwei alternativen Methoden. Es werden die
Füllstrukturen Luft, Haut, Weichteile und Knochen für das visuo-haptische Echtzeit-
Rendering (1000 bis 2000 Hz) geeignet geschätzt.

2.1.1.1 Bayes-Transferfunktionen

Der Ansatz der Transferfunktionen mit stückweise linearen 1D-Funktionssegmenten erlaubt durch die kompakte tabellarische Darstellung der Stützpunkte und lineare Interpolation den Echtzeitzugriff auf die visuo-haptischen Eigenschaften. Diese Eigenschaft
prädestiniert ihn für das direkte visuo-haptische Volumen-Rendering modellbasiert defor-
mierter, atembewegter Patientenbilddaten.

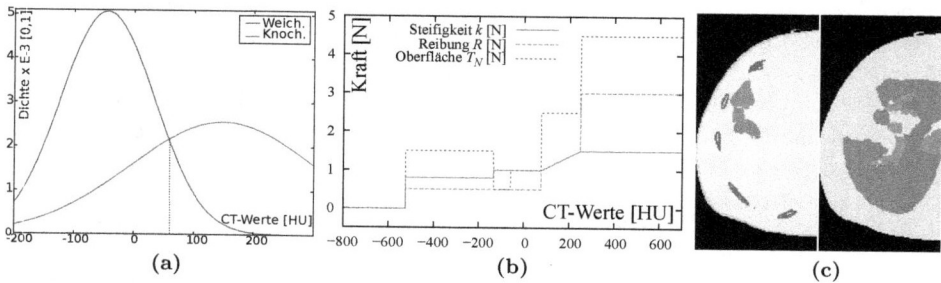

(a)   (b)   (c)

Abbildung 2.3: Bestimmung von Transferfunktionen: (a) Bayes-Schwelle von Weichgewebe (blaue Linie) zu Knochen (grüne Linie). (b) Typische haptische (k, R, T_N)-Transferfunktionen mit linear geneigtem (k, R)-Segment um 200 HU. (c) Zu lernende Label-Karten L_g für zwei Random-Forest-Klassifikatoren mit Luft außerhalb des Körpers in Schwarz: (Links) Großvolumige RFK-Lernstrukturen für RFK_{lar} (Haut: orange, Weichgewebe: gelb, Knochen: lila, Risikostruktur: rot, ignorierte Strukturen: grau). (Rechts) Leberstrukturen für RFK_{liv} (Leber: braun, Gallengänge: grün, Leberblutgefäße: rot, andere Objekte: orange). Aus [6, 4, 8].

Für die Definition des GPA wurden haptische und visuelle Transferfunktionen $h = h_{bay}$ für voluminöse Gewebe wie Haut, Fett oder Knochen intervallweise definiert:

$$h_{bay}(\mathbf{x}, d) = \begin{cases} l_{risk}, & I(\mathbf{x}) \in [-\infty, t_{skin}^{soft}) \wedge d > \delta \\ l_{skin}, & I(\mathbf{x}) \in [t_{air}^{skin}, t_{skin}^{soft}) \wedge d \le \delta \\ l_{soft}, & I(\mathbf{x}) \in [t_{skin}^{soft}, t_{soft}^{bone}) \text{ mit } t_{soft}^{bone} = \begin{cases} \check{t}_{soft}^{bone}, & d \le \delta \\ \hat{t}_{soft}^{bone}, & d > \delta \end{cases} \\ l_{bone}, & I(\mathbf{x}) \in [t_{soft}^{bone}, \infty] \quad \text{mit } t_{soft}^{bone} = -''- \\ l_{air}, & \text{sonst} \end{cases} \quad (2.3)$$

Die drei Abszissenstützpunkte t_{von}^{zu} (von $\in \{$air, skin, soft$\}$, zu $\in \{$skin, soft, bone$\}$) für die Transferfunktionsintervalle wurden mittels einer Bayesschen Diskriminanzanalyse anhand eines ausgewählten vollsegmentierten Referenzpatienten ermittelt [1, 2, 4, 8]. Bei den sich schneidenden aus den Referenzsegmentierungsmasken geschätzten Normalverteilungen (Abb. 2.3a) wird jeweils die Abszisse des höher gelegenen Ordinatenschnittpunkts als t_{von}^{zu} gewählt. Die entsprechenden haptischen Ordinatenstützstellen wurden empirisch mittels wiederholter Punktionsversuche der Gewebe mit punktionserfahrenen Ärzten bestimmt [2, 78]. δ deutet in Gl. (2.3) lokal die Nadelweglänge bis zur virtuellen Faszienhaut (§ 2.1.2.1) an. Mittels der Lage der Nadelspitze relativ zur explizit modellierten Faszienhaut (Abb. 2.2b, Magenta), wird eine Fallunterscheidung zwischen subkutan-peripheren (Abb. 2.2b(1)) und viszeralen Strukturen (Abb. 2.2b(2)) getroffen. Diese resultiert erstens in einer Wahl der Übergangsschwelle t_{soft}^{bone} als untere Schwelle $\check{t}_{soft}^{bone}$ oder obere Schwelle $\hat{t}_{soft}^{bone}$ [4]. Zweitens triggert der Fasziendurchstoß die Umdeutung einzelner Intervalle im Intensitätsbereich $[-\infty, t_{skin}^{soft})$ als äußere Luft ($d \le \delta$) oder körperinnere Risikostrukturen ($d > \delta$). Problemspezifisch realisierbar sind auch visuo-haptische Transferfunktion mit fuzzyfizierenden [126], nicht konstantwertigen Intervallsegmenten wie in [8] vorgeschlagen. Dies ist in Abb. 2.3b beispielhaft illustriert. Neue Patientenbilddaten eines NPA können nun mit einem optimierten Histogramm-Matching-Verfahren [127] mit einer bijektiven, monoton steigenden, stückweise linearen Abbildung an die Abszissenintervallkonfiguration des GPA angepasst werden. Die Intensitätswerte der neuen Patientenbilddaten werden intervallweise auf diejenigen des GPA skaliert. Die hier verwendete Variante verwendet fünf Intervallrandpunkte (5 %-, 25 %-, 50 %-, 75 %-, 95 %-Quartile). Idealerweise werden die drei lokalen Histogramm-Maxima von Fett (25 %), Weichteilgewebe (50 %) und Knochen (75 %) der Intensitätsdaten im oberen Abdomen beider Patientendatensätze aufeinander abgebildet.

Das klassische Transferfunktionskonzept mit eindimensionalem Intensitätsdefinitionsbereich wurde in diesem Abschnitt um eine binäre Dimension der Fallunterscheidung bezüglich der Lage des zu segmentierenden Voxels inner- oder außerhalb umfassender Strukturen erweitert (peripher vs. viszeral). Dies mündet in das Konzept lokal gültiger Transferfunktionen. Mit der Interpretation einer Ortsangabe als zusätzlicher Dimension ist auch das Thema höherdimensionaler Transferfunktionen h angeschnitten und wird in § 2.1.1.2 mit der Methode des maschinellen Lernens untersucht.

2.1.1.2 Random-Forest-Transferfunktionen

Eine alternative Methode zur Bestimmung von h aus Gl. (2.1) besteht in der Definition maschinell gelernter Transferfunktionen über mehrdimensionalen Merkmalsräumen mit einem trainierten Random-Forest-Klassifikator (RFK): $h = h_{RF}$ [128]. Der Ansatz wurde in [6] für bis zu dreidimensionale Merkmalsräume untersucht. Ausgehend von manuellen Goldstandardsegmentierungen wurden je ein Multi-Label-Bild L_g zusammen mit einem Merkmalsbildtupel $\mathbf{m}$ von einem RFK gelernt und kann als zugriffseffiziente Transferfunktion abgetastet ($\sqsubseteq$) bzw. tabelliert werden:

$$h_{RF} \sqsubseteq RFK\left(L_g;\, \mathbf{m} \in \{(f_j, \ldots, f_k) \mid j < k,\, 0 < k \leq 2\}\right). \tag{2.4}$$

Aufgrund der technischen Grenzen u. a. der Dimensionen des verwendeten hocheffizienten GPU-Texturspeichers ($\leq$3D) beim Rendering [129] wurden in [6] maximal drei Merkmalsbilder $f_j (j = 0..2)$ gelernt. Diese können für jeden Positionsindex i und Ortsvektor $\mathbf{x}_i$ berechnet werden:
- f_0: Die normalisierte Intensität des Voxels an der Position i: $f_0^i = I(\mathbf{x}_i)$,
- f_1: Der Euklidische Abstand zur Hautoberfläche: $f_1^i = d = D_{skin}(\mathbf{x}_i)$,
- f_2: Der Betrag des Gradienten: $f_2^i = |\nabla I(\mathbf{x}_i)|$.

Die Kompatibilität der Intensitätsdaten zwischen GPA und NPA wird auch hier zunächst durch die normalisierende Histogrammanpassung aus § 2.1.1.1 erreicht. Entsprechend Gl. (2.1) wurden zwei RFKn gelernt: Es wurde (1) ein Klassifikator $RFK_{lar} \sqsupseteq h$ für großvolumige Strukturen und (2) ein gesonderter Klassifikator $RFK_{liv} \sqsupseteq L$ für Leberstrukturen trainiert, um auch für Zielstrukturen diesen Ansatz zu bewerten. Die Label-Karten für das Training der beiden strukturspezifischen Klassifikatoren sind in Abb. 2.3c exemplarisch dargestellt. Dabei wurden die verschiedenen zweidimensionalen (f_0, f_1), (f_0, f_2), (f_1, f_2) und eine dreidimensionale Merkmalskombination (f_0, f_1, f_2) untersucht. Training und Test erfolgten in zwei Varianten einer Leave-Some-Out-Kreuzvalidierung (90 %, 30 %). Klassifikatoren mit (1) jeweils einem (neun vom Training ausgelassen) bzw. (2) sieben Patienten (drei ausgelassen) wurden trainiert.

2.1.2 Organspezifisch optimierte Segmentierungsverfahren

Im Patientenmodellierungskonzept wurden neben den mächtigen jedoch z. T. unspezifischen Transferfunktionen für großvolumige Füllstrukturen noch explizit generierte genaue-

re Segmentierungsmasken für Schlüsselstrukturen benötigt. Im fokussierten Anwendungs-
kontext der Leberpunktion sind Faszien der interkostalen Muskulatur, Leber, Gallengänge
und hepatische Blutgefäße relevant.

2.1.2.1 Spline-Modellierung einer virtuellen Faszienhaut

Der GPA enthält in den Hilfsdaten ein Spline-Oberflächenmodel der interkostalen Faszien [1, 4], welche die Besonderheit eines deutlich spürbaren Duschstoßereignisses in der
Kraftausgabe aufweisen. Zudem wird die Unterscheidung zwischen peripher und viszeral
gelegenen Nadelspitzenpositionen möglich, wie in Abb. 2.2b angedeutet und Gl. (2.3) formuliert (§ 2.1.1.1). Auf eine anatomisch genaue Segmentierung der zum Muskelapparat
gehörigen Faszienstrukturen wurde aufgrund ihrer diffusen Darstellung in CT-Bildern verzichtet. Eine haptisch spürbare Grenzfläche zwischen den Rippen wurde durch eine die
Rippenbögen interpolierende B-Spline-Oberfläche:

$$\mathbf{r}\left(\phi, h\right) = \begin{pmatrix} B_x\left(\phi, h\right) \\ B_y\left(\phi, h\right) \\ B_z\left(\phi, h\right) \end{pmatrix}, \ 0 \leq \phi \leq 2\pi, \ h_0 \leq h \leq h_1 \tag{2.5}$$

mit der Höhe h und dem Winkel ϕ in Zylinderkoordinaten approximiert. Die Funktionen
B_x, B_y und B_z sind B-Spline-Flächen über dem rechteckigen Gebiet (ϕ, h).
Schließlich wird die an einen NPA angepasste Fläche $\mathbf{r}\left(\phi, h\right)$ in den Multi-Label-Datensatz
L mit dem Label l_{fascia} einkodiert und für das hinreichend plausible haptische Rendering
der Faszien und die Unterscheidung subkutan-peripherer und viszeraler Strukturen in
neuen Bilddaten verwendet (vgl. § 2.1.1.1).

2.1.2.2 Multi-Atlas-Segmentierung der Leber

Zur organspezifisch optimierten Segmentierung der Leber wurden Multi-Atlas-basierte
Segmentierungs- (MAS) und neuartige effiziente Patch-basierte Label-Fusionierungsme-
thoden entwickelt [1, 7]. Die Atlasdatenbank aus Atlanten mit Intensitäts- und Segmen-
tierungsdaten befindet sich in den Hilfsdaten des GPA. Als Atlasdatenbank standen aus
der bisherigen klinischen Kooperation mit der Klinik für Radiologie und Nuklearmedizin
des Universitätsklinikums Schleswig-Holstein, Campus Lübeck, 60 3D-CT-Datensätze mit
bereits von Radiologen segmentierten Lebern zur Verfügung.
Die Multi-Atlas-Segmentierung der Leber passt eine Auswahl affin vorregistrierter Atlanten (Abb. 2.4a) der Atlasdatenbank des GPA morphologisch genauer an den NPA an.
Sie wurde im Hinblick auf Robustheit und Zeiteffizienz optimiert [1, 7]. Nach der affinen
Vorregistrierung wurden 60 % (Abb. 2.4b) der verfügbaren Atlanten aus der Atlasdatenbank gütemaßbasiert verworfen [1]. Die Multi-Atlas-Segmentierung ist danach ein Prozess
mit wenigen gut parallelisierbaren nicht-linearen Single-Atlas-Registrierungen (Abb. 2.4c),
deren multiple Segmentierungsschätzmasken am Ende zu einer mittleren Gesamtsegmen-
tierung fusioniert wurden (Abb. 2.4d). Ein weiterer wesentlicher Aspekt der effizienten
MAS liegt in der Beschleunigung des Label-Fusionierungsschritts am Ende der Prozess-
kette durch spärliche Berücksichtigung von Patch-Nachbarschaften [7]. Weitere Ergeb-
nisoptimierungen erfolgten durch GraphCut-Postprocessing [130] (GC) mit optionalen,
interaktiv spärlich gesetzten Korrekturen (iGC) [1].

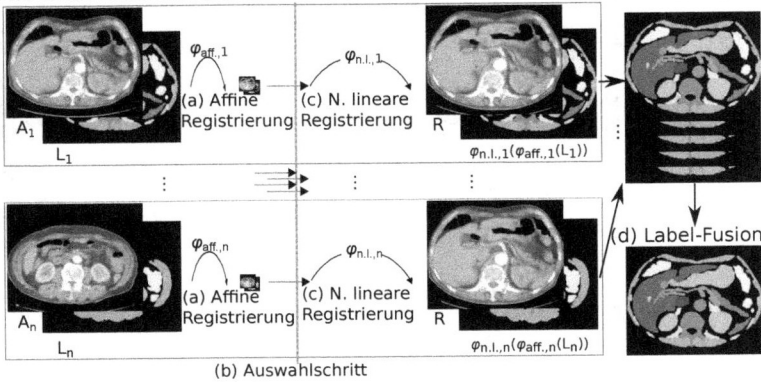

Abbildung 2.4: Schema der Multi-Atlas-Segmentierung mit Auswahlschritt: (a) Für jeden Atlas aus der Label-Atlas-Datenbank wird eine affine und (b) nach Auswahl ggf. (c) nicht-lineare Single-Atlas-Registrierung durchgeführt. Die aufwendigen nicht-linearen Registrierungen wurden auf je einem von 24 PC-Knoten parallel berechnet. Die Label-Fusion (d) erfolgt auf einem PC. Aus [1].

2.1.2.3 Segmentierung der Lebergefäße

Auch die Segmentierung von Gefäßstrukturen innerhalb der Leber wurde organspezifisch optimiert. Der GPA enthält hierfür in den Hilfsdaten Standardparameter, die empirisch auf einer Reihe von pathologischen Testdaten gelernt wurden [1].

Für einen NPA wurden die in der PTC/D wichtigen Blutgefäße (Risikostruktur) und Gallengänge (Zielstruktur) innerhalb der nun aus § 2.1.2.2 vorliegenden Lebersegmentierung lokal-adaptiv segmentiert. Es wurde ein Vesselness-Verfahren [1] entwickelt, mit dem bei ausreichend Bildkontrast für Blutgefäße und cholestatisch ausgeprägten Gallengängen sehr gute Ergebnisse erreicht wurden. Abb. 2.5 stellt die Schrittfolge der Lebergefäßsegmentierung zusammenfassend dar [1].

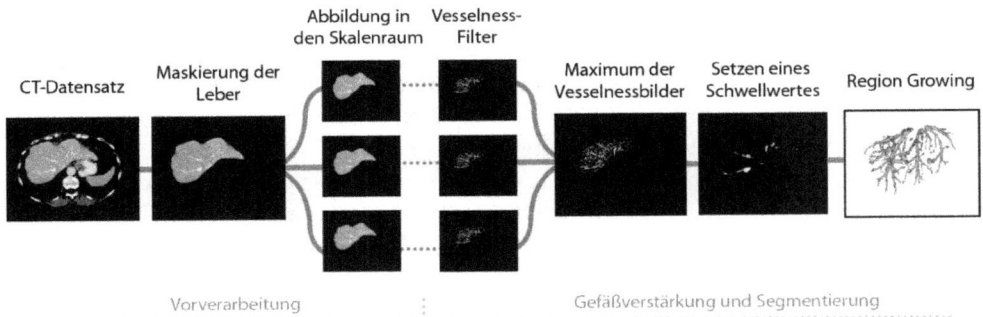

Abbildung 2.5: Visualisierung der sechs Schritte der Segmentierung heller Lebergefäße, die sich von links nach rechts aus Vorverarbeitung, Gefäßverstärkung und Segmentierung zusammensetzt. Dunkle Gallengefäße wurden durch Invertierung vor der Maskierung segmentiert. Aus [14].

Nach Maskierung der Leber resultiert mittels Multi-Skalen-Vesselness-Filterung [51], Maximumfilterung sowie anschließender strukturspezifisch optimierter Schwellwertoperation, Volumenwachstum mit automatisch generierten Saatpunkten und morphologischer Nachbearbeitung ein Gefäßbaum. Für die Segmentierung der dunklen Gallengänge wird der CT-Datensatz eingangs invertiert.

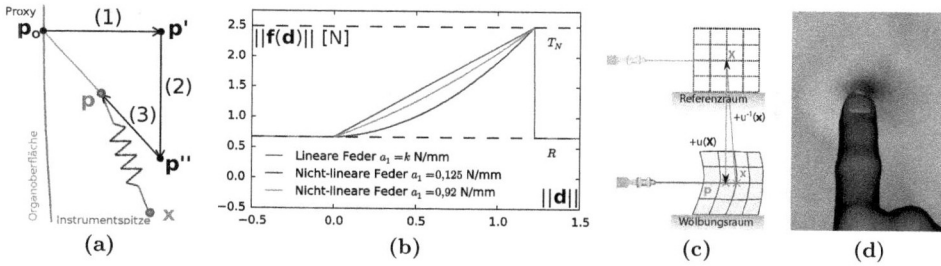

Abbildung 2.6: Haptik (a, b) und Deformation (c, d): (a) Dreischrittverfeinerung der Proxyposition **p** [114]. (b) Kraftanstiege verschiedener Federn an einer Organkapsel. (c) Im Wölbungsraum definieren Nadelspitze (Geräteposition) **x** sowie virtueller Proxy **p** die Deformationen in der Umgebung der Nadel. (d) Palpatorische Deformation der Haut unter Verwendung eines Multi-Proxy-Arrays an der Fingerkuppe. Adaptiert aus [2, 4].

2.2 Multi-Proxy-basierte visuo-haptische Methoden

Es wurden neue Proxy-basierte haptische Algorithmen [8] und Evaluationsmethoden [4] für die Simulation von Nadelpunktionen in partiell segmentierten Daten entwickelt [2, 4]. Die Proxy- und bildgradientenbasierte Kraftausgabe [113, 114, 131] mittels CT-Bildgradienten (Abb. 2.6a) wurde hier unter Benutzung des Konzepts partiellen Segmentierungen mit lückenfüllenden Transferfunktionen aus § 2.1 neu formuliert [8]. Die an den Benutzer ausgegebenen Kraftkomponenten werden in sechs Freiheitsgraden (degrees of freedom, DOF) durch die Divergenz der Geräteposition zu Kraftwiderstände modellierenden virtuellen Proxies berechnet. Die Erweiterung des Ein-Proxy-Nadelmodells zu Multi-Proxy-Methoden [2, 13] erlaubt die Simulation größerer Kontaktflächen, wie z. B. bei Fingern oder US-Köpfen (Abb. 2.6d). Unter Betrachtung eines einzelnen Proxies wird der Gerätpunkt (Nadelspitze) und die Gerätelage (Nadelschaft) im virtuellen Raum mit einem entsprechenden virtuellen 6DOF-Proxy (Position und Torques) mittels fiktiver Zug- und Drehmomentfedern verbunden. Position und Lage des zurückhaltenden Proxies werden durch die Gewebeparameter bestimmt. Bezüglich der drei Positionsfreiheitsgrade wird ein Proxy **p** dabei von Strukturrändern detektiert durch $\frac{d}{d\mathbf{x}}l(\mathbf{x}, d) \neq 0$ zurückgehalten (Gl. 2.1; Abb. 2.6a), während sich die vom haptischen Eingabegerät bestimmte Nadelspitzenposition **x** benutzergesteuert weiterbewegt. Die ab jetzt ausgegeben Gegenkräfte durch sich virtuell aufspannende Federn vor allem in der axialen Nadelvorschubrichtung werden für den Benutzer deutlich als Strukturwiderstand spürbar. Nadelangulationen werden durch finite Stabelemente (vgl. Abb. 2.7), die durch Drehmomentfedern verbunden sind, nachgebildet [12].

Bei der linearen Kraftausgabe, wird der Distanz- bzw. Nadelvorschubvektor $\mathbf{d} = \mathbf{x} - \mathbf{p}$ zwischen Proxy **p** und Nadelspitze **x** mit der linearen Federkonstante a nach Hooke $\mathbf{f}(\mathbf{d}) = -a \cdot \mathbf{d}$ zur Kraftberechnung gegen den Nadelvorschub herangezogen.

Nicht-lineare Kraftanstiege (Abb. 2.6b) an Organkapseln stellen eine haptisch realitätsnähere Kraftrückgabe dar [2]. Folgende Modellformel mit linearen und quadratischen Kraftanteilen und speziellen Parametern $a_{0..2}$ wurde vorgeschlagen:

$$\mathbf{f}(\mathbf{d}) = -\frac{\mathbf{d}}{\|\mathbf{d}\|} \left(a_2 \|\mathbf{d}\|^2 + a_1 \|\mathbf{d}\| + a_0 \right). \tag{2.6}$$

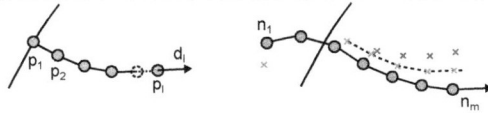

Abbildung 2.7: Diskretisierung von Nadelpfaden in Stab- und Proxy-Elemente: Links: koinzidierende Nadelschaftstellen und Kopplungsproxies $\mathbf{p}_i$. An der Nadelspitze werden diese Kopplungspunkte während des Einschiebens in Richtung $\mathbf{d}_l$ neu eingesetzt. Rechts: Die Proxies (Kreuze) werden zu aktiven Lateralkräfte generierenden Proxies (rot) durch materialabhängige Federverbindungen mit den korrespondierenden Nadelschaftstellen $\mathbf{n}_i$. Die Proxies werden durch Atembewegungsvektoren (u) weiter verschoben (blau) und ziehen die Nadel in Richtung der Atembewegung. Aus [3].

Kraftanstiege mit quadratischen Termen stellen eine gefühlt und quantitativ *in vivo* gezeigte [132, 133] plausiblere Alternative zur linearen Federkraftausgabe dar.

Zur Kopplung zwischen haptischem und visuellem Rendering dient der Nadelvorschubrichtungsvektor $\mathbf{d}$ als Eingabe (Deformationsrichtung) für die Weichteilgewebedeformationsalgorithmen (Abb. 2.6c), die im folgenden Abschnitt zusammengefasst werden. Andererseits haben die im nächsten Abschnitt besprochenen zeitveränderlichen Atemmodellvektorfelder Einfluss auf die Kraftausgabe. Die Verbindung eines z. B. sinusoidalen Pseudo-Atembewegungsvektorfeldes $u(t) = (0, A \cdot \sin(t), 0)^\top$ mit der Atemamplitude A [mm] mit dem Nadelschaft wird über spezielle Kopplungsproxies erreicht, die sich perlenschnurartig (Abb. 2.7) entlang der eingeschobenen Nadel aufreihen [3]. Die Berechnung der atembedingten Kraftkomponenten findet durch die Divergenz der durch u verschobenen Nadelschaft-Proxies von korrespondierenden Nadelschaftstellen im nachfolgend vorgestellten undeformierten Referenzraum statt.

2.3 Visuelles Rendering US-gestützter Punktionen

An dieser Stelle werden unter Berücksichtigung von Atembewegungen zeitvariante Methoden für die 3D/4D-Visualisierung und 2D-Visualisierungstechniken für Schnitt- und Projektionsbilder zusammengefasst. Dem Ansatz des direkten Volumen-Rendering [119] folgend wurden echtzeitfähige parallele Raycasting-Algorithmen in Nvidia CUDA entwickelt. Durch spezielle Implementierungen der zugrunde liegenden Strahlverfolgung und des Rendering-Integrals [134] können verschiedene bildgebende Verfahren für atembewegte virtuelle Patientenkörper simuliert werden.

Die Weichteildeformationen durch Instrumenteneinsatz und Atmung wird mit der Haptiksimulation wechselwirkend verkoppelt, indem die Verbindungsvektoren zwischen Gerätnadelstellen und Proxies (vgl. Abb. 2.7, rechts) wie u. a. im Fall der Nadelspitze in das aus numerischen Gründen verwendete inverse Deformationsfeld als $u^{-1}(\mathbf{x}) = -\mathbf{d}$ einfließen (Abb. 2.6c). Das inverse Deformationsfeld vermeidet Definitionslücken im verformten Zustand, da es lückenlos auf der Bilddomäne definiert ist. Danach wird es angelehnt an die Temperaturdiffusion regularisiert und liefert effizient plausibel propagierte Nadeldeformationen [9]. Zusätzlich zur Simulation der in [135, 3, 9] vorgestellten Weichteilverformung durch Nadelpunktionseingriffe wurden Multi-Proxy-Methoden zur Visualisierung von Deformationen z. B. durch Palpation (Abb. 2.6d) und Ultraschalluntersuchungen in den Simulator integriert [13, 16].

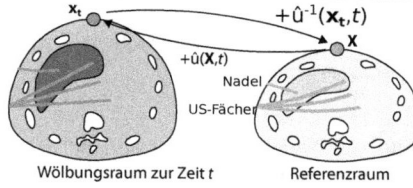

Abbildung 2.8: Schematische Darstellung einer axialen Schicht im visuo-haptischen Deformations-Framework: Jeder Punkt im Wölbungsraum $\mathbf{x}_t$ kann auf einen Punkt $\mathbf{X}$ im statischen Referenzraum abgebildet werden und umgekehrt. Dies wird hier beispielsweise für einen Punkt auf der Hautoberfläche sowie Punkte entlang eines Nadelpfads und eines US-Abtaststrahlfächers gezeigt. Adaptiert aus [3].

2.3.1 Deformationen durch 4D-Bewegungssimulation

4D-CT-Datensätze bestehen aus einer Folge von n 3D-CT-Phasenbildern $I_{j \in 1,...,n} : \Omega \to \mathbb{R}$ ($\Omega \subset \mathbb{R}^3$), welche die Anatomie des Patienten in verschiedenen Zuständen eines einzigen Atemzyklus darstellen, sprich schrittweise jeweils von maximaler Inhalation zu Exhalation. Nicht-lineare Verformungen $\varphi_j : \Omega \to \Omega$ zwischen den Phasen I_j und einer ausgewählten Referenzphase I_{ref} wurden durch organspezifisch optimierte Bildregistrierungsverfahren [136] bestimmt, um Voxel-weise Korrespondenzen herzustellen. Die erhaltene Bewegungsinformation zwischen verschiedenen Phasen war die Grundlage der Modellbildung eines zeitveränderlichen Bewegungsmodells.

In diesem Verfahren [5, 3, 110] wird das aus der Bildakquise vorhandene 1D-Spirometriesignal $s(t)$ mit der zeitlichen Ableitung erweitert zu einem 2D-Signal $\hat{\mathbf{z}}(t) = (s(t), s'(t))$, das unterschiedliche Tiefen der Atmung (Interzyklusvariabilität) repräsentiert und zwischen Ein- und Ausatmung unterscheidet (Hysterese). Es dient zur Parametrisierung des Atembewegungsmodells. Unter der Annahme der Linearität zwischen dem Atmungssignal und der internen Bewegung wurden die zuvor ermittelten n Transformationen φ_j mit dem Atemsignal $\hat{\mathbf{z}}(t_j)$ für die zeitvariante Interpolation simulierter 4D-Daten mit einem multivariaten linearen Bewegungsmodell verwendet [5]:

$$\hat{\varphi}(\mathbf{X}, t) = \bar{a}_1(\mathbf{X}) \cdot s(t) + \bar{a}_2(\mathbf{X}) \cdot s'(t) + \bar{a}_3(\mathbf{X}), \quad \mathbf{X} \subset \Omega, \tag{2.7}$$

dessen Koeffizienten $\bar{a}_{1..3}$ (Vektorfelder) durch lineare Regression bestimmt wurden. Angewandt auf die Bilddaten $I_{ref}(\mathbf{X})$ über den undeformierten Stützstellen $\mathbf{X}$ (Referenzraum), vermag die der gelernten Transformation $\hat{\varphi}(\mathbf{X}, t) = id + \hat{u}(\mathbf{X}, t)$ entsprechende additive Bewegungsvektorfeldfunktion $\hat{u}(\mathbf{X}, t)$ das zugehörige zeitvariant verformte Referenzbild im Wölbungsraum $\mathbf{x} \subset \Omega$ kontinuierlich darzustellen:

$$I_t(\mathbf{x}) = I_{ref}(\mathbf{X}) \circ \hat{\varphi}(\mathbf{X}, t) \overset{!}{=} I_{ref}(\mathbf{X}) \text{ s.t. } \mathbf{x} = \mathbf{X} + \hat{u}(\mathbf{X}, t). \tag{2.8}$$

Stützpunkteweise (Voxel-Gitterpunkte) ausgedrückt ergibt sich ein atmungsbedingt gekrümmter zeitvarianter Wölbungsraum: $\mathbf{x}_t = \mathbf{X} + \hat{u}(\mathbf{X}, t)$, dessen abzutastende ungekrümmte Unterräume (Ebenen, Linien, Slabs) im Referenzraum gekrümmt sind und dort abgetastet werden können (Abb. 2.8). Somit ist zur Effizienzsteigerung des direkten 4D-Volumen-Renderings mit diesem zeitvarianten Bewegungsvektorfeld alternativ ein Raycasting mit zeitvariant gekrümmten Abtaststrahlen im 3D-CT-Bild des Referenzraums möglich, ohne die teure Verformung der statischen 3D-CT-Bilddaten und der Multi-Label-

Daten aus Gl. (2.8) explizit zu berechnen. Zur Berechnung der verbogenen Strahlen ist das inverse Bewegungsvektorfeld $\hat{u}^{-1}(\mathbf{x}_t, t)$ notwendig:

$$\mathbf{X} = \mathbf{x}_t + \hat{u}^{-1}(\mathbf{x}_t, t). \tag{2.9}$$

Dieses existiert jedoch nicht global bei nicht-linearen Deformationen mit Gleitspaltrandbedingungen (Pleura) als glatte und eineindeutige Funktion [136]. Daher wird als Näherung auf die Approximation $\hat{u}^{-1}(\mathbf{x}_t, t) = -\hat{u}(\mathbf{X}, t)$ zurückgegriffen und eine konvergierende Iterationsgleichung definiert: $\mathbf{X}_n = \mathbf{x}_t - \hat{u}(\mathbf{X}_{n-1}, t)$, die bei festgehaltener Zeit t nach ca. $n = 10$ Schritten die Anwendung von $\hat{u}^{-1}(\mathbf{x}_t, t)$ robust approximiert [137]. In [3] wird dies geschickt mit den kleinen Positionsvorschüben $\mathbf{d}_l$ auf einem Raycastingstrahl kombiniert, ohne die stabile Konvergenz zu beinträchtigen:

$$\mathbf{X}_n = \mathbf{x}_t + \mathbf{d}_l - \hat{u}(\mathbf{X}_{n-1} + \mathbf{d}_l, t). \tag{2.10}$$

2.3.2 Spezielle Verfahren des Raycastings

Die implizit bzw. explizit deformierten CT-Daten I_t des virtuellen Patientenatlas bilden die Grundlage für das Raycasting mit einem in die Szene geschickten Sehstrahl mit je nach betrachtetem Raum (Abb. 2.8) deformierten bzw. entsprechenden geradlinig angeordneten Abtastpunkten $\mathbf{X}_i \hat{=} \mathbf{x}_i$ zur Generierung der zeitvarianten stereoskopischen 3D/4D-Ansichten und 2D-Projektionen (Röntgen) und Schnittbilder (MPR, US). Grundlage für die Einfärbung der Rasterpunkte auf der Bildebene war das Render-Integral [119, 134] entlang der Sehstrahlen, das für die menschliche Augwahrnehmung oder die hier Kontrollbildgebungsverfahren ausgestaltet wurde [2].
Bei der Röntgensimulation wurde das Raycasting dazu genutzt, die totale Absorption entlang eines Strahls auf Grundlage der in den CT-Daten enthaltenen Abschwächungswerte zu berechnen. Die Summe der Abschwächungswerte entlang des Sehstrahls mit Berücksichtigung der simulierten Kontrastmittelausbreitung wurde zur Bestimmung der Intensität für den Rasterpunkt auf der Bildebene herangezogen. Die Ausbreitung eines injizierten Kontrastmittels in den segmentierten Gallengängen wurde lokal mittels eines maskierten diffusiven Ausbreitungsprozesses im Referenzraum simuliert [2].

2.3.2.1 Ultraschallsimulation in atmenden virtuellen Patienten

Ein Schwerpunkt der publizierten Arbeiten ist die Nvidia CUDA-gestützte Ultraschallsimulation basierend auf atembewegten CT-Daten [5], die in Abb. 2.9 schematisch gezeigt wird. Die einzelnen Schritte werden genauer erläutert. Es wurde ein spezielles siebenschrittiges Raycasting- und Bildkompositionsverfahren mit dem zeitabhängig gebogenen Abtaststrahlenfächer verwendet:

(1) Zunächst werden zu einem Zeitpunkt t auf den einzelnen Strahlen mit Abtastpunkten $\mathbf{X}_i$ eines entsprechend der Orientierung des US-Kopfes ausgerichteten 2D-Strahlenfächers Hounsfield-Intensitäten $I_t(\mathbf{X}_i)$ parallel abgetastet. Mit einer Falltabelle aus [138] werden diese in Dichtewerte ρ konvertiert. Der Strahlenfächer besteht aus 256 Strahlen (CUDA-Blocks) mit je 512 Punkten (CUDA-Threads).

(2) Die Schallkennimpedanz $Z(\mathbf{X}_i)$ im Punkt $\mathbf{X}_i$ eines Strahls wird kubisch zwischen bekannten Stützpunkten interpoliert [139]:

$$Z(\mathbf{X}_i) = (349.281 \cdot \rho(\mathbf{X}_i) - 0.151261 \cdot \rho(\mathbf{X}_i)^2 + 0.00117651 \cdot \rho(\mathbf{X}_i)^3) \tag{2.11}$$

Abbildung 2.9: US-Simulations-Pipeline: (1) A-Mode Abtastung der 3D-CT-Daten auf einem ggf. gebogenen Strahlenfächer, (2) Abschätzung der Schallkennimpedanz, (3) Schätzung der Reflexions-, Transmissions- und Absorptionskoeffizienten, (4) Berechnung der Transmission, (5) tiefenabhängige Verstärkung - Time-Gain-Control (TGC) und (6) B-Mode-Komposition des US-Bildes. (7) Das simulierte Bild wurde mit Hilfsinformationen augmentiert. Darunter fällt auch eine Dopplersimulation durch Farbmodulation einer eingeblendeten Blutgefäßmaske. Aus [5].

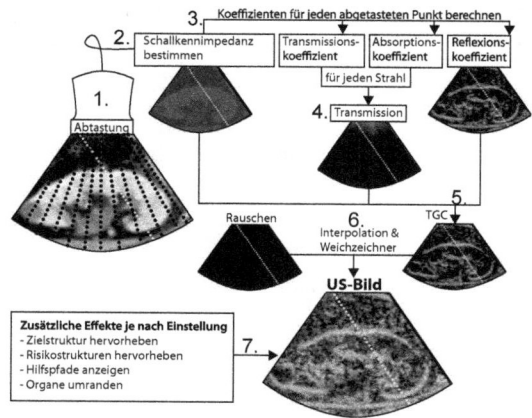

Die Sollwerte aus der Literatur [140] werden durch diese Abschätzung für einzelne Strukturen nicht immer genau genug angenähert. Daher werden für Lunge, Knochen und Gefäße die partiellen Segmentierungen und dort strukturspezifisch lokal gültige Impedanzen aus dem Patientenatlas herangezogen.

(3) Reflexions- und die Transmissionskoeffizienten werden mit den Schallkennimpedanzen Z und den Richtungsvektoren der Strahlen an Gewebeübergängen (Bildgradient) berechnet. Der Einfallswinkel kann mit dem Skalarprodukt des Richtungsvektors des einfallenden Strahls und der Oberflächennormalen (Bildgradient) berechnet werden [141]. Schließlich werden in diesem Teilschritt Absorptionskoeffizienten geschätzt. HU-Werten bzw. ggf. lokal vorhandenen Teilsegmentierung werden Richtwerte aus der Literatur [140] zugeordnet. Für nicht segmentiertes Weichteilgewebe wird ein Absorptionskoeffizient von $0,55$ dB/cm angenommen [140].

(4) Ausgehend von einer angenommenen normierten Intensität $I_0 = 1$ wird diese mit zunehmender Eindringtiefe in das Gewebe durch Absorption und Reflexion schrittweise abgeschwächt. Auf der GPU wird in diesem Schritt zur parallelen Berechnung ein Block mit 256 Threads für 256 Strahlen erzeugt. Die Restenergie $I_i(\mathbf{X}_i)$ nimmt mit der Eindringtiefe ab und wird rekursiv berechnet. Damit kann die reflektierte Intensität $I_r(\mathbf{X}_i)$ über den Reflexionskoeffizienten geschätzt werden, indem vereinfachend der Weg der der einfallenden Intensität zurückverfolgt und die am Transducer empfangene Intensität $I_e(\mathbf{X}_i)$ nochmals gleich vom Gewebe abgeschwächt wurde.

(5) Mit zunehmender Entfernung der Reflexionsorte vom Transducer werden die Signale durch das durchlaufene Gewebe stärker abgeschwächt. Wünschenswert ist jedoch die gleichmäßige Darstellung der Strukturen ohne den systematischen Unterschied durch die Eindringtiefe. Der Time-Gain-Control (TGC) zur tiefenabhängigen Verstärkung des empfangenen Signals kompensiert dies. Die zur Simulation verwendete Verstärkung $v(d)$ berücksichtigt die US-Frequenz f und kann durch den Faktor c vom Anwender in der Simulator-GUI analog zu einem realen US-Gerät angepasst werden:

$$v(d) = \exp\left(-\frac{c \cdot d \cdot f}{10}\right)^2 \tag{2.12}$$

Schließlich kann das verstärkte Signal $I_v(\mathbf{X}_i)$ mit der Entfernung d zum Schallkopf berechnet werden:

$$I_v(\mathbf{X}_i) = \frac{I_e(\mathbf{X}_i)}{v(d)} \cdot I_0 \qquad (2.13)$$

Die konstant angenommene Abschwächung in einem Gewebe bewirkt eine Aufhellung im Bild hinter schwach absorbierendem Gewebe. Dieses Artefakt kann z. B. hinter einer gefüllten Harnblase durch den kleinen Abschwächungskoeffizienten von Wasser von ca. $< 0,002$ dB/cm [140] beobachtet werden.

(6) Die heuristische Zusammensetzung des B-Mode-Bildes verwendet eine Bildkomposition [142] und kann über eine GUI vom Benutzer angepasst werden. Bildkompositorische Elemente sind künstliches Perlin-Rauschen und Weichzeichenfilter.

(7) Weitere Hilfsvisualisierungen, wie z. B. die farbige Umrandung von Schlüsselstrukturen einer Punktionsanwendung (Zielstrukturen: Gallengänge, Läsionen) erhöhen den didaktischen Wert der US-Simulation. Zudem kann Dopplerultraschall durch Farbmodulation der segmentierten Blutgefäße eingeblendet werden [2], sodass auch diese nicht zu punktierenden Risikostrukturen sichtbar werden. Die Punktionsnadel wird im US-Bild grau und die Zielführung gelb gestrichelt als Linie dargestellt.

2.4 Evaluationsaspekte und -methodik

Die Bewertung der Modellierung virtueller Patienten durch Segmentierungsmethoden greift hauptsächlich auf die DICE-Metrik [20] sowie z. T. auf mittlere und maximale Oberflächenabstände zurück [143]. Für den Modellierungsprozess virtueller Patienten (Abb. 2.1, S. 7) wurde außerdem der Zeitaufwand gemessen [1]. Zur Bewertung dienten 10 Testdatensätze und Kreuzvalidierungsmethoden. Zur allgemeinen Bewertung des VR-Trainingssystems wurde auf der qualitativen Seite eine Benutzerstudie durchgeführt. Quantitativ wurde neben der Segmentierungsgüte der virtuellen Patienten vor allem die Kraftausgabe mit mittleren quadratischen und maximalen Fehlern bewertet. Das visuo-haptische Rendering wurde qualitativ in der Benutzerstudie und quantitativ durch Berechnung von bildweisen Rendering-Zeiten- [ms] bzw. -Frequenzen (Bilder pro Sekunde, engl. frames per second, FPS [Hz]) bewertet.

In dem neu publizierten planungsgestützten Evaluations-Framework für haptische Kraftausgabemethoden [4] wurde eine große Anzahl von plausiblen Punktionspfaden (Referenzpfade) GPU-gestützt Raycasting-basiert geplant. Entlang dieser Referenzpfade wurde die Nadel mit konstanter Geschwindigkeit und Berechnung der Ausgabe der zu vergleichenden Kraftalgorithmen simuliert bewegt (siehe Abb. 2.10).

In der Planungsphase wird als hartes Kriterium die Erreichbarkeit der Zielstruktur (z. B. Gallengänge, Läsionen) in Nadellänge ausgehend von der Ausgangsstruktur (Hautoberfläche) bestimmt. Undurchdringlich deklarierte Strukturen wie Knochen und andere Risikostrukturen werden nicht berührt. Weiche Kriterien (Pfadlänge, Abstand zu Risikostrukturen, Einstichwinkel in Zielgefäßast) in einem gewichteten Mittelwert dienen zu Qualitätsbewertung (Scoring) und Ranking der möglichen Pfade [4]. Für einen Haut-Voxel maximiert der gewählte Pfadkandidat die Bewertung. Zur Kraftausgabebewertung wird an jeder Position eines Referenzpfades an der Nadelspitze ein Kraftausgabepaar berechnet: (1) die durch den Referenzalgorithmus mit Vollsegmentierungen (AcusVR) [18, 78] und (2) die durch das neu entwickelte Verfahren mit partiellen Segmentierungen resultierende Kraft [1, 4, 8] (AcusVR2). Als Metriken um die Kraftausgabewertepaare zu bewerten,

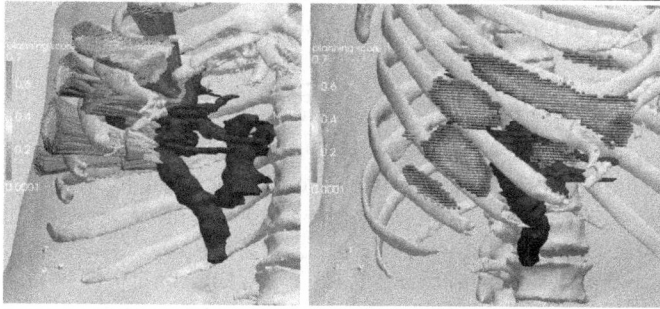

Abbildung 2.10: Gefundene Referenzpfade (farbig), Haut (beige) und Knochen (weiß): (Links) Pfade von der Haut zur Zielstruktur der äußeren Gallengänge (lila). (Rechts) Testpfade mit dem Ziel Gallengänge: Die Farbcodierung entspricht der Qualität der Trajektorie (grün: hohe Pfadqualität). Aus [4].

wurden der „mittlere quadratische Fehler" ((root) mean squared error, (R)MSE) und der „maximale absolute Fehler" (maximal absolute error, MAE) verwendet. Für die statistische Auswertung der ortsabhängig festgestellten Fehler wurde der p-Wert von zweiseitigen t-Tests herangezogen.

In der Benutzerstudie kamen als probate Zielgruppe für das Punktionstraining in der medizinischen Ausbildung 16 Medizinstudierende des 10. Semesters kurz vor dem praktischen Jahr infrage. Ihnen wurde der Simulator in einem standardisierten Studienprotokoll und Zeitrahmen (30-60 Minuten) vorgeführt bis die gleiche Bedienfähigkeit des Systems gegeben war. Der VR-Trainer in der Variante mit schienengeführter US-Punktion wurde ihnen dann zu insgesamt sechs selbstständig durchgeführten bewerteten Punktionsversuchen überlassen: (1) drei Punktionsversuche entlang vorgegebener Referenzpfade und (2) drei freie Punktionen. Anschließend wurde ein standardisierter Fragebogen (Tab. 3.3, S. 32) ausgefüllt und die Fragen auf einer vierstufigen Likert-Skala [144] beantwortet, um eine klare Tendenz in der Bewertung zu provozieren. Aus der Menge der 18 Fragen zielten zwei eingestreute Fragen auf die Bewertung des Trainingseffekts in Gestalt des gestiegenen Selbstvertrauens ab (Motivation), eine solche Punktion selbstständig durchführen zu können. Der vermeintliche Trainingseffekt wurde durch Antwortvergleich dieser beiden Fragen (F1 vs. F16) statistisch mit dem Wilcoxon-Vorzeichen-Rang-Test bewertet [145].

3 Ergebnisse

Die bei anderen Simulatoren notwendige manuelle Vollsegmentierung [18, 19, 78, 39] wurde durch einen zeiteffizienten semi-automatischen Prozess mit Hintergrundteilprozessen ersetzt (Abb. 2.1, S. 7). Es werden im Folgenden die erzielten Gütemaßwerte für die Füllstrukturen und für die Schlüsselstrukturen dargestellt.

Anschließend werden Ergebnisse für das haptische und visuelle Rendering gezeigt. Abschließend werden die Zeiteffizienz der Patientenmodellierung und qualitative Resultate einer Benutzerstudie für das Training von Gallengangpunkten dargelegt.

3.1 Modellierung patientenspezifischer Atlanten

Der GPA bzw. NPA wurde als hierarchische Datenstruktur angelegt und im XML-Format gespeichert (Abb. 2.2a, S. 8). Der GPA enthält alle Kernattribute, um einen beliebigen virtuellen PTC/D-Patienten zu beschreiben. Daneben enthält er Hilfsattribute wie eine Parametertabelle [1], die Leberatlasdatenbank und das B-Spline-Modell zur Faszienmodellierung. Der GPA kann selbst als Demopatient in den Simulator geladen werden, da ihm ein ausgewählter Intensitätsdatensatz inkl. Segmentierungen zugrunde liegen. In [1] wurden mehrere GPAn erstellt und an 10 NPAn kreuzvalidierend erfolgreich angepasst.

3.1.1 Transferfunktionsbasierte Segmentierung

Die Transferfunktionen aus § 2.1.1 eignen sich zum Echtzeitzugriff auf die visuo-haptische Parameter während der Simulation. Die Segmentierungsqualitäten der alternativ untersuchten Transferfunktionsansätze werden in den folgenden Abschnitten dargelegt.

3.1.1.1 Bayes-Transferfunktionen

Zur Definition der Transferfunktionsstützstellen für h_{bay} in Gl. (2.3, S. 10) für den GPA wurden unter Normalverteilungsannahme initial die statistischen Parameter Mittelwert und Standardabweichung großräumiger, gegebener Segmentierungen (Luft, Haut, Weichteilgewebe und Knochen) analysiert. Die manuell vollsegmentierten Patientendaten standen aus Vorarbeiten zur Verfügung [18, 19]. Paarweise wurden nun für die Übergänge (von-zu) Luft-Haut, Haut-Weichteile, Weichteile-Knochen Intervallgrenzen t_{von}^{zu} nach Bayes als Schnittpunkt gewebespezifischer Normalverteilungen zur Klassentrennung errechnet (Abb. 2.3a, S. 10).

Die auf dieser Analyse aufbauenden stückweise definierten visuellen und haptischen Transferfunktion sind exemplarisch in Abb. 3.1a und angewandt in Abb. 3.1b (peripher) und Abb. 3.1c (viszeral) dargestellt.

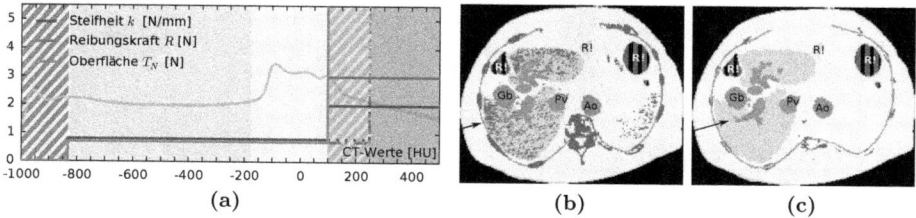

Abbildung 3.1: Visuo-haptische Transferfunktion (a) aus Gl. (2.3, S. 10) und Anwendung (b, c): (a) Intensitätshistogramm (grau) mit farbcodierten Intervallen von Luft (hellgrau), Haut (orange), Fett (gelb) und Knochen (lila). Das grau-weiß schraffierte Intervall wird entweder als Luft oder Risikostruktur in Abhängigkeit von der Nadelspitzenposition klassifiziert. Der gelb-lila schraffierte Bereich zeigt die Fälle „Nadelschaft außerhalb" bzw. „innerhalb" der virtuellen Faszienhaut ((b) bzw. (c)). (b) Subkutan-periphere Lage: Axiales Schichtbild mit farbcodiertem Gewebe: Luft (schwarz), Haut (orange), Fett (gelb), Knochen (lila) und teilweise Segmentierungen. (c) Viszerale Lage der Nadelspitze. Legende: R=Risikostruktur, Gb=Gallenblase, Ao=Aorta und Pv=Pfortader. Aus [1].

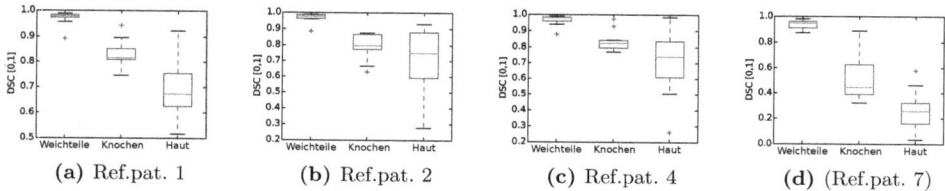

Abbildung 3.2: Boxplots der DICE-Koeffizienten (DSC) sortiert nach Medianwert: (a-c) Referenzpatienten abhängige großvolumige Strukturen. Die Weichteilsegmentierung war am besten, während dünne Strukturen schwerer zu segmentieren waren (Haut). (d) Der korpulente Referenzpatient 7 lieferte die schlechtesten Ergebnisse bei allen anderen Zielpatienten und sollte nicht im GPA für diese Patientengruppe verwendet werden. Aus [1].

In [1] wurde eine Robustheitsstudie durchgeführt, indem der dem GPA zugrunde liegende CT-Datensatz innerhalb der Testgruppe der 10 Patienten viermal anders gewählt wurde. Die Segmentierung neuer CT-Bilddaten für einen NPA kann wie in § 2.1.1.1 gezeigt nach erfolgter bijektiver Histogrammanpassung auf den Intensitätsdatensatz des GPA mit seiner Label-Transferfunktion erfolgen.

Unter kreuzvalidierender Variation der auf zehn Testpatienten sinnvoll angewendeten drei GPAn (1, 2, 4) wurden beste mittlere (mediane) DICE-Werte für die Strukturen Haut, Weichteile und Knochen von 0,79±0,09 (0,75), 0,97±0,03 (0,98) und 0,83±0,06 (0,80) (Abb. 3.2a-c) mit Referenzpatient 2 erreicht [1]. Der korpulente Referenzpatient 7 für einen GPA diente als Gegenbeispiel (Abb. 3.2d).

3.1.1.2 Random-Forest-Transferfunktionen

Als alternativer vollautomatischer Ansatz wurden Random-Forest-Klassifikatoren als gelernte Transferfunktionen (Abb. 3.3, oben) untersucht, die nach dem Training ebenfalls eine sehr zeiteffiziente Segmentierung der Füllstrukturen erlauben. Beispielhafte qualitative Ergebnisse der robustesten gefunden Klassifikatoren mit Trainingsgruppen zu sieben Patienten und drei Features werden in Abb. 3.3 unten dargestellt.

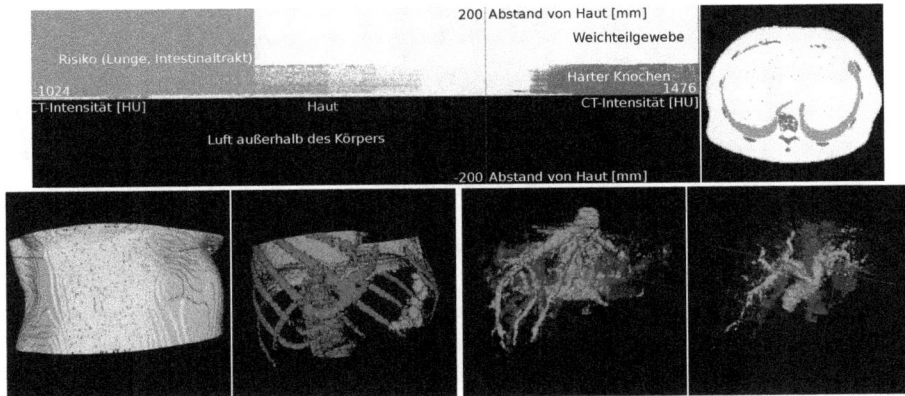

Abbildung 3.3: (Oben) Typische zweidimensionale von RFK_{lar} abgetastete Transferfunktion h (links) und Anwendungsergebnis (rechts). (Unten) In RA-Ansicht: (Links) Haut, Knochen und Risikostrukturen durch Anwendung der Transferfunktion. (Rechts) Blut- und Gallengefäße. Aus [6].

Die Verwendung dieser mehrdimensionalen Transferfunktionen ist für das visuo-haptische Rendering analog zur Bayes-Tf. aus § 3.1.1.1 sehr zeiteffizient möglich [6].

Beste Mittel- (Median-) DICE-Werte von 0,79±0,14 (0,84) für die Haut, 0,97±0,01 (0,97) für das Weichteilgewebe, 0,63±0,11 (0,62) für Knochen und 0,83±0,23 (0,92) für Risikostrukturen konnten für eine Referenzpatientenlerngruppe mit sieben Patienten erreicht werden. Für die Leber selbst wurde 0,90±0,14 (0,95) und für die Leberstrukturen wurden 0,37±0,13 (0,41) für Blutgefäße und 0,39±0,14 (0,35) für die schwierigen Gallengefäße vollautomatisch ohne manuelle Nachbearbeitung erzielt [6]. Die Klassifikatoren mit der in [6] empfohlenen größeren Lerngruppe und drei Merkmalen waren tendenziell etwas robuster bei etwas besseren Medianwerten.

Auf einem Intel Xeon W3530@2.8 GHz Prozessor, mit acht Kernen und einer Lerngruppe mit sieben Patienten und allen drei Merkmalen waren mittlere Trainingszeiten von nur 10 Sekunden möglich. Bei der Klassifikation wurden 1.6E-06 Sekunden pro Voxel (625.000 Hz) gemessen. Dieses Laufzeitverhalten passt sehr gut zu direkten haptischen Volumen-Rendering-Ansätzen, die von der Nadel berührte Voxel mit 1000-2000 Hz auf der CPU klassifizieren müssen [2].

3.1.2 Organspezifisch optimierte Segmentierungsverfahren

Es werden zunächst qualitative Ergebnisse für die Modellierung der haptisch wichtigen Struktur der Faszien gezeigt. Es folgen die quantitativen Ergebnisse zur semi-automatischen Segmentierung der Leber und der Leberblut- und -gallengefäße.

3.1.2.1 Spline-Modellierung einer virtuellen Faszienhaut

Die Modellierung einer Faszienhaut, die (1) zur haptisch plausiblen Simulation eines salienten Nadeldurchstoßereignisses auf dem Weg ins Leberinnere und (2) zur Unterscheidung peripherer und viszeraler Strukturen in Gl. (2.3, S. 10) dient, wurde mit zylindrischen B-Spline-Funktionen realisiert. Das Referenzmodell ist passgenau zu den jeweiligen im GPA

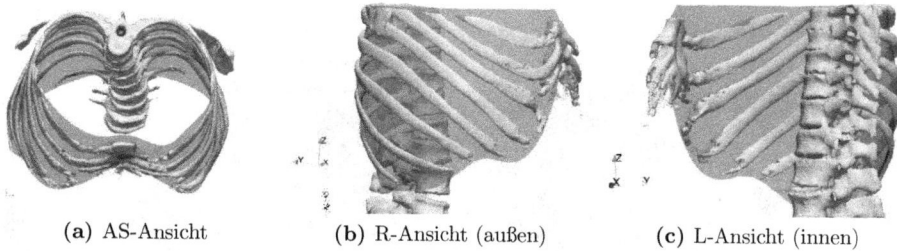

(a) AS-Ansicht　　　　(b) R-Ansicht (außen)　　　　(c) L-Ansicht (innen)

Abbildung 3.4: Die Referenz-B-Spline-Oberfläche (Magenta) genau in die Rippenbögen des Brustkorbs (grau) eingepasst: (a) komplette Ansicht der zylindrischen B-Spline-Fläche. (b) Ansicht von außerhalb der rechten Hälfte des Brustkorbs. (c) Innenansicht des rechten Brustkorbs. Aus [1].

Abbildung 3.5: Oberflächenabstände für die Leber eines Patienten in LP-Ansicht. Bei den hier dargestellten, gemittelten einseitigen Hausdorffabständen zeigte sich, dass die größten Abstände in punktionsirrelevanten Bereichen an den caudalen und medialen Leberspitzen befinden. Aus [7].

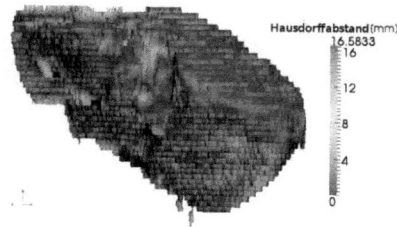

enthaltenen Referenzpatientendaten und bietet genug Freiheitsgrade, um auf jeden ungesehenen Patientendatensatz (NPA) angepasst zu werden.

Es wurde ein Modell mit 75 3D-Kontrollpunkten und drei kubischen B-Spline-Basisfunktionen gewählt [1]. Die längs gerichtete mindestens C^0-stetige Saumlinie des Zylinders ($\phi = 0$ bzw. $\phi = 2\pi$) wurde in die Wirbelsäule gelegt, dieser Bereich war irrelevant für die PTC/D-Punktionsanwendung. Dieses Modell wurde für den ausgewählten Referenzpatienten-CT-Datensatz erstellt und steht im jeweiligen GPA zur Verfügung. Für NPAn wurden die 3D-Kontrollpunkte der zylindrischen B-Spline-Fäche so eingestellt, dass die schwellwertsegmentierten Rippen mittig geschnitten wurden und der Zylinderbodenrand mit den Rippenbögen abschloß. Der Zeitaufwand für diesen Schritt betrug pro Patient maximal 40 Minuten ermittelt mit 10 Testpatienten [1]. Im Hintergrund liefen auf 24 Rechnern Atlas-Segmentierungen der Leber (Abb. 2.4, S. 13).

3.1.2.2 Multi-Atlas-Segmentierung der Leber

Nach erfolgter Single-Atlas-Registrierung gegebener Segmentierungsmasken der GPA-Atlasdatenbank auf einen ungesehenen Zielpatienten (NPA) wird eine konsolidierende Wahrscheinlichkeitskarte der Leber durch einen Patch-basierten Fusionsansatz der multiplen Schätzmasken generiert [1, 7]. Dieser arbeitete zeiteffizienter und lieferte bessere Ergebnisse als andere, etablierte Fusionsmethoden (z. B. SIMPLE, STAPLE, Vote- und Sum-Rule) aus der Literatur [146, 147, 148, 149]. Das entwickelte Fusions-Verfahren wurde detailliert in einer Leave-One-Out-Kreuzvalidierung mit 12 Patienten [7] getestet. Mittlere Oberflächenabstände von 2,6 mm, Hausdorffdistanzen von maximal 27,5 mm [7] und DICE-Koeffizienten von bis zu 0,95 konnten erreicht werden. Bei den Hausdorffabständen zeigte sich in der Studie, dass sich die größten Abstände im punktionsirrelevanten Bereich an den Leberspitzen (Abb. 3.5) befinden [7].

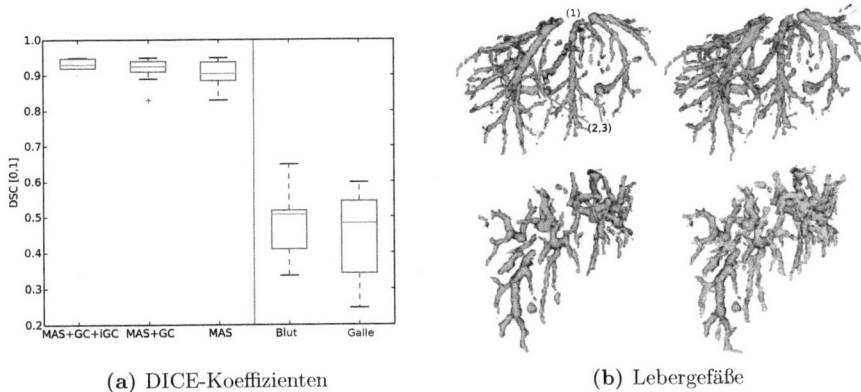

(a) DICE-Koeffizienten   (b) Lebergefäße

Abbildung 3.6: Ergebnisse für Schlüsselstrukturen: (a) Boxplots der DICE-Koeffizienten der Schlüsselstrukturen nach Medianwert sortiert: MAS=Multi-Atlas-Segmentierung, GC=GraphCut-Nachverarbeitung, iGC=interaktive GC-Nachbearbeitung. (b) Gefäßsegmentierung mit Vesselness-Methode: obere Reihe: (Links) Blutgefäße aus der automatischen Segmentierung und (rechts) überlagert mit roter Referenzsegmentierung. (1) Verbindungsstelle der Lebervenen; (2,3) linke und rechte hepatische Arterien und Venen. Untere Reihe: entsprechende Bilder mit den Gallengängen (Referenzsegmentierung in Hellgrün). Aus [1].

Später wurde in [1] eine optimierte MAS-Strategie anhand von 10 Testpatienten unter Verwendung einer Atlasdatenbank mit 59 Atlanten evaluiert, die Ergebnisse sind in Abb. 3.6a zusammengefasst. Die Leber wurde hier präzise mit DICE-Koeffizienten von 0,93±0,01 segmentiert. Der Vorteil mit Einbezug spärlicher interaktiver Korrekturen (MAS+GC+iGC) war signifikant besser als ohne jegliche GraphCut-Korrektur (MAS), jedoch nicht signifikant besser als die vollautomatische Schrittfolge MAS+GC. Die Laufzeit dieses Schrittes wurde auf maximal zwei Stunden begrenzt.

3.1.2.3 Segmentierung der Lebergefäße

Es wurden DICE-Koeffizienten für Leberblut- und Lebergallengefäße maximal bis zu 0,65 und 0,60 ermittelt. Der Mittelwert (Median) der DICE-Koeffizienten liegt für Blutgefäße bei 0,47±0,09 (0,51) und für Gallengänge bei 0,44±0,12 (0,48) (Abb. 3.6a). Die besten Ergebnisse wurden unter Einbezug von Satos [51] Vesselness-Merkmalen erzielt. Beispielhafte Ergebnisse sind in Abb. 3.6b dargestellt. Die Laufzeit dieses Teilschritts beträgt maximal 15 Minuten [1].

3.2 Quantitative Bewertung der Haptik

In [4] wurde eine neue Kraftausgabebewertungsmethodik vorgestellt und die Kraftausgabe [2, 8] mit 3508 automatisch geplanten Pfaden (vgl. Kap. 2.4) an einem Referenzpatienten evaluiert.

Es zeigten sich RMSE (MSE) bzw. MAE von 0.07±0,098 N (0,0056±0,0097 N^2) bzw. maximal 0,73±0,15 N. Statistisch bedeutende Fehler ($p <0,05$) wurden bei nur 0,8 % aller Referenzpfade gefunden (Abb. 3.7). Ein systematischer Fehler von 0,7 N in der

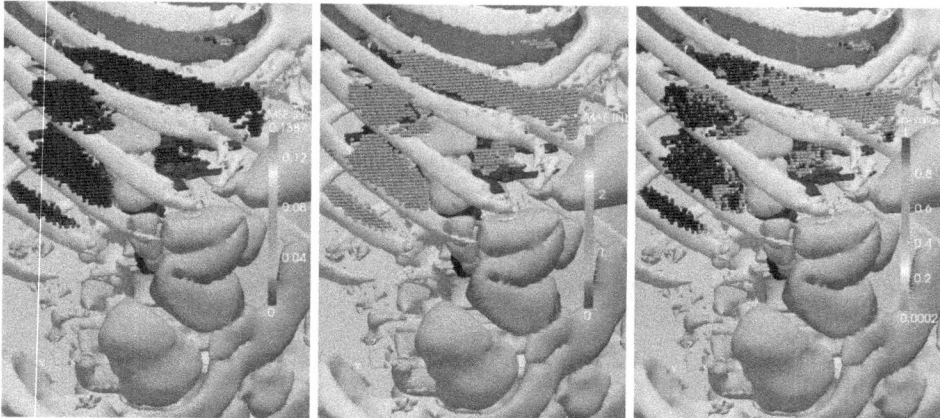

(a) Mittlere quadratische Fehler   (b) Maximale absolute Fehler   (c) p-Wert

Abbildung 3.7: Farbcodierte Fehlermetriken der Referenzpfade: (a) MSE: Blaue Pfadstartpunkte bezeichnen sehr geringe mittlere quadratische Fehler. (b) MAE: Hellblau zeigt einen haptisch irrelevanten systematischen Fehler von 0,7 N an der Hautoberfläche. (c) P-Werte in Rot zeigen wenige signifikante Fehler. Die Risikostrukturen Lunge (mattblau) und Darm (dunkelbeige) werden von den Raycasting-geplanten Pfaden gemieden. Aus [4].

Abbildung 3.8: Kraftkurven für einen typischen Pfad mit maximalem absoluten Fehler von 0,7 N: Referenzkraft (blau) vs. neuer Algorithmus (magenta): Die Kraftverläufe für den Pfad waren strukturell identisch, bis auf einen Fehler an der Haut. Dies war durch eine haptisch irrelevante um 1 bis 2 mm versetzte Detektion von Hautstrukturen bedingt. Aus [4].

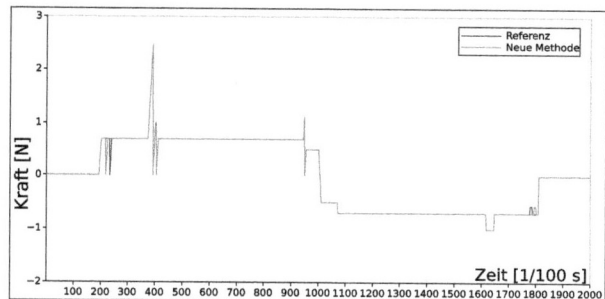

MAE-Metrik wurde beobachtet (Abb. 3.8), der auf eine leicht zum Goldstandard versetzte Detektion von Hautstrukturen zurückführbar war.

Für die artefaktfreie haptische Kraftausgabe muss die Abfrage der haptischen Parameter vom NPA und die Kraftberechnung zwingend hocheffizient (1000-2000 Hz) zur Laufzeit ausgewertet werden. Die Label-Abfrage und ggf. folgende Transferfunktionsauswertung aus aus Gl. (2.1, S. 9) sowie die Kraftberechnung aus Gl. (2.6, S. 14) erfüllen diese Bedingung leicht auf einem CPU-Kern aktueller Desktop-Computer-Prozessoren (Intel i7, 3 GHz).

3.3 Bewertung des visuellen Renderings

Die visuelle Plausibilität und Echtzeitfähigkeit der Methoden wurde qualitativ und quantitativ untersucht und bestätigt [5, 2, 3]. Für die Glättung und Propagierung der Nadeldeformationen im inversen Deformationsfeld wurde kein signifikanter Unterschied eines effizienten Temperaturdiffusionsansatzes zu einem physikalisch besser motivierten linear

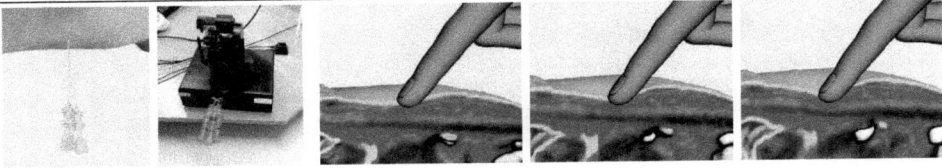

Abbildung 3.9: Visualisierung des Einflusses der Atmung auf die Kraftausgabe (links) und eines tastenden, fixierten Fingers auf den einatmenden virtuellen Patienten (rechts). Aus [3].

elastischen Regularisierungsansatz gefunden [9]. Goldstandard waren hierbei *in silico*-FEM-Simulationen der Gewebedeformation.

3.3.1 Deformationen durch 4D-Bewegungssimulation

Die Ergebnisse des Ansatzes wurden für die Simulation allgemein in [3] und für den patientenspezifischen US-gestützten Nadeleingriff in atembewegten Patienten in [5] vorgestellt. Qualitativ wird die 4D-Atembewegungssimulation in Abb. 3.12 auf S. 29 im Zusammenhang mit der US-Simulation veranschaulicht. Videomaterial, das im Internet hinterlegt ist, zeigt das Rendering und die Atembewegung in der VR-Simulation. In Abb. 3.9 liegt ein fixierter Finger auf der Haut eines atmenden virtuellen Patienten und das Gewebe schiebt sich in Richtung der Atembewegung zusammen.

Die Rendering-Performance unter Atemanimation genügt auf der Nvidia GTX 680 mit 37,52 ms pro Bild (27 FPS) sehr gut der Echtzeitanforderung [3].

3.3.2 Spezielle Verfahren des Raycastings

Visuelle Rendering-Ergebnisse für verschiedene Visualisierungsmodi sind in Abb. 3.10a, 3.10b und im Video[1] dargestellt. Durch die Flexibilität der Transferfunktionen kombiniert mit einem Clipping-Verfahren entlang frei wählbarer Schnittebenen wurden verschiedene didaktisch sinnvolle Darstellungen erreicht.

Das zeitliche Verhalten der visuellen Rendering-Module im Zusammenspiel der Gesamtsimulation wird in Abb. 3.10c deutlich. Auf der verwendeten GPU-Grafikkarte Nvidia GTX 680 war lediglich das selten benötigte Modul der Fluoroskopiesimulation (X-Ray, Abb. 3.13b, S. 30) mit Kontrastmittelsimulation nicht regelmäßig echtzeitfähig (18 Hz<25 Hz). Für Einzelbilder und eine akzeptable Darstellung der Kontrastmittelausbreitung reicht diese FPS-Performanz jedoch (>15 Hz) [150].

Abb. 3.10b stellt ein reales US-Bild der Niere (links) einem mit der vorgestellten Methode simulierten US-Bild gegenüber (rechts). Die Form der Niere ist auf beiden Bildern gut erkennbar, jedoch hat das reale Bild weichere Kanten, ein charakteristischen Organrauschen und weist eine radiale Unschärfe auf. Abb. 3.11 zeigt ein simuliertes US-Bild der Leber mit verschiedenen Hilfsvisualisierungen zur didaktisch klaren Darstellung der Gefäße und Zielstrukturen. Die simulierten Deformationen durch die Nadel an Gewebegrenzen werden in Abb. 3.11 (Mitte) am Beispiel einer Punktion der Leberkapsel verdeutlicht. Auch die simulierte Schattenbildung hinter Rippen ist erkennbar. In der PTC/D-Simulation wird eine Führungsschiene an der US-Sonde simuliert, um eine haptisch geführte Punktion in

---

[1]Videomaterial: `https://goo.gl/Lgn9du`

(a)

(b)

(c)

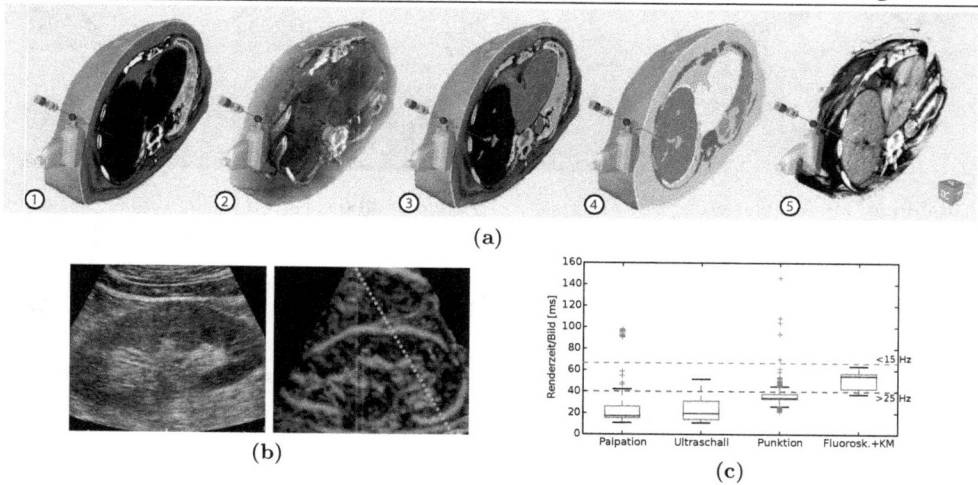

Abbildung 3.10: Qualitative und quantitative Visualisierungsergebnisse: (a) Verschiedene Volumen-Renderings eines virtuellen Patientenatlas mit aktiviertem Clipping-Modus: (1) mit Transferfunktion, (2) unterschiedliche Opazitätswerte für die Transferfunktionen, (3) Ziel und Risikostruktur eingeblendet, (4) Label-Funktion und (5) eine Intensitätsfensterung. (b) Beispiel eines realen (links) und eines simulierten (rechts) Ultraschallbildes der Niere. (c) Boxplotresultate der Bildaufbaugeschwindigkeiten auf einer Nvidia GTX 680: Werte unterhalb der blauen Linie bedeuten echtzeitfähige Aktualisierungsraten (>25 Hz), KM: Kontrastmittelsimulation. Siehe auch Fußnote [1]. Aus [5, 2].

der US-Ebene entlang der virtuellen Ziellinie (gelb gestrichelt) zu ermöglichen. Die Nadel wird in grau dargestellt.

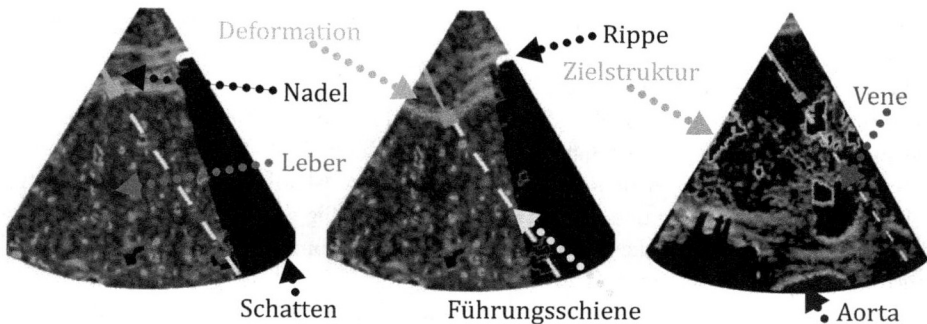

Abbildung 3.11: Ultraschallsimulation: Links: Nadel vor Einstich in die Leber. Mitte: Veranschaulichung der Deformationen beim Einstich in die Leber. Rechts: Hilfsvisualisierungen. Didaktisch hilfreich ist hier auch die optional verdickte Darstellung der Nadelspitze. Aus [15].

3.3.2.1 Ultraschallsimulation in atmenden virtuellen Patienten

Durch die Berücksichtigung der Atmung wird die Trainingssimulation der US-Bildgebung und der US-gestützten Nadelpunktion in der Führungsschiene noch anspruchsvoller für den Trainierenden. Dieser Simulationsaspekt wurde in [5] vorgestellt. Anhand eines 4D-CT-Datensatzes wurde ein patientenspezifisches Atemmodell erstellt und die US-gestützte Nadelpunktion hiermit gekoppelt.

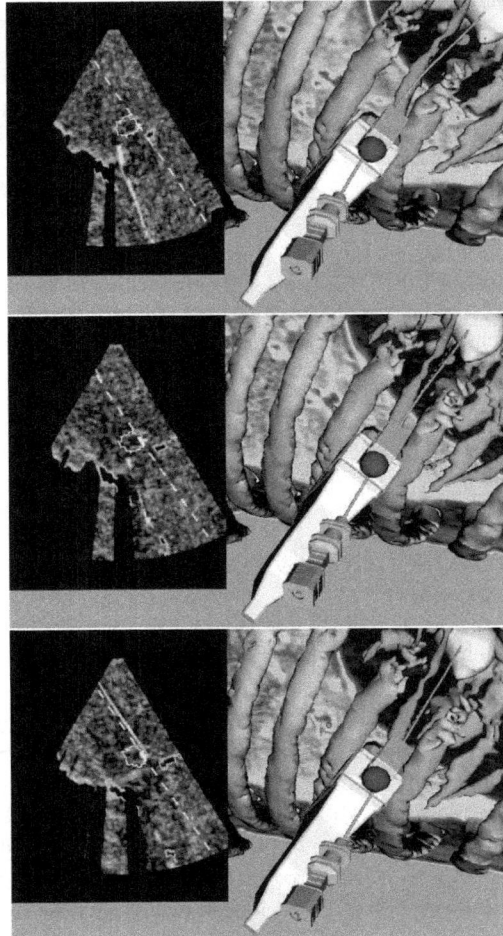

Abbildung 3.12: Drei Zeitpunkte der US-gestützten Leberpunktion und verschiedene Strukturen beim Ausatmen des virtuellen Patienten: Rippen (grau), Gallengänge (links im US: grün, rechts in 3D: blass rot), Zielläsion (gelb). Die optionale Dopplersimulation für Blutgefäße ändert mit einer realistischen Frequenz die Farbe (im US: rot-gelb). Dunkle Bereiche auf der unteren linken Seite des US-Bildes entsprechen Lungenbereichen, die Schall nicht reflektieren. Siehe auch Fußnote [2]. Aus [5].

Abb. 3.12 und das im Internet verfügbare Videomaterial[2] aus [5] zeigen simulierte US-Bilder unter Patientenatmung. Verschiedene farbig eingeblendete didaktische Visualisierungen sind zu sehen (Lebergefäße: grün/rot, Doppler: orange pulsierend, Zielläsion: gelb). Dunkle Bereiche ohne Schallreflexion in der linken unteren Ecke des simulierten US-Bildes aus Abb. 3.12 entsprechen den Lungen (Risikostruktur), die nicht punktiert werden und aufgrund des hohen Luftgehalts den Schall nicht reflektieren. Für ein US-Bild der Ausgabegröße 256x256 Pixel, wurden 256 Strahlen in parallelen CUDA-Blöcken werden mit jeweils 512 Punkten in 512 CUDA-Threads berechnet. Der isoliert betrachtete Render-

---

[2]Videomaterial: `https://goo.gl/AvXjQd`

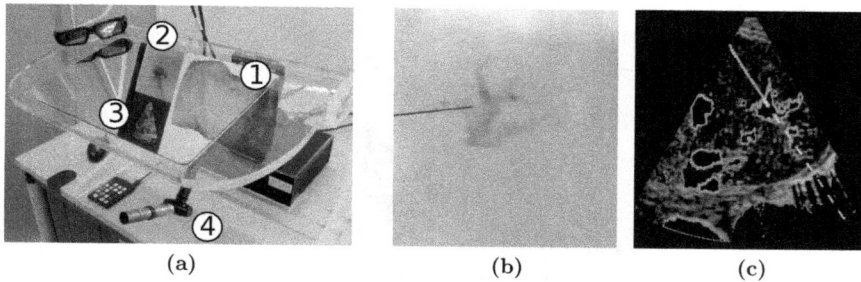

(a)   (b)   (c)

Abbildung 3.13: Simulator im Überblick: (a) Benutzerschnittstelle: (1) Volumen-Rendering, (2) Röntgensimulation, (3) Ultraschallsimulation und (4) Steuergriff des Kraftrückgabegeräts. (b) Detailansicht des Röntgenbilds (2) bei Kontrastmittelgabe in den Gallengängen. (c) Ultraschallsimulation (3) mit Hilfsvisualisierungen (grün/rot=Ziel-/Risikostrukturen). Aus [2].

Kernel für die US-Simulation erforderte 8 ms pro Bild mit der hierbei verwendeten Nvidia Quadro 4000 und erreichte somit ein Maximum von 124 FPS [5].

3.4 Zusammenfassende Evaluation

Es wurde ein innerhalb einer VR-Workbench[3] integriertes System bestehend aus einem Geomagic Phantom 1.5 6DOF HighForce Kraftrückkopplungsgerät und einem 3D-Stereo-Display verwendet (Abb. 3.13). Die visuelle Immersion mit Shutter-Brillen erfolgt mit einem unterhalb des Stereomonitors montierten halbdurchlässigen Spiegel zur erhöhten Auge-Hand-Koordination (Abb. 3.13a(1-3)). Unter dem Spiegel befindet sich der Arbeitsraum des haptischen Gerätes (Abb. 3.13a(4)). Die simulierte Fluoroskopie- und US-Kontrollbildgebung, wie sie im klinischen Alltag vorhanden ist, assistiert bei der Navigation (Abb. 3.13b, 3.13c). Das System eignet sich für zwei patientenspezifische Planungs- und Trainingsszenarien US-gestützter Punktionseingriffe: Erstens für das Punktieren der aufgestauten Gallengänge der Leber (PTC/D) [2] und zweitens für die Biopsie- und Ablationspunktion [5]. Die Atemsimulation für die US-gestützte Punktionssimulation mit 4D-CT-Daten wurde in [5, 3] publiziert.
Die Ergebnisse der alternativ untersuchten Ansätze zur Segmentierung der Strukturen mit Bayes- und Random-Forest-Transferfunktionen bzw. organspezifischen Methoden [1, 6] sind in Tab. 3.1 gegenübergestellt. Für Knochen wurden signifikant bessere Ergebnisse für den Bayes-Ansatz gefunden. Tendenziell waren die Bayes-basierten und organspezifisch optimierten Methoden genauer und präziser.

3.4.1 Zeiteffizienz der Modellierung virtueller Patienten

Durch die entwickelten Modellierungsmethoden wurde insgesamt eine deutlich geringere Gesamtzeit für die Erstellung eines neuen virtuellen Patientenmodells erreicht. Statt der vorher benötigten 32 bis 63 Stunden [18, 19], waren mit der vorgestellten Methodik nur

---

[3]SenseGraphics AB, Kista, Schweden, http://www.sensegraphics.com

Methode: DICE-	Bayes-Tf. Mittelwert	RF-Tf. Mittelwert	Methode: DICE-	Organspez. Mittelwert	RF-Tf. Mittelwert
Haut	0,79±0,09	0,79±0,14	Leber	0,93±0,01	0,90±0,14
Weichteile	0,97±0,03	0,97±0,01	Blutgefäße	0,47±0,09	0,37±0,13
Knochen	0,83±0,06*	0,63±0,11	Gallengef.	0,44±0,12	0,39±0,14

Tabelle 3.1: Segmentierungsergebnisse mit den Bayes-Transferfunktionen (links) und organspezifisch optimierten Methoden (rechts) jeweils gegenüber Random-Forest-Transferfunktionen. *: $p < 0,0001$. DICE-Werte empfohlener Methoden aus Tab. 2 und 3 (#2) aus [1] und Tab. 2d aus [6].

Aufgabe	Auto.	Semi.	Zeit [h:mm] MAS	GC	iGC
(1) Multi-Atlas-Segmentierung	x		2:00	2:00	2:00
(2) Faszienhautmodellierung		x	0:40	0:40	0:40
Summe (sequentiell 1-2)			2:40	2:40	2:40
Maximum (parallel 1-2)			2:00	2:00	2:00
(3) GraphCut-Postprocessing	x		N/A	0:10	0:10
(4) Interaktiver GraphCut		x	N/A	N/A	0:20
(5) Gefäßsegmentierung	x		0:15	0:15	0:15
Summe (sequentiell 3-5)			0:15	0:25	0:45
Summe sequentielle Bearbeitung			2:55	3:05	3:25
Summe mit 1 im Hintergrund			2:15	2:25	2:45

Tabelle 3.2: Zeitaufwände für die hauptsächlich automatischen (MAS, GC) und vermehrt interaktive Variante (iGC) für einen PC-Cluster mit ≥ 24 Knoten und einen Bediener. Aufgabe (1) wurde im Hintergrund ausgeführt, während die Faszien (2) bearbeitet wurden. Die Aufgaben (3-5) mussten nacheinander mit der resultierenden Lebermaske (1) verarbeitet werden. Aus [1].

noch etwa 2 bis 3 Stunden [1] Zeitaufwand für robuste Ergebnisse erforderlich (Tab. 3.2). Die Faszienhautmodellierung aus § 2.1.2.1 ist in Tab. 3.2 der manuell aufwendigste Teil im Modellierungskonzept (vgl. Kap. 3.4.1), wurde jedoch geschickt parallel zu den rechenaufwendigen Schritten der Multi-Atlas-Lebersegmentierung durchgeführt. Für diesen zeitkritischsten Schritt wurde ein parallel rechnender PC-Cluster mit 24 Workstations verwendet [1].

3.4.2 Benutzerevaluation

Während der Entwicklung des VR-Punktionstrainingssimulators haben zwei in Leberpunktionen erfahrene Mediziner die Arbeiten regelmäßig beratend unterstützt und bewertet. Zur Bewertung der Trainingsqualität des Simulators wurde eine Benutzerstudie mit 16 Studierenden der Medizin des 10. Semesters durchgeführt. Die Ergebnisse der Auswertung des Fragenkatalogs sind in Tab. 3.3 dargestellt.

Sehr positiv wurde die Sinnhaftigkeit (F4) und technische Umsetzung eingeschätzt (F5-13). Die Interaktion mit dem haptischen Gerät (F5-7) war für einige Probanden ungewohnt. Subjektiv wurde F6 am kritischsten gesehen. Nach dem Training (F14-18) wurde das Punktionsbewertungssystem am schlechtesten bewertet (F14). Das Training am Simulator führte schließlich zu einer signifikanten Steigerung des Benutzerselbstvertrauens (F1 vs. 16), anschließend eine Punktion praktisch durchzuführen. Dies wurde mit dem Wilcoxon-Vorzeichen-Rang-Test ($p < 0.01$) bestätigt [145]. Alle Antworten zum VR-System tendieren zum positiven Bereich bis 2,5.

Nr.	Frage	Median	Mittelw.	Std'abw.
1.	Eine PTCD hätte ich mir auch vor dem Training zugetraut.	3	2.88	0.96
2.	Das Absolvieren einer virtuellen Trainingseinheit vor der realen PTCD hatte ich generell für sinnvoll.	1	1.50	0.73
3.	Die Simulation könnte für einen neuen Patienten eine gute Planungsmöglichkeit bieten.	1	1.44	0.63
4.	Die Simulation könnte die Qualität eines bevorstehenden Eingriffs verbessern und die Belastung des Patienten verringern.	1	1.44	0.63
5.	Die Kraftrückgabe erscheint mir realistisch.	2	1.94	0.77
6.	Ich konnte durch die Kraftrückgabe die entscheidenden Strukturen erfühlen.	2	2.25	0.93
7.	Die Steuerung der virtuellen Instrumente mit dem haptischen Gerät war intuitiv.	2	2.00	0.82
8.	Die Darstellung der Körperoberfläche (Haut) erscheint mir realistisch.	2	2.00	0.63
9.	Die stereoskopische 3D-Darstellung vereinfacht das Training.	1.5	1.56	0.63
10.	Die Darstellung von Schatten vereinfacht die räumliche Orientierung.	2	1.81	0.75
11.	Die Kontrastmittelgabe und Ausbreitung ist in der Röntgensimulation gut zu erkennen.	1.5	1.56	0.63
12.	Die Ultraschallsimulation hilft bei der Navigation und dem Auffinden der Zielstruktur.	1	1.19	0.54
13.	Die Korrekturvorschläge des Simulators waren hilfreich.	2	1.86	0.77
14.	Das Bewertungssystem des Simulators ist aussagekräftig.	2	2.13	0.74
15.	Das Training mit dem PTCD-Simulator ist sinnvoll.	1	1.50	0.63
16.	Nach Absolvieren des Trainingsprogramms würde mir die erste Punktion leichter fallen.	2	1.94	0.85
17.	Durch das Training kann ich mir die anatomischen Strukturen des Leberbereichs besser vorstellen.	2	2.06	0.68
18.	Die technische Umsetzung des Simulators ist gut gelungen.	1	1.38	0.50

Legende:
Ja
1.0-1.5
1.5-2.0
2.0-2.5
2.5-3.0
3.0-3.5
3.5-4.0
Nein

Tabelle 3.3: Fragebogen für die 16 Medizinstudierenden mit resultierenden Medianen, Mittelwerten und Standardabweichungen der Bewertungen. Aus [2].

4 Diskussion und Ausblick

Das Konzept zur US-gestützten Punktionssimulation atembewegter virtueller Patienten wurde unter dem Leitgedanken der maximal erreichbaren Plausibilität mit den zur Verfügung stehenden Hardwaremitteln erfolgreich umgesetzt [5, 2]. Die neu entwickelten visuo-haptischen Rendering-Methoden reizten den aktuellen Stand der Technik aus (Nvidia GTX680) und können zukünftig von neuer GPU-Hardware stark profitieren [2]. Die hinreichende Realitätsnähe wurde qualitativ und quantitativ untersucht [2, 4]. Der Systementwicklungsprozess wurde durch in der PTC/D erfahrene Mediziner begleitet, die z. B. die haptischen Simulationsparameter der Kraftausgabe der einzelnen Gewebe in wiederholten Probepunktionen fein eingestellt haben. Eine Testnutzergruppe studierender Mediziner hat das System in einer Benutzerstudie technisch als sehr gelungen und sehr motivierend bewertet [2].

Die für die patientenspezifische Anwendbarkeit des Simulators notwendige Modellierung der Strukturen wurde in einem neuartigen Prozessablauf mit sequenziellen und parallelen Teilschritten erstellt [1]. Die wünschenswerte Vollautomatisierung war für die virtuelle Faszienhaut nicht möglich, jedoch wurde eine deutliche Verringerung der Segmentierungszeitaufwände (vgl. Tab. 3.2, S. 31) von 32 bis 63 auf zwei bis drei Stunden erreicht [18, 19, 39]. Der Stand der Forschung und die Erfahrung zeigen, dass im klinischen Alltag für bestimmte Segmentierungsprobleme noch auf absehbare Zeit manuelle Interaktionsmöglichkeiten insbesondere bei Besonderheiten wie Pathologien einzelner Patienten notwendig sein werden. Nur so kann aktuell die Genauigkeit der virtuellen Modelle für das patientenspezifische Planungstraining garantiert werden.

Das Konzept der effizienten Patientenmodellierung ausgehend von einem eine Patientengruppe repräsentierenden generischen Patientenatlas (GPA) zu ähnlichen ungesehenen neuen Patientenatlanten (NPA) wurde erfolgreich eingesetzt und publiziert [1]. Die hierarchische Datenstruktur des attributierten Baumes eignet sich für die begriffliche Darstellung von Beinhaltungsbeziehungen und ermöglicht den Echtzeitzugriff der für das Rendering benötigten Parameter. Ein simulationsfähiger GPA könnte konzeptionell auch gemittelt aus mehreren, ausgewählten repräsentativen Patientenbilddaten oder synthetisch modelliert werden [151, 152]. Eingehender untersucht werden könnten zukünftig auch interaktive Ansätze, die über die patientenspezfische Anpassung visuo-haptischer Transferfunktionen mittels einer vereinfachten GUI eine sofortige Visualisierung und schnelle Modellierung bestimmter Strukturen des virtuellen Patienten erlauben [153]. Der generische Patientenatlas würde hierbei als Attribute statistisch modellierte, gewebespezifische n-dimensionale Transferfunktionsschablonen beinhalten und ihre Hauptmodengewichtung auf GUI-Bedienelemente abbilden (Schieberegler).

Die für die Modellbildung notwendige Segmentierung der großvolumigen Füllstrukturen Haut, Weichteilgewebe, Knochen und luftgefüllter Risikostrukturen (Darm, Magen, Lunge) wurde mit zwei alternativen Transferfunktionsansätzen untersucht, die jeweils sehr schnell akkurate Ergebnisse erzeugten. Auf der einen Seite wurde der Bayes-Transferfunktions- [1, 8] und andererseits der Random-Forest-Klassifikator-Transferfunktionsansatz (RFK) über einem mehrdimensionalen Merkmalsraum untersucht [6]. Im Vergleich beider Verfahren ergaben sich im Rahmen der durchgeführten Studien außer für Knochen zugunsten der Bayes-Tfn. keine signifikanten Unterschiede, auch da die Standardabweichungen der Ergebnisse bei der RFK-Methode tendenziell recht groß waren. Vorteil des Random-Forest-Ansatzes ist die generelle Anwendbarkeit für alle Füll- und Zielstrukturen, deren DICE-Koeffizienten nachteilig tendenziell jedoch etwas schlechter bzw. weniger robust waren, d. h. deutlich höheren Standardabweichungen aufwiesen. Zur Verbesserung zu untersuchen wären daher höherdimensionale Merkmalsräume ($n > 3$) und die Ableitung von Merkmalen in der unmittelbaren Nachbarschaft eines Voxels (Patches). Sobald die GPUs hocheffiziente n-dimensionale Speicherzugriffsmöglichkeiten (Texturspeicher) anbieten, würde das visuelle Rendering auch mit entsprechenden n-dimensionalen Random-Forest-Transferfunktionen effizient möglich sein. Aktuelle z. T. bereits GPU-implementierte Methoden des Deep-Learning und Convolutional-Neural-Networks könnten als alternative Verfahren des maschinellen Lernens [154, 155] untersucht werden.

Bei den Bayes-Transferfunktionen könnten sich GPAs für verschiedene Patientengewichtsklassen besser eignen, um eine akkurate Modellierung der großvolumigen Füllstrukturen (Haut, Weichteilgewebe, Knochen) zu erreichen. Außerdem sollte zukünftig die Unterteilung des Weichteilgewebekompartiments in die darin enthaltenen Strukturen wie bspw. Fett und Muskeln untersucht werden. Da dies in CT-Bildern mit unterschiedlichen lokalen Kontrastmittelzuständen eine schwierige Thematik darstellt [8], wurde im Rahmen dieser Arbeit schließlich aus Robustheitsgründen darauf verzichtet. Die bereits in [19, 113, 114] vorgestellte zusätzliche Berücksichtigung der CT-Werte beim haptischen Rendering durch gewichtete Überlagerung kann für eine realistischere unregelmäßige Kraftdarstellung faserhaltiger Gewebe sorgen. Sie kann jedoch insbesondere im Fall von CT-Bildartefakten auch für den Trainierenden irritierend sein. Für die harten interkostalen Faszienfasern wurde jedoch auf den Hinweis der medizinischen Berater eingehend mit der virtuellen B-Spline-Faszienhaut ein Modell erstellt, das im haptischen Rendering ein plausibles Durchstoßereignis dieser Struktur zwischen den Rippen liefert. Die mit der RFK ebenfalls untersuchten Leberstrukturen wurden fallweise sehr gut, jedoch oft nicht robust genug gefunden. Insgesamt ist zum aktuellen Stand der Forschung der Bayes-Transferfunktionsmethode der Vorzug zugeben, insbesondere aufgrund der signifikant besseren Segmentierung der wichtigen Risikostruktur Knochen (Tab. 3.1, S. 31). Es wurden für Schlüsselstrukturen in der Zielumgebung der PTC/D-Punktion organ- bzw. strukturspezifisch optimierte Verfahren entwickelt.

Bei den organspezifisch optimierten Verfahren war die Faszienhautmodellierung für die Unterscheidung peripherer und viszeraler Strukturen und das haptische Rendering das manuell zeitaufwendigste Verfahren. Die Segmentierung der Leber mit der Multi-Atlas-Segmentierung (MAS) war die zeit- und rechenaufwendigste Methode. Auch durch den parallelen Ablauf dieser beiden Teilschritte wurde eine deutliche Zeitersparnis erreicht [1, 7]. Das Zeitfenster von maximal zwei Stunden für die vollautomatische MAS war ausreichend bemessen, auch um gleichzeitig semi-automatisch eine sehr plausible Fasziensegmentierung zu erhalten. Diese war bei Einübung des dafür einzuplanenden medizinisch-technischen Personals innerhalb von maximal ca. 40 Minuten erledigt. Sicherlich sind in Zukunft weitere Automatisierungsschritte an dieser Stelle angebracht, die mathematisch die Approximation einer 3D-Punktwolke über zylindrischen Parameterbereichen erfordern. Solche Spline-Approximationsprobleme können methodisch als gelöst betrachtet werden [156], müssten jedoch für die konkrete Problemstellung vorverarbeitend optimiert parametrisiert werden. Für die rechenintensiven MAS-Methoden wurden vollautomatische Methoden entwickelt, die eine beschleunigte Fusion - im letzten Teilschritt der MAS - der einzelnen Segmentierungsschätzungen ermöglichte [7]. GPU-beschleunigte nicht-linearen Registrierungen standen in [157] noch nicht zur Verfügung, mit der Implementierung wurde jedoch bereits begonnen [158]. Zukünftiges Ziel wäre zunächst vor dem Hintergrund der noch manuellen Faszienmodelladaptierung, die Multi-Atlasregistrierung ebenfalls garantiert in ein maximales Zeitfenster von ca. 40 Minuten zu integrieren. Dies könnte in naher Zukunft auch mit den verwendeten CPU-basierten nicht-linearen Registrierungsverfahren möglich sein, vor allem auch da die Anzahl der CPU-Kerne ständig zunimmt. Die untersuchte Segmentierung der Leberstrukturen in [6] mit der RFK-Methode (vgl. § 3.1.1.2) lieferte auch hier weniger robust schlechtere mittlere DICE-Koeffizienten von 0,9, 0,37 und 0,39 als die organspezifisch optimierten Methoden aus § 2.1.2.2 und § 2.1.2.3 und hat daher das Nachsehen (Tab. 3.1, S. 31). Letztendlich wurde für die Lebergefäße auf strukturspezifisch optimierte Vesselness-basierte Methoden zurückgegriffen, die jedoch teilweise unterbrochene Gefäßverläufe liefern. Es könnten für die zukünftig vorgesehene Simulation von Blutflüssen lückenschließende Gefäßbaummodelle [159] eingepasst werden.

In der in [4] veröffentlichten Haptikstudie wurde zunächst eine neue Kraftbewertungsmethodik vorgestellt und die Kraftausgabe mit 3508 automatisch geplanten zielführenden Pfaden (vgl. § 2.4) an einem Referenzpatienten evaluiert. Diese *in silico*-Bewertungsmethode verwendet einen mit punktionserfahrenen Ärzten haptisch kalibrierten Referenzpatienten mit einer manuell erstellten Vollvolumensegmentierung [18, 19] im Vergleich zu den neuen Methoden der mit priorisierten partiellen Segmentierungen kombinierten Transferfunktionsheuristik. Mit diesem empirischen Evaluationsansatz werden Probleme durch Ethikkommissionen und haptische Messapparaturen elegant vermieden. In der *in silico*-Evaluation aus [4] zeigten sich mittlere quadratische (Gesamt-) Fehler (RMSE) von 0,07±0,098 N und maximale absolute Fehler (MAE) von 0,73±0,15 N. Der systematische MAE-Fehler von ca. 0,7 N war auf eine leicht zum Goldstandard versetzte Detektion der Hautoberfläche zurückführbar. Bezogen auf Fehlerschwellen, die von gerade noch spürbaren Unterschieden (engl. just noticeable differences, JNDs) für Länge und Kraft des Hand-Arm-Systems [160, 161] abgeleitet werden können und sich prozentual auf einen Referenzreiz beziehen, waren die Fehler haptisch nicht relevant. Hand-Arm-System-Kraft-JNDs rangieren zwischen 15 bis 26 % für hohe (-6 N) bis niedrige (-0,5 N) Referenzgegenkräfte [161]. Ein Hand-Arm-Kraft-JND von 18,1 % (β_1-Gelenk für -0,87 N, siehe Tab. II in [161]) kann nun auf die gemessene durchschnittliche Gegenkraft von 0,8 N im Inneren des Körpers während der Nadeleinführung bezogen werden und liefert einen Schwellwert von 0,145 N. Die in [4] gemessenen RMSE-Fehler lagen deutlich unter diesem Wert. Die MAE-Fehler durch die im Millimeterbereich (Voxel-Länge) versetzte Detektion der Hautoberfläche können mit den JNDs (11 %) für Längenunterschiede [160] bewertet werden. Aufgrund der vorigen freien, benutzergesteuerten Nadelbewegung in der Luft, der damit fehlenden Referenzlänge (und Referenzkraft) und simulierten Patientenatmung sind diese Fehler haptisch kaum von Bedeutung. Statistisch bedeutende Fehler ($p < 0,05$) wurden bei nur 0,8 % aller Referenzpfade gefunden. Das haptische Rendering an Organgrenzen erfolgte erstmals mit einem plausibleren quadratischen Anstieg [2], der ein realistischer elastisches Nadelgefühl an Organkapseln ermöglichte.

Das visuelle Rendering unter Berücksichtigung der Deformation des Weichteilgewebes durch Instrumentenansatz und Atmung wurde erstens durch die Kopplung der Proxy-basierten Kraftausgabe mit der visuellen Deformations-Rendering-Methode erreicht [2].

Zweitens wurde durch die Berücksichtigung von patientenspezifischen Atemmodellen [5, 3] eine realitätsnahe Simulation der US-gestützten Nadelpunktion unter Atmung vorgestellt. Diese Atemmodelle könnten zukünftig populationsbasiert [162] definiert werden und durch nicht-lineare Registrierungsverfahren [136] auf andere 3D-Patientendaten adaptiert werden. Hiermit soll für Trainings- und Planungszwecke bei neuen atembewegten Patienten die Patientendosis für die Akquisition von 4D-CT-Daten obsolet werden. In Zukunft könnte auch die Unregelmäßigkeit der Atmung durch ggf. extrapolierende Atembewegungsfeldmodulation erreicht werden. Gesteuert werden würde ein solches Atemmodell durch ein simuliertes Spirometersignal mit Zufallseinfluss bspw. in der Atemamplitude und Atemzyklusdauer [111, 110]. Die Fluoroskopiesimulation mit Kontrastmittelausbreitung erreichte mit der verwendeten GPU (Nvidia GTX 680) mit akzeptablen 18 Hz kein Echtzeitverhalten, dies ist aktuell jedoch durch die sich signifikant steigernde GPU-Leistung ein absehbar lösbarer, kleiner Nachteil. Eine Bildrate von 15 Hz gilt gemeinhin als noch akzeptabel für eine flüssige Wahrnehmung [150]. Die Fluoroskopiesimulation wird nur für einzelne Kontrollbildaufnahmen und kurze Sequenzen bei vermuteter erfolgreicher Punktion von Gallengefäßen verwendet. Eine besser echtzeitfähige Simulation mit sich ausbreitendem Kontrastmittel ist nicht wirklich relevant wenn auch wünschenswert. Dagegen lieferte die kontinuierlich verwendete Ultraschallsimulation Bildraten im Echtzeitbereich (Abb. 3.10c, S. 28).

In einer Benutzerstudie mit 16 Medizinstudierenden des 10. Semesters vor dem praktischen Jahr (PJ) wurde nach einem standardisierten Trainingsdurchlauf ein Fragebogen mit 18 Fragen (F) ausgewertet. Die Evaluation des Simulators durch die Versuchsteilnehmer war durchgehend positiv. Es wurde hinsichtlich der technischen Umsetzung gutes bis sehr gutes Feedback erreicht. Die Antworten auf F6 in Tab. 3.3 auf S. 32 waren von der überhöhten Erwartungshaltung geprägt, die Leberzielstrukturen wirklich deutlich fühlen zu können. Unsere medizinischen Experten wiesen jedoch darauf hin, dass der Leberrand und die Lebergefäße im Vergleich zum Fasziendurchstoß nur sehr subtil spürbar sind. Zwei der Fragen (F1, 16) stellten auf die Bewertung des Benutzerselbstvertrauens bez. der PTC/D vor und nach der Sitzung ab. Das Training wurde als sinnvoll (F4, 15) angesehen und das Selbstvertrauen, eine solche Punktion selbst durchzuführen, stieg deutlich an (F1, 16). Zwar war die Differenz zwischen F1 gegenüber F16 signifikant und ein möglicher Trainingseffekt deutete sich an (Abb. 3.3, S. 32), jedoch konnte dies aufgrund des kleinen Studienrahmens nicht abschließend belegt werden. Immerhin konnte von einem subjektiv empfundenen Motivationseffekt gesprochen werden. Betrachtete man jeweils sequentiell drei Punktionsversuche in einem der Trainingsmodi, wurde in späteren Versuchen der Serie eine tendenzielle Steigerung der Leistungspunktzahlen beobachtet. Diese Aussagen könnte in einer umfangreicheren Studie auch gegenüber einer nicht-trainierten Kontrollgruppe statistisch erhärtet werden. Es wurde insgesamt die technische Realisierung der Kontrollbildgebungssimulation, d. h. das visuo-haptische Rendering und die den Vorgang deutlich unterstützende Ultraschallsimulation mit Schienenführung und Zieltrajektorie (F12), als sehr positiv empfunden. Am kritischsten wurde das Punktionsbewertungssystem (F14) beurteilt, das verbessert werden sollte.

Das vorgestellte VR-Trainings- und Planungssystem für Leberpunktionen liefert einen sinnvollen Beitrag. Es zeigt neue Perspektiven der risikolosen räumlich-mentalen Trainings und der Interventionsvorbereitung einerseits für Medizinstudierende in der Ausbildung und andererseits potenziell für praktizierende Mediziner im klinischen Alltag auf. Der Anwendungsfall der PTC/D-Punktion diente als interessantes Beispiel, bei dem zwei unterstützende Kontrollbildgebungsverfahren benutzt wurden: Es waren dies die Fluoroskopie und die US-Bildgebung. Damit ist das VR-System bereits für weitere Anwendungsszenarien wie die Radio-Frequenz-Ablationssimulation von Leberherden hervorragend gerüstet. Es müsste dabei um die entsprechenden Methoden der Simulation der Temperaturausbreitung unter Berücksichtigung von Atmung und Blutfluss sowie Zelltodzonen um die Nadelspitze im Gewebe erweitert werden. Zudem sind entsprechende Bewertungsmethoden für die Benutzerversuche zu überlegen. Technisch gesehen lässt sich das System zukünftig stetig durch den Einsatz neu auf den Markt kommender GPU-Hardware und VR-Brillen immersiv verbessern [34].

Der vorgestellte 4D-VR-Simulator hat das Potential aus dem Prototypstadium hinaus in die Ausbildung von Medizinstudierenden sinnvoll einsetzbar zu sein und den praktizierenden Mediziner bei der mental-visuo-haptischen Vorbereitung auf konkret anstehende Eingriffe zu unterstützen. Durch die Entwicklung und Evaluation der beschriebenen Methoden und Algorithmen sollte das allgemeine und patientenindividuelle Punktionstraining bei anspruchsvollen Eingriffen wie z. B. der Gallengangs- oder Leberläsionspunktion zeitnah ermöglicht werden. Dieses Ziel wurde hinreichend plausibel vollumfänglich erreicht. Das Systemkonzept kann zudem in Zukunft auf andere Nadelinterventionen wie simulierte Leberbiopsien und Ablationen von Leberherden erweitert werden.

Die PTC/D-Punktion diente als interessantes Anwendungsbeispiel. Das Modellierungskonzept für virtuelle Patientenkörper läßt sich jedoch kanonisch auf andere Anwendungsfälle erweitern, indem für neue Zielstrukturen Transferfunktionsintervalle, organspezifisch optimierte Methoden und Bewegungsmodelle ergänzt werden. Idealerweise könnte in Zukunft durch das vorgestellte prototypische Systemkonzept in einer professionellen Implementierung die Patientensicherheit erhöht, Patientengenese verkürzt und Kosteneffizienz durch verbesserte Eingriffsqualität gesteigert werden. Konkret kann der im Vorfeld eines Eingriffs trainierte Arzt ggf. die Belastung des Patienten vermindern. Einerseits könnte sich die Anzahl der fluoroskopischen Kontrollaufnahmen und andererseits mehr noch die Invasivität des Eingriffs, d. h. die Anzahl der Nadelrepositionierungen, signifikant verringern. Weiterhin werden zukünftig Dosis sparend existierende patientenspezifische oder populationsbasierte 4D-Atembewegungsmodelle auf neue 3D-Patientendaten adaptiert, um die Bildakquise für die Atemmodellbildung zu vermeiden.

5 Zusammenfassung

Einleitung: Das vorgestellte VR-Trainings- und -Planungssystem umfasst (1) Konzepte zur personalisierten Patientenkörpermodellierung mit partiell segmentierten Bilddaten [1, 6, 7, 8], (2) Methoden zur Weichteildeformationssimulation durch Instrumenteneinsatz und Körperfunktionen wie Atmung und (3) damit gekoppelte visuo-haptische Rendering-Methoden [5, 2, 3, 4]. Der Schwerpunkt dieser Arbeit lag auf effizienten Methoden zur Modellierung virtueller Patienten und ausgewählten visuo-haptischen Rendering-Verfahren für ultraschallgestützte Nadelpunktionen.

Die hier als Anwendungsbeispiel betrachtete Cholestase entsteht durch intrahepatische Aufstauungen von Gallensäften bedingt durch Abfluss behindernde Gallensteine, Tumoren oder Narbenbildung, welche den endoskopischen Zugang verlegen können. Leitsymptom ist eine Gelbsucht sowie blasser Stuhl begleitet von Befindlichkeitsstörungen wie Appetitlosigkeit, Müdigkeit, Juckreiz und Übelkeit [26]. Minimal-invasiv fluoroskopisch dargestellt, diagnostiziert und therapiert wird die Krankheit bspw. durch Kontrastmittel einleitende Gallengangspunktion und -drainage (PTC, PTCD).

Ziel der Arbeit war ein VR-Systemkonzept für das virtuelle patientenspezifische Training der Nadelnavigation zu einer intrahepatischen Zielstruktur. Die Simulation üblicher zur Navigation und Kontrolle verwendeter Bildgebungsverfahren wie Ultraschall (US) und Fluoroskopie war ein wichtiger Teilaspekt. Dabei wurden auch Weichteilgewebsdeformationen durch Instrumenteneinsatz und Atmung berücksichtigt. Wünschenswert für eine möglichst hohe Immersion in die virtuelle Realität war eine möglichst plausible Simulation der relevanten visuo-haptischen Phänomene unter technisch-infrastrukturellen Randbedingungen [2]. Als Kompromiss zwischen Rechenaufwand, Echtzeitanforderungen und realitätsgetreuer Darstellung (Rendering) bot sich das Konzept der „hinreichenden Plausibilität" als Zielkriterium an [123, 124, 125]. Dieses Konzept erlaubt Vereinfachungen der Modelle und Simulationsverfahren bedingt durch die finanziellen und technischen Rahmenbedingungen, solange ein Nutzen gegeben ist.

Material und Methoden: Es wurden im Themenbereich der Modellierung virtueller Patienten neuartige Segmentierungsmethoden einerseits für die von der Nadel passierten Füll- bzw. zu vermeidende Risikostrukturen (Haut, Weichteilgewebe, interkostale Faszien bzw. Knochen, Lunge, Intestinaltrakt, Leberblutgefäße) und andererseits für Zielstrukturen (Leber, Gallengänge) vorgestellt [1, 6, 7, 8]. Zur zeiteffizienten Segmentierung der benötigten Strukturen wurde ein Gesamtkonzept mit parallelen Arbeitsabläufen entwickelt [1]. In diesem laufen aufwendige organspezifische, automatische Prozesse im Hintergrund (Lebersegmentierung) ab [1, 7] und gehen mit Benutzereingaben an anderen Strukturen (Faszienmodell) parallel einher [1].

Ausgehend von einem bereits simulierbaren generischen Patientenatlas (GPA) wurde dieser als neuer Patientenatlas (NPA) an neue CT-Daten adaptiert. Ein solcher NPA dient als personalisiertes, simulierbares Modell und beschreibt patientenindividuell alle simulationsrelevanten visuo-haptischen Eigenschaften [1, 2].

Für die Segmentierung großräumiger Füllstrukturen wurden mit zwei alternativen Ansätzen Transferfunktionen definiert: (1) die Bayes- [1] und (2) die Random-Forest-Klassifikatortransferfunktionen (RFK) [6] über einem maximal kubischen Definitionsgebiet. Beide Methoden erlauben einen GPU-kompatiblen Echtzeitzugriff auf die visuo-haptischen Simulationsparameter der Gewebe [129].

Explizit angefertigte partielle Segmentierungen für Schlüsselstrukturen überlagern die Transferfunktionssegmentierung. Für die saliente Kraftausgabe beim Fasziendurchstoß wurde ein dreidimensionales B-Spline-Modell gewählt [1]. Für die Leber wurde ein Multi-Atlas- [1, 7] und für Lebergefäße ein Vesselness-Verfahren vorgeschlagen.

Es wurden neue direkte haptische Rendering-Algorithmen [2] auch unter Berücksichtigung der Patientenatmung [3] und *in silico*-Kraftevaluationsmethoden für die Simulation von Nadelpunktionen in partiell segmentierten Daten entwickelt [4, 8]. Mit dieser Arbeit steht für die VR-Simulation mittels nicht-linearer Kraftanstiege an Organkapseln erstmals eine haptisch realitätsnähere Kraftrückgabe im Konzept des direkten haptischen Volumen-Rendering zur Verfügung [2] .

Dem Ansatz des direkten visuellen Volumen-Rendering folgend wurden echtzeitfähige parallele Raycasting-Algorithmen in Nvidia CUDA entwickelt [2]. Diese dienen zur Erzeugung realistischer zweidimensionaler Projektions- und Schnittbilder sowie dreidimensionaler, zeitvarianter Stereobildansichten des ggf. modellgesteuert atembewegten virtuellen Patientenkörpers. Atemmodelle wurden patientenspezifisch aus 4D-CT-Bilddaten generiert [6, 3, 110]. Durch spezielle Implementierungen einer gekrümmten Strahlverfolgung [3] und des Rendering-Integrals wurden Fluoroskopie- und Ultraschallbilder [5] der durch Atmung deformierten CT-Daten effizient simuliert [2, 9].

Zur allgemeinen Bewertung des Systems wurde auf der qualitativen Seite eine Benutzerstudie mit auf einer Likert-Skala zu beantwortenden Fragen durchgeführt [2]. Mit verschiedenen quantitativen Metriken wurden Segmentierungsgüte, Kraftausgabe und Rendering-Performanz bewertet. Die Entwicklung des Systems wurde von leberpunktionskundigen Ärzten aus der Medizinischen Klinik I, Bereich Gastroenterologie/Hepatologie, und der Klinik für Radiologie und Nuklearmedizin, Universitätsklinikum Schleswig-Holstein, Campus Lübeck, beratend begleitet und optimiert.

Ergebnisse: Es wurde eine neue für die Leberpunktionssimulation optimierte Modellierungsmethodik virtueller Patientenkörper entwickelt [1, 7, 8]. Die rechenintensive Leber-Multi-Atlas-Segmentierung lief auf einem PC-Cluster ab. Währenddessen widmete sich der menschliche Bediener der Faszienhautmodelladaption. Insgesamt wurde ein signifikant attraktiverer Modellierungszeitrahmen von zwei bis drei Stunden (Tab. 3.1, S. 31) im Vergleich zu 32 bis 63 Stunden aus [18, 19] erreicht [1].

Die Atlasdatenstruktur wurde als hierarchische Baumstruktur mit Vererbung angelegt. Ein generischer Patientenatlas (GPA) enthält alle Attribute und Modelle, um nach einem Adaptionsprozess einen beliebigen virtuellen PTCD-Patienten als neuen Patientenatlas (NPA) zu beschreiben [1].

Für die Füllstrukturen Haut, Weichteile und Knochen wurden mit der Bayes-transferfunktionsbasierten Segmentierung virtueller Patientenkörper vollautomatisch unter studienbedingter Variation der für den GPA verwendeten Referenzbilddaten mittlere DICE-Koeffizienten von 0,79, 0,97 und signifikant bessere 0,83 (vs. RFK) bei kleineren Standardabweichungen erreicht [1]. Die Bayes-Transferfunktion schnitt verglichen zu RFKs tendenziell besser ab (Tab. 3.1 links, S. 31).

Im Methodenkanon der organspezifisch optimierten Methoden für Schlüsselstrukturen wurde zur Multi-Atlas-Segmentierung (MAS) der Leber zunächst eine vollautomatische

Methode mit einer neuen effizienten, Patch-basierten Labelfusionsmethode entwickelt [7]. Die Methode lieferte bessere Ergebnisse als andere, etablierte Fusionsmethoden (z. B. SIMPLE, STAPLE, Vote- und Sum-Rule) [146, 147, 148]. DICE-Koeffizienten von durchschnittlich 0,91±0,02 wurden in [7] erreicht. In [1] wurde diese Methodik um Atlasselektion- und Postprocessingschritte erweitert und anhand von 10 Testpatienten unter Verwendung einer Atlasdatenbank mit 59 Atlanten evaluiert. Es ergab sich im Vergleich zur RFK mit 0,9±0,14 eine wesentlich präzisere Segmentierung der Leber mit einem DICE-Koeffizienten von 0,93±0,01 (Tab. 3.1 rechts, S. 31).

Die Leberblutgefäße bzw. die Gallengänge wurden in [1] strukturspezifisch mit medianen DICE-Koeffizienten von 0,51 bzw. 0,48 segmentiert. Mit der sehr schnellen Random-Forest-Klassifikation wurden hier keine Vorteile festgestellt (0,41 bzw. 0,35) [6]. Auch hier sind die strukturspezifisch optimierten Methoden vorzuziehen.

Bezüglich des haptischen Rendering wurde in [4] eine neue *in silico*-Evaluationsmethodik vorgestellt und die Kraftausgabe damit bewertet. In den Ergebnissen aus [4] zeigten sich kaum wahrnehmbare mittlere Fehler (RMSE) von 0,07 N bzw. wohlbegründbare maximale absolute Fehler (MAE) von 0,7 N. Statistisch bedeutende Fehler ($p < 0,05$) wurden bei nur 0,8 % aller Referenzpfade gefunden.

Die visuelle Plausibilität und Echtzeitfähigkeit der Visualisierungsmethoden für die 3D-Ansicht und die Kontrollbildgebung wurde qualitativ und quantitativ untersucht und bestätigt [2]. Lediglich die Simulation der Kontrastmittelausbreitung erzeugte auf der Nvidia GTX 680 innerhalb der Fluoroskopiesimulation Bildraten unterhalb von 25 Hz, die jedoch mit akzeptablen 18 Hz oberhalb der kritischen Grenze von 15 Hz [150] noch akzeptabel waren. Rendering-Ergebnisse für verschiedene Visualisierungsmodi sind in Abb. 3.10, Seite 28 und Abb. 3.12, S. 29 dargestellt.

Zur Bewertung der Trainingsqualität des Simulators wurde eine Benutzerstudie mit 16 Studierenden der Medizin des 10. Semesters durchgeführt. Das Selbstvertrauen der Studienteilnehmer, eine Leberpunktion selbst durchzuführen, stieg nach einer einstündigen, standardisierten Trainingssitzung signifikant an ($p < 0,01$).

Diskussion und Ausblick: Die effiziente Patientenmodellierung - ausgehend von einem eine Patientengruppe repräsentierenden Punktionsatlas (GPA) - neuer Patientenatlanten (NPA) wurde erfolgreich eingesetzt [1]. Die für die patientenspezifische Anwendbarkeit des Simulators notwendigen Segmentierungsmethoden der Strukturen wurde in einen effizienten Prozessablauf eingegliedert [1]. Verbleibender zeitlicher Engpass in der MAS sind die nicht-linearen Registrierungen auf der CPU [157]. Arbeiten zur GPU-gestützten Verbesserungen wurden bereits gestartet [158]. Der optimierte Gesamtprozessablauf der Einzelmethoden [1] lieferte einen Beschleunigungsfaktor von mehr als 10 [18, 19, 39] mit einer Reduzierung von 32 bis 63 auf zwei bis drei Stunden wie Tab. 3.2 auf S. 31 dokumentiert.

Die für die Modellbildung notwendige Segmentierung der großvolumigen Füllstrukturen Haut, Weichteilgewebe (Fett-Bindegewebe-Muskel-Organ-Kompartiment) und Knochen wurde mit zwei alternativen Transferfunktionsansätzen untersucht, die jeweils effizient akkurate und plausible Ergebnisse erzeugen [1, 6]. Es könnten in diesem Kontext zukünftig höher dimensionale Merkmalsräume und weitere maschinelle Lernverfahren untersucht werden [154]. Die Aufteilung des Weichteilgewebekompartiments in die darin enthaltenen Unterstrukturen wie z. B. Fett und Muskeln in CT-Daten könnte ebenfalls genauer erforscht werden. Eine haptisch relevante Faszienhaut als Teil der interkostalen Muskeln zwischen den Rippen wurde auf Anregung der medizinischen Berater für die Kraftausgabe explizit semi-automatisch modelliert. Diese zukünftig zu automatisierende Modellierung erlaubte außerdem die wichtige Unterscheidung peripherer und viszeraler Strukturen in den Bayes-Transferfunktionen. Der Durchstoß dieser Struktur ist das salienteste haptische Ereignis bei der PTCD.

In der quantitativen Evaluierung der haptischen Kraftausgabe mit einer neu vorgeschlagenen Evaluierungsmethodik [4] zeigten sich kleine mittlere Fehler. Ein systematischer maximaler absoluter Fehler von 0,7 N entlang einzelner Testpfade konnte wohlbegründet werden, ist jedoch spatial-haptisch nicht relevant [160, 161]: Erstens dringt die Nadel in den Körper durch eine kleine Hautinzision ein. Zweitens war er auf eine im Millimeterbereich zum Goldstandard versetzte Lage der segmentierten Hautoberfläche zurückführbar, die praktisch beim atembewegten Patienten nicht relevant ist.

Das visuelle Rendering in Kombination mit der Deformation des Weichteilgewebes durch Instrumentenansatz und Atmung wurde einerseits durch die Divergenzkopplung mit den haptischen Multi-Proxy-basierten Methoden erreicht. Andererseits wurde durch die Animation statischer 3D-Daten mit patientenindividuellen Atemmodellen ein realistischer Eindruck atmender Körpermodelle erzeugt [2, 3]. Die im Vergleich zur Fluoroskopie wichtigere, kontinuierlich während der US-gestützten Nadelnavigation verwendete Ultraschallsimulation [5] erreichte die Echtzeitbedingung (FPS>25 Hz) sehr gut [2]. In einer Benutzerstudie mit 16 Medizinstudierenden des 10. Semesters wurde nach standardisierten Trainingssitzungen ein Fragebogen mit 18 Fragen zu verschiedenen Aspekten des VR-Systems ausgewertet. Es wurde hinsichtlich der technischen Umsetzung gutes bis sehr gutes Feedback erreicht (Abb. 3.3, S. 32) [2]. Zwei der Fragen (F1, 16) stellten hierbei auf die Bewertung des Benutzerkonfidenz bez. der Durchführung einer PTCD vor und nach der Sitzung ab. Zwar war die Differenz zwischen F1 und F16 signifikant und ein möglicher Trainingseffekt deutete sich an, jedoch kann dies aufgrund des Studienumfangs nicht abschließend belegt werden.

Das vorgestellte VR-Trainings- und Planungssystem zeigt neue Perspektiven des risikolosen, haptisch- und räumlich-mentalen Trainings für Ausbildungszwecke sowie der patientenspezifischen Planung und Interventionsvorbereitung (Case-Preview) auf. Die PTCD-Punktion diente als interessantes Anwendungsbeispiel. Das Modellierungskonzept für virtuelle Patientenkörper läßt sich kanonisch auf andere Anwendungsfälle erweitern, indem für neue Zielstrukturen organspezifisch optimierte Methoden ergänzt werden. Das Systemkonzept kann in Zukunft auch auf andere Nadelinterventionen wie simulierte Leberbiopsien und Ablationen von Leberherden erweitert werden. Hierbei sollen Wärmeabtransporteffekte durch Blutfluss und Atmung berücksichtigt werden. Der vorgestellte 4D-VR-Simulator hat das Potenzial, aus dem Prototypstadium hinaus in die Ausbildung von Medizinstudierenden sinnvoll einzugehen. Zudem könnte er den praktizierenden Mediziner bei der mentalen Vorbereitung auf konkret anstehende Eingriffe zu unterstützen, um die Belastung durch Nadelrepositionierungen und fluoroskopische Kontrollbildgebungsdosis zu verringern.

Danksagung

Mein Dank gilt in erster Linie Prof. Heinz Handels und Dirk Fortmeier für ihre Unterstützung der unter meiner Federführung durchgeführten Arbeiten.

Weiterhin danke ich den Kollegen Matthias Wilms und Oskar Maier für die Zusammenarbeit in wichtigen Einzelfragen.

Dank gilt auch den Studierenden aus den von mir zur Thematik betreuten Master-Arbeiten Martin Röseler und Ehsan Maghsoudi.

Ebenfalls danken möchte ich den thematisch involvierten Studierenden der von mir betreuten Bachelor-Arbeiten: Julian Schröder, Tobias Hecht, Peter Behringer und Jonas Beuke.

Danken möchte ich auch Johanna Degen, Sandra Schulz und Christian Lukas für das Gegenlesen der Kurzzusammenfassung.

Abbildungsverzeichnis

Tabellenverzeichnis

Literaturverzeichnis

[1] A. Mastmeyer, D. Fortmeier, H. Handels, "Efficient patient modeling for visuo-haptic VR simulation using a generic patient atlas," *Computer Methods and Programs in Biomedicine*, Bd. 132, S. 161–175, 2016.

[2] D. Fortmeier, A. Mastmeyer, J. Schröder, H. Handels, "A virtual reality system for PTCD simulation using direct visuo-haptic rendering of partially segmented image data," *IEEE Journal of Biomedical and Health Informatics*, Bd. 20, Nr. 1, S. 355–366, 2016.

[3] D. Fortmeier, M. Wilms, A. Mastmeyer, H. Handels, "Direct visuo-haptic 4D volume rendering using respiratory motion models," *IEEE Transactions on Haptics*, Bd. 8, Nr. 4, S. 371–383, 2015.

[4] A. Mastmeyer, T. Hecht, D. Fortmeier, H. Handels, "Ray-casting based evaluation framework for haptic force-feedback during percutaneous transhepatic catheter drainage punctures," *International Journal of Computer Assisted Radiology and Surgery*, Bd. 9, S. 421–431, 2014.

[5] A. Mastmeyer, M. Wilms, D. Fortmeier, J. Schröder, H. Handels, "Real-time ultrasound simulation for training of US-guided needle insertion in breathing virtual patients," in *Medicine Meets Virtual Reality 22, MMVR 2016*, Bd. 220 of *Studies in Health Technology and Informatics*, S. 219–226, IOS Press, 2016.

[6] A. Mastmeyer, D. Fortmeier, H. Handels, "Random forest classification of large volume structures for visuo-haptic rendering in CT images," in *Proc. SPIE Medical Imaging: Image Processing*, Bd. 9784, S. 97842H–1–8, International Society for Optics and Photonics, 2016.

[7] A. Mastmeyer, D. Fortmeier, E. Maghsoudi, M. Simon, H. Handels, "Patch-based label fusion using local confidence-measures and weak segmentations," in *Proc. SPIE Medical Imaging: Image Processing*, (Orlando, USA), S. 86691N–1–11, International Society for Optics and Photonics, 2013.

[8] A. Mastmeyer, D. Fortmeier, H. Handels, "Direct haptic volume rendering in lumbar puncture simulation," in *Medicine Meets Virtual Reality 19, MMVR 2012*, Bd. 173 of *Studies in Health Technology and Informatics*, S. 280–286, IOS Press, 2012.

[9] D. Fortmeier, A. Mastmeyer, H. Handels, "Image-based soft tissue deformation algorithms for real-time simulation of liver puncture," *Current Medical Imaging Reviews*, Bd. 9, Nr. 2, S. 154–165, 2013.

[10] K. Engelke, A. Mastmeyer, V. Bousson, T. Fuerst, J.-D. Laredo, W. A. Kalender, "Reanalysis precision of 3D quantitative computed tomography (QCT) of the spine," *Bone*, Bd. 44, Nr. 4, S. 566–572, 2009.

[11] A. Mastmeyer, K. Engelke, C. Fuchs, W. A. Kalender, "A hierarchical 3D segmentation method and the definition of vertebral body coordinate systems for QCT of the lumbar spine," *Medical Image Analysis*, Bd. 10, Nr. 4, S. 560–577, 2006.

[12] A. Mastmeyer, G. Pernelle, L. Barber, S. Pieper, D. Fortmeier, S. Wells, H. Handels, T. Kapur, "Model-based catheter segmentation in MRI-images," in *MICCAI Workshop on Interactive Medical Image Computing, IMIC 2015, 18th International Conference on Medical Image Computing and Computer-Assisted Intervention - MICCAI 2015*, (München), S. 110–118, 2015.

[13] D. Fortmeier, A. Mastmeyer, H. Handels, "An image-based multiproxy palpation algorithm for patient-specific VR-simulation," in *Medicine Meets Virtual Reality 21, MMVR 2014*, Studies in Health and Information Technology, S. 107–113, IOS Press, 2014.

[14] P. A. Behringer, A. Mastmeyer, D. Fortmeier, C. Biermann, H. Handels, "Segmentierung intrahepatischer Gefäße mit Vesselness-Verfahren," in *Bildverarbeitung für die Medizin 2014* (T. M. Deserno, H. Handels, H.-P. Meinzer, T. Tolxdorff, Ed.), Informatik aktuell, S. 150–155, Springer Berlin Heidelberg, 2014.

[15] J. Schröder, A. Mastmeyer, D. Fortmeier, H. Handels, "Ultraschallsimulation für das Training von Gallengangspunktionen," in *Bildverarbeitung für die Medizin 2014* (T. M. Deserno, H. Handels, H.-P. Meinzer, T. Tolxdorff, Ed.), Informatik aktuell, (Aachen), S. 222–227, Springer, Berlin Heidelberg, Springer, Berlin Heidelberg, 2014.

[16] D. Fortmeier, A. Mastmeyer, H. Handels, "Image-based palpation simulation with soft tissue deformations using chainmail on the GPU," in *Bildverarbeitung für die Medizin 2013* (H.-P. Meinzer, T. M. Deserno, H. Handels, T. Tolxdorff, Ed.), (Heidelberg), S. 140–145, Springer Verlag, Berlin, Springer Verlag, Berlin, 2013.

[17] D. Fortmeier, A. Mastmeyer, H. Handels, "Optimized image-based soft tissue deformation algorithms for visualization of haptic needle insertion," in *Medicine Meets Virtual Reality 20 - NextMed, MMVR 2013, San Diego, California, USA, February 20-23, 2013*, S. 136–140, 2013.

[18] D. J. Dalek, *Erstellung von Fallbeispielen für einen Virtual Reality Lumbalpunktionssimulator und Evaluation der Trainingseffekte.* Dissertation, Medizinische Fakultät der Universität Hamburg, 2014.

[19] M. Färber, *Entwicklung eines Virtual-Reality-Frameworks zur Simulation von Punktionseingriffen.* Dissertation, Sektion Informatik/Technik, Universität zu Lübeck, 2009.

[20] L. R. Dice, "Measures of the amount of ecologic association between species," *Ecology*, Bd. 26, Nr. 3, S. 297–302, 1945.

[21] T. Okada, M. G. Linguraru, M. Hori, R. M. Summers, N. Tomiyama, Y. Sato, "Abdominal multi-organ segmentation from CT images using conditional shape–location and unsupervised intensity priors," *Medical Image Analysis*, Bd. 26, Nr. 1, S. 1 – 18, 2015.

[22] L. Wang, C. Hansen, S. Zidowitz, H. K. Hahn, "Segmentation and separation of venous vasculatures in liver CT images," in *Proc. SPIE Medical Imaging: Computer-Aided Diagnosis*, S. 90350Q–1–8, International Society for Optics and Photonics, 2014.

[23] P. M. Schlag, S. Eulenstein, T. Lange, *Computerassistierte Chirurgie.* Elsevier, 2010.

[24] Y. Seppenwoolde, H. Shirato, K. Kitamura, S. Shimizu, M. van Herk, J. V. Lebesque, K. Miyasaka, "Precise and real-time measurement of 3D tumor motion in lung due to breathing and heartbeat, measured during radiotherapy," *International Journal of Radiation Oncololgy, Biology, Physics*, Bd. 53, S. 822–834, Jul 2002.

[25] N. Zorger S. Feuerbach, "Technik der perkutanen transhepatischen Cholangio-Drainage (PTCD)," *Journal für Gastroenterologische und Hepatologische Erkrankungen*, Bd. 8, Nr. 4, S. 21–26, 2010.

[26] W. Pschyrembel S. Amberger, *Pschyrembel Klinisches Wörterbuch.* de Gruyter, 2004.

[27] K. Kandarpa L. Machan, *Handbook of interventional radiologic procedures.* Lippincott Williams & Wilkins, 2011.

[28] L. Lin, *Practical Clinical Ultrasonic Diagnosis.* World Scientific, 1997.

[29] Z. Luyao, X. Xiaoyan, X. Huixiong, X. Zuo-Feng, L. Guang-Jian, L. Ming-de, "Percutaneous ultrasound-guided cholangiography using microbubbles to evaluate the dilated biliary tract: initial experience.," *Eur Radiol*, Bd. 22, S. 371–378, Feb. 2012.

[30] C. F. Dietrich D. Nürnberg, Ed., *Interventioneller Ultraschall - Lehrbuch und Atlas für die Interventionelle Sonografie.* Thieme, 2011.

[31] S. M. Rowe, "Plausible reality for real-time immersion in the virtual arena," in *ICCV 99 Workshop on Frame-rate Vision*, S. 1–6, 1999.

[32] M. A. Gutiérrez, F. Vexo, D. Thalmann, *Stepping into Virtual Reality: A Practical Approach.* Springer, Berlin, 2008.

[33] S. K. Sarker B. Patel, "Simulation and surgical training," *International Journal of Clinical Practice*, Bd. 61, Nr. 12, S. 2120–5, 2007.

[34] R. Dörner, W. Broll, P. Grimm, B. Jung, "Virtual Reality und Augmented Reality (VR/AR)," *Informatik-Spektrum*, Bd. 39, Nr. 1, S. 30–37, 2014.

[35] J. M. Rosen, S. A. Long, D. M. McGrath, S. E. Greer, "Simulation in plastic surgery training and education: the path forward," *Plastic and Reconstructive Surgery*, Bd. 123, Nr. 2, S. 729–38; discussion 739–40, 2009.

[36] K. Gurusamy, R. Aggarwal, L. Palanivelu, B. R. Davidson, "Systematic review of randomized controlled trials on the effectiveness of virtual reality training for laparoscopic surgery," *British Journal of Surgery*, Bd. 95, Nr. 9, S. 1088–1097, 2008.

[37] N. Schenkman, "Virtual reality training in urology," *Journal of Urology*, Bd. 180, Nr. 6, S. 2305–6, 2008.

[38] J. S. Tsang, P. A. Naughton, S. Leong, A. D. Hill, C. J. Kelly, A. L. Leahy, "Virtual reality simulation in endovascular surgical training," *Surgeon*, Bd. 6, Nr. 4, S. 214–20, 2008.

[39] Y. Wu L. Yencharis, "Commercial 3D imaging software migrates to PC medical diagnostics," *Advanced Imaging Magazine*, S. 16–21, 1998.

[40] Y. Kang, K. Engelke, W. A. Kalender, "A new accurate and precise 3D segmentation method for skeletal structures in volumetric CT data," *IEEE Transactions on Medical Imaging*, Bd. 22, Nr. 5, S. 586–598, 2003.

[41] R. Adams L. Bischof, "Seeded region growing," *IEEE Transactions on Pattern Analysis and Machine Intelligence*, Bd. 16, Nr. 6, S. 641–647, 1994.

[42] Z. Xu, R. P. Burke, C. P. Lee, R. B. Baucom, B. K. Poulose, R. G. Abramson, B. A. Landman, "Efficient multi-atlas abdominal segmentation on clinically acquired CT with SIMPLE context learning," *Medical Image Analysis*, Bd. 24, Nr. 1, S. 18 – 27, 2015.

[43] T. Heimann, B. Van Ginneken, M. A. Styner, Y. Arzhaeva, V. Aurich, C. Bauer, A. Beck, C. Becker, R. Beichel, G. Bekes, *et al.*, "Comparison and evaluation of methods for liver segmentation from CT datasets," *IEEE Transactions on Medical Imaging*, Bd. 28, Nr. 8, S. 1251–1265, 2009.

[44] J. E. Iglesias M. R. Sabuncu, "Multi-atlas segmentation of biomedical images: A survey," *Medical Image Analysis*, Bd. 24, Nr. 1, S. 205 – 219, 2015.

[45] R. Wolz, C. Chu, K. Misawa, M. Fujiwara, K. Mori, D. Rueckert, "Automated abdominal multi-organ segmentation with subject-specific atlas generation.," *IEEE Transactions on Medical Imaging*, Bd. 32, S. 1723–30, 2013.

[46] C. Chu, M. Oda, T. Kitasaka, K. Misawa, M. Fujiwara, Y. Hayashi, Y. Nimura, D. Rueckert, K. Mori, "Multi-organ segmentation based on spatially-divided probabilistic atlas from 3D abdominal CT images," Bd. 8150, S. 165–172, 2013.

[47] T. Okada, M. Linguraru, M. Hori, R. Summers, N. Tomiyama, Y. Sato, "Abdominal multi-organ CT segmentation using organ correlation graph and prediction-based shape and location priors," in *Medical Image Computing and Computer-Assisted Intervention – MICCAI 2013*, Bd. 8151 of *Lecture Notes in Computer Science*, S. 275–282, Springer Berlin Heidelberg, 2013.

[48] R. Wolz, C. Chu, K. Misawa, K. Mori, D. Rueckert, "Multi-organ abdominal CT segmentation using hierarchically weighted subject-specific atlases," *Medical Image Computing and Computer Assisted Intervention – MICCAI*, Bd. 7510, S. 10–17, 2012.

[49] T. Okada, M. G. Linguraru, M. Hori, Y. Suzuki, R. M. Summers, N. Tomiyama, Y. Sato, "Multi-organ segmentation in abdominal CT images," in *2012 Annual International Conference of the IEEE Engineering in Medicine and Biology Society*, S. 3986–3989, Aug 2012.

[50] M. Oda, T. Nakaoka, T. Kitasaka, "Organ segmentation from 3D abdominal CT images based on atlas selection and graph cut," *Abdominal Imaging*, Bd. 7029, S. 181–188, 2011.

[51] Y. Sato, S. Nakajima, N. Shiraga, H. Atsumi, S. Yoshida, T. Koller, G. Gerig, R. Kikinis, "Three-dimensional multi-scale line filter for segmentation and visualization of curvilinear structures in medical images," *Medical Image Analysis*, Bd. 2, S. 143–168, 1998.

[52] A. F. Frangi, W. J. Niessen, K. L. Vincken, M. A. Viergever, "Multiscale vessel enhancement filtering," in *Medical Image Computing and Computer-Assisted Interventation—MICCAI'98*, S. 130–137, Springer, 1998.

[53] K. Drechsler C. L. Oyarzun, "Comparison of vesselness functions for multiscale analysis of the liver vasculature," *Proc. 10th IEEE International Conference on Information Technology and Applications in Biomedicine*, S. 1–5, 2010.

[54] X. Qian, M. P. Brennan, D. P. Dione, W. L. Dobrucki, M. P. Jackowski, C. K. Breuer, A. J. Sinusas, X. Papademetris, "A non-parametric vessel detection method for complex vascular structures," *Medical Image Analysis*, Bd. 13, Nr. 1, S. 49–61, 2009.

[55] F. Conversano, R. Franchini, C. Demitri, L. Massoptier, F. Montagna, A. Maffezzoli, A. Malvasi, S. Casciaro, "Hepatic vessel segmentation for 3D planning of liver surgery: experimental evaluation of a new fully automatic algorithm," *Academic radiology*, Bd. 18, Nr. 4, S. 461–470, 2011.

[56] W. Müller-Wittig R. Kramme, "Virtuelle Realität in der Medizin," in *Medizintechnik: Verfahren – Systeme – Informationsverarbeitung*, S. 847–858, Springer Berlin Heidelberg, 2011.

[57] T. Coles, D. Meglan, N. John, "The role of haptics in medical training simulators: A survey of the state of the art," *IEEE Transactions on Haptics*, Bd. 4, S. 51–66, Jan. 2011.

[58] W. I. M. Willaert, R. Aggarwal, I. Van Herzeele, N. J. Cheshire, F. E. Vermassen, "Recent advancements in medical simulation: Patient-specific virtual reality simulation," *World Journal of Surgery*, Bd. 36, S. 1703–12, Juli 2012.

[59] L. Soler J. Marescaux, "Patient-specific surgical simulation," *World Journal of Surgery*, Bd. 32, Nr. 2, S. 208–212, 2008.

[60] C. Forest, O. Comas, C. Vaysiere, L. Soler, J. Marescaux, "Ultrasound and needle insertion simulators built on real patient-based data," *Studies in Health Technology and Informatics*, Bd. 125, S. 136–9, 2007.

[61] J. Allard, S. Cotin, F. Faure, P.-J. Bensoussan, F. Poyer, C. Duriez, H. Delingette, L. Grisoni, "Sofa-an open source framework for medical simulation," in *MMVR 15-Medicine Meets Virtual Reality*, Bd. 125, S. 13–18, IOP Press, 2007.

[62] C. Basdogan, M. Sedef, M. Harders, S. Wesarg, "VR-based simulators for training in minimally invasive surgery," *IEEE Computer Graphics and Applications*, Bd. 27, Nr. 2, S. 54–66, 2007.

[63] W. D. Cannon, D. G. Eckhoff, W. E. Garrett, R. E. Hunter, H. J. Sweeney, "Report of a group developing a virtual reality simulator for arthroscopic surgery of the knee joint," *Clinical Orthopedics*, Bd. 442, S. 21–29, 2006.

[64] M. Harders, U. Spaelter, P. Leskovsky, G. Szekely, H. Bleuler, "Haptic interface module for hysteroscopy simulator system," *Studies in Health Technology and Informatics*, Bd. 125, S. 167–169, 2007.

[65] P. Maillard, L. Flaction, E. Samur, D. Hellier, J. Passenger, H. Bleuler, "Instrumentation of a clinical colonoscope for surgical simulation," *Proc. IEEE Engineering in Medicine and Biology Society*, S. 70–73, 2008.

[66] D. Ilic, T. Moix, N. M. Cullough, L. Duratti, I. Vecerina, H. Bleuler, "Real-time haptic interface for VR colonoscopy simulation," *Studies in Health Technology and Informatics*, Bd. 111, S. 208–212, 2005.

[67] A. Zivanovic, E. Dibble, B. Davies, L. Moody, A. Waterworth, "Engineering requirements for a haptic simulator for knee arthroscopy training," *Studies in Health Technology and Informatics*, Bd. 94, S. 413–418, 2003.

[68] J. D. Mabrey, S. D. Gillogly, J. R. Kasser, H. J. Sweeney, B. Zarins, H. Mevis, W. E. Garrett, R. Poss, W. D. Cannon, "Virtual reality simulation of arthroscopy of the knee," *Arthroscopy*, Bd. 18, Nr. 6, S. E28, 2002.

[69] M. J. Manyak, K. Santangelo, J. Hahn, R. Kaufman, T. Carleton, X. C. Hua, R. J. Walsh, "Virtual reality surgical simulation for lower urinary tract endoscopy and procedures," *Journal of Endourology*, Bd. 16, Nr. 3, S. 185–190, 2002.

[70] U. Kühnapfel, H. K. Cakmak, H. Maass, "Endoscopic surgery training using virtual reality and deformable tissue simulation," *Computers & Graphics*, Bd. 24, Nr. 5, S. 671–682, 2000.

[71] S. J. O'Leary, M. A. Hutchins, D. R. Stevenson, C. Gunn, A. Krumpholz, G. Kennedy, M. Tykocinski, M. Dahm, B. Pyman, "Validation of a networked virtual reality simulation of temporal bone surgery," *Laryngoscope*, Bd. 118, Nr. 6, S. 1040–1046, 2008.

[72] N. Kusumoto, T. Sohmura, S. Yamada, K. Wakabayashi, T. Nakamura, H. Yatani, "Application of virtual reality force feedback haptic device for oral implant surgery," *Clinical Oral Implants Research*, Bd. 17, Nr. 6, S. 708–713, 2006.

[73] A. Petersik, P. B., T. U., H. K.H., M. Heiland, H. H, T. Buzug, T. Lueth, "Realistic haptic interaction for computer simulation of dental surgery," in *Perspective in Image-Guided Surgery*, (Singapore), S. 261–269, World Scientific, 2004.

[74] B. Sae-Kee, R. Riener, M. Frey, T. Pröll, R. Burgkart, "Phantom-based interactive simulation system for dental treatment training," *Studies in Health Technology and Informatics*, Bd. 98, S. 327–332, 2004.

[75] G. J. Wiet, D. Stredney, D. Sessanna, J. A. Bryan, D. B. Welling, P. Schmalbrock, "Virtual temporal bone dissection: an interactive surgical simulator," *Otolaryngology and Head and Neck Surgery*, Bd. 127, Nr. 1, S. 79–83, 2002.

[76] G. J. Wiet, J. Bryan, E. Dodson, D. Sessanna, D. Stredney, P. Schmalbrock, B. Welling, "Virtual temporal bone dissection simulation," *Studies in Health Technology and Informatics*, Bd. 70, S. 378–384, 2000.

[77] M. Färber, T. Dahmke, C. A. Bohn, H. Handels, "Needle bending in a VR-puncture training system using a 6DOF haptic device," *Studies in Health Technology and Informatics*, Bd. 142, S. 91–3, 2009.

[78] M. Färber, F. Hummel, C. Gerloff, H. Handels, "Virtual reality simulator for the training of lumbar punctures," *Methods of Information in Medicine*, Bd. 48, Nr. 5, S. 493–501, 2009.

[79] M. Färber, J. Ehrhardt, H. Handels, "Live-wire-based segmentation using similarities between corresponding image structures," *Computerized Medical Imaging and Graphics*, Bd. 31, S. 549–560, Oktober 2007.

[80] U. Dreifaldt, Z. Kulcsar, P. Gallagher, "Exploring haptics as a tool to improve training of medical doctors in the procedure of spinal anaesthetics," *Proc. Eurohaptics*, 2006.

[81] J. Magill, B. Anderson, G. Anderson, P. Hess, S. Pratt, "Multi-axis mechanical simulator for epidural needle insertion," in *Medical Simulation*, S. 267–276, Springer, 2004.

[82] T. Dang, T. M. Annaswamy, M. A. Srinivasan, "Development and evaluation of an epidural injection simulator with force feedback for medical training," *Studies in Health Technology and Informatics*, Bd. 81, S. 97–102, 2001.

[83] L. L. Holton, "Force models for needle insertion created from measured needle puncture data," *Studies in Health Technology and Informatics*, Bd. 81, S. 180–186, 2001.

[84] P. Gorman, T. Krummel, R. Webster, M. Smith, D. Hutchens, "A prototype haptic lumbar puncture simulator," *Studies in Health Technology and Informatics*, Bd. 70, S. 106–109, 2000.

[85] L. Hiemenz, D. Stredney, P. Schmalbrock, "Development of the force-feedback model for an epidural needle insertion simulator," *Studies in Health Technology and Informatics*, Bd. 50, S. 272–277, 1998.

[86] P. F. Villard, F. P. Vidal, L. Ap Cenydd, R. Holbrey, S. Pisharody, S. Johnson, a. Bulpitt, N. W. John, F. Bello, D. Gould, "Interventional radiology virtual simulator for liver biopsy," *International Journal of Computer Assisted Radiology and Surgery*, S. 1–13, 2014.

[87] D. Ni, W. Chan, J. Qin, Y. Chui, "A virtual reality simulator for ultrasound-guided biopsy training," *IEEE Computer Graphics and Applications*, Bd. 31, Nr. 2, S. 143–150, 2011.

[88] D. Ni, W.-Y. Chan, J. Qin, Y. Qu, Y.-P. Chui, S. S. Ho, P.-A. Heng, "An ultrasound-guided organ biopsy simulation with 6DOF haptic feedback," *International Conference on Medical Image Computing and Computer-Assisted Intervention – MICCAI*, S. 551–559, 2008.

[89] S. Tandon, V. Devarajan, E. Richter, "Design and simulation of a visual and haptic assisted biopsy (ViHAB) system," *Studies in Health Technology and Informatics*, Bd. 132, S. 514–516, 2008.

[90] D. Magee D. Kessel, "A computer based simulator for ultrasound guided needle insertion procedures," *Proc. IET*, S. 301–308(7), Januar 2005.

[91] C. Lathan, K. Cleary, R. Greco, "Development and evaluation of a spine biopsy simulator," *Studies in Health Technology and Informatics*, Bd. 50, S. 375–376, 1998.

[92] J. B. Ra, S. M. Kwon, J. K. Kim, J. Yi, K. H. Kim, H. W. Park, K. U. Kyung, D. S. Kwon, H. S. Kang, S. T. Kwon, L. Jiang, J. Zeng, K. Cleary, S. K. Mun, "Spine needle biopsy simulator using visual and force feedback," *Computer Aided Surgery*, Bd. 7, Nr. 6, S. 353–363, 2002.

[93] S. Ullrich T. Kuhlen, "Haptic palpation for medical simulation in virtual environments," *IEEE Transactions on Visualization and Computer Graphics*, Bd. 18, Nr. 4, S. 617–25, 2012.

[94] T. Coles, N. John, D. Gould, D. Caldwell, "Integrating haptics with augmented reality in a femoral palpation and needle insertion training simulation," *IEEE Transactions on Haptics*, Bd. 4, Nr. 3, S. 199–209, 2011.

[95] M. W. Scerbo, J. P. Bliss, E. A. Schmidt, S. N. Thompson, "The efficacy of a medical virtual reality simulator for training phlebotomy," *Human Factors*, Bd. 48, Nr. 1, S. 72–84, 2006.

[96] M. W. Scerbo, E. A. Schmidt, J. P. Bliss, "Comparison of a virtual reality simulator and simulated limbs for phlebotomy training," *Journal of Infusion Nursing*, Bd. 29, Nr. 4, S. 214–224, 2006.

[97] M. Ursino, J. L. Tasto, B. H. Nguyen, R. Cunningham, G. L. Merril, "CathSim: an intravascular catheterization simulator on a PC," *Studies in Health Technology and Informatics*, Bd. 62, S. 360–366, 1999.

[98] S. Ullrich, T. Frommen, R. Rossaint, T. Kuhlen, "Virtual reality-based regional anaesthesia simulator for axillary nerve blocks," *Studies in Health Technology and Informatics*, Bd. 142, S. 392–394, 2009.

[99] Y.-J. Lim, P. Valdivia, C. Chang, N. Tardella, "Mr fluid haptic system for regional anesthesia training simulation system," *Studies in Health Technology and Informatics*, Bd. 132, S. 248–253, 2008.

[100] P. P. Banerjee, S. Rizzi, C. Luciano, "Virtual reality and haptic interface for cellular injection simulation," *Studies in Health Technology and Informatics*, Bd. 125, S. 37–39, 2007.

[101] C.-K. Chui, J. Teo, Z. Wang, J. Ong, J. Zhang, K.-M. Si-Hoe, S.-H. Ong, C.-H. Yan, S.-C. Wang, H.-K. Wong, J. H. Anderson, S.-H. Teoh, "Integrative haptic and visual interaction for simulation of PMMA injection during vertebroplasty," *Studies in Health Technology and Informatics*, Bd. 119, S. 96–98, 2006.

[102] O. Goksel, K. Sapchuk, W. J. Morris, S. E. Salcudean, "Prostate brachytherapy training with simulated ultrasound and fluoroscopy images," *IEEE Transactions on Biomedical Engineering*, Bd. 60, Nr. 4, S. 1002–12, 2013.

[103] R. Alterovitz, J. Pouliot, R. Taschereau, I. C. Hsu, K. Goldberg, "Simulating needle insertion and radioactive seed implantation for prostate brachytherapy," *Studies in Health Technology and Informatics*, Bd. 94, S. 19–25, 2003.

[104] C. Villard, L. Soler, A. Gangi, D. Mutter, J. Marescaux, "Toward realistic radiofrequency ablation of hepatic tumors 3D simulation and planning," in *Proc. SPIE Medical Imaging: Visualization, Image-Guided Procedures, and Display*, Bd. 5367, S. 586–595, International Society for Optics and Photonics, 2004.

[105] T. Livraghi, L. Solbiati, M. F. Meloni, G. S. Gazelle, E. F. Halpern, S. N. Goldberg, "Treatment of focal liver tumors with percutaneous radio-frequency ablation: Complications encountered in a multicenter study 1," *Radiology*, Bd. 226, Nr. 2, S. 441–451, 2003.

[106] T. Livraghi, S. N. Goldberg, S. Lazzaroni, F. Meloni, L. Solbiati, G. S. Gazelle, "Small hepatocellular carcinoma: Treatment with radio-frequency ablation versus ethanol injection," *Radiology*, Bd. 210, Nr. 3, S. 655–661, 1999.

[107] P. F. Villard, P. Boshier, F. Bello, D. Gould, "Virtual reality simulation of liver biopsy with a respiratory component," *Liver Biopsy*, 2011.

[108] P. F. Villard, F. P. Vidal, C. Hunt, F. Bello, N. W. John, S. Johnson, D. A. Gould, "A prototype percutaneous transhepatic cholangiography training simulator with real-time breathing motion," *International Journal of Computer Assisted Radiology and Surgery*, Bd. 4, S. 571–578, 2009.

[109] S. F. Gibson, "3D chainmail: A fast algorithm for deforming volumetric objects," in *Proc. Interactive 3D Graphics*, S. 149–154, ACM, 1997.

[110] M. Wilms, R. Werner, J. Ehrhardt, A. Schmidt-Richberg, H.-P. Schlemmer, H. Handels, "Multivariate regression approaches for surrogate-based diffeomorphic estimation of respiratory motion in radiation therapy," *Physics in Medicine and Biology*, Bd. 59, Nr. 5, S. 1147–1164, 2014.

[111] M. Wilms, J. Ehrhardt, R. Werner, M. Marx, H. Handels, "Statistical analysis of surrogate signals to incorporate respiratory motion variability into radiotherapy treatment planning," in *Proc. SPIE Medical Imaging: Image-Guided Procedures, Robotic Interventions, and Modeling*, (San Diego), S. 90360J–1–8, 2014.

[112] N. Jensen, G. Gaus, G. von Voigt, S. Olbrich, "Design and psychophysical study of volume compression for haptic rendering," in *Second Joint EuroHaptics Conference and Symposium on Haptic Interfaces for Virtual Environment and Teleoperator Systems (WHC'07)*, S. 261–267, IEEE, 2007.

[113] K. Lundin, B. Gudmundsson, A. Ynnerman, "General proxy-based haptics for volume visualization," *Proc. Eurohaptics*, S. 557–560, 2005.

[114] K. Lundin, A. Ynnerman, B. Gudmundsson, "Proxy-based haptic feedback from volumetric density data," in *Proc. Eurohaptics*, S. 104–109, 2002.

[115] T. Hayasaka, H. Liu, R. Himeno, T. Yamaguchi, "A MRI based semi-automatic modeling system for computational biomechanics simulation," in *Medical Imaging and Augmented Reality, 2001. Proceedings. International Workshop on*, S. 282–285, IEEE, 2001.

[116] P. Ljung, J. Krüger, E. Groller, M. Hadwiger, C. D. Hansen, A. Ynnerman, "State of the art in transfer functions for direct volume rendering," in *Computer Graphics Forum*, Bd. 35, S. 669–691, Wiley Online Library, 2016.

[117] B. Preim, A. Baer, D. Cunningham, T. Isenberg, T. Ropinski, "A survey of perceptually motivated 3D visualization of medical image data," in *Computer Graphics Forum*, Bd. 35, 2016.

[118] B. Wang, "Direct volume rendering of 4D deformable volume images," März 2009. US Patent 7,505,037.

[119] K. Engel, M. Hadwiger, J. M. Kniss, A. E. Lefohn, C. R. Salama, D. Weiskopf, *Real-time Volume Graphics*. A K Peters, 2006.

[120] J. Kruger R. Westermann, "Acceleration techniques for GPU-based volume rendering," in *Proceedings of the 14th IEEE Visualization 2003 (VIS'03)*, S. 38, IEEE Computer Society, 2003.

[121] B. Cabral, N. Cam, J. Foran, "Accelerated volume rendering and tomographic reconstruction using texture mapping hardware," in *Proceedings of the 1994 symposium on Volume visualization*, S. 91–98, ACM, 1994.

[122] S. R. Beane, Z. Davoudi, M. J. Savage, "Constraints on the universe as a numerical simulation," *The European Physical Journal*, Bd. 50, Nr. 9, S. 1–9, 2014.

[123] T. Kuhlen, *Exploring Virtuality: Virtualität im interdisziplinären Diskurs*, Kap. Virtuelle Realität als Gegenstand und Werkzeug der Wissenschaft, S. 133–147. Wiesbaden: Springer Fachmedien Wiesbaden, 2014.

[124] D. Jackèl, S. Neunreither, F. Wagner, "Modellierung und Animation von Naturerscheinungen," *Methoden der Computeranimation*, S. 193–246, 2006.

[125] D. Jackel, S. Neunreither, F. Wagner, *Methoden der Computeranimation*. Springer-Verlag, 2006.

[126] L. A. Zadeh, "Fuzzy sets," *Information and Control*, Bd. 8, Nr. 3, S. 338–353, 1965.

[127] L. Nyúl, J. K. Udupa, X. Zhang, "New variants of a method of MRI scale standardization," *IEEE Transactions on Medical Imaging*, Bd. 19, Nr. 2, S. 143–150, 2000.

[128] A. Criminisi J. Shotton, *Decision forests for computer vision and medical image analysis*. Springer Science & Business Media, 2013.

[129] J. Sanders E. Kandrot, *CUDA by Example: An Introduction to General-Purpose GPU Programming*. Addison-Wesley Professional, 1st ed., 2014.

[130] Y. Boykov V. Kolmogorov, "An experimental comparison of min-cut/max-flow algorithms for energy minimization in vision," *IEEE Transactions on Pattern Analysis and Machine Intelligence*, Bd. 26, S. 1124–1137, Sept. 2004.

[131] D. C. Ruspini, K. Kolarov, O. Khatib, "The haptic display of complex graphical environments," *Proc. 24th annual conference on Computer graphics and interactive techniques SIGGRAPH 97*, S. 345–352, 1997.

[132] D. J. v. Gerwen, J. Dankelman, J. J. v. d. Dobbelsteen, "Needle-tissue interaction forces–a survey of experimental data.," *Medical Engineering and Physics*, Bd. 34, Nr. 6, S. 665–80, 2012.

[133] N. Abolhassani, R. Patel, M. Moallem, "Needle insertion into soft tissue: A survey.," *Medical Engineering and Physics*, Bd. 29, Nr. 4, S. 413–31, 2007.

[134] J. T. Kajiya, "The rendering equation," in *Proceedings of the 13th Annual Conference on Computer Graphics and Interactive Techniques*, SIGGRAPH '86, (New York, NY, USA), S. 143–150, ACM, 1986.

[135] D. Fortmeier, *Direct Volume Rendering Methods for Needle Insertion Simulation*. Doktorarbeit an der Sektion Informatik/Technik, Universität zu Lübeck, 2016.

[136] A. Schmidt-Richberg, R. Werner, H. Handels, J. Ehrhardt, "Estimation of slipping organ motion by registration with direction-dependent regularization," *Medical Image Analysis*, Bd. 16, Nr. 1, S. 150 – 159, 2012.

[137] M. Chen, W. Lu, Q. Chen, K. J. Ruchala, G. H. Olivera, "A simple fixed-point approach to invert a deformation field," *Medical physics*, Bd. 35, Nr. 1, S. 81–88, 2008.

[138] U. Schneider, E. Pedroni, A. Lomax, "The calibration of CT Hounsfield units for radiotherapy treatment planning," *Phys Med Biol*, Bd. 41, Nr. 1, S. 111, 1996.

[139] T. Reichl, J. Passenger, O. Acosta, O. Salvado, "Ultrasound goes GPU: Real-time simulation using CUDA," in *Proc. SPIE Medical Imaging: Visualization, Image-Guided Procedures, and Modeling*, S. 726116-1–10, International Society for Optics and Photonics, 2009.

[140] J. Bushberg, J. Seibert, E. Leidholdt, J. Boone, *The Essential Physics of Medical Imaging*. Wolters Kluwer Health, 2011.

[141] T. Reichl, J. Passenger, O. Acosta, O. Salvado, "Echtzeit-Ultraschallsimulation auf Grafik-Prozessoren mit CUDA," in *Bildverarbeitung für die Medizin 2009*, Springer Berlin Heidelberg, 2009.

[142] A. Karamalis, *GPU Ultrasound Simulation and Volume Reconstruction*. Masterarbeit an der Fakultät für Informatik der Technischen Universität München, 2009.

[143] Y. Zhang, "A survey on evaluation methods for image segmentation," *Pattern Recognition*, Bd. 29, S. 1335–1346, 1996.

[144] R. Likert, "A technique for the measurement of attitudes," *Archives of Psychology*, Bd. 140, 1932.

[145] J. Bortz, G. Lienert, K. Boehnke, *Verteilungsfreie Methoden in der Biostatistik.* Springer-Lehrbuch, Springer, 2000.

[146] T. R. Langerak, U. a. van der Heide, A. N. T. J. Kotte, M. a. Viergever, M. van Vulpen, J. P. W. Pluim, "Label fusion in atlas-based segmentation using a selective and iterative method for performance level estimation (SIMPLE)," *IEEE Transactions on Medical Imaging*, Bd. 29, S. 2000–8, Dez. 2010.

[147] T. Rohlfing, R. Brandt, R. Menzel, D. B. Russakoff, C. R. Maurer, "Quo vadis , atlas-based segmentation ?," 2005.

[148] S. K. Warfield, K. H. Zou, W. M. Wells, "Simultaneous truth and performance level estimation (STAPLE): an algorithm for the validation of image segmentation.," *IEEE Transactions on Medical Imaging*, Bd. 23, S. 903–21, 2004.

[149] J. Kittler F. Alkoot, "Sum versus vote fusion in multiple classifier systems," *IEEE Transactions on Pattern Analysis and Machine Intelligence*, Bd. 25, Nr. 1, S. 110–115, 2003.

[150] M. V. Sanchez-Vives M. Slater, "From presence to consciousness through virtual reality," *Nature Reviews Neuroscience*, Bd. 6, S. 332–339, April 2005.

[151] W. Segars, G. Sturgeon, S. Mendonca, J. Grimes, B. M. Tsui, "4D XCAT phantom for multimodality imaging research," *Medical Physics*, Bd. 37, Nr. 9, S. 4902–4915, 2010.

[152] A. Guimond, J. Meunier, J.-P. Thirion, "Average brain models: A convergence study," *Computer Vision and Image Understanding*, Bd. 77, Nr. 2, S. 192–210, 2000.

[153] C. Rezk-Salama, M. Keller, P. Kohlmann, "High-level user interfaces for transfer function design with semantics," *IEEE Transactions on Visualization and Computer Graphics*, Bd. 12, Nr. 5, S. 1021–1028, 2006.

[154] Y. LeCun, Y. Bengio, G. Hinton, "Deep learning," *Nature*, Bd. 521, Nr. 7553, S. 436–444, 2015.

[155] Y. Jia, E. Shelhamer, J. Donahue, S. Karayev, J. Long, R. Girshick, S. Guadarrama, T. Darrell, "Caffe: Convolutional architecture for fast feature embedding," in *Proc. 22nd ACM International Conference on Multimedia*, S. 675–678, ACM, 2014.

[156] P. Dierckx, *Curve and surface fitting with splines.* Oxford University Press, 1995.

[157] A. Schmidt-Richberg, R. Werner, H. Handels, J. Ehrhardt, "A flexible variational registration framework," *Insight Journal*, S. http://hdl.handle.net/10380/3460, 2014.

[158] S. Köhnen, J. Ehrhardt, A. Schmidt-Richberg, H. Handels, "CUDA Optimierung von nicht-linearer oberflächen- und intensitätsbasierter Registrierung," in *Bildverarbeitung für die Medizin 2011: Algorithmen - Systeme - Anwendungen Proceedings des Workshops vom 20. - 22. März 2011 in Lübeck* (H. Handels, J. Ehrhardt, M. T. Deserno, H.-P. Meinzer, T. Tolxdorff, Ed.), (Berlin, Heidelberg), S. 99–103, Springer Berlin Heidelberg, 2011.

[159] P. Tan, G. Zeng, J. Wang, S. B. Kang, L. Quan, "Image-based tree modeling," in *ACM Transactions on Graphics (TOG)*, Bd. 26, S. 87, ACM, 2007.

[160] F. E. van Beek, W. M. Bergmann Tiest, A. M. L. Kappers, "Haptic discrimination of distance," *PLoS ONE*, Bd. 9, S. 1–9, 08 2014.

[161] M. Vicentini, S. Galvan, D. Botturi, P. Fiorini, "Evaluation of force and torque magnitude discrimination thresholds on the human hand-arm system," *ACM Trans. Appl. Percept.*, Bd. 8, S. 1:1–1:16, Nov. 2010.

[162] J. Ehrhardt, R. Werner, A. Schmidt-Richberg, H. Handels, "Statistical modeling of 4D respiratory lung motion using diffeomorphic image registration.," *IEEE Transactions on Medical Imaging*, Bd. 30, S. 251–265, Sept. 2011.

Glossar und Abkürzungsverzeichnis

1D, 2D	Eindimensional, zweidimensional: Vorhandene Freiheitsgrade.
3D, 4D	3D: Dreidimensional, räumlich. 4D: Vierdimensional, raum-zeitlich.
Abb., Tab.	Abbildung, Tabelle.
Ansicht-AS	Anterior-superior: Sicht von oben vorn.
Ansicht-LP	Links-posterior: von links-hinten.
Ansicht-R, -L	Rechts, links: Sicht von rechts, links.
Ansicht-RA	Rechts-anterior: Sicht von rechts-vorn.
CT	Computed Tomography: Computer-Tomografie, Röntgenverfahren zur Aufnahme von Volumenbilddaten.
DICE-Koeffizient	Dice Similarity Coefficient (DSC): Gütemaß zur Bewertung von Volumenüberlappung zwischen Goldstandardsegmentierung und geschätzter Segmentierung: 0 keine Übereinstimmung, 1 perfekte Übereinstimmung. Der DICE-Koeffizient wird gelegentlich auch in Prozent angegeben.
DOF	Degrees Of Freedom: Freiheitsgrade.
F	Fragen aus dem Fragenkatalog der Benutzerevaluation.
FEM	Finite-Element-Methoden dienen zur Simulation physikalischer Vorgänge auf stückweise unterteilten, endlichen Definitionsgebieten.
FPS	Frames Per Second: Bilder pro Sekunde ist ein Gütewert für die flüssige Darstellung bewegter Bilder, so dass beim Betrachter der Eindruck eines realistischen Bewegungsablaufs entsteht. Eine kritische untere Grenze stellen 15 Hz dar.
GC, iGC	GraphCut, interaktiver GraphCut: Ein nachverarbeitendes Segmentierungsverfahren, dass ein Bild als Graf modelliert und den Nachbarschaftskanten Kosten zuweist. Die Segmentierung findet durch einen kostenminimierenden Kantenschnitt des Grafen. Hintergrund und zu segmentierendes Objekt werden vorher (interaktiv) grob markiert (Saatregionen).
GPA	Generischer Patientenatlas: Ein allgemeiner simulierbarer Atlas, der mit neuen Patientenbilddaten personalisiert werden kann. Der GPA ist konzeptuell vergleichbar mit einem virtuellen Patientenmannequin.
GPGPU-Computing	General Purpose Graphics Processing Unit-Computing: Die Prozessorleistung aktueller Grafikhardware wird auch für allgemeine Zwecke (nicht Computerspiele) verwendet.
GPU	Graphics Processing Unit: Grafikprozessor für die spezialisierte und optimierte Berechnung von Grafiken und zeitveränderlichen Visualisierungen in Computern, Spielkonsolen und Smartphones.
GUI	Graphical User Interface: Grafische Benutzeroberfläche zur Bedienung eines Computer-Programms.

JND	Just Noticeable Difference: Gerade noch spürbare Reizunterschiede für Kräfte und Längen des Hand-Arm-Systems. Diese werden in Prozent ausgedrückt und sind abhängig von Referenzreizen.
Likert-Skala	Diskrete Skala mit Bewertungsstufen von Zustimmung zu Ablehnung.
MAE	Maximal Absolute Error: Maximaler absoluter Fehler.
MAS	Multi-Atlas-Segmentierung: Ein rechenaufwendiges jedoch robustes Segmentierungsschätzverfahren, bei dem mehrere Intensitätsdatensätze mit korrespondierenden apriori-Segmentierungen auf neue Intensitätsdaten mittels nichtlinearer Registrierungsverfahren verformt werden. Die verformten apriori-Segmentierungen werden am Ende gemittelt (fusioniert) und ergeben eine robuste Gesamtschätzung der gesuchten Segmentierung.
MPR	Multi-Planare-Reformation: Schnittbilder, die durch einen Volumendatensatz gelegte und abgetastete Ebenen entstehen.
NPA	Neuer Patientenatlas: Ein neuer simulierbarer Atlas, enspricht einer personalisierten Version des GPA mit neuen Patientenbilddaten.
Patch	Bildstück: Nachbarschaftlich zusammenhängender, kleiner Unterbereich eines Bildes.
Proxy	Virtueller Stellvertreterpunkt zur Berechnung von Nadelkräften und Weichteildeformationen.
PTC	Perkutane Transhepatische Cholangiografie: Minimalinvasives Verfahren, bei dem mit Hilfe einer dünnen Hohlnadel unter Durchleuchtungskontrolle perkutan (durch die Haut) durch Punktion der Leber und langsame Nadelretraktion Röntgenkontrastmittel in die Gallengänge eingebracht wird.
PTC/D	Gemeinsame Abkürzung für die Nadeleingriffe PTC und PTCD.
PTCD	Perkutane Transhepatische Cholangiodrainage: Bei der PTC ist es möglich, über den gelegten Zugang eine Ableitung der Gallenflüssigkeit nach außen über eine Drainage herzustellen, um einen Rückstau in den Gallenwegen zu beseitigen. Diese Erweiterung der PTC wird PTCD genannt.
RF, RFK	Random-Forest(-Klassifikator): Dieser weist einem n-dimensionalen Merkmalstupel eine semantische Aussage zu (hier: Label stellvertretend für ein Gewebe, Organ oder Struktur).
RMSE, MSE	(Root) Mean Squared Error: (Gewurzelter) mittlerer quadratischer Fehler: $RMSE = \sqrt{MSE}$.
Slab	Quaderförmiger Auschnitt eines Volumenbildes zur Erzeugung von dickschichtigen Multi-Planaren-Reformationen (MPR); definiert durch den Zwischenraum zweier Ebenen.
Tf.	Transferfunktion.
TGC	Time Gain Control: Tiefenabhängige Verstärkung des reflektierten US-Signals.
US	Ultraschall: Schall mit Frequenzen oberhalb des menschlichen Hörfrequenzbereichs.
Voxel, Pixel	Volume Element: Ein Volumenelement ist der elementare quaderförmige Baustein eines 3D-Volumenelementgitters. Picture Element: Elementarer rechteckiger Baustein eines 2D-Bildelementgitters (Bildpunkt).
VR	Virtual Reality: Interaktive Darstellung und Wahrnehmung einer Nachahmung der Wirklichkeit in einer physikalisch bzw. für die menschlichen Sinne plausiblen Computer-Simulation.

Symbolverzeichnis

Symbol:	Bedeutung:
§	Abschnitt.
$\mathbf{x}$	Ortsvektor.
$h_{...}\left(\mathbf{x}, d\right)$	Label-Transferfunktionen zur effizienten Segmentierungsschätzung.
bay	Index zur Andeutung Bayesscher-Transferfunktionen h_{bay}.
d	Eindringtiefe des Nadelwegs von der Hautoberfläche bzw. eines simulierten US-Strahls [mm].
l_{risk}	Label-Wert der Risikostrukturen.
l_{skin}	Label-Wert der Hautschicht.
l_{soft}	Label-Wert des Weichteilgewebes (Fett, Bindegewebe, Muskeln, innere Organe).
l_{bone}	Label-Wert der Knochenstrukturen.
l_{air}	Label-Wert der Luft (Hintergrund).
$L\left(\mathbf{x}\right), L_g$	Priorisierter Multi-Label-Datensatz, Referenzsegmentierung.
l_{fascia}	Label-Wert der interkostalen Faszienschicht.
l_{liver}	Label-Wert der Leber.
l_{blood}	Label-Wert der Leberblutgefäße.
l_{bile}	Label-Wert der Lebergallengefäße.
$l\left(\mathbf{x}, d\right)$	Label-Schätzfunktion, benutzt $h_{...}\left(\mathbf{x}, d\right)$ und $L\left(\mathbf{x}\right)$.
$I\left(\mathbf{x}\right)$	Bildfunktion: Intensität eines Bildes I zum Ortsvektor $\mathbf{x}$ [HU].
r, g, b	Farbintensität eines Kanals im RGBA-Farbmodell $\in [0, 1]$.
a	Opazität der im RGBA-Modell angegebenen Farbe $\in [0, 1]$.
k	Federsteifigkeit der Proxy-Feder für eine Struktur [N/mm].
R	Reibungskraft für eine Struktur [N].
T_N	Oberflächendurchstoßkraft einer Organ-/Strukturkapsel [N].
t_{skin}^{soft}	Bayes-Schwellwert für den Übergang von Haut zu Weichteilgewebe [HU].
δ	Abstand des Faszienmodells zur Hautoberfläche entlang des Nadelpfads.
t_{air}^{skin}	Bayes-Schwellwert für den Übergang von Luft zu Haut [HU].
t_{soft}^{bone}	Bayes-Schwellwert für den Übergang von Weichteilgewebe zu Knochen [HU].
$\check{t}_{soft}^{bone}$	Niedriger Bayes-Schwellwert für den Übergang zu Knochen [HU].
$\hat{t}_{soft}^{bone}$	Erhöhter Bayes-Schwellwert für den Übergang zu Knochen [HU].
t_{von}^{zu}	Platzhalter für die genannten Bayes-Schwellwerte (von $\in$ {air, skin, soft}, zu $\in$ {skin, soft, bone}).
$L = RFK\left(\mathbf{m}\right)$	RF-Klassifikations-Aufruf mit Merkmalsbildern, ergibt Label-Bild. Spezialfall von $L \sqsubseteq RFK$.
$RFK\left(L; \mathbf{m}\right)$	RFK-Aufruf mit Label-Bild und Merkmalsbildern zum Training.
$\mathbf{m}$	Merkmalsbildtupel z. B. mit $(f_j, f_{j+1}, \ldots)$.
$\sqsubseteq, \sqsupseteq$	Verwendet zur Andeutung von Abtastung, analog zu Teilmenge. Je nach Kontext Abtastung eines Bild- bzw. Merkmalsraums.
lar, liv	Index zur Andeutung von RFKn/Transferfunktionen für großvolumige Strukturen, Leberstrukturen.
f_j, f_k	Merkmalsbilder für den Random-Forest-Klassifikator.

Symbol:	Bedeutung:
j, k	Bildindizes: Merkmalsbilder (j, k), Atlanten (k) oder CT-Phasenbilder aus Atemzyklus (j).
i	Positionsindex in einer definierten Durchlaufrichtung einer Leitstruktur (Voxel-Modell, Strahl), Index von Ortsvektoren $\mathbf{x}$, $\mathbf{X}$ oder Bildmerkmalen f_j.
f_0 (f_0^i)	Basismerkmal der normalisierten Bildintensitäten (an Position i).
f_1 (f_1^i)	Erstes, abgeleitetes Merkmal, hier Euklidischer Abstand zur Hautoberfläche (an Position i) [mm].
$D_{skin}(\mathbf{x})$	Euklidischer Abstand zur Hautoberfläche [mm].
f_2 (f_2^i)	Zweites, abgeleitetes Merkmal, hier Gradientenbetrag (Position i).
$\nabla, \lvert\nabla\ldots\rvert$	Gradient, Gradientenbetrag.
$\mathbf{r}(\phi, h)$	Eine die Rippenbögen interpolierende vektorwertige B-Spline-Funktion (3D-Fläche) in Zylinderkoordinaten.
ϕ	Winkel im Zylinderkoordinatensystem $\in [0 \leq \phi \leq 2\pi]$.
h	Höhe in definiertem Intervall im Zylinderkoordinatensystem $\in [h_0, h_1]$.
B_x, B_y, B_z	Koordinatenkomponenten der 3D-B-Spline-Fläche über dem rechteckigen Definitionsbereich (ϕ, h).
φ, φ^{-1}	Deformationsabbildung eines Raums und Invertierung.
$\varphi_{aff,k}$	Affine Deformationsabbildung für den k-ten Atlas.
$\varphi_{n.l.,k}$	Nicht-lineare Deformationsabbildung für den k-ten Atlas.
$\mathbf{p}, (\mathbf{p_0}, \mathbf{p}', \mathbf{p}'')$	Virtuelle Proxy-Position, der Proxy bleibt an Gewebestrukturen hängen und spannt mit der Nadelposition $\mathbf{x}$ eine virtuelle Feder auf (Zwischenpositionen bei der iterativen Proxy-Berechnung).
$\mathbf{d}, \mathbf{d}_l$	Nadelvorschubvektor, kleine Positionsvorschübe.
$\mathbf{n}$	Nadelschaftstellen bei Diskretisierung der Nadel in Stabelemente.
$\mathbf{f}$	Dem Nadelvorschubvektor entgegen wirkender Kraftvektor.
$a, (a_0, a_1, a_2)$	Federkonstante(n) zur Berechnung (nicht-)linearer Federkräfte.
u, u^{-1}	Additives Verschiebungsvektorfeld, welches eine Deformation φ in einer Momentaufnahme approximiert und Invertierung.
t	Zeit [s].
A	Atemamplitude in Pseudo-Atmungs-Verschiebungsvektorfeld [mm].
Ω	Definitionsbereich des Bildvolumens $(\Omega \subset \mathbb{R}^3)$.
I_{ref}	Ausgewählte Referenzbildphase aus einem Atemzyklus.
$s(t)$	1D-Spirometriesignal.
$\hat{\mathbf{z}}(t)$	2D-Spirometriesignal zur Unterscheidung zwischen Ein- und Ausatmung (Hysterese).
$\hat{\varphi}(\mathbf{X}, t)$	Multivariates lineares Bewegungsmodell.
$\mathbf{X}$	Ortsvektor im Referenzraum.
$\mathbf{x_t}$	Zeitabhängig verschobener Ortsvektor (im Wölbungsraum).
$\bar{a}_1, \bar{a}_2, \bar{a}_3$	Vektorfeldkoeffizienten des linearen Atembewegungsmodells.
I_t	Verformtes Referenzbild I_{ref} zu einem Zeitpunkt t.
$\circ$	Verknüpfungoperator für Deformationsabbildungen mit anderen Deformationen oder Bildern.
$\hat{u}(\mathbf{X}, t)$	Additives der Deformation $\hat{\varphi}$ momentan entsprechendes Verschiebungsvektorfeld des Bewegungsmodells.
$\hat{u}^{-1}(\mathbf{x_t}, t)$	Additives inverses Verschiebungsvektorfeld des Bewegungsmodells.
ρ	Dichte [kg/m³].
Z	Schallkennimpedanz [N s/m³].
I_i, I_r, I_e, I_v	Rest-, reflektierte, am US-Transducer empfangene, TGC-verstärkte Energieintensität
f	Ultraschallfrequenz [MHz].
v	Verstärkung der TGC-Korrektur [dB].
p-Wert	Signifikanzwert eines statistischen Tests $\in [0, 1]$.
$\pm$	Prefix für eine statistische Standardabweichung, genannt nach einem Mittelwert.

Publikationsverzeichnis und Lizenzierung

---

[1]gleichberechtigte Erstautoren A. Mastmeyer und D. Fortmeier

Efficient Patient Modelling for Visuo-Haptic VR Simulation

Andre Mastmeyer[a,1], Dirk Fortmeier[a,b], Heinz Handels[a,2]
[a] Institute of Medical Informatics, University of Lübeck, Lübeck, Germany
[b] Graduate School for Computing in Medicine and Life Sciences, University of Lübeck, Lübeck, Germany
[1] Corresponding author
[2] This work is supported by the German Research Foundation (DFG HA 2355/11-2).

Abstract

Background and Objective: This work presents a new time-saving virtual patient modeling system by way of example for an existing visuo-haptic training and planning virtual reality (VR) system for percutaneous transhepatic cholangio-drainage (PTCD).
Methods: Our modeling process is based on a generic patient atlas to start with. It is defined by organ-specific optimized models, method modules and parameters, i.e. mainly individual segmentation masks, transfer functions to fill the gaps between the masks and intensity image data. In this contribution, we show how generic patient atlases can be generalized to new patient data. The methodology consists of patient-specific, locally-adaptive transfer functions and dedicated modeling methods such as multi-atlas segmentation, vesselness filtering and spline-modeling.
Results: Our full image volume segmentation algorithm yields median DICE coefficients of 0.98, 0.93, 0.82, 0.74, 0.51 and 0.48 regarding soft-tissue, liver, bone, skin, blood and bile vessels for ten test patients and three selected reference patients. Compared to standard slice-wise manual contouring time saving is remarkable.
Conclusions: Our segmentation process shows out efficiency and robustness for upper abdominal puncture simulation systems. This marks a significant step towards establishing patient-specific training and hands-on planning systems in a clinical environment.

1 Introduction and Related Work

Needle insertion simulation for liver biopsy [1, 2] or into blood vessels [3, 4] is an active research area. Among visuo-haptic rendering, the just-in-time and accurate virtual patient modeling process is of major importance, but largely unaddressed in the literature so far. Training and planning of needle interventions just before the actual procedure is to the benefit of the patient (lower number of needle repositionings), lowers time spent on an actual case and consequently decreases treatment cost. Other simulator approaches to needle insertion simulation use full volume manual segmentations and corresponding explicit surface or volume mesh models to represent the organs and tissues, which may be subject to online remeshing [5]. Patient-specificity in a short time frame [6], i.e. the

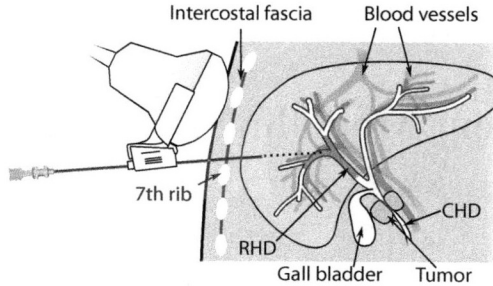

Figure 1: Ultrasound guided PTCD just before puncturing the target region (RHD, in green): Coronal cross section of the target anatomy with dilated hepatic duct (target structure). The needle can be guided on a trail attached to the probe. Puncturing of risk structures such as blood vessels should be avoided.

ability to simulate an intervention facing new patient data, is the main topic focused in this publication.

In [7], a simulator for ultrasound (US)-guided liver lesion needle punctures using two haptic devices for US-device and needle respectively is described. They use surface models created by the marching cubes algorithm and refrain from direct volume rendering due to slow processing times. In [8], a simulator for percutaneous transhepatic cholangiography (PTC) is presented. There, surface models have to be created as well and neither direct haptic nor visual rendering of patient image data is available.

In our previous work, the lumbar puncture simulator "AcusVR" [9] proved to be a valuable planning and training system. The hardware setup of this tool comprised a Geomagic Phantom Premium 1.5 6DOF haptic device, a combination of shutter glasses as well as a stereoscopic display for virtual reality immersion. Training was shown effective in a study with several users [9]. Unfortunately, AcusVR and other systems to this day still need a time consuming manual contouring process aiming at complete full volume segmentation of the CT data, which can take 20-40 hours [10] depending on the anatomical site, used methods and level of detail. Recently we have presented a new voxel-model-based VR simulation framework [11], for which the patient modeling process is decribed here.

Regarding our targeted procedures, percutaneous transhepatic cholangio-drainage (PTCD) extends percutaneous transhepatic cholangiography (PTC, for visualizing the bile ducts by contrast agent), towards the goal of relieving the patient from pain by drainage of cholestatically dilated bile ducts [12]. Cholestasis is accompanied by obstructions in the common hepatic bile duct (CHD) such as lesions or gallstones. To drain the "right hepatic bile duct" (RHD) and the rest of the bile system, a needle is positioned between the 6th and 7th ribs through the intercostal spaces and the liver into the duct using ultrasound guidance. Fig. 1 briefly describes the PTC/D-procedure.

To motivate the contributions of this work, we also briefly summarize our new virtual reality simulation framework [11] and its visuo-haptic rendering concepts depending on several visuo-haptic parameters. The visuo-haptic parameter determine the visual appearance of rendered organs in terms of color and transparency and the haptic force feedback in terms of e.g. surface penetration force or organ internal friction. These parameters are attached to a label in a multi-label data set, the construction process of which we describe here. Our simulator AcusVR2 (Fig. 2a) is an reinvention of its predecessors (AcusVR) concepts [9] in many aspects. AcusVR was a classic simulator for lumbar punctures using

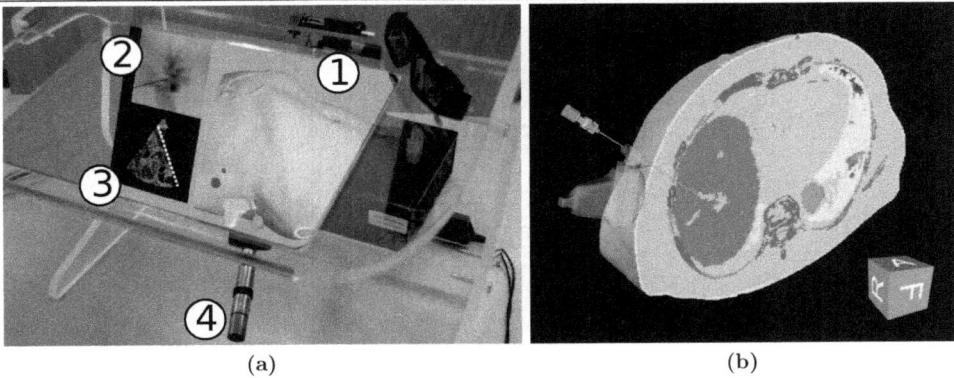

(a)   (b)

Figure 2: Haptic workbench with semi-transparent mirror below a stereoscopic display: (a) (1) Main rendering window, (2) X-ray rendering window, (3) ultrasound rendering window and (4) haptic device handle. (b) Tagged volume rendering of the patient using "clipping mode".

virtual patients with explicit rigid polygonal organ models for every relevant structure, which were segmented manually.

In our new voxel-model-based simulator [11], the virtual PTCD intervention can be trained and planned subject to the following workflow using various virtual tools: (1) palpation, (2) ultrasound (US) probing and (3) US-guided needle puncture. Needle guidance and force feedback when penetrating the patient are displayed to the user via a Geomagic Phantom Premium 6DOF HighForce haptic force feedback device.

Compared to AcusVR and other systems [13], in our current simulator we only need a small part of the image volume (Fig. 2b, e.g. liver) to be segmented explicitly. We use direct volume rendering by ray-casting [14], which is able to visualize major parts of the image data without preprocessing steps. Our renderer accepts an arbitrary piecewise-linear visual RGBA transfer function or tagging function augmented by multi-label segmentation data (see corresponding colored areas in Figs. 2b and 5).

In contrast to the related work mentioned above, our new system concept using a Generic Patient Atlas (GPA) features methods and attributes such as the mentioned augmented multi-label visuo-haptic parameter transfer functions. Generally, a complete segmentation of the image volume is needed for the simulation. Here, for a New Patient Atlas (NPA) instance, only a partial segmentation of the image volume using dedicated methods has to be explicitly created to provide a usable patient model. The remaining segmentation background is filled by label transfer function estimation based on the image intensity values. The isolated segmentation of bones [15, 16], liver [17] and vessels [18] has been adressed by other authors. In this paper, we present an integrative full image volume modeling concept for air, bone and soft-tissue based on a case-based transfer function model, Multi-Atlas Segmentation (MAS) of the liver and liver-specific vessel segmentation algorithms. All shown individual methods collude in an overall framework, include interesting novel aspects and are optimized for robustness. We propose a new pipeline with parallel tasks for the fast segmentation of key and background structures.

The contributions focused here consist of a virtual patient modeling process featuring only partially segmented intensity data where for other state of the art simulators a full explicit manual volume segmentation is in fact necessary. Secondly, we dramatically reduce time efforts in comparison to manual full image volume segmentation, while still achieving high simulation quality [11]. Thirdly, the whole volume segmentation pipeline shown here contains novel individual steps and is kept general to be easily expandable to other liver puncture intervention scenarios, such as tumor ablation.

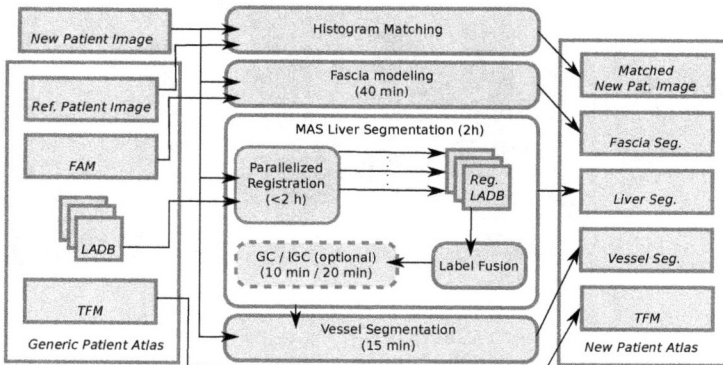

Figure 3: Scheme of our Generic Patient Atlas (GPA) to New Patient Atlas (NPA) adaptation process (LADB=liver atlas data base; TFM=transfer function model; FAM=fascia model; GC=graph cut; iGC=interactive GC). Normal boxes contain data objects, round cornered boxes represent processes.

The article is organized as follows: In section 2, the methods for the generation of patient atlases are presented. Section 3 shows our implementation details and evaluation methodology. Finally, we show the modeling and time efficiency results in section 4 and discuss them in section 5.

2 Methods

In our system concept, we start using a fully manually segmented and reviewed reference patient to define the core of the generic atlas. It is then augmented by helping attributes such as an atlas database containing a certain number of liver segmentations and an empirically learned parameter set for several organ-specific segmentation methods. Generally speaking, the generic patient atlas's attributes are then generalized to new patient atlases, the process is shown in a nutshell in Fig. 3.

Conceptually, for new unsegmented patient images, the new intensity data is first adapted to a selected reference patient by a histogram matching technique. Then, the fascia, the liver and its vessels are segmented using organ-specifically optimized methods.

The following detail sections consist of two major parts: First, we describe the concept of the generic patient atlas as a start point and the modeling process of it (based on the selected reference patient). Second, the process for the generalization to new patient atlases is presented.

2.1 Generation of a Generic Patient Atlas

A normally weigthed reference patient serves to define a Generic Patient Atlas (GPA), consisting of static attributes in form of a property node tree [11] and exchangeable attributes. Users of our methodology should start defining such a GPA first. In this publication, only the material leaf nodes are important which can be viewed in a simple "material node dictionary". The default for the exchangeable data is set to attributes representing a reference patient. Each new patient atlas instance that represents a new patient image then consists of the static attributes inherited from the generic patient atlas and the replaced exchangeable attributes based on processing the new patient intensity data.

Additionally to the intensity and full volume segmentation data of the reference patient, we use a Liver Atlas Data Base (LADB) for liver segmentation. Details can be found in the implementation and experiments section 3.

A GPA's material node dictionary consist of material label (key) and visuo-haptic parameter tuples $(R, G, B, A; T_N, R, k)$ as value. The tuples are valid in transfer function intervals (intensity ranges) and segmentation masks associated with a few key structures. (R, G, B, A) describes the visual appearance (color, transparency) of the object, and (T_N, R, k) denotes haptic characteristics, i.e. a cutting force threshold T_N, friction R and stiffness k. Two medical experts have punctured the relevant tissues and empirically tuned the haptic parameters for the simulation [11]. Some transfer function intervals (cf. Figs. 4, 5) are subject to a distinction of cases dependent on the needle tip position $\mathbf{x}$ described later (local adaptation). The GPA's exchangeable data comprises volume intensity, multi-label segmentation data and coefficients from the fascia spline model.

In case a label tag inside a segmentation mask is found for a voxel, it is matched with the material tuple from the node dictionary. Since we use only partially segmented data (Fig. 4a), the remaining labels have to be estimated.

Selection Criteria for Reference Patient Intensity Data   As it will turn out, it is indicated to use non-over weighted reference patients. The field-of-view especially concerning the z-range must contain the key structures. In our current application, the upper abdomen containing the liver is the targeted area. When contrast agent is used in a procedure, the reference patient data should reflect the typical phase and level of contrast agent.

Set-up of Transfer-Function Model Points   Using a fully segmented reference patient, the normal distributions of the gray levels are calculated for air, skin, soft-tissue (fat) and bone. For these classes we determine the intersections of the distribution curves $t_{\text{air}}^{\text{skn}}$, $t_{\text{skn}}^{\text{sft}}$ and $t_{\text{sft}}^{\text{bn}}$ [19]. Bayes-optimal model points $t_{\text{air}}^{\text{skn}}$, $t_{\text{skn}}^{\text{sft}}$ and $t_{\text{sft}}^{\text{bn}}$ [HU] result from this step, the latter threshold is refined as low $t_{\text{sft};lo}^{\text{bn}} = t_{\text{sft}}^{\text{bn}} + t_{off;lo}^{bn}$ and high $t_{\text{sft};hi}^{\text{bn}} = t_{\text{sft};lo}^{\text{bn}} + t_{off;hi}^{bn}$ with bone threshold offsets. The thresholds are used to define the compiled visuo-haptic parameter transfer function shown in Fig. 5. Note, the local adaptive bone model point $t_{\text{sft}}^{\text{bn}}(\mathbf{x})$ is dependent on the needle tip location $\mathbf{x}$ relative to the fascia and can be either $t_{\text{sft};lo}^{\text{bn}}$ or $t_{\text{sft};hi}^{\text{bn}}$:

$$t_{\text{sft}}^{\text{bn}}(\mathbf{x}) = \begin{cases} t_{\text{sft};lo}^{\text{bn}} & \text{if needle shaft inside fascia} \\ t_{\text{sft};hi}^{\text{bn}} & \text{otherwise} \end{cases} \tag{1}$$

By this means, bone vs. soft-tissue classification is locally adaptive: Rib cage and costal cartilage are classified in our labeling function using the peripheral sensitive bone threshold of $t_{\text{sft};lo}^{\text{bn}}$ (see Fig. 4b). In case the needle tip $\mathbf{x}$ has passed the fascia, we use the much more specific conservative hard bone threshold of $t_{\text{sft};hi}^{\text{bn}}$ (see Fig. 5, yellow hatched interval).

The tagging function l_{t} can now be defined for position $\mathbf{x}$, a given image intensity $v = I(\mathbf{x})$ and label $l_{\text{sgm}} = L(\mathbf{x})$ from the multi-label image L containing fascia, liver and vessel labels as:

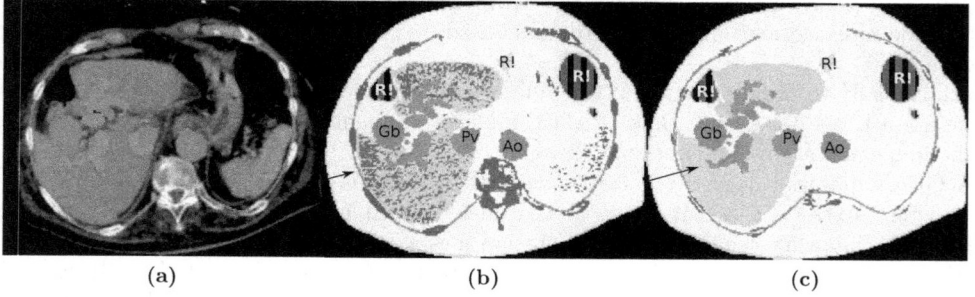

(a)   (b)   (c)

Figure 4: Three times the same axial slice of patient #1: (a) Intensity image slice augmented by color-coded partial segmentations: fascia (magenta), liver (transparent brown), ducts (green), blood vessels (red). (b) Slice augmented with color-coded tissue label classes air (black), skin (orange), fat (yellow), bone (purple) and partial segmentations. (c) Slice augmented with color-coded tissue label classes in case the needle has passed the fascia label (arrow). The following acronyms indicate: R!=risk structure, Gb=gall bladder, Ao=aorta and Pv=portal vein.

$$l_t(\mathbf{x}) = \begin{cases} l_{\text{sgm}} & \text{if } l_{\text{sgm}} \neq 0 \\ l_{\text{rsc}} & \text{elsif } \left(v < t_{\text{skn}}^{\text{sft}}\right) \wedge (d > \delta) \\ l_{\text{air}} & \text{elsif } v < t_{\text{air}}^{\text{skn}} \\ l_{\text{skn}} & \text{elsif } v \in \left[t_{\text{air}}^{\text{skn}}, t_{\text{skn}}^{\text{sft}}\right) \\ l_{\text{sft}} & \text{elsif } v \in \left[t_{\text{skn}}^{\text{sft}}, t_{\text{sft}}^{\text{bn}}(\mathbf{x})\right) \\ l_{\text{bn}} & \text{elsif } v \geq t_{\text{sft}}^{\text{bn}}(\mathbf{x}) \end{cases} \tag{2}$$

with the current needle insertion depth d, and δ is a minimal insertion depth after which the detection of unspecified risk structures l_{rsc} starts. Such an efficiently evaluable equation is necessary for visuo-haptic rendering at 2000 Hz on a single CPU-core.

This way, we yield a quick classification of voxels, which can be visually checked using color-tagging of the CT data (see Figs. 2b, 4, 5). Important risk structures (l_{rsc}) such as the pleural space including recesses are detected in real-time by the following strategy: An air cavity lined with skinny tissue occurring at the needle tip inside the body is generally suspicious and is indicated as unspecified risk structure to the user (cf. Eq. 2; Figs. 4b; 5, grey hatched interval).

Fascia Modeling for Haptic Rendering   Apart from the image data and segmentation masks of a patient, a spline model for the fascia is set-up. Accurate muscle and fibrous tissue layer segmentation in CT data is very hard to accomplish and we mainly aim at plausible haptic rendering of an artificial thin resistant internal intercostal fascia layer between the ribs. In reality, the fascia cut-through feeling is the most salient haptic incident on the needle path. Thus, we decided to use a B-spline surface [20] to close the intercostal spaces where the layers of fascial muscles are located and consider it as a exchangeable part of the GPA that has to be adapted when creating a new atlas instance. Fig. 6 shows the reference fascia model-fit between the ribs; a spline surface $s(\phi, h) = (B_x(\phi, h), B_y(\phi, h), B_z(\phi, h))^T$ is fit through a rib cage segmentation obtained using a conservative bone threshold [21], where the normalized height $0 \leq h \leq 1$ and girth angle $0 \leq \phi \leq 2\pi$ are cylinder coordinates [22]. The functions B_x, B_y and B_z are individual B-spline surfaces defined over the rectangular (ϕ, h)-domain:

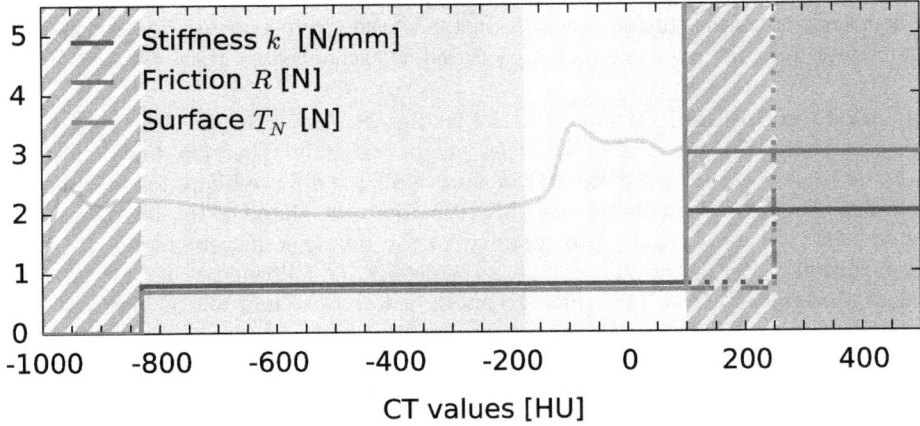

Figure 5: Compiled visuo-haptic transfer function for reference patient #1 overlayed to the histogram curve (gray) of the reference patient #1 with color coded intervals of air (light-gray), skin (orange), fat (yellow) and bone (purple) as used in the tagging function. The grey white-hatched interval is either classified as air or "inside risk" structure depending on the needle insertion depth. The ends of the yellow-purple hatched area indicate the cases needle tip outside resp. passed fascia ($t_{sft}^{bn} = t_{sft;lo}^{bn}$ resp. $t_{sft;hi}^{bn}$).

$$B(\phi, h) = \sum_{n=0}^{N_{kn}} \sum_{m=0}^{M_{kn}} c_{n,m} \cdot N_{n,k+1}(\phi) \cdot N_{m,l+1}(h) \tag{3}$$

with N_{kn} (girth) and M_{kn} (height) as the number of knots, $c_{n,m}$ are the control coefficients, k and l are the degrees of the B-Spline base functions $N_{n,k+1}(\phi)$ and $N_{m,l+1}(h)$. Now, the $c_{n,m}$ define the control points of the reference fascia model to be adapted to new patients.

2.2 Process for a New Patient Atlas

The following section describes the creation of a NPA instance. In a first phase, an intensity value normalization of the new patient image data to the reference patient takes place, which makes the generic atlas's transfer function model applicable. Second, the new

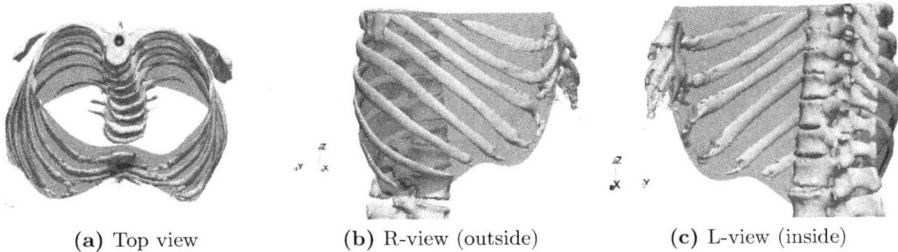

(a) Top view　　　(b) R-view (outside)　　　(c) L-view (inside)

Figure 6: The reference B-Spline surface (transparent magenta) fitted accurately through the rib cage (gray) of patient #1: (a) complete cylindrical spline, (b) outside of the right half of the rib cage in lateral view from right, (c) inside of rib cage.

patient data undergoes a dedicated modeling process with several specific methods for the liver and its vessels. In the new atlas instance, the newly generated data replaces the default data from the reference patient declared as exchangeable in the GPA.

Transfer Function and Fascia Model Fitting Strictly speaking, the model points defined in section 2.1 are valid for the reference patient only. Therefore first, a histogram matching procedure proposed for MR images by [23] is adapted here for CT images to generalize the transfer functions. By this technique, the shape of the histogram of the targeted new patient data $T(x)$ is adapted to the reference patient image $R(x)$. Our customization of the method for CT data consists of the following steps: (1) Histogram outliers are removed from both histograms by a low near zero and a high near 100% percentile threshold. Hence, the very low and high end voxels are removed from the histogram of the reference and new patient data sets. (2) Gray values $g_{R,i}$ resp. $g_{T,i}$ ($i = 0..N_{pc} - 1$) at N_{pc} fixed percentile levels monotonically increasing from 0% to 100% are determined in both data sets and can be regarded as corresponding match points. (3) With $T(x)$ inside the interval $[g_{T,i-1}, g_{T,i}]$, piecewise linear transforms ($i = 1..N_{pc} - 1$)

$$M_i(x) = g_{R,i-1} + \frac{g_{R,i} - g_{R,i-1}}{g_{T,i} - g_{T,i-1}} \cdot (T(x) - g_{T,i-1}) \qquad (4)$$

of the intervals in between the landmarks of the new patient (target), yield the desired matching of the histograms. By changing the image intensities of the targeted new patient all used transfer function model points from the GPA get specific to the new patient image (Fig. 3, first process box). Note, this invertible procedure is equivalent to fitting the model points (thresholds) to the new patient image. We propose this step under the reasonable assumptions of matching image data of non-over weighted patients, same field-of-views (here: full cross-sections) and anatomical z-range (here: upper abdomen).
Second, the fascia template B-spline model from the GPA is interactively adapted to the new patients rib cage by manipulating the control points. The spline model finally is converted to a label mask representation and included into the multi-label segmentation L of the new patient data (Fig. 3, second process box).

Segmentation using a Liver Atlas Database To this day, for surgery planning and training, the results of automatic segmentation methods still have to be manually inspected and corrected even if the methods claim to be fully automatic and high quality. Briefly, we propose a precise three step procedure to robustly improve results and guarantee sufficient quality also in terms of maximal distances: (1) Automatic four sub-step multi-atlas-segmentation; (2) automatic refining post-processing of the segmentation with GraphCuts; (3) if necessary, manual editing of GraphCut constraints and re-iterating GraphCut (Fig. 3, third process box).
Step 1: Regarding multi-atlas segmentation, we have recently presented a complete framework and a new accurate and efficient label-fusion method in [24]. Typically, multi-atlas segmentation aims at using a database of atlases each consisting of an intensity image with corresponding segmentation masks (Fig. 7, left). Each intensity image of an atlas of the database is deformed by registration methods to the intensity image of the new targeted patient intensity image (single atlas steps, Fig. 7, middle). Applying the found deformation to the database atlas segmentation label map yield one segmentation guess for the targeted patient. The candidate segmentation guesses finally undergoe a fusion step resulting in one augmented average segmentation guess (Fig. 7, right). The intensity images from the LADB atlases to be registered first undergo a histogram normalization towards the new patient image (cf. Sec. 2.2).

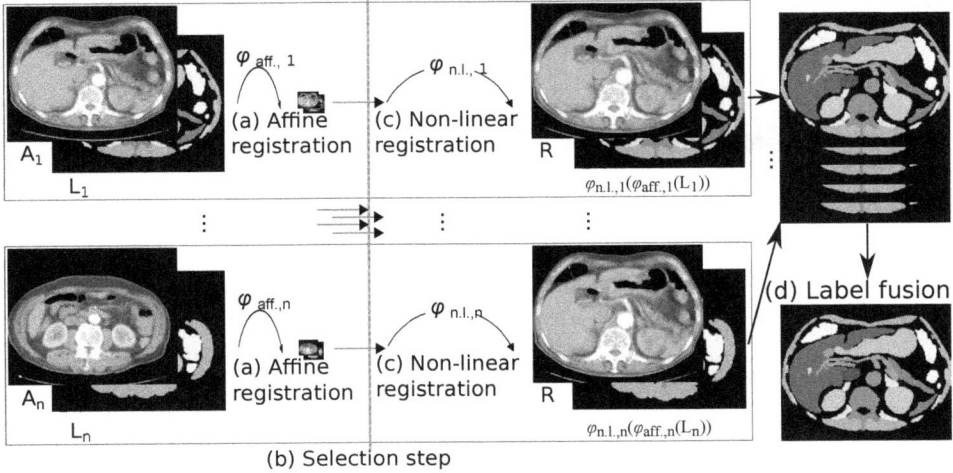

(b) Selection step

Figure 7: Multi-Atlas-Segmentation scheme with sub-steps. For each atlas from the label atlas data base, a registration step consisting of affine and non-linear registration is performed. These steps are performed in parallel, each distributed to one of 24 cluster nodes. The label fusion step takes place on one PC. The letters in brackets correspond to the steps in the text.

An atlas from the GPA's LADB database with a number of subjects greater than 20 [25] consists of an intensity image and a liver segmentation mask. Our improved multi-atlas-segmentation scheme presented here consists of four sub-steps (Fig. 7): (a) an affine registration, (b) a selection by similarity ranking, (c) a non-linear registration and (d) a new fast and accurate label mask fusion step (cf. letters in Fig. 7):

(a) The result of the coarse affine registration step is a transformation matrix, which is then applied to the liver masks. In this step during registration, we minimize the Sum of Squared intensity Differences (SSD) metric on binary image pairs containing hard bone structures.

(b) The selection of a percentage below <50% of the best atlases in terms of the SSD metric speeds up the following sub-steps (c, d) significantly [25] while keeping or even improving the segmentation quality. The metric is computed locally in an intensity image pair inside the affinely transformed atlas liver masks.

(c) Refining the coarse affine registration, the selected atlas data sets are non-linearly registered to the new image data using diffeomorphic demons [26, 27]. The resulting smooth deformation fields are applied to the selected atlas liver segmentation masks and serve as a set of guessed organ segmentations in the new patient image. They have to be fused now.

(d) Majority Voting and Sum Rule fusion [28] are by far the fastest fusion methods and deliver good results, however, at lesser quality than our new Patch Based Local Confidence measure (PBLC) method [24]. SIMPLE (Selective and Iterative Method for Performance Level Estimation) and STAPLE (Simultaneous Truth and Performance Level Estimation) [29, 30] are advanced methods, but do not necessarily offer benefits [24]. PBLC is complementary to the formerly published methods, as it uses sparse neighborhoods and the underlying intensity data in weights w_{pc} in the label mask fusion process [24]:

$$\hat{L}\left(x_i\right) = \frac{\sum_{s=1}^{|A|} \sum_{j \epsilon N_{\mathrm{off}}} w_{\mathrm{pc}}\left(x_i, x_{s,i+j}\right) \cdot L\left(x_{s,i+j}\right)}{\sum_{s=1}^{|A|} \sum_{j \epsilon N_{\mathrm{off}}} w_{\mathrm{pc}}\left(x_i, x_{s,i+j}\right)} \tag{5}$$

In this equation $\hat{L}$ is the continuous label estimate for a voxel x_i, $|A|$ is the number of atlases, N_{off} refers to a set of index offsets defining a sparse neighborhood and the voxel $x_{s,i+j}$ is placed in atlas s at neighbor position j. Regarding a voxel, inside

$$w_{\text{pc}}(x_i, x_{s,j}) = exp\left(-\frac{1 - J\left(P_{\text{wsg}}(x_i),\ P_{\text{sg}}(x_{s,i+j})\right)}{h}\right) \tag{6}$$

this label fusion technique compares displaced local patches $P_{\text{sg}}(x_{s,i+j})$ from the registered atlas segmentation to weakly segmented patches $P_{\text{wsg}}(x_i)$ using an organ-specific segmentation of the targeted image data with the Jaccard ratio $J\epsilon[0, 1]$ [24]. h is a decay parameter which is chosen lower than 0.5 to place more weight on good patch correspondences, i.e. $J > 0.5$. Organwise locally weighted averaging of the deformed segmentations yields local confidences, i.e. a final voxel score $\hat{L}$ in the interval $[0, L]$. Thresholding by $t_{fus} \cdot L$ of this score decides on the voxel's class with $t_{fus}\epsilon[0.5, 1]$ [24].

Step 2: GraphCut segmentation [31] models the image voxel grid as a graph, lets the user attach sink and source nodes (tagging) to its nodes and searches a max-flow min-cut by joint energy minimization of functionals: (1) by measuring costs of assigning a label to a voxel and (2) by penalizing high label differences. The cost of the graphs edges is determined by local contrast along connected components borders, usually neighbored voxels. Here, the components are regions resulting from a watershed preprocessing step as the method has proven to be successful for interactive liver lesion and heart segmentation [32, 33]. Our new GraphCut (GC) post-processing is initialized with automatically generated constraints. In a first step, we use the result from the multi-atlas segmentation and define a search band for the GraphCut near to the border of the liver mask by morphological dilation and erosion with a reasonable number of iterations. Per iteration a shell with the thickness of one voxel is added (dilation) or removed (erosion) from the object. Hence, the search band has a diameter of twice the number of erosions (or dilations) to correct for over- and under-segmentations. Depending on the voxel size the number of morphological operations in one direction has to be chosen such that a reasonable search band diameter is reached (see Fig. 8). The eroded segmentation is added to the foreground constraints, the inverted dilated segmentation forms the background constraint. Finally, to improve the segmentation in the search band, we use watershed region merging GraphCuts for lower memory consumption and enhanced speed.

Step 3: As indicated, the segmentation needs reviewing, which in our concept optionally goes along with the manual adaptation of the GraphCut constraints. The user can decide, if the segmentation is sufficient and accept the result. Alternatively, scrolling through the slices and perceiving obvious flaws in the segmentations, the user can adapt the automatically defined constraints, e.g. set additional constraints in the heart region. In Fig. 8, over-segmentation is corrected by manually adding appropriate background markers in the search band. The user can take advantage of the GraphCuts feature to add constraints in a few representative slices only. We coin the term interactive GraphCut for this concept (iGC).

Vessel Segmentation using the Liver Mask   Blood vessels (risk structures) and bile ducts (target) located inside the liver are now ready to be addressed. They should either be avoided or reached with the needle (RHD/CHD).

To alleviate the segmentation of the vessel-tree, we propose a vessel highlighting and selection method based on vesselness filtering [18]. The procedure uses several empirically learned constant parameters (GPA) and comprises 6 mainly automatic steps: (1) soft-border liver masking, (2) image pyramiding, (3) detection of tubular structures in scale space, (4) fusion of scales space results, (5) thresholding and (6) connected component selection. Details of this stage (Fig. 3, fourth process box) follow:

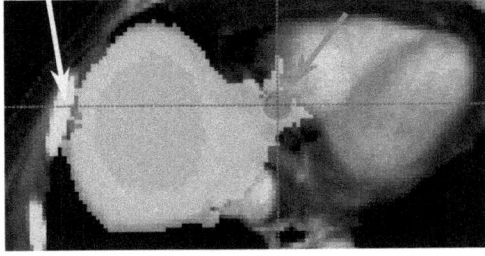

Figure 8: CT slice augmented with background constraint (red), foreground constraint (green), GraphCut segmentation result (cyan). In the search band, the segmentation leaks into the heart area (red arrow) and away behind the ribs (yellow arrow). Manually, background constraints can be added before restarting the GraphCut (red circle).

Step 1: The liver segmentation from the previous section is used to obtain an image with voxels outside the liver mask set to the mean intensity value of voxels on the fringe of the liver, while keeping the original intensities inside the liver. This is motivated by the high sensitivity of the vesselness filter: it detects too many structures outside the liver and at its fringe that do not correspond to liver vessels.

Step 2: Sato's vesselness-filter [18] is applied to a Gaussian image pyramid of the result image of step 1: the masked-out liver undergoes Gaussian filtering with a sequence of three standard deviations $\sigma_s^{1,2,3}$ mm to allow the vesselness filter to detect tubular structures of different diameters.

Step 3: Using the Gaussian image pyramid, we use the vesselness detection formulation by [18] working on the second derivative (Hessian) of the image. The three eigenvalues $\lambda_{1,2,3}$ of the local Hessian for a voxel $\mathbf{x}$ are used to define a local score for a voxel to belong to a tubular structure:

$$V(\sigma_s, \mathbf{x}) = \begin{cases} \exp\left(\frac{-\lambda_1^2}{2(\alpha_1 \lambda_c)^2}\right) \lambda_c, & \lambda_1 \leq 0, \ \lambda_c \neq 0 \\ \exp\left(\frac{-\lambda_1^2}{2(\alpha_2 \lambda_c)^2}\right) \lambda_c, & \lambda_1 > 0, \ \lambda_c \neq 0 \\ 0, & \lambda_c = 0 \end{cases} \tag{7}$$

with $\lambda_c = \min(-\lambda_1, -\lambda_2)$ and $\alpha_1 < \alpha_2$ being user adjustable parameters. From the GPA's method parameter table, we look up α_1 and α_2.

Step 4: The fused vesselness image holds the maximum vesselness value from three scales:

$$V(\mathbf{x}) = \max_{\sigma_s^{1,2,3}} V(\sigma_s, \mathbf{x}) \tag{8}$$

Step 5: Thresholding by a vesselness score of t_{vess}^{blood} resp. t_{vess}^{bile} for blood vessels resp. bile ducts sorts out many false positive voxels, but still many isolated small voxel groups remain, which not necessarily can be assigned to a vessel.

Step 6: Connected component analysis build upon standard seeded region growing [34] removes small isolated islands. To this aim, we measure the volume of all detected components with a certain neighborhood size. In case of the blood vessels resp. bile vessels a percentile smaller than 10% of the small components are dismissed from the segmentation.

Conceptually, the bile ducts undergo the same procedure with an inverted image. The parameter table of the GPA is shown in the next section.

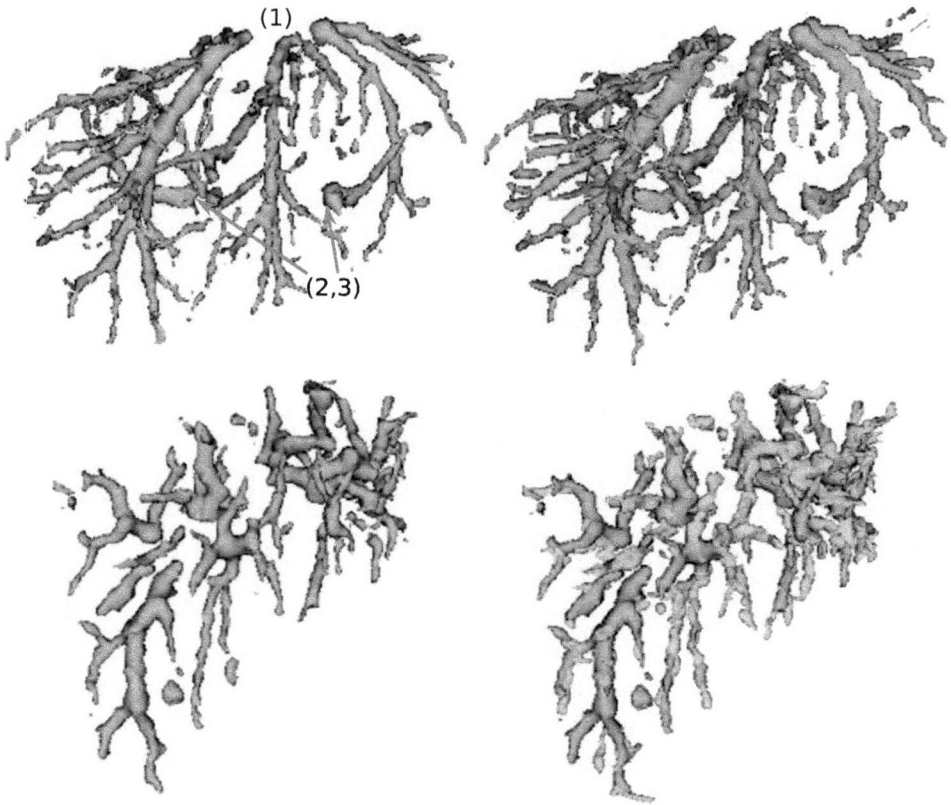

Figure 9: Vessel segmentation using our vesselness procedure: upper row (pat. 7): blue blood vessels automatic segmentation (left) and overlayed with red reference segmentation (right). (1) Juncture of hepatic veins; (2,3) left and right hepatic arteries and veins. Lower row (pat. 8): images corresponding to the bile ducts (reference segmentation in light green).

3 Implementation and Evaluation

Using the parameters from Tab. 1 and workflows from Figs. 3 and 7 the presented patient modeling approach for new atlas instances is assessed quantitatively separately for every structure and regarding performance in a study as described in the following. The hard- and software setup of the PC cluster can be seen in Fig. 11b.

3.1 Segmentation

Generally for all used data sets, non body objects from image aqcuisition such as patient table, cables and medical devices attached to the patient's body, have to be removed from the CT and label data. To this aim, we use a morphological procedure consisting of erosions, dilations, connected component analysis, hole filling and masking. Only the biggest component, i.e. the patient's body, is kept for further processing.

We applied our methods to 10 patients, some suffering from dilated bile ducts (cholestasis). Each patient's CT image was resampled to 256 voxels in x- and y-direction and 236-256 voxels in z-direction. The voxel size in the data sets is between 1.55-1.85 mm in x- and y-direction and 1.65-2.00 mm in z-direction. CT images were acquired in portal venous phase. For evaluation purposes, necessary manual expert segmentations were carried out by a team of three experts. Targeted patient intensity data can be easily cut to match the z field of view of the reference patient. As we generally use torso data with same z field-of-views to prove robustness of our histogram matching method, this step was not necessary at this juncture with our patient cohort.

For liver multi-atlas-segmentation, we use an atlas database consisting of 59 atlases with intensity images and liver masks. It consists of 59 clinical routine scans with 512×512 voxels and 4-5 mm slice distance. The number of slices ranges from 51 to 63 in the abdominal area from the iliac crest to the caudal slices of the heart; voxel xy-sizes fall into the range from 0.637 to 0.835 mm. Livers were manually segmented once by a team of two clinical experts. Facing a targeted new patient with the proposed system, preparation consists of manually cropping the z-range to contain the liver [24].

To assess the robustness of the approach under the aspect of chosing different reference patients, we use three appropriate reference patients (#1, #2, #4) using the selection criteria outlined in section 2.1 and one counter-example reference patient #7 with a large fat compartment volume.

Our 10 test patients including a selected reference patient undergo the patient-specific case-based classification dependent on the voxel position $\mathbf{x}$ from Eq. 2 and the dedicated method steps with parameters as summarized in Tab. 1.

For segmentation evaluation, we compare gold standard manual segmentations to the results using the DICE segmentation overlap coefficient (DSC, max. 1.0) [35]. The gold standard segmentations for ten test patients were created by a team of three experts for the ten PTCD patients. To overview the segmentation errors we choose Box-Plots. For median image selection, we define $\lfloor median \rfloor$ to denote the image with the median value just below the mathematical median.Repeated measurement ANOVA on ranks (Friedman RMANOVA followed by Tukey post-hoc test) is used to compare the DICE ratio resulting from the automatic liver multi-atlas segmentation (MAS) and the two postprocessing phases (GC, iGC).

3.2 Efficiency

The performance of the proposed segmentation system is based on typical amounts of time used for the individual steps. We neglect time-efforts for easy or very efficients tasks such as manually cropping data or histogram matching. The time amounts for steps requiring manual interactions are based on empirical measurements taken by the operators doing the job. The times for the automatic steps are extracted from algorithm log files. This way we supply five minute interval rounded upper boundary time measures $\hat{t}_i$ for the pipeline steps (1) time-boxed MAS liver segmentation, (2) fascia modeling, (3) GraphCut post-processing, (4) interactice GraphCut and (5) vessel segmentation, (2-5) worst case each. Generous time-boxing of the registration tasks in step (1) is motivated by empirically observed quasi-convergence of the registration. Due to some oszillation of the convergence criterium, the convergence detector did not always react accordingly. In the results, we also report the number of registrations for which convergence was detected earlier and after which time span. In the segmentation protocol, the operator starts either task (1) in the background or waits for its results (idles).

By this means, a total upper boundary of sequential processing time including 24 parallel single atlas tasks can be given as:

$$\hat{T}_{seq} = \left\lceil \frac{24}{N_{PCnod}} \right\rceil \cdot \hat{t}_1 + \sum_{i=2}^{5} \hat{t}_i \tag{9}$$

In the second variant, the manual operator never idles and works on task (2) in parallel to task (1) running in the background:

$$\hat{T}_{par} = max \left(\left\lceil \frac{24}{N_{PCnod}} \right\rceil \cdot \hat{t}_1, \hat{t}_2 \right) + \sum_{i=3}^{5} \hat{t}_i \tag{10}$$

In the results we give upper bounds for $N_{PCnod} \geqq 24$ and a chart for $N_{PCnod} \leq 24$ concerning the term $\left\lceil \frac{24}{N_{PCnod}} \right\rceil \cdot \hat{t}_1$ to also display worst case MAS performance for smaller node set-ups. Furthermore, we provide detailed time measurements for important node configuration experiments from five runs with $N_{PCnod} = 1, 2, 4, 6, 8, 12$ and optimally 24 nodes and report them as mean, standard deviation (error bars) and boxplots.

4 Results

4.1 Segmentation Results

In Tab. 1 the three tissue thresholds are dependent on the chosen reference patient. Qualitatively, the skin layer can be clearly distinguished from other soft tissue and bony structures (Fig. 2b). Visual rendering side effects occur at borders of the risk structures that are filled with air (lungs, intestine): these are rendered similar to the skin surface. This side effect is important for the detection of air cavity fringes (risk structure) in Eq. 2. For the fascia (cf. Fig. 6), we evaluated the outcome visually only and could always obtain plausible spline surfaces through the rib bones in all cases. Furthermore, we lack gold-standard segmentations of the fascia to compare to. More result images with comparison to a manual reference segmentation are shown in Figs. 9 and 10. We can observe plausible overlaps in the right column of Fig. 9 and top and middle row in Fig. 10. The worst-case results for vessels (bottom row) arise when the pathology of dilated bile ducts or well contrasted blood vessels are not present or prominent enough in the patients. Quantitatively, for liver vessel segmentation (see Tab. 2), the median DSC that can be obtained by our proposed procedure are 0.48 for bile ducts and 0.51 for blood vessels, which are as expected smaller than for liver segmentations. Our method step compares equal to recently published liver vessel segmentation approaches [36]. The segmentation of these fine tree-like structures is still a big challenge. To our best knowledge no segmentation

Table 1: Parameter table stored in the GPA: Proposed parameters for the individual modeling steps. *Low or high bone threshold used with needle shaft outside or inside the fascia. +The thresholds abbreviated by "th." are dependent on the chosen reference patient. # abbreviates "Number of".

Method \ Parameter	Description	Value			
		Ref.pat.#1	Ref.pat.#2	Ref.pat.#4	(Ref.pat.#7)
	Risk structure detection depth	$\delta = 5\,mm$			
	Air-Skin th. [HU]	t_{air}^{skn} =-833	-899	-810	-770
	Skin-Fat th. [HU]	t_{skn}^{sft} =-175	-229	-167	-198
Transfer func.+	Threshold offsets [HU]	$t_{off;lo\|\|hi}$= 40 || 150			
	Fat-Bone th. [HU]*	$t_{sft;lo\|\|hi}^{bn}$ =98 || 248	151 || 300	156 || 306	224 || 374
	Percentile thresholds	5%, 95%			
	# percentiles / levels	N_{pc}=5 / 0%, 25%, 50%, 75%, 100%			
	Spline-Degrees	$k = l = 3$			
3D-B-Spline-Fit	Bone th. [HU]	~250			
	# knots	$N_{kn} = 14$			
	# knots	$M_{kn} = 4$			
	# LADB atlases	59			
	Atlas selection % (#)	40% (24)			
Multi-Atlas-Seg.	Fusion method	PBLC5 [24]			
	Fusion decay	$h = 0.1$			
	Fusion score th. factor	$t_{fus} = 0.62$			
Graph-Cut	Search band diam.	2x5=10 Voxels, i.e. 15.5-20 mm			
	# scales	3			
	Standard deviations	$\sigma_s^{1,2,3} = 2,\ 3,\ 4\ mm$			
Vesselness	Vesselness weigths	$\alpha_1 = 0.5,\ \alpha_2 = 2.$			
	Blood/Bile score th.	t_{vess}^{blood}=1.2 / t_{vess}^{bile}=1.3			
	Vol. meas. neighborhood size	3D 18-neigborhood			
	Blood/bile volume percentile	1 % / 8 %			

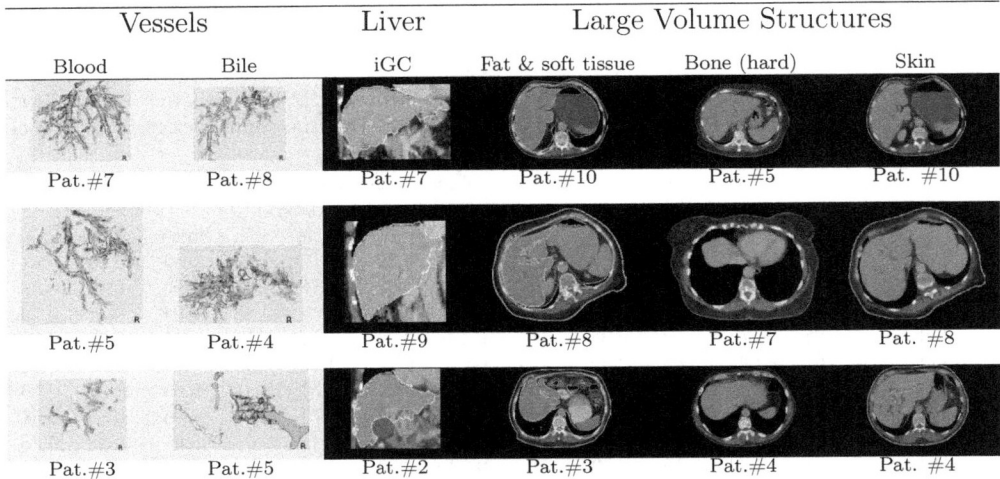

Vessels		Liver	Large Volume Structures		
Blood	Bile	iGC	Fat & soft tissue	Bone (hard)	Skin
Pat.#7	Pat.#8	Pat.#7	Pat.#10	Pat.#5	Pat. #10
Pat.#5	Pat.#4	Pat.#9	Pat.#8	Pat.#7	Pat. #8
Pat.#3	Pat.#5	Pat.#2	Pat.#3	Pat.#4	Pat. #4

Figure 10: Exemplary best (top row) / ⌊median⌋ (middle row) / worst (bottom row) segmentation results for reference patient #1. The following color legend is used: cyan color=reference segmentation, yellow=result segmentation, green=correct overlap between the segmentations. Window and center are set to 600/75 HU in the MPR images. The 3D renderings are presented in RL-view.

Table 2: Segmentation results: Reference patient independent DSC values for the liver segmentation variants and the other tissues. Regarding Multi-atlas segmentation (MAS) the results improve steadily using graph cuts (GC, iGC). *Results with additional interactive GraphCut (iGC) are significantly better ($p < 0.05$) compared to MAS.

Pat.	Vessels		Liver		
	Blood	Bile	MAS	+GC	+iGC
Pat. 1	0.36	0.38	0.83	0.83	0.92
Pat. 2	0.52	0.56	0.88	0.89	0.92
Pat. 3	0.34	0.33	0.93	0.94	0.94
Pat. 4	0.41	0.46	0.90	0.93	0.93
Pat. 5	0.50	0.25	0.95	0.95	0.95
Pat. 6	0.52	0.55	0.91	0.91	0.92
Pat. 7	0.65	0.29	0.94	0.94	0.95
Pat. 8	0.52	0.60	0.90	0.92	0.92
Pat. 9	0.51	0.51	0.87	0.91	0.93
Pat. 10	0.42	0.52	0.95	0.95	0.95
Mean	0.47	0.44	0.91	0.92	0.93
±SD	0.09	0.12	0.04	0.04	0.01
Median	0.51	0.48	0.91	0.93	0.93*
⌊Median⌋	0.50	0.46	0.90	0.92	0.93

Table 3: Segmentation results: Reference patient dependent DSC values for large volume structures: In contrast to the selected reference patients (#1, 2, 4), the counter example reference patient #7 downgrades the results for bone and skin significantly.

Pat.	Large Volume Structures											
	Ref.pat.#1			Ref.pat.#2			Ref.pat.#4			(Ref.pat.#7)		
	Soft-t.	Bone	Skin	Soft-t.	Bone	Skin	Soft-t.	Bone	Skin	Soft-t.	Bone	Skin
Pat. 1	0.89	0.80	0.62	0.89	0.87	0.59	0.88	0.77	0.63	0.87	0.68	0.11
Pat. 2	0.98	0.86	0.76	0.99	0.87	0.87	0.98	0.84	0.83	0.95	0.46	0.28
Pat. 3	0.97	0.90	0.60	0.97	0.79	0.83	0.97	0.93	0.82	0.91	0.54	0.23
Pat. 4	0.98	0.75	0.52	0.98	0.63	0.49	0.98	0.80	0.50	0.96	0.39	0.33
Pat. 5	0.99	0.94	0.63	0.99	0.87	0.67	0.99	0.97	0.66	0.95	0.66	0.30
Pat. 6	0.96	0.81	0.71	0.96	0.77	0.88	0.95	0.78	0.84	0.89	0.32	0.18
Pat. 7	0.97	0.81	0.78	0.96	0.85	0.28	0.94	0.79	0.26	0.98	0.89	0.58
Pat. 8	0.98	0.81	0.64	0.98	0.67	0.61	0.98	0.83	0.60	0.97	0.38	0.46
Pat. 9	0.98	0.82	0.75	0.99	0.80	0.93	0.98	0.82	0.91	0.94	0.40	0.15
Pat. 10	0.99	0.83	0.92	0.98	0.78	0.93	0.99	0.83	0.98	0.92	0.43	0.03
Mean	0.97	0.83	0.69	0.97	0.83	0.79	0.96	0.84	0.70	0.93	0.51	0.27
±SD	0.03	0.06	0.11	0.03	0.06	0.09	0.03	0.07	0.22	0.04	0.18	0.16
Median	0.98	0.82	0.67	0.98	0.80	0.75	0.98	0.82	0.74	0.95	0.45	0.26
⌊Median⌋	0.98	0.81	0.64	0.97	0.79	0.67	0.97	0.80	0.66	0.95	0.43	0.23

Table 4: Time effort estimates for automatic vs. semi-automatic steps for a PC cluster with ≥ 24 nodes and one operator. Task 1 can be run in the background, while the fascia (2) are addressed. Tasks 3-5 must be processed in sequence using the resulting liver mask (1).

Task	Auto.	Semi.	Time [h:mm]$\pm$SD MAS	GC	iGC
1. Multi-atlas segmentation $\hat{t}_1$	x		2:00	2:00	2:00
2. Fascia modeling $\hat{t}_2$		x	0:40	0:40	0:40
Sum (sequential tasks 1-2)			2:40	2:40	2:40
Maximum (parallel tasks 1-2)			2:00	2:00	2:00
3. GraphCut post-processing $\hat{t}_3$	x		N/A	0:10	0:10
4. Interactive GraphCut $\hat{t}_4$		x	N/A	N/A	0:20
5. Vessel segmentation $\hat{t}_5$	x		0:15	0:15	0:15
Sum (sequential tasks 3-5)			0:15	0:25	0:45
Total for sequential processing $\hat{T}_{seq}$			2:55	3:05	3:25
Total with task 1 in background $\hat{T}_{par}$			2:15	2:25	2:45

challenges addressing the topics of liver vessel, fascia, whole body skin, soft-tissue and bone segmentation have been launched yet.

In contrast, DICE coefficients up to 0.933[1] are obtained in the most recent MICCAI and VISCERAL Anatomy 3 challenges [37, 17] resulting from automatic or semi-automatic schemes for the liver to which our results compare well.

In our method comparison, we obtain significantly better mean results of 0.93 with a low standard deviation of 0.01 ($p < 0.01$, post: $p < 0.05$) with the iGC compared to the MAS step alone (Tab. 2). The errors for structures with smaller volume are higher as can be observed in Fig. 12. Tree-like structures with the smallest volume such as vessels are found on the right side of the figure. The bile ducts have the smallest volume compared to all other structures. For the small volume vessel structures, we achieve DSC values around 0.5. W.r.t. large volume structures (Tabs. 2, 3), the skin is segmented with a DSC overlap of 0.73 on average excluding the counter example reference patient #7. It possesses the lowest volume from the large volume structures. The most frequent error is undersegmentation, i.e. a too thin skin with spurious voxels (Fig. 10, low row, rightmost). Bone and soft-tissue are segmented best, with median DSCs of 0.82 and 0.98. Regarding the liver, many errors extending into the medial area can be corrected by the iGC step. However, they do not impede accurate training in the liver periphery. Inspecting the location of the problem areas where GraphCut constraints were altered or added, some adaptations were also carried out at the lower and right apexes of the liver. In medial areas, where adjacent organs to the liver are present such as heart, stomach and kidneys, over-segmentation can occur. Under-segmentations are much less frequent and typically show out behind ribs or in the liver apexes. A closer investigation reveals that because of the already high quality of the automatic multi-atlas and GraphCut postprocessed segmentation the necessity of the tedious correction of the constraints for our training purposes is rare.

---

[1]looked up 12/20/2015: http://visceral.eu:8080/register/Leaderboard.xhtml

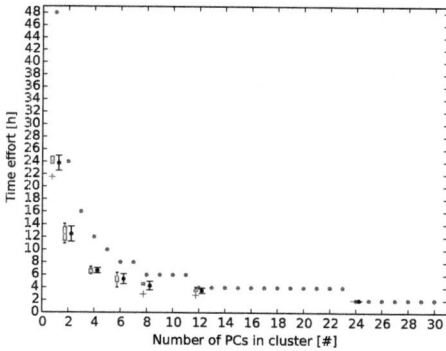

(a) Number of PC nodes vs. max. time for $\hat{t}_1$

Spec.	Value
Brand	Dell Precision
Modell	T3500 WorkStation
CPU	IntelXeon(R)W3530
	2.80GHz, Cores (ht): 8
OS	Ubuntu Linux 14.04 LTS
Memory	24GiB System Memory
Disk	1TB Hitachi HDS72101
Compiler	Gnu C++ 4.8.0
Software	Registration Toolbox [26]
Libraries	Insight Toolkit (V4.4.0)
File sync.	Netw. File Sys. (V1.2.8)

(b) Set-up of our node cluster PCs

Figure 11: Characteristics and performance of the proposed system: (a) It is advised to use the lowest number of PCs in a horizontal line. Mean execution times (boxplots/error bars) are about halfway for node numbers <4. (b) Hard- and software specifications of our PC cluster nodes. ht: Hyper threading.

4.2 Efficiency

Time efforts for the major steps of the patient modeling process are shown in Tab. 4 for $N_{PCnod} \geqq 24$. Regarding the work-flow, the user can start comfortably with tasks (2) in parallel to the long running multi-atlas segmentation (1). In task two, the control points of the reference fascia model from patient #1 are adapted to a new patient using 3D CAD software[2]. In the optimal environment with $N_{PCnod} = 24$, we end up with time efforts ranging from two to three hours. Note, 84% percent of the registration tasks in the MAS step finish before the end of the time-box, time effort for them is 0:43±0:22 [h:mm]. As we are using 24 registration tasks in parallel, there is good chance that at least one task uses the maximum amount of time and determines the net time used for the MAS step. This motivates us to give upper boundary times in our results in Tab. 4. For smaller node numbers in the PC cluster, we provide Fig. 11a with worst case estimates and time measurements from experiments with 1, 2, 4, 6, 8, 12 and 24 PC nodes with mean±standard deviation of 23.76±1.20, 12.44±1.20, 6.66±0.45, 5.31±0.80, 4.25±0.68, 3.52±0.41 and 2.00±0.00. The hardware set-up of our PC cluster is shown in Fig. 11b. Compared to a single node set-up, the practically achievable speedup is 12. Compared to slice-wise complete manual segmentation (40h) [10] and our own experience (70h), we are able to reduce time efforts for virtual patient modeling significantly with our proposed system configuration.

5 Discussion

In this paper, starting from a generic patient atlas virtual patient modeling is carried out via robust transfer-function-based label-estimator using three patient-specific thresholds augmented by the segmentation of certain key structures. The result of this new task-parallel pipeline process delivers a robust full volume segmentation of the upper abdomen, hardly addressed in the literature so far. Our induction strategy to start with one patient

---

[2]www.blender.org

to build a generic patient atlas and instantiate a new atlas from new patient image intensity data has the potential to be a valid concept for CT data in the future. Liver segmentation errors concentrate in the medial area, the apexes or behind ribs and are smaller in the peripheral regions of the patients where the puncture needle can access the structures. The semi-automatic segmentation system presented here is proven fast and valid for our purposes. Additionally, semi-automatic GraphCut post-processing can improve the multi-atlas segmentation significantly. In the literature, abdominal organ segmentation has gained considerable attention recently. Several organ segmentation techniques have been benchmarked in challenges [37, 17]. However, the very large inter-patient shape variations and pathologies constitute the still unresolved challenge in this area and point out the need for reviewing and interactive corrections as we propose. However, by our means, we can guarantee adequate liver segmentation in general and the time efforts for post-processing are moderate.

Regarding geometry and volume, the size and shape of an organ are important factors for the DSC outcome of the algorithms. Larger organs tend to have higher DSCs while especially small tree-like structures yield lower DSCs, already offering good quality at levels around 0.5 and a coherent look of the puncture relevant larger vessels (Figs. 9, 10). However, some detected vessel branches may show out some gaps, for which another post-processing method should be invented. It remains to be said, that for successful vessel segmentation we need prominently dilated bile ducts and well contrasted blood vessels for the accurate segmentation of these difficult structures. For the liver we achieve high DSCs up to 0.95. Liver segmentation results with DSCs greater than 0.9 are sufficient in our context. The improvements of 0.02 on average that is brought by interactive GC in the context of transhepatic percutaneous needle insertions is worth the effort and our recommendation is to use the semi-automatic iGC step if necessary after reviewing the result. Thus, if still needed with the interactive GC corrections we are able to deal with difficult patients, and can achieve significant improvements in certain individuals (outlier correction). Using the interactive GraphCut procedure more rigorously, we could enforce even higher quality results at the cost of increased interaction time. For normal cases, mainly sparse constraint additions in the search band are required, which do not need to be carried out slice-wise, a hint in every 5-10th slice is sufficient. Our new label fusion technique used here is favorable in terms of accuracy and speed to other state-of-the art techniques [24].

With regards to skin, soft-tissue and hard cortical bone, the DSC errors obtained and number of outliers are small, and the segmentation is robust as has been confirmed by visual inspection (Fig. 10). Minimally a DSC of 0.26 for the skin in the problematic patient #7 can be noted. This is due to a systematic undersegmentation of it, which is caused by the morphological peeling preprocessing (table and device removal). Also, sometimes the manual segmentation is a bit smaller than the skin detected by the threshold-based estimation [22]. The error is not severe in our context, as the needle enters the body through a small skin incision made by the surgeon, thus its haptic rendering can be neglected. For the plausible visual rendering impression in case of the too thin skin, in our context morphological postprocessing of the can be used to artificially mitigate this issue. Regarding the problematic reference patient #7, significant fat volume in a reference patient tends to shift the centroid of the histograms of the matched (thin) patients to dark intensities. However, such an overweighted inappropriate reference patient can still be reasonably used as target patient. Skin segmentation is worst here, but on grounds of the small incision and key structure, soft tissue and bone segmentations still working well the patient #7 as target is reasonably usable.

Along with increasing the size of our PC cluster (24 PCs) or commercially available cloud-based cluster solutions, the atlas data base could be augmented by more cases for

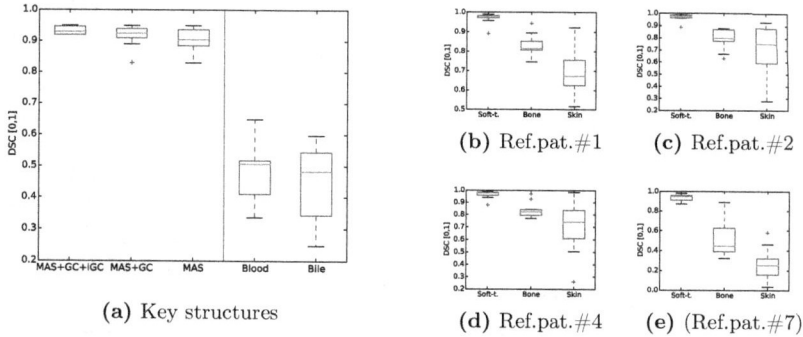

Figure 12: Boxplots of DICE coefficients sorted by median value: (a) Reference patient independent key structures. (b-e) Reference patient dependent large volume structures. Soft tissue segmentation is best while thin structures are harder to segment (skin). The overweighted reference patient #7 yields the worst results when applied to all other target patients and should not be used.

the sake of higher segmentation quality. Any optimization in hard- or software concerning e.g. the GPU implementation of the registration algorithms potentially decreases the mean time needed for the MAS step and consequently the necessary time-box to limit this step. The time-boxing approach for the MAS step is important for clinical usability, as the results must be provided in a certain time frame.

Choosing appropriate reference patients, our system concept has the potential to significantly reduce the time needed for the creation of new virtual patients from medical image data compared to standard slice-wise manual contouring [10].

The limitations of this work can be summarized as follows. There are currently two bottleneck tasks in the process. First, it is necessary to speed up the non-linear registration process to converge reliably at least in the time frame the fascia model is manually adapted. Second, the manual steps especially the fascia modeling needs to be automated and then interactively corrected as already possible in the MAS liver segmentation.

6 Conclusion and Future Work

Our analysis showed out that our new patient modeling system using partially segmented image data and patient-specific case- and transfer-function-based label estimator are valid for the efficient creation of new virtual patient models in a liver puncture scenario. The patient modeling approach works reliable, and drastically reduces the time for patient preparation, in our experience from 40-70h for tedious manual full segmentation to less than half a work day. Of course, we aim at automating the manual longer lasting steps in our pipeline (see Tab. 4), e.g. the fascia modeling, which we intend to formulate as the solution of an approximation problem through a point cloud from a rib skeleton. Regarding the generic patient atlas, the intensity distribution of the reference patient is important to be generalizable. A mean image intensity patient atlas from a cohort could serve well inside the GPA. Furthermore, we would like to develop an atlas-based approach for vessel tree segmentation. Efficiency could well be further adressed by implementing the non-linear registration methods on the GPU, which currently is the main bottleneck task.

Acknowledgment

The authors would like to thank our clinical partner Prof. Dr. J. Barkhausen, clinics for radiology and diagnostics, Dr. med. P. Wellhöner, clinics for internal medicine, both UKSH Luebeck, our colleague O. Maier, our students P. Behringer, J. Beuke, T. Hecht and S. Köhnen.

Conflict of Interest

Hereby the authors of this submission: Andre Mastmeyer, Dirk Fortmeier and Heinz Handels assure, we are free from conflicts of interest.

Ethics

No ethical conflicts are associated to this work, all patient data were acquired and anonymized before and apart from this study.

References

[1] P. F. Villard, F. P. Vidal, L. Ap Cenydd, R. Holbrey, S. Pisharody, S. Johnson, a. Bulpitt, N. W. John, F. Bello, and D. Gould, "Interventional Radiology Virtual Simulator for Liver Biopsy," *Int. J. Comput. Assist. Radiol. Surg.*, vol. 9, pp. 255–267, Mar. 2014.

[2] D. Ni, W. Chan, J. Qin, and Y. Chui, "A Virtual Reality Simulator for Ultrasound-guided Biopsy Training," *IEEE Compu. Graph. Appl.*, pp. 143–150, 2011.

[3] S. Ullrich and T. Kuhlen, "Haptic Palpation for Medical Simulation in Virtual Environments," *IEEE Trans. Vis. Comput. Graphics*, vol. 18, no. 4, pp. 617–25, 2012.

[4] T. Coles, N. John, D. Gould, and D. Caldwell, "Integrating Haptics with Augmented Reality in a Femoral Palpation and Needle Insertion Training Simulation," *IEEE Trans. Hapt.*, vol. 4, no. 3, pp. 199–209, 2011.

[5] R. Alterovitz, D. Ritchie, U. C. Berkeley, L. Cho, J. F. O. Brien, K. K. Hauser, K. Goldberg, and J. R. Shewchuk, "Interactive Simulation of Surgical Needle Insertion and Steering," pp. 1–10, 2009.

[6] W. I. M. Willaert, R. Aggarwal, I. Van Herzeele, N. J. Cheshire, and F. E. Vermassen, "Recent Advancements in Medical Simulation: Patient-specific Virtual Reality Simulation," *World J. Surg.*, vol. 36, pp. 1703–12, July 2012.

[7] F. P. Vidal, N. W. John, A. E. Healey, and D. A. Gould, "Simulation of Ultrasound Guided Needle Puncture using Patient Specific Data with 3D Textures and Volume Haptics," *Comput. Animat. Virtual Worlds*, vol. 19, no. 2, pp. 111–127, 2008.

[8] P.-F. Villard, F. P. Vidal, C. Hunt, F. Bello, N. W. John, S. Johnson, and D. A. Gould, "A Prototype Percutaneous Transhepatic Cholangiography Training Simulator with Real-time Breathing Motion," *Int. J. Comput. Assist. Radiol. Surg.*, vol. 4, pp. 571–578, 2009.

[9] M. Färber, F. Hummel, C. Gerloff, and H. Handels, "Virtual Reality Simulator for the Training of Lumbar Punctures," *Meth. Inf. Med.*, vol. 48, no. 5, pp. 493–501, 2009.

[10] Y. Wu and L. Yencharis, "Commercial 3-d Imaging Software Migrates to Pc Medical Diagnostics," *Adv. Imag. Mag.*, pp. 16–21, 1998.

[11] D. Fortmeier, A. Mastmeyer, J. Schröder, and H. Handels, "A virtual reality system for ptcd simulation using direct visuo-haptic rendering of partially segmented image data," *IEEE Journal of Biomedical and Health Informatics*, vol. 20, pp. 355–366, Jan 2016.

[12] L. Lin, *Practical Clinical Ultrasonic Diagnosis*. World Scientific, 1997.

[13] T. Coles, D. Meglan, and N. John, "The Role of Haptics in Medical Training Simulators: A Survey of the State of the Art," *IEEE Trans. Hapt.*, vol. 4, pp. 51–66, Jan 2011.

[14] K. Engel, M. Hadwiger, J. M. Kniss, A. E. Lefohn, C. R. Salama, and D. Weiskopf, *Real-time Volume Graphics*. A K Peters, 2006.

[15] K. Engelke, A. Mastmeyer, V. Bousson, T. Fuerst, J.-D. Laredo, and W. A. Kalender, "Reanalysis precision of 3d quantitative computed tomography (QCT) of the spine," *Bone*, vol. 44, no. 4, pp. 566–572, 2009.

[16] A. Mastmeyer, K. Engelke, C. Fuchs, and W. A. Kalender, "A hierarchical 3d segmentation method and the definition of vertebral body coordinate systems for qct of the lumbar spine," *Med. Image Anal.*, vol. 10, no. 4, pp. 560–577, 2006.

[17] T. Heimann, B. Van Ginneken, M. A. Styner, Y. Arzhaeva, V. Aurich, C. Bauer, A. Beck, C. Becker, R. Beichel, G. Bekes, *et al.*, "Comparison and Evaluation of Methods for Liver Segmentation from CT Datasets," *IEEE Trans. Med. Imag.*, 2009.

[18] Y. Sato, S. Nakajima, N. Shiraga, H. Atsumi, S. Yoshida, T. Koller, G. Gerig, and R. Kikinis, "Three-dimensional multi-scale Line Filter for Segmentation and Visualization of Curvilinear Structures in Medical Images," *Med. Image Anal.*, vol. 2, pp. 143–168, 1998.

[19] A. Mastmeyer, D. Fortmeier, and H. Handels, "Direct Haptic Volume Rendering in Lumbar Puncture Simulation," in *Medicine Meets Virtual Reality 19, MMVR 2012*, vol. 173 of *Stud. Health. Technol. Inform.*, pp. 280–286, IOS Press, 2012.

[20] P. Dierckx, *Curve and Surface Fitting with Splines*. Oxford University Press, 1993.

[21] E. Neri, D. Caramella, and C. Bartolozzi, "Image processing in radiology," *Medical Radiology. Diagnostic Imaging. Baert AL, Knauth M., Sartor K. Editors, Springer*, 2008.

[22] A. Mastmeyer, T. Hecht, D. Fortmeier, and H. Handels, "Ray-casting Based Evaluation Framework for Haptic Force-Feedback During Percutaneous Transhepatic Catheter Drainage Punctures," *Int. J. Comput. Assist. Radiol. Surg.*, vol. 9, pp. 421–431, 2014.

[23] L. Nyúl, J. K. Udupa, and X. Zhang, "New Variants of a Method of MRI Scale Standardization," *IEEE Trans. Med. Imag.*, vol. 19, no. 2, pp. 143–150, 2000.

[24] A. Mastmeyer, D. Fortmeier, E. Maghsoudi, M. Simon, and H. Handels, "Patch-based Label Fusion using Local Confidence-measures and Weak Segmentations," in *Proc SPIE*, (Orlando, USA), pp. 86691N–1–86691N–11, 2013.

[25] P. Aljabar, R. Heckemann, A. Hammers, and J. V. Hajnal, "Classifier Selection Strategies for Label Fusion," in *Proc MICCAI*, pp. 523–531, 2007.

[26] A. Schmidt-Richberg, R. Werner, H. Handels, and J. Ehrhardt, "A flexible variational registration framework," *Insight Journal*, p. http://hdl.handle.net/10380/3460, 2014.

[27] J. Ehrhardt, R. Werner, A. Schmidt-Richberg, and H. Handels, "Statistical Modeling of 4D Respiratory Lung Motion Using Diffeomorphic Image Registration.," *IEEE Trans. Med. Imag.*, vol. 30, pp. 251–265, Sept. 2011.

[28] T. Rohlfing, R. Brandt, R. Menzel, and C. R. Maurer, "Evaluation of Atlas Selection Strategies for Atlas-based Image Segmentation with Application to Confocal Microscopy Images of Bee Brains," *NeuroImage*, vol. 21, pp. 1428–1442, Apr 2004.

[29] S. K. Warfield, K. H. Zou, and W. M. Wells, "Simultaneous Truth and Performance Level Estimation (STAPLE): An Algorithm for the Validation of Image Segmentation," *IEEE Trans. Med. Imag.*, vol. 23, pp. 903–21, July 2004.

[30] T. R. Langerak, U. a. van der Heide, A. N. T. J. Kotte, M. a. Viergever, M. van Vulpen, and J. P. W. Pluim, "Label Fusion in Atlas-based Segmentation using a Selective and Iterative Method for Performance Level Estimation (SIMPLE)," *IEEE Trans. Med. Imag.*, vol. 29, pp. 2000–8, Dec. 2010.

[31] Y. Boykov and V. Kolmogorov, "An Experimental Comparison of Min-cut/max-flow Algorithms for Energy Minimization in Vision," *IEEE Trans. Pattern Anal. Mach. Intell.*, vol. 26, pp. 1124–1137, Sep 2004.

[32] J. Stawiaski, E. Decenciere, and F. Bidault, "Interactive Liver Tumor Segmentation using Graph Cuts and Watershed," in *In Workshop on 3D Segmentation in the Clinic: A Grand Challenge II. Liver Tumor Segmentation Challenge. MICCAI*, 2008.

[33] O. Maier, D. J. Carretero, A. de Santos Lleo, and M. J. L. Carbayo, "Segmentation of RV in 4D Cardiac MR Volumes using Region-merging Graph Cuts," *Comput. Cardiol.*, vol. 39, pp. 697–700, 2012.

[34] R. Adams and L. Bischof, "Seeded Region Growing," *IEEE Trans. Pattern Anal. Mach. Intell.*, vol. 16, no. 6, pp. 641–647, 1994.

[35] L. R. Dice, "Measures of the amount of ecologic association between species," *Ecology*, vol. 26, no. 3, pp. 297–302, 1945.

[36] L. Wang, C. Hansen, S. Zidowitz, and H. K. Hahn, "Segmentation and separation of venous vasculatures in liver ct images," 2014.

[37] "Visual concept extraction challenge in radiology-visceral.," 2015.

A Virtual Reality System for PTCD Simulation using Direct Visuo-haptic Rendering of Partially Segmented Image Data

Dirk Fortmeier[1], *Student Member, IEEE*, Andre Mastmeyer[1], Julian Schröder, and Heinz Handels, *Member, IEEE*
[1] Equal main contribution by two first authors
This work is supported by the German Research Foundation (DFG, HA 2355/11-1)

Abstract

This work presents a new visuo-haptic virtual reality (VR) training and planning system for percutaneous transhepatic cholangio-drainage (PTCD) based on partially segmented virtual patient models. We only use partially segmented image data instead of a full segmentation and circumvent the necessity of surface or volume mesh models. Haptic interaction with the virtual patient during virtual palpation, ultrasound probing and needle insertion is provided. Furthermore, the VR simulator includes X-ray and ultrasound simulation for image-guided training. The visualization techniques are GPU-accelerated by implementation in Cuda and include real-time volume deformations computed on the grid of the image data. Computation on the image grid enables straightforward integration of the deformed image data into the visualization components. To provide shorter rendering times, the performance of the volume deformation algorithm is improved by a multigrid approach. To evaluate the VR training system, a user evaluation has been performed and deformation algorithms are analyzed in terms of convergence speed with respect to a fully converged solution. The user evaluation shows positive results with increased user confidence after a training session. It is shown that using partially segmented patient data and direct volume rendering is suitable for the simulation of needle insertion procedures such as PTCD.
Keywords: Virtual reality, Visualization, Haptic Rendering, Needle Insertion.

1 Introduction

Virtual reality (VR) surgery simulation with needle insertion [1, 2, 3, 4] is a current field of research, which deals with the topics of visual and haptic rendering (visuo-haptics) as well as the generation of virtual patient models. The downside of most systems is their lack of being able to simulate an intervention on new patient data image just in time because of the need for detailed segmentation and modeling of the patient's anatomy.

Previously, we have presented a lumbar puncture simulator "AcusVR" [5] being a valuable training and planning tool. This system consisted of a Geomagic Phantom Premium 1.5 6DOF haptic device and a combination of shutter glasses and a CRT-monitor for VR immersion. A user study was conducted and training was shown to be effective

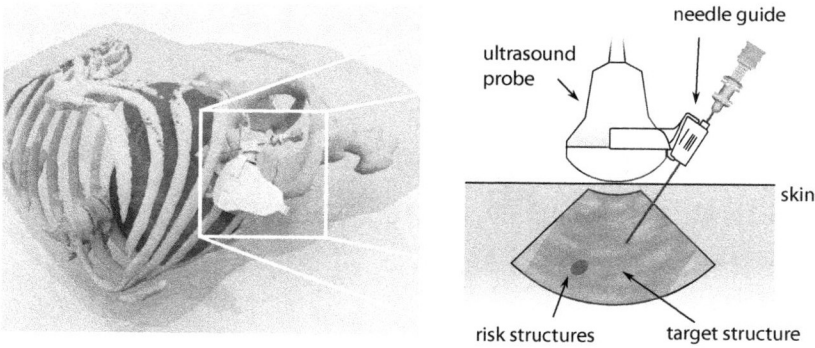

Figure 1: Schematic visualization of the virtual patient model, showing needle and ultrasound probe placement in the intercostal spaces for PTCD and cross section coplanar to the US-imaging plane with dilated hepatic duct (target structure). The needle can be guided on a trail attached to the probe. Puncturing of risk structures such as blood vessels should be avoided.

[5]. However, AcusVR relied on a time-consuming complete manual segmentation of the patients anatomy, which can take up to 40 hours for a single patient data set. Visualization of dynamic effects such as the deformation of tissue during interventions was not available and fixed 3D polygonal models were used.

Percutaneous transhepatic cholangio-drainage (PTCD) is a needle insertion intervention in which dilated bile ducts, caused by cholestasis, are punctured to relieve the patient by a drainage [6]. Cholestasis can be caused by e.g. gallstones or tumors in the common hepatic bile duct (CHD). To reach the target (right hepatic bile duct, RHD), the needle often is inserted between the 6th and 7th ribs (intercostal spaces) and through the liver. Up-to-date intervention techniques make use of an ultrasound probe with an attached needle guide (Fig. 1) that helps to keep the needle on a path inside the US image plane. This paper concentrates on a visuo-haptic simulation framework for the training and planning of the first steps of PTCD regarding needle navigation. A prerequisite is 3D CT imaging of the liver before the intervention. The motivation to train this intervention patient-specifically beforehand with a VR system is that VR training is considered to be a benefit for apprentices and can improve the preparation of the surgeon for real interventions. Following this assumption, it can reduce the number of needle repositionings, and thus the duration of the intervention and healing times, as well as patient dose because of lower X-ray exposure.

For haptic and visual immersion, we present the implementation of image-based deformation algorithms into the framework with interactive direct volume rendering of patient data, ultrasound and X-ray simulation with contrast agent injection. The framework uses partially segmented 3D CT image data for direct visual and haptic rendering without relying on the creation of surface representations or volumetric meshes.

In contrast to mesh based approaches of needle insertion simulation [7, 8, 9, 10], our methods do not use meshes, but rather approaches that are directly computed on regular grids. Favorably, no meshing procedure is needed and no re-meshing operations have to be performed at run-time. Also, patient image data is given as regular grids and graphics hardware can deal efficiently with this kind of structure.

The major contributions of this work are a comprehensive presentation of the direct visuo-haptic rendering components and an improvement of the method used for computation of soft tissue deformations, which can be applied for needle or palpation induced deformations. Additionally, a user study supporting the utility of our framework was performed. It is shown that direct visuo-haptic rendering approaches are valid means for simulation of PTCD. To our knowledge, our system is the first featuring a complete needle insertion simulation framework solely using a voxel based representation for all visuo-haptic interaction and includes simulation of deformation caused by interaction in all visual representations.

The article is organized as follows: First, related work is described. In the following section 3, an overview of the VR simulator and its hardware and software components is given. Then, in section 4 methods for the haptic simulation and visualization of needle insertion, palpation and ultrasound probing based on partially segmented data are presented. Section 5 gives details on the evaluation of the framework including a user study. Finally, results are presented in section 6 and discussed in section 7.

2 Related Work

Simulation of haptic interaction in surgery training is discussed in [11] and different haptic devices and fields of application are presented. General patient-specific simulation systems are reviewed in [12].

Regarding needle puncture, current simulations feature insertion of needles into blood vessels [1, 2], for liver biopsy [3, 4] or prostate brachytherapy [13]. Closely related to the system presented here is the ImaGiNe-S system [14], detailed in [15] and [16]. In [15], a simulator for ultrasound (US)-guided liver lesion needle punctures using two haptic devices for US probe and needle respectively is described. They use surface models created by the marching cubes algorithm and refrain from direct volume rendering due to slow processing times. In [16], a simulator for percutaneous transhepatic cholangiography (PTC) is presented, which relies on surface models as well. The major differences in comparison to our system are that our set-up uses partially segmented image data and direct volume rendering with visualization of local deformations in all visualization components.

The haptic force feedback modeling of needle insertion has been surveyed in [17]. A method for volume based rendering of needle insertion is presented in [5]. Recent simulations concerning virtual palpation by using a haptic device include [1, 2, 18, 19]. In [1], palpation is used to determine the insertion site for femoral artery puncture leading to regional anesthesia using a Phantom Omni 3DOF haptic device. A special palpation pad has been created as a custom replacement of the stylus interface of the Omni and it has been shown that this pad approach is more natural than using the stylus. For the same kind of intervention, a different approach is taken in [2]. There, palpation is simulated in an augmented reality scene and the user directly palpates an artificial silicone interface with his fingers. The haptic response of the interface is provided by two Novint Falcon devices and a hydraulic end effector.

Simulation of soft tissue deformations is a major research area by itself. For needle insertion simulation, the works of [7, 8] are of major importance. There, the finite element method is used and thus the virtual patients are represented by a tetrahedrical mesh data structure. Remeshing, i.e. manipulation of the tetrahedrical structure, at run-time is used to make the needle comply to the structure of the mesh and to provide more elements close to the needle. Since FE methods are computationally intensive, update rates as needed for haptic interaction (500-2000 Hz) are hard to achieve. To mitigate the problem and enable high update rates, multirate compliant mechanisms [10] can be used making it possible to use FEM simulation for haptic force feedback computation. A framework for interactive simulation of cutting and deformations using FEM and direct volume rendering was recently presented in [20].

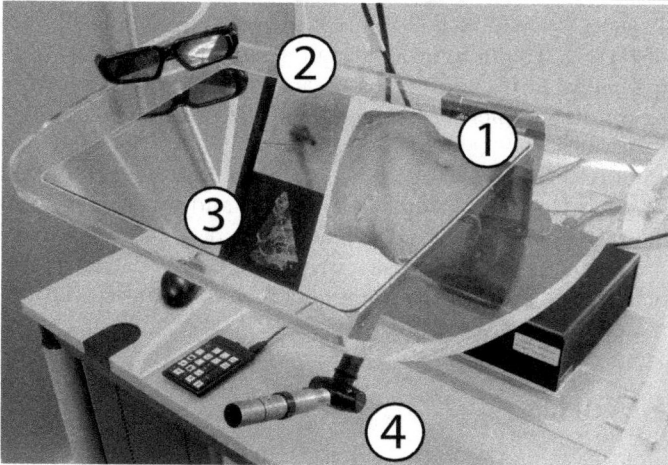

Figure 2: Haptic workbench and simulation: (1) Main rendering window, (2) X-ray rendering window, (3) ultrasound rendering window and (4) haptic device handle.

Real-time simulation of angiography was adressed by [21] and real-time fluoroscopy simulation for PTC in [16]. Simulation of ultrasound imaging based on CT data is presented in [22, 23, 24].

3 Simulator Overview

The hardware setup of the simulation system consists of a visuo-haptic workbench using stereoscopic 3D (see Fig. 2). Using the haptic input device a user can steer virtual tools in the VR environment.

After the creation of a new patient model in a preprocessing step, the crucial parts of a virtual PTCD intervention can be trained and planned. The workflow consists of the following sequence: (1) virtual palpation, (2) US probing and (3) puncturing with the needle. Finally, (4) a button press checks for the emission of contrast agent into the bile ducts by using X-ray simulation. After changing from palpation to the US tool, the needle can be snapped into a guide at the side of the US probe and the puncture is performed by guided advance of the needle into the patient's body. When a risk structure is hurt by the needle tip, the user is notified by turning the simulation window background red, a successful insertion is indicated by a green background and contrast agent spreading out in the bile ducts is visualized in the X-ray viewport. This way, a successful puncture of the bile ducts is indicated, and the training ends. In reality, the replacement of the needle by a catheter for drainage would follow, which is much easier than the needle placement and therefore neglected.

The deformation of soft tissue in the CT volume data using palpation, US device and needle insertion is computed and displayed in real-time.

To assess skill improvement using the system, two different modes are offered to the user: The first is a "free planning mode", where the operator can search for needle trajectories. Scoring is then based on needle insertion duration and hit/miss of the target structure. In the second mode, needle trajectory accuracy while puncturing along predefined reference paths can be assessed ("reference path mode"). Reference paths can be generated by a path planning concept [25] or specified by medical experts and are kept as "bookmarks".

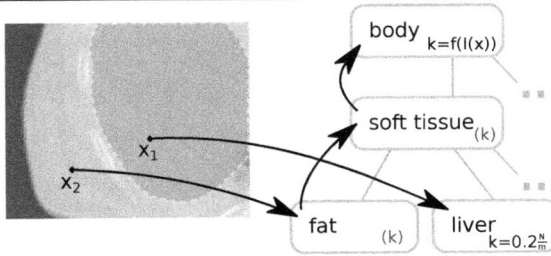

Figure 3: Explanation of the property tree: If a parameter of a voxel is needed, first, the corresponding structure is determined by a present segmentation (x_1) or heuristic (x_2). Then the parameter is looked up in the tree. In this example, k is defined as a fixed value for the liver segmentation or otherwise as a transfer function for the root element. The transfer function is evaluated using the CT value of the voxel.

4 Visuo-Haptic Rendering of Partially Segmented Image Data

After the creation of a virtual patient model, it is presented to a trainee in a visuo-haptic environment using direct rendering of the volume data. In the following, first the representation of the patient data is described and then we present the haptic algorithms and methods for real-time visual rendering, X-ray and ultrasound simulation.

4.1 Patient Data and Property Tree

The patient data representations used in the simulation consist of a tree-like description of tissue properties, partial segmentations of a patient's volumetric image data and the CT image data itself. Each node in the tree corresponds to a distinct tissue type or class of tissues. Furthermore, transfer functions can be defined for individual nodes of the property tree, relating Hounsfield values to haptic simulation parameters or color information for the volume rendering. Inheritance from parent nodes make it unnecessary to define tissue properties for each element of the tree (see Fig. 3). The haptic parameters were tuned by two medical experts with profound experience in PTCD punctures to ensure face validity for a reference patient. Different tissues and interfaces have been punctured repeatedly on reproducible application relevant paths and the parameters have been adjusted by request of the experts.

Additionally, tissue thresholds $t_{\text{fat}}^{\text{bone}}$, $t_{\text{skin}}^{\text{fat}}$ and $t_{\text{air}}^{\text{skin}}$ have to be determined, which are used to roughly classify a voxel given its Hounsfield value. Since these thresholds are patient-specific, new patient data has to be prepared by histogram matching of the new CT image onto the reference image data. Furthermore, creation of partial segmentations is necessary. This step consists of the segmentation and modeling of key structures by manual or semi-automatic methods, i.e. liver, liver vessels (bile ducts, blood vessels) and intercostal fascia.

4.2 Needle Haptics with Proxy-Based Rendering of Partially Segmented Data

For rendering of needle forces, a proxy based approach [26] is used. The virtual needle tip $\mathbf{x}$ is connected to a virtual proxy $\mathbf{p}$ via a spring and Hooke's law $\mathbf{f}(\mathbf{d}) = k \cdot \mathbf{d}$ with $\mathbf{d} = \mathbf{p} - \mathbf{x}$ and spring constant k is used to compute force feedback. The needle is assumed

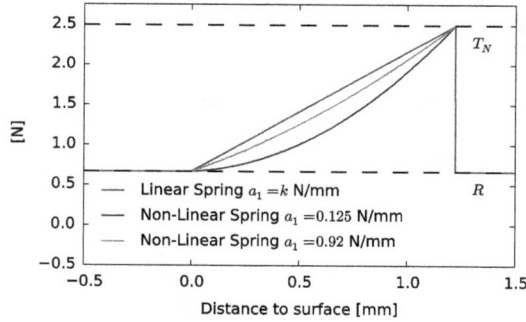

Figure 4: Force output for a surface using the non-linear spring with different settings for a_1.

to be bending free, which is a reasonable simplification for ultrasound guided PTCD where relatively stiff needles ($\leq$ 18 gauge) are used.

Characteristic forces as occurring in needle insertion are simulated by manipulation of the proxy's position [5]. Needle shaft forces are modeled by projecting the proxy position onto the direction of insertion, which results in forces fixing the haptic device handle on the virtual insertion path.

Simulation of the resistance of tissue surfaces to needle puncture is achieved by keeping the proxy on the tissue's surface until the spring generates a force higher than a tissue specific threshold T_N. According to Hooke's law, the spring model has a linear characteristic when needle tip and proxy positions diverge at a tissue border. Another variant for computation of needle forces is a more realistic non-linear spring force [27]. Following this approach, we use a second degree polynomial

$$\mathbf{f}(\mathbf{d}) = \frac{\mathbf{d}}{\|\mathbf{d}\|}\left(a_2\|\mathbf{d}\|^2 + a_1\|\mathbf{d}\| + a_0\right) \tag{1}$$

with $\mathbf{d} = \mathbf{p} - \mathbf{x}$ being the indentation of the surface at a tissue border. As a novelty, the parameters a_0, a_1 and a_2 are set in a way that the surface puncture event occurs at the same indentation and with the same force as it would happen with the linear spring, which was evaluated to provide realistic force output at organ borders in our reference system [5]. Between first contact of the needle tip with a tissue border and the puncture event, forces below the linear spring forces are computed with a non-linear slope (see Fig. 4). The maximum friction force R when moving the needle within a homogeneous tissue corresponds and determines the parameter $a_0 = R$, whereas the user-specified parameter $a_1 \in [0, k]$ given in [N/m] influences the linear term and has to be estimated heuristically. The last parameter, namely

$$a_2 = \frac{k \cdot (k - a_1)}{|T_N - a_0|} \tag{2}$$

results from the parameters a_0 and a_1, the spring stiffness constant k of the linear model and the surface resistance force T_N. A low value for a_1 thus enforces a lower slope at the beginning of the force curve, i.e. increases the influence of the quadratic term. Using this spring model we aim to achieve a more realistic haptic rendering at organ capsules with a force curve that corresponds better to the model and ex-vivo bovine liver needle insertion measurements from [27]. Note that setting $a_1 = k$ is equivalent to using a linear spring.

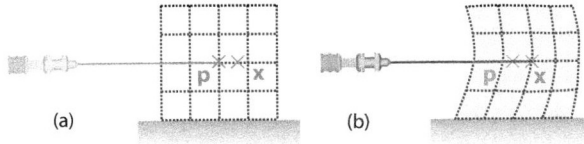

Figure 5: Needle in undeformed state of the virtual patient as defined by the proxy (a) and needle steered by the haptic device in the current deformed configuration of the tissue (b). Connecting **x** and **p** by a spring is used to calculate force feedback.

Inside an organ, friction of different tissues is rendered by delaying the proxy movement and adjusting the spring constant k of the virtual spring and a maximal friction force value R by a stick-slide approach [28] in the form

$$\mathbf{p}' = \begin{cases} \mathbf{x} + \frac{R}{k}\frac{\mathbf{d}}{\|\mathbf{d}\|} & \text{if } \|\mathbf{d}\| \cdot k > R \\ \mathbf{p} & \text{otherwise} \end{cases} \tag{3}$$

with $\mathbf{p}'$ being the new proxy position and with $\mathbf{d} = \mathbf{p} - \mathbf{x}$ being the offset of the old proxy position and device position.

As explained in Fig. 3, the property tree provides the parameters R, k and T_N in form of a transfer function or constant values valid in a classified region. In the case of a fully segmented patient, where each tissue in the patient's image has a distinct label, the tissue parameters are looked up in the property tree: First, the current label $l(\mathbf{p})$ and CT image value $\mathbf{I}(\mathbf{p})$ is determined at the proxy position. For each haptic parameter the following is done: Starting at the tree node that matches the label, the tree is traversed upwards until a node with a constant value or transfer function defining the parameter of interest is found. If during traversal a node containing a transfer function is found, then it is evaluated for the CT value at the proxy position, giving the haptic parameter. The proxy position corresponds to the needle tip in the undeformed state of the virtual patient, i.e. the undeformed image of the patient at time of image acquisition, as illustrated in Fig. 5. Another possibility would be to determine the parameters at the device tip. The reason the proxy is preferred is the assumption that the spatial relation of tip and proxy define the deformation of the tissue. Thus, fetching the parameters at the proxy position in the undeformed image data is equivalent to fetching the parameters in a deformed state of the image.

To reduce the preparation time needed for segmentation in practice, partially segmented data $\mathbf{L}_{pt}$ can be used for determination of the label and the matching tree node. For segmented regions, the lookup of parametric values is done as in the fully segmented case. In image regions where the label information is incomplete, a heuristic is used to guess the missing labels. This heuristic requires CT image data for which the intensities have been adapted to the reference patient image data, making the used thresholds implicitly patient-specific. It depends on the image gray value $\mathbf{I}(\mathbf{p})$, and the current insertion depth d:

$$h(\mathbf{I}(\mathbf{p}), d) = \begin{cases} l_{\text{risk}} & \text{if } \mathbf{I}(\mathbf{p}) \in [-\infty, t_{\text{skin}}^{\text{fat}}) \wedge d > \delta \\ l_{\text{skin}} & \text{if } \mathbf{I}(\mathbf{p}) \in [t_{\text{air}}^{\text{skin}}, t_{\text{skin}}^{\text{fat}}) \wedge d \leq \delta \\ l_{\text{fat}} & \text{if } \mathbf{I}(\mathbf{p}) \in [t_{\text{skin}}^{\text{fat}}, t_{\text{fat}}^{\text{bone}}) \\ l_{\text{bone}} & \text{if } \mathbf{I}(\mathbf{p}) \in [t_{\text{fat}}^{\text{bone}}, \infty] \\ l_{\text{air}} & \text{otherwise} \end{cases} \tag{4}$$

The constant δ is a minimal insertion depth after which the detection of unspecified risk structures l_{rsc} should start. This is necessary to prevent the algorithm to classify the patient's skin surface as a risk structure. Here, the value used in our evaluation have been empirically set to $\delta = 5.0$ mm.

With this heuristic, the final equation to estimate a distinct label in real-time (2000 Hz) for a position $\mathbf{p}$ in the image is:

$$l(\mathbf{p}, d) = \begin{cases} \mathbf{L}_{pt}(\mathbf{p}) & \text{if } \mathbf{L}_{pt}(\mathbf{p}) \neq 0 \\ h(\mathbf{I}(\mathbf{p}), d) & \text{otherwise} \end{cases} \tag{5}$$

Tissue borders are rendered in case two different labels are detected in two successive rendering steps. From the haptics perspective, this motivates to have explicit segmentation models available for structures involved in haptically important tissue transitions, e.g. the fascia.

4.3 Haptic Simulation of Palpation and Ultrasound Probe Interaction

In practice, palpation is applied to determine the insertion point of the needle, while ultrasound or X-ray imaging is used to guide the needle inside the human body [6]. Therefore, a method for haptic rendering of intercostal space palpation is needed.

Using the ultrasound device, the probe is aligned on the skin between the rib bones (intercostal space). Our approach [19] is based on Euclidean distance maps of threshold segmented structures. These can be obtained by segmentation thresholds t_{air}^{skin} and t_{fat}^{bone} giving the distance maps D_{skin} and D_{bone}. They are used to calculate forces acting on fixed points that are distributed on the surfaces of tools or the tip of the virtual finger. For each of these points $\mathbf{x}$, penalty force terms $\mathbf{f}_{skin}$ and $\mathbf{f}_{bone}$ that model the surface of the patient and bone structures are applied. Each of the forces is in the form

$$\mathbf{f}_i = \mathbf{v}_i \cdot f_i \left(D_i \left(\mathbf{x} \right) \right) \tag{6}$$

with $\mathbf{v}_i$ being the direction of the force and f_i a non-linear function relating the Euclidean distance of the point $\mathbf{x}$ to the surface $i \in \{skin, bone\}$ to the force's magnitude.

For the skin surface force, the normalized gradient of the distance map D_{skin} is used. Similarly, for the force direction of the hard structure force, the normalized gradient of D_{bone} is reoriented towards the skin surface in case it points in the opposite direction of $\mathbf{v}_{skin}$, giving the force direction.

Furthermore, their friction on the surfaces is computed by a proxy based scheme, which is similar to the simulation of friction of the needle. The relation of proxy and contact node then again is used to calculate a force $\mathbf{f}_{friction}$. Based on these three components, the total force on a node is the sum

$$\mathbf{f} = \mathbf{f}_{skin} + \mathbf{f}_{bone} + \mathbf{f}_{friction} \tag{7}$$

By using this force, torque can be computed by the cross product of the force and the lever arm formed by the haptic device position and the position of the node. Averaging the forces and torques of all nodes in contact gives the force and torque displayed to the user via the haptic device.

4.4 Direct Volume Rendering of the Deformable Patient's Body

Most recent surgery simulations use indirect volume rendering methods (polygonal models) for the visualization of a patient's medical image data. Indirect volume rendering relies on the creation of a surface representation in a preprocessing step, often based on a segmentation of anatomical structures. On the contrary, direct volume rendering by ray casting is a well known field [29] and can be used to visualize image data without preprocessing steps.

To improve realism, visualization of soft tissue deformations occurring during the interaction with the patient is desirable. Since these deformations are limited to a small neighborhood around the interacting tools, we use our method presented in [30] to compute deformations of a cubical voxel sub-volume $\mathbf{J}$ consisting of 64^3 voxels on the grid Ω. There, deformations on the image data are computed by a physically motivated linear-elastic or diffusive relaxation process influenced by a material function that prohibits the deformation of hard structures. Generally speaking, the result of the algorithms is a displacement field $u : \Omega \rightarrow \mathbb{R}^3$ computed by minimizing an energy functional using iterative explicit integration by application of a differential operator T:

$$u_{i+1} = u_i + Tu_i \tag{8}$$

The displacement field has to be inverted and then can be used to resample $\mathbf{J}$ by trilinear interpolation. Instead of calculating u, the inverse u^{-1} can be computed directly. The method's main limitation are relatively long run times needed for convergence. To reduce the time needed for convergence, two methods are used to speed up the relaxation process of needle or palpation induced deformations: (1) The ChainMail algorithm and (2) a multigrid method. The ChainMail method is an efficient way to simulate deformations on regular grids [31, 32] and was used for palpation induced deformations in [19, 33]. The main idea is to assume that the movement of elements of a soft body is spatially limited by constrains similar to rings of chain mail. Despite being efficient, the plausibility in terms of physical correctness of the resulting deformations is limited and typical visual diamond shaped artifacts arise.

In contrast to this, the multigrid approach relies on the deformation models as proposed in our previous work [30]. Multigrid methods are often applied in image registration [34, 35] or finite element simulation [36]. Instead of only computing on a single mesh or grid, different resolutions are used for computation and the intermediate solutions from lower resolutions are used as initial solutions for the higher resolutions. Here, the multigrid method is implemented using three levels (L_0, L_1, and L_2) and works as follows: In each time step of the simulation, the grid of deformations from the previous iteration in the same resolution as the image data ($L_0 = 64^3$) is resampled twice by reducing the resolution by a factor of two. With i being the grid level and w_i the associated grid dimension, the resampling can be defined recursively as

$$L_i(x, y, z) = L_{i-1}(2x, 2y, 2z), x, y, z \in \{1, ..., w_i\} \tag{9}$$

This way, the grid of deformations L_1 with 32^3 elements and L_2 with 16^3 elements respectively are computed.

Then, the relaxation algorithm of [30] is applied to L_2 several times followed by a redistribution of the deformations onto L_1. After applying the relaxation to L_1 and redistribution onto L_0, final relaxation steps are performed on L_0. The redistribution can be defined as

$$L_i(x, y, z) = L_{i+1}\left(\frac{x}{2}, \frac{y}{2}, \frac{z}{2}\right), x, y, z \in \{1, ..., w_i\} \tag{10}$$

To visualize the deformed volume data, a custom volume renderer was developed to render the resulting deformed sub-volume combined with the original undeformed image by ray casting. This renderer uses a piecewise-linear visual RGBA transfer function $c(v) = (r(v), g(v), b(v), a(v))^\top$, which is composed of visual transfer functions from the property tree, to relate the Hounsfield values along a viewing ray to color information. The weight $\alpha_i \in [0..1]$ of each of the n transfer functions from the property tree can each be adjusted by the user. The combined transfer function is defined as

$$c(v) = \sum_{1 \leq i \leq n} \alpha_i a_i(v) \left[\begin{pmatrix} r_i(v) \\ g_i(v) \\ b_i(v) \\ 0 \end{pmatrix} + \begin{pmatrix} 0 \\ 0 \\ 0 \\ 1 \end{pmatrix} \right] \tag{11}$$

for a given gray value v.

To give the user the possibility to inspect the internal structures of the patient interactively, an additional "clipping mode" can be used: A plane, which is defined by the position and orientation of the current tool is used to hide parts of the patients that lie on one side of the plane. Elements on the plane can be tagged by the labeling function as used in the haptic rendering and displayed according to the element's color given by the property tree or by a color coding of target (green) and risk structures (red). Another rendering mode is provided, which uses a simple windowing function for the volume rendering, which is supposed to be intuitive for users familiar with windowing of medical image data.

To improve depth perception, simple shadow rendering of the tools is incorporated in the volume rendering.

4.5 Simulation of X-ray and Contrast Agent Injection

The ray casting method is adapted for an additional simulation of fluoroscopy imaging with contrast agent injection based on the patient's partial segmentations and 3D CT image data. The contrast agent is injected by the needle during insertion to augment visibility of the punctured liver vessels.

Here, we model the resulting image intensity of the pixels as a function of the total attenuation factor a from the Beer-Lambert law $I = I_0 e^{-a}$ as proposed by [37]: The total attenuation factor $a = \sum_{x_i \in R} \mu(x_i) \Delta x$ is given by the attenuation coefficient $\mu(x_i)$ for each point on a ray R and the distance Δx between the sampling points. Attenuation coefficients are computed from Hounsfield units based on the attenuation coefficient for water [38]. Given a photon energy of 0.1 MeV, we use the attenuation coefficient $\mu_{\text{water}} = 0.17 \text{ m}^{-1}$ as a basis. Furthermore, attenuation of injected contrast agent has to be estimated at run-time. In fluoroscopy, iodine is often used as a contrast agent since it has a high attenuation coefficient of $\mu_c(x) = 1.9 \frac{\text{cm}^2}{\text{g}} \rho(x)$ for a given density $\rho(x)$ of the contrast agent. We model the density of the contrast agent by a diffusion process on a grid given by the hepatic duct segmentation, which gives a total attenuation factor

$$a = \Delta x \sum_{x_i \in R} (\mu(x_i) + \mu_c(x_i)) \tag{12}$$

for a single ray.

Initially, all density values of the grid representing the hepatic duct segmentation are set to zero. In case the puncture needle enters the hepatic duct, contrast agent is automatically injected by increasing the density of the contrast agent at the needle tip by a fixed amount. In each time step of the simulation, the contrast agent propagation is simulated by explicit integration of the diffusion equation $\rho_{t+\tau} = \rho_t + \tau \Delta \rho_t$ on the grid of contrast agent density with ρ_t being the density of contrast agent at time t and τ being the time step.

4.6 Simulated Ultrasound

Ultrasound guided needle puncture is often used for accessing peripheral lesions and vessels in the liver [6]. In contrast to using X-ray techniques, no radiation dose is applied and this technique lowers the number of needle repositionings noticeably. In our simulator, the virtual US head features a needle guide. Training and planning with this advanced tooling can improve the efficiency and effectiveness of the operator on a new patient.

The methods of [22], [23] and [24] served as references for our US simulation based on CT data. We added the use of partial segmentations to further enhance the realism of the simulation. Moreover, for didactic reasons assisting visualization of certain object borders and Doppler mode simulation is available. Basically, we use a parallelized ray casting technique implemented in Cuda for the US image fan, which is composed of many radially emerging rays. For one ray and the final image, the computation can be divided into six steps, which can be found in the appendix. One new aspect in the simulation pipeline is the amplification of the returned signal using simulated time gain control (see step 4, Eq. 15 in the appendix). Moreover, optional color overlays and colored borders indicating target and risk structures can be enabled for various structures.

Using Doppler-mode, the dynamic flow of blood can be seen inside the arteries and veins, which is important for the surgeon's needle navigation around these structures. In our simplified Doppler-US simulation, we use a blood pressure $p\left(t\right)$ curve as a velocity indicator

$$v\left(t\right) = \sqrt{2 \cdot \left(p(t)/\rho_{\text{blood}}\right)} \tag{13}$$

and in a HSL color model modulate the hue of the color overlay following the time dependent velocity. Arteries are presented in a red-to-yellow color gradient, and veins are displayed in a blue-to-cyan gradient. At the segmented blood vessel voxels, the Doppler color overlay flashes with a pulse rate of 80 beats per minute and a phase shift of $1/3$ periods between arteries and veins.

4.7 Implementation Details

As illustrated in Fig. 6, all described visualization components are implemented and parallelized using Nvidia Cuda. The parallelization for the computation of deformations is described in [30], columns of $\mathbf{J}$ are assigned to Cuda blocks, with threads for each element of a column. For the ray casting, blocks are defined as rectangular image regions with each thread corresponding to a ray. In our implementation of ultrasound simulation, one ray corresponds to a block, with a thread for each sampling point. The results from the visualizations are copied to the framebuffer using OpenGL/Cuda interoperability. To achieve this, custom rendering elements have been implemented that fit into the rendering pipeline of the Visualization Toolkit (VTK) library. Based on the properties of the haptic device and haptic algorithms, the virtual tools also are rendered using VTK/OpenGL by rasterization. This combined visualization runs on a single thread at interactive rates.

A CPU thread executes the haptic algorithms at a high rate of 2000 Hz. The haptic algorithms are implemented in C++ with an interface to the haptic device using the OpenHaptics low-level API (HDAPI) [39].

The main obstacle we faced during the integration of the components was the combination of the volume rendering with the rasterization. This was mainly caused by the fact that Cuda does not give direct access to the depth buffer. It was solved by copying the resulting depth buffer from the volume rendering to the render buffer by using a GLSL fragment shader.

5 Evaluation

For needle insertion force calculations, the targeted rendering rate of 2000 Hz is easily achieved and is not worth a detailed performance study. An evaluation of palpation

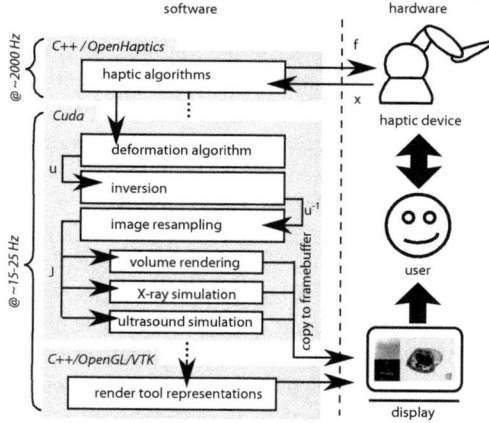

Figure 6: Overview of software and hardware components of the simulator.

rendering performance can be found in [19]. In contrast, the visualization aspects regarding volume rendering of deformations, X-ray and ultrasound simulation deserve detailed evaluation in terms of rendering performance and visual plausibility. Furthermore, the whole system is assessed in a user study.

5.1 Performance Evaluation of Visual Rendering

The performance of the visual rendering has been tested on a workstation with Nvidia GTX 680 graphics hardware in terms of rendering time per frame. To this aim, a scripted sequence of the initial PTCD steps palpation, ultrasound probing, needle insertion and X-ray inspection has been performed $n = 10$ times. The duration of each of the steps is set to 6 seconds. Volume rendering uses a resolution of 512^2 pixels and X-ray rendering a resolution of 256^2 pixels. The size of the sub-volume used for deformation computation is set to 64^3 voxels.

To compare and analyze the benefits gained from the ChainMail algorithm and the multigrid approach, the behavior in a setting that reflects intercostal space palpation with an indentation of the skin surface of 14 mm and 36 contact nodes distributed on the virtual finger's tip is analyzed. To this aim, we compare our unoptimized method from [30] to the speedup gained by the ChainMail and multigrid approach. This comparison is performed separately for both the diffusive approximation and the linear-elastic relaxation formulation for soft tissue deformations as proposed in [30]. Overall, we compare six relaxation methods (unoptimized, ChainMail and multigrid; each with the diffusive and linear elastic relaxation). For both the ChainMail and multigrid optimizations, a single, initial iteration is followed by unoptimized steps, because further iteration did not change the result.

For $u(x, t)$ being the elements of the displacement field after a processing time t using one of the six methods for computing deformations, we measured the mean squared difference (MSD) of the successive steps and a fully converged unoptimized solution:

$$e_{\mathrm{msd}}(t) = \frac{1}{|\Omega|} \sum_{x \in \Omega} \|u(x, t) - u(x, \infty)\|^2 \tag{14}$$

with $u(x, \infty)$ corresponding to a fully converged solution of the unoptimized processes (see also equation 8). We use $u(x, \infty)$ under the assumption that it represents valid ground truth, which is reasonable since processing speed is evaluated here and not deformation accuracy. In this experiment, the ChainMail and the multigrid methods are applied once, followed by a series of unoptimized relaxation steps. This is done to show that the algorithms indeed have found an initial solution that can be improved in further iterations. In the actual simulator, only the ChainMail approach would be handled in this fashion since the multigrid method already includes several unoptimized relaxation steps. For the multigrid method, the number of iterations on the levels L_0, L_1 and L_2 are set to 4, 8 and 16.

Additionally, qualitative results of the rendering methods and relaxation approaches are given.

5.2 Qualitative User Evaluation

A user study covering visuo-haptic rendering and to further confirm general validity and user acceptance was conducted with 16 (9 female, 7 male) medical students (5th year) prior to their one year practical hospital training. Medical students well represent a target user group in terms of medical training with our simulator. Each trainee was given a time window of 30 to 60 minutes. Before starting with the training, each subject has been introduced to the simulator to reach the same level of ability. The instructor showed a single puncture in "free" and "reference path mode" to the trainee. The trainees then were able to get scores from three tries in both modes each.

After the training, each subject was handed out a four point Likert-scale questionnaire [40] to evaluate the simulation system. The motivation for using four points on the scale is to have the subjects clearly decide for a more positive or negative tendency regarding the question.

The questionnaire shown in Tab. 1 is divided into the three sections:

1. User previous knowledge, experience and confidence (Q1-Q3).
2. User perception of the system including visual and haptic rendering (Q4-Q13).
3. General final user evaluation of the system and confidence after training (Q14-Q19).

For comparison of user confidence before and after the training session we use the Wilcoxon signed rank test (Q1 vs. Q16). The user evaluation has been performed on a workstation running on an Intel Xeon W3550@ 3.07GHz with 32 GB RAM with a Nvidia Quadro 4000 Graphics Card. The image data for the virtual patient model had a resolution of 256x256x236 elements. Volume rendering uses an image plane resolution of 512^2 pixels and X-ray rendering a resolution of 256^2 pixels. For simulation of deformations, the ChainMail method has been used.

6 Results

6.1 Visual Rendering Performance

6.1.1 Quantitative

Fig. 7 shows box-plotted rendering times in the described sequence (see section 5.1). In the first phase, the patient's tissue is deformed by palpation, which increases the processing times noticeable. The same holds for the second phase with additional computations needed for ultrasound simulation. Deformations caused by the needle and contrast agent diffusion are responsible for the increase in computation time in the third phase. The X-ray simulation needs increased computation time as clearly can be seen in the last phase. Generally, the rendering is capable of real-time resp. interactive rendering using the GTX 680 graphics card.

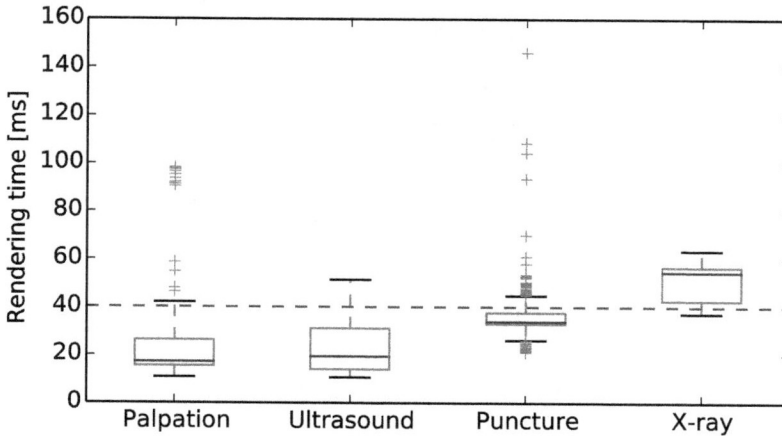

Figure 7: Boxplots of rendering times during a scripted test sequence. Everything below the blue line indicates real-time capable update rates (25Hz).

Deformation algorithm performance is presented in Fig. 8. To reflect the real-time capable behavior of the algorithms, only the first 50 milliseconds are plotted. It is shown that the multigrid approach easily outperforms both the ChainMail and the unoptimized version.

6.1.2 Qualitivate

Screenshots of the visualization components are shown in Fig. 9 and 10: we show volume rendering with enabled "clipping mode" using (1) the combined visual transfer function from the property tree, (2) a different combination of transfer functions with decreased opacity values for the transfer functions of 'skin' and 'soft tissue', (3) an overlay of target and risk structures, (4) the labeling function and (5) a rendering based on a windowing transfer function. Using the visual transfer function, the skin layer can be clearly distinguished from other soft tissue and bony structures. Visual rendering side effects occur at borders of the structures that are filled with air (lungs, intestine): these are rendered similar to the skin surface but are classified as risk structure (see Eq. 4). This effect is also visible when using the overlay and labeling functions.

In the X-ray simulation (Fig. 10a), the needle has been inserted in the bile duct for several seconds and contrast agent already has spread out.

Fig. 10b shows a sample image of the US simulation. The shape of the bile ducts can be well perceived. They are characterized by dark, reflection-free areas. There also is a bony structure in the field of view, the rib, behind which a typical shadow shows out.

The image in Fig. 10b is simulated with a transducer frequency $f = 3$ MHz and a fan-beam angle of 30 degrees.

Concerning deformations caused by palpation, Fig. 11 shows the benefit of the multigrid method, which avoids the diamond shaped artifacts shown by the ChainMail approach. Also, the unoptimized method after a fixed number of 16 relaxation steps has been applied is shown. A higher number of relaxation steps would inhibit real-time capabilities and thus the need for optimization in case of palpation is demonstrated.

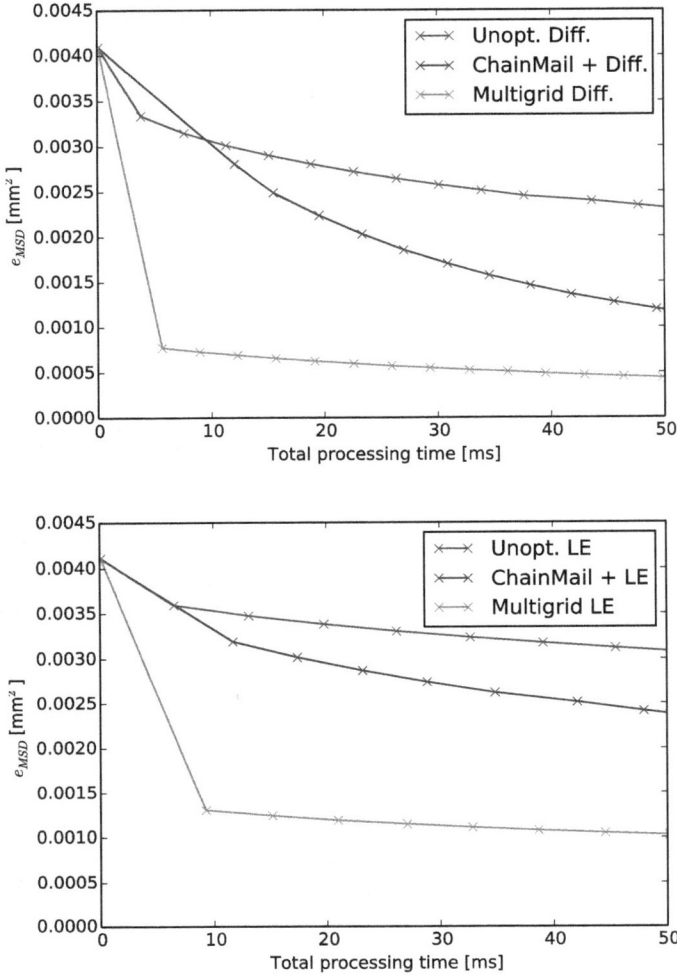

Figure 8: Mean squared differences of deformations between stepwise solutions of the deformation algorithms and a fully converged solution during a 50 ms period for diffusive relaxation (upper) and linear-elastic relaxation (lower). One initial step of the ChainMail and the multigrid approach is followed by a series of unoptimized relaxation steps.

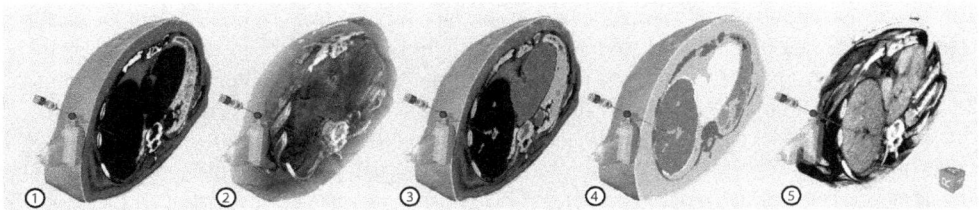

Figure 9: Different volume renderings of the virtual patient with enabled "clipping mode": (1) using a combined transfer function, (2) using different opacity values for the transfer functions, (3) target and risk structure overlay, (4) labeling function and (5) a windowing transfer function.

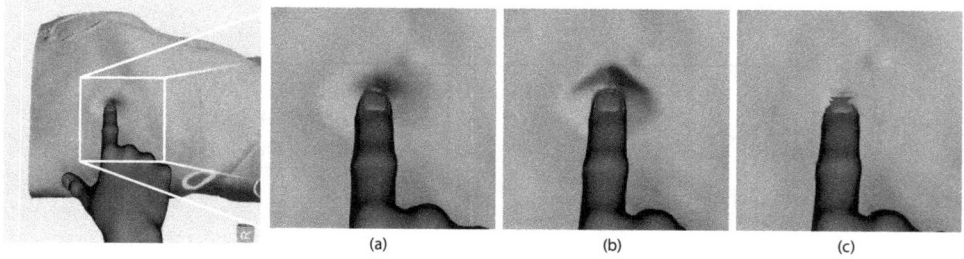

Figure 11: Rendering of the palpation from the simulation, deformations computed by (a) a multigrid method, (b) ChainMail and (c) unoptimized version with a number of relaxation steps that still enables real-time interaction. Obviously, (a) is the best result since (b) contains diamond shaped artifacts resulting from the ChainMail algorithm and the number of relaxation steps in (c) do not result in realistic deformation, demonstrating the need for an optimization.

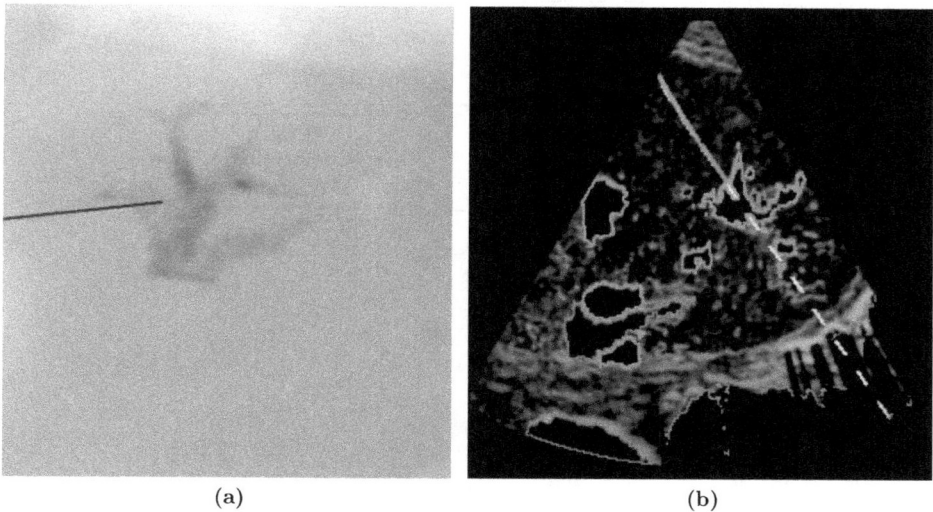

Figure 10: (a) Simulated X-ray image with contrast agent spreading in the bile ducts. (b) Simulated US image with augmented target (green) and risk (red) structures, the yellow dotted line shows the predicted path of the inserted needle.

6.2 User Evaluation

Tab. 1 shows the results of the user evaluation. Most students were unconfident to perform a real first PTCD (Q1). Questions judging the simulator have been answered positively, i.e. the median and mean of each answer is below the 4-point Likert-scale midpoint of 2.5 (Q2-Q18). The attitude towards intuitiveness and realism of the force-feedback of the simulation has been judged the least favorable (Q5-Q7) with the highest standard deviations. Visual rendering of the skin surface is still positively judged, but has the lowest score regarding visual rendering (Q8). Improvements of the visual perception by stereoscopic 3D and shadow rendering is overall rated as good (Q9-Q10). The X-ray and ultrasound simulation were rated very good regarding the purpose of training and planning (Q11-Q12). The scoring system is regarded helpful (Q13) but not as meaningful (Q14). Application of the simulator in the real world is viewed as promising (Q2-Q4, Q15-Q16).

Table 1: Questionnaire given to the medical students (n = 16) with resulting median, mean and standard deviations of the scores.

No. Question	Median	Mean	Std. Dev.
1 I would have dared to do a PTCD before the training.	3	2.88	0.96
2 In general, I consider performing a virtual training session prior to a real intervention to be reasonable.	1	1.50	0.73
3 For a new patient, the simulation could provide a good planning possibility.	1	1.44	0.63
4 The simulation could increase the quality of an upcoming intervention and reduce stress for the patient.	1	1.44	0.63
5 The force-feedback seems realistic to me.	2	1.94	0.77
6 The force-feedback enabled me to feel the important structures.	2	2.25	0.93
7 Control of the haptic device was intuitive.	2	2.00	0.82
8 The visual rendering of the patient surface (skin) seems realistic.	2	2.00	0.63
9 The stereoscopic 3D simplifies the training.	1.5	1.56	0.63
10 Rendering of shadows simplifies the spatial orientation.	2	1.81	0.75
11 The injection and diffusion of contrast agent is well recognizable in the X-ray simulation.	1.5	1.56	0.63
12 The ultrasound simulation helps while navigating and finding the target region.	1	1.19	0.54
13 The advice of the evaluation component has been helpful.	2	1.86	0.77
14 The evaluation component is meaningful.	2	2.13	0.74
15 Training with the simulator makes sense.	1	1.50	0.63
16 After performing a training session, a first real puncture would be easier for me.	2	1.94	0.85
17 Using the simulation, I can better imagine the anatomical structures in the region of the liver.	2	2.06	0.68
18 The technical realization is well done.	1	1.38	0.50

Legend:
Fully agree
1.0-1.5
1.5-2.0
2.0-2.5
2.5-3.0
3.0-3.5
3.5-4.0
Fully disagree

Overall, the technical realization has been judged very positively (Q18). To estimate the training effect and trainee confidence before and after the training, the results of Q1 and Q16 are statistically compared using a Wilcoxon signed rank test. The result is significant ($p < 0.01$).

7 Discussion

In the following, we will discuss general findings concerning the visuo-haptic system and the results from the user evaluation.

Deformations are clearly visible on the surface of patients when palpating or using the US tool, and internal deformations caused by lateral movements or tissue indentation can clearly be seen when using the "clipping mode" or US probing. Deformation methods for needle insertion without using ChainMail have been presented in [30] and deformations caused by palpation using ChainMail in [33]. Here, we combined these approaches and introduced a multigrid approach into our framework and showed its favorable visual plausibility and computational speed. Besides, ChainMail causes diamond shaped artifacts and is not physically motivated making the multigrid approach the appropriate choice.

Regarding the X-ray simulation, the quality of the rendered bile ducts augmented by contrast agent is limited by the resolution of the image data. The diameter of the segmented vessels usually is only a few voxels wide and thus the rendered structures have blocky edges. Nevertheless, the X-ray simulation creates convincing output and would profit from higher CT image resolution.

For the raycasting, relatively small resolutions of the resulting image were used in the user evaluation setup but the rasterization-based rendering of the interacting tools is done in the full resolution of the display, mitigating the impression of low-resolution rendering.

Well-known US-typical artifacts, such as speed-displacement and multiple reflexion are not modeled in our US simulation, but it delivers realistic image quality well suited for training and planning use. However, for the US visualization as for the whole concept of the simulator the dedicated segmentation of some key structures is still necessary.

The user evaluation shows that haptic interaction and force feedback is rated differently by 16 students (Tab. 1, Q6-Q7). We consider 16 individuals and two medical experts to be sufficient to give a valid first impression of the system. The high standard deviation shows that the ease of using the device differs for individual students. Another aspect confirmed by the supervising instructors is a slightly easier introduction of the simulator to male students. This might be due to the increased computer gaming affinity and experience of our male student sample. Furthermore, the feedback that important structures are not felt distinctively could be explained by the fact that in contrast to the puncturing of the fascia, a strongly salient haptic feature, the surface forces of the liver and the bile ducts are not as high. The test persons had no puncture experience before using the simulator and tend to have a high expectation to feel all tissue interfaces very saliently. However, our medical experts confirmed the salient fascia puncture event and the much less pronounced puncture events of the other structures. Construct validity was not evaluated explicitly in this study, but the instructors observed a prominent difference, when our PTCD-experienced medical experts used the system compared to the students. As our system currently only features one haptic device, switching from the virtual US tool to the needle tool fixes the former at its current position. It is difficult to model a coupled ultrasound probing and needle insertion adequately with a single haptic device. Using a single device also limits the application of specifically adapted interfaces. The Phantom Omni used in other works [1, 2] better supports customization, i.e. replacing the stylus by a needle base or using a palpation pad, but lacks 6DOF haptic feedback. In our simulation, palpation takes place first. Using a stylus for this is not optimal (see [1]), but since palpation is mainly used for coarse orientation to successfully find intercostal spaces, we think it will not lead to negative training effects. The palpation is followed by ultrasound probing, for which a stylus interface is appropriate. We are confident that more advanced haptics hardware (with multiple 6DOF haptic devices) could mitigate the problem in the future. The confidence of the user is shown to increase significantly during the training process, which is a good hint for effective training. In terms of visual rendering, the users did not consider the rendering of the patients skin surface fully realistic (Tab. 1, Q8), but nevertheless, visualization of the patient by volume rendering is successful, both regarding the visual quality as well as frame rate of visual rendering. Real-time rendering is achieved easily using a Nvidia GTX 680, interactive rates are guaranteed for the workbench setup used in the user study. The methods for increasing depth perception, namely stereoscopic 3D and tool shadow rendering, can be regarded to be helpful. In general, the supporting imaging simulations (X-ray, ultrasound) were received very well by the students and can be considered a valuable part of the simulation (Q11, Q12). However, not all aspects relevant to real US are modeled, i.e. multiple reflexions or speed displacement correction per ray-tracing instead of ray-casting. Overall, it is shown that direct visuo-haptic rendering can be performed by completely relying on image data defined on its underlying natural regular grid data structure without the traditional representation by surface or volume meshes and rasterization based rendering. For a truly patient specific simulation framework, a method for the fast modeling of the virtual patient is needed. Using manual segmentation methods, this can take several hours, but methods for time-efficient semi-automatic segmentation are currently under development.

As for the predecessor of the system, the 6DOF high force haptic device and workbench is still the dominant cost factor ($50k) in terms of hardware components. It can easily cost more than ten times the sum of the other components, which are usual consumer electronics.

8 Conclusion and Future Work

In this paper, we showed that our new visuo-haptic rendering techniques for puncture atlases are valid means for PTCD simulation. A larger user evaluation study regarding concept and face validity is on our schedule as well as a thorough evaluation of the haptic force output with an already proposed framework [25]. Virtual patient modeling is a further aspect to be addressed in a separate publication.

Visuo-haptic rendering solely based on image data and segmentation without incorporation of surface and tetrahedral meshes is shown to be successful, and we are confident that future graphic hardware generations will enable usage of full resolution CT image data (512^2 pixels, thin slices). Also, more powerful graphics hardware could lay the foundations for faster and more accurate image-based deformation algorithms with more complex constitutive models and unique material properties to handle heterogeneities of different soft tissue types; currently, only hard and soft tissues are distinguished.

Given a fast visual rendering, the possibilities of using head-mounted displays could be investigated. Current developments as the Oculus Rift or Sony's Project Morpheus might enable low-cost solutions applicable within our framework. Another interesting aspect would be the comparison of surface based virtual patients and our new approach in a user study. Within our framework we are able to represent both variants. The ultrasound simulation methods could be augmented by a ray-tracing technique and by incorporating Navier-Stokes fluid simulation for more realistic Doppler-mode simulation. The contrast agent simulation could be also adapted to the blood vessels. Finally, respiratory motion using 4D CT data or 4D motion models [41] of the lungs and the adjacent liver will be included in the visuo-haptic simulation.

Acknowledgment

The authors would like to thank our clinical partner Dr. med. P. Wellhöner, our colleague O. Maier, our students P. Behringer, J. Beuke, T. Hecht and S. Köhnen and all participants of the user study.

Appendix

For completeness, the five steps that are performed for one ray of a ray fan and the final ultrasound image compilation step are given here:

Step 1: First the conversion from Hounsfield values to densities $\rho(x_i)$ at ray position x_i takes place using the distinction of cases from [42], where HU intervals are converted to densities ρ by piecewise linear functions.

The impedance, i.e. Z-values in each pixel are calculated using the formerly obtained densities ρ:

$$Z(x_i) = \alpha_1 \rho(x_i) + \alpha_2 \rho(x_i)^2 + \alpha_3 \rho(x_i)^3$$

with $\alpha_1 = 349.281$, $\alpha_2 = -0.151261$ and $\alpha_3 = 0.00117651$ [22].

The transmission is given by [43] assuming normal inclination:

$$T(x_i) = \frac{4 \cdot Z(x_i) \cdot Z(x_{i+1})}{Z(x_{i+1}) + Z(x_i)}$$

The values of $Z(x_i)$ and $Z(x_{i+1})$ are taken from neighbored points on the ray, $Z(x_i)$ corresponds to the current point x_i and $Z(x_{i+1})$ to its successor more inside the body.

For the absorption $\mu(x_i)$, the partial segmentations resp. the interval heuristics are used, detailed value ranges for μ are given in [43]. In case of intervals given in [43], we choose the interval midpoint as μ-value.

Step 2: The algorithm used for the normalized local energy calculation I_a after absorption, using $I_a(x_0) = 1$, spacing s between the samples and frequency f, is:

$$I_a(x_i) = I_a(x_{i-1}) \cdot T(x_i) \cdot \exp(-\mu(x_i) \cdot s \cdot f/10)$$

Step 3: The reflection coefficient $R(x_i)$ is estimated as proposed by [22] assuming normal inclination to a tissue interface

$$R(x_i) = \left(\frac{Z(x_{i+1}) - Z(x_i)}{Z(x_{i+1}) + Z(x_i)} \right)^2$$

The $\cos(\phi)^2$ term for the modified Lambert's cosine law $I_r = I_a \cdot \cos(\phi)^n$ [22] is estimated as

$$\cos(\phi)^2 = \left(\frac{\mathbf{d} \cdot \nabla Z(x_i)}{\|\mathbf{d}\| \cdot \|\nabla Z(x_i)\|} \right)^2$$

where $\mathbf{d}$ is the direction vector of the ray and $\nabla Z(x_i)$ is the gradient of local impedance neighborhood $Z(x_i)$. Thus, ϕ corresponds to the angle between the ray and the surface gradient. The Lambert's cosine law with the modified term using $n = 2$ tries to model a mixture of diffuse and accentuated specular reflection.

According to [22], using Lambert's modified cosine law for diffuse reflection and the reflection coefficient R, the terms can be combined yielding the reflected energy

$$I_r(x_i) = I_a(x_i) \cdot \cos(\phi)^2 \cdot R(x_i)$$

The resulting energy at the transducer I_e and the intensity before time gain control finally is

$$I_e(x_i) = I_r(x_i) \cdot I_a(x_i)$$

Step 4: For simulated time gain control (TGC), a heuristic function $f(d) = \exp(-c \cdot d \cdot f/10.0)^2$ is used, where the time gain factor initialized as $c = 0.55$ can be set by the user on the GUI, d describes the distance to the transducer and f is the transducer frequency used. The resulting amplified signal to display at a pixel x_i is set to:

$$I_{\text{tgc}}(x_i) = I_0 \cdot \frac{I_e(x_i)}{f(|x_i - x_0|)} \tag{15}$$

Step 5: Logarithmic rescaling delivers better visualization of low energies and is defined as [22, 23]

$$I_{\text{out}}(x_i) = \frac{\log(a \cdot I_{\text{tgc}}(x_i) + 1)}{\log(a + 1)}$$

with $a = 10^6$ determining the amplification of weak signals.

Step 6: The fan image is linearly interpolated from the individual rays and post-processing for additive Perlin noise [44] and blurring by folding with a standard Gaussian filter kernel ($\sigma = 2$ mm) takes place.

References

[1] S. Ullrich and T. Kuhlen, "Haptic Palpation for Medical Simulation in Virtual Environments," *IEEE Trans. Vis. Comput. Graphics*, vol. 18, no. 4, pp. 617–25, 2012.

[2] T. Coles, N. John, D. Gould, and D. Caldwell, "Integrating Haptics with Augmented Reality in a Femoral Palpation and Needle Insertion Training Simulation," *IEEE Trans. Hapt.*, vol. 4, no. 3, pp. 199–209, 2011.

[3] P. F. Villard, F. P. Vidal, L. Ap Cenydd, R. Holbrey, S. Pisharody, S. Johnson, a. Bulpitt, N. W. John, F. Bello, and D. Gould, "Interventional Radiology Virtual Simulator for Liver Biopsy," *Int. J. Comput. Assist. Radiol. Surg.*, pp. 1–13, July 2013.

[4] D. Ni, W. Chan, J. Qin, and Y. Chui, "A Virtual Reality Simulator for Ultrasound-guided Biopsy Training," *IEEE Compu. Graph. Appl.*, pp. 143–150, 2011.

[5] M. Färber, F. Hummel, C. Gerloff, and H. Handels, "Virtual Reality Simulator for the Training of Lumbar Punctures," *Meth. Inf. Med.*, vol. 48, no. 5, pp. 493–501, 2009.

[6] L. Lin, *Practical Clinical Ultrasonic Diagnosis*. World Scientific, 1997.

[7] N. Chentanez, R. Alterovitz, D. Ritchie, L. Cho, K. K. Hauser, K. Goldberg, J. R. Shewchuk, and J. F. O'Brien, "Interactive Simulation of Surgical Needle Insertion and Steering," in *Proc. ACM SIGGRAPH 2009*, pp. 88:1–10, Aug 2009.

[8] S. DiMaio and S. Salcudean, "Needle Steering and Motion Planning in Soft Tissues," *IEEE Trans. Biomed. Eng.*, vol. 52, pp. 965–974, June 2005.

[9] C. Duriez, C. Guebert, M. Marchal, S. Cotin, and L. Grisoni, "Interactive Simulation of Flexible Needle Insertions Based on Constraint Models," in *Medical Image Computing and Computer-Assisted Intervention - MICCAI 2009* (G.-Z. Yang, D. Hawkes, D. Rueckert, A. Noble, and C. Taylor, eds.), vol. 5762 of *Lecture Notes in Computer Science*, pp. 291–299, Springer Berlin Heidelberg, 2009.

[10] I. Peterlik, M. Nouicer, C. Duriez, S. Cotin, and A. Kheddar, "Constraint-Based Haptic Rendering of Multirate Compliant Mechanisms," *IEEE Trans. Hapt.*, vol. 4, pp. 175–187, May 2011.

[11] T. Coles, D. Meglan, and N. John, "The Role of Haptics in Medical Training Simulators: A Survey of the State of the Art," *IEEE Trans. Hapt.*, vol. 4, pp. 51–66, Jan 2011.

[12] W. I. M. Willaert, R. Aggarwal, I. Van Herzeele, N. J. Cheshire, and F. E. Vermassen, "Recent Advancements in Medical Simulation: Patient-specific Virtual Reality Simulation," *World J. Surg.*, vol. 36, pp. 1703–12, July 2012.

[13] O. Goksel, K. Sapchuk, W. J. Morris, and S. E. Salcudean, "Prostate Brachytherapy Training with Simulated Ultrasound and Fluoroscopy Images," *IEEE Trans. Biomed. Eng.*, vol. 60, no. 4, pp. 1002–12, 2013.

[14] F. Bello, A. Bulpitt, D. A. Gould, R. Holbrey, C. Hunt, N. W. John, S. Johnson, R. Phillips, A. Sinha, F. P. Vidal, P.-F. Villard, and H. Woolnough, "ImaGiNe-S: Imaging Guided Needle Simulation," in *Proceedings of Eurographics 2009 Short and Areas Papers and Medical Prize Awards*, pp. 5–8, Eurographics Association, 2009.

[15] F. P. Vidal, N. W. John, A. E. Healey, and D. A. Gould, "Simulation of Ultrasound Guided Needle Puncture using Patient Specific Data with 3D Textures and Volume Haptics," *Comput. Animat. Virtual. Worlds.*, vol. 19, no. 2, pp. 111–127, 2008.

[16] P. F. Villard, F. P. Vidal, C. Hunt, F. Bello, N. W. John, S. Johnson, and D. A. Gould, "A Prototype Percutaneous Transhepatic Cholangiography Training Simulator with Real-time Breathing Motion," *Int. J. Comput. Assist. Radiol. Surg.*, vol. 4, pp. 571–578, 2009.

[17] N. Abolhassani, R. Patel, and M. Moallem, "Needle Insertion into Soft Tissue: A Survey.," *Med. Eng. Phys.*, vol. 29, no. 4, pp. 413–31, 2007.

[18] S. Yasmin and A. Sourin, "Image-Based Virtual Palpation," in *Transactions on Computational Science XVIII* (M. Gavrilova, C. Tan, and A. Kuijper, eds.), vol. 7848 of *Lecture Notes in Computer Science*, pp. 61–80, Springer Berlin Heidelberg, 2013.

[19] D. Fortmeier, A. Mastmeyer, and H. Handels, "An Image-Based Multiproxy Palpation Algorithm for Patient-Specific VR-Simulation," in *Medicine Meets Virtual Reality 21, MMVR 2014*, vol. 196 of *Stud. Health Technol. Inform.*, pp. 107–113, IOS Press, 2014.

[20] S. Li, Q. Zhao, and S. Wang, "Interactive Deformation and Cutting Simulation Directly using Patient-specific Volumetric Images," *Comput. Anim. Virtual Worlds*, vol. 25, no. 2, pp. 155–169, 2014.

[21] X. Wu, J. Allard, and S. Cotin, "Real-time Modeling of Vascular Flow for Angiography Simulation," in *Medical Image Computing and Computer-Assisted Intervention–Miccai 2007*, pp. 557–565, Springer, 2007.

[22] T. Reichl, J. Passenger, O. Acosta, and O. Salvado, "Ultrasound goes GPU: Real-time Simulation using CUDA," in *Proc. SPIE*, p. 726116, 2009.

[23] O. Kutter, A. Karamalis, W. Wein, and N. Navab, "A GPU-based Framework for Simulation of Medical Ultrasound," in *Proc. SPIE*, vol. 7261, p. 726117, 2009.

[24] W. Wein, S. Brunke, A. Khamene, M. Callstrom, and N. Navab, "Automatic CT-ultrasound Registration for Diagnostic Imaging and Image-guided Intervention," *Med. Image Anal.*, vol. 12, no. 5, pp. 577 – 585, 2008.

[25] A. Mastmeyer, T. Hecht, D. Fortmeier, and H. Handels, "Ray-casting Based Evaluation Framework for Haptic Force-Feedback During Percutaneous Transhepatic Catheter Drainage Punctures," *Int. J. Comput. Assist. Radiol. Surg.*, vol. 9, pp. 421–431, 2014.

[26] D. C. Ruspini, K. Kolarov, and O. Khatib, "The Haptic Display of Complex Graphical Environments," *Proc. ACM SIGGRAPH 97*, pp. 345–352, 1997.

[27] A. M. Okamura, C. Simone, and M. D. O'Leary, "Force Modeling for Needle Insertion into Soft Tissue," *IEEE Trans. Biomed. Eng.*, vol. 51, pp. 1707–1716, Oct. 2004.

[28] V. Hayward and B. Armstrong, "A New Computational Model of Friction Applied to Haptic Rendering," *Experimental Robotics VI*, pp. 404–412, 2000.

[29] K. Engel, M. Hadwiger, J. M. Kniss, A. E. Lefohn, C. R. Salama, and D. Weiskopf, *Real-time Volume Graphics*. A K Peters, 2006.

[30] D. Fortmeier, A. Mastmeyer, and H. Handels, "Image-based Soft Tissue Deformation Algorithms for Real-time Simulation of Liver Puncture," *Curr. Med. Imaging. Rev.*, vol. 9, no. 2, pp. 154–165, 2013.

[31] S. F. Gibson, "3D Chainmail: A Fast Algorithm for Deforming Volumetric Objects," in *Proc. Inter. 3D Graph.*, pp. 149–154, ACM, 1997.

[32] F. Rössler, T. Wolff, and T. Ertl, "Direct GPU-based Volume Deformation," in *Proc. Curac 2008*, pp. 65–68, 2008.

[33] D. Fortmeier, A. Mastmeyer, and H. Handels, "Image-based Palpation Simulation with Soft Tissue Deformations using ChainMail on the GPU," in *German Conference on Medical Image Computing (BVM 2013)* (H.-P. Meinzer, T. M. Deserno, H. Handels, and T. Tolxdorff, eds.), pp. 140–145, Heidelberg: Springer Verlag, Berlin, 2013.

[34] E. Haber and J. Modersitzki, "A Multilevel Method for Image Registration," *SIAM J. Sci. Comput.*, vol. 27, no. 5, pp. 1594–1607, 2006.

[35] J. Ashburner, "A Fast Diffeomorphic Image Registration Algorithm," *Neuroimage*, vol. 38, no. 1, pp. 95–113, 2007.

[36] C. Dick, J. Georgii, and R. Westermann, "A Real-time Multigrid Finite Hexahedra Method for Elasticity Simulation using CUDA," *Simul. Model. Prac. Theo.*, vol. 19, no. 2, pp. 801–816, 2011.

[37] D. B. Russakoff, T. Rohlfing, K. Mori, D. Rueckert, A. Ho, J. R. Adler Jr, and C. R. Maurer Jr, "Fast Generation of Digitally Reconstructed Radiographs using Attenuation Fields with Application to 2D-3D Image Registration," *IEEE Trans. Med. Imag.*, vol. 24, pp. 1441–54, Nov. 2005.

[38] G. Sherouse, K. Novins, and E. Chaney, "Computation of Digitally Reconstructed Radiographs for Use in Radiotherapy Treatment Design," *Int. J. Rad. Onc. Biol. Phys.*, no. July 1989, pp. 651–658, 1990.

[39] B. Itkowitz, J. Handley, and W. Zhu, "The OpenHaptics Toolkit: A Library for Adding 3D Touch Navigation and Haptics to Graphics Applications," in *Eurohaptics Conference, 2005 and Symposium on Haptic Interfaces for Virtual Environment and Teleoperator Systems, 2005. World Haptics 2005. First Joint*, pp. 590–591, IEEE, 2005.

[40] R. Likert, "A Technique for the Measurement of Attitudes," *Arch. Psych.*, vol. 140, 1932.

[41] J. Ehrhardt, R. Werner, A. Schmidt-Richberg, and H. Handels, "Statistical Modeling of 4D Respiratory Lung Motion Using Diffeomorphic Image Registration.," *IEEE Trans. Med. Imag.*, vol. 30, pp. 251–265, Sept. 2011.

[42] U. Schneider, E. Pedroni, and A. Lomax, "The Calibration of CT Hounsfield Units for Radiotherapy Treatment Planning," *Phys. Med. Biol.*, vol. 41, no. 1, p. 111, 1996.

[43] J. Bushberg, J. Seibert, E. Leidholdt, and J. Boone, *The Essential Physics of Medical Imaging*. Wolters Kluwer Health, 2011.

[44] K. Perlin, "Improving Noise," *ACM Trans. Graph.*, vol. 21, pp. 681–682, July 2002.

Direct Visuo-Haptic 4D Volume Rendering using Respiratory Motion Models

Dirk Fortmeier, Student Member, IEEE, Matthias Wilms, Andre Mastmeyer, Heinz Handels, Member, IEEE
This work is supported by the German Research Foundation (DFG, HA 2355/11-2)

Abstract

This article presents methods for direct visuo-haptic 4D volume rendering of virtual patient models under respiratory motion. Breathing models are computed based on patient-specific 4D CT image data sequences. Virtual patient models are visualized in real-time by ray casting based rendering of a reference CT image warped by a time-variant displacement field, which is computed using the motion models at run-time. Furthermore, haptic interaction with the animated virtual patient models is provided by using the displacements computed at high rendering rates to translate the position of the haptic device into the space of the reference CT image. This concept is applied to virtual palpation and the haptic simulation of insertion of a virtual bendable needle. To this aim, different motion models that are applicable in real-time are presented and the methods are integrated into a needle puncture training simulation framework, which can be used for simulated biopsy or vessel puncture in the liver. To confirm real-time applicability, a performance analysis of the resulting framework is given. It is shown that the presented methods achieve mean update rates around 2000 Hz for haptic simulation and interactive frame rates for volume rendering and thus are well suited for visuo-haptic rendering of virtual patients under respiratory motion.
Keywords: Visuo-haptics, Volume Rendering, Breathing motion, Needle insertion simulation

1 Introduction

Visuo-haptic simulation of needle insertion is an active field of research. Its aim is to provide a virtual environment in which a surgeon can train an intervention without harming real patients or relying on costly and non-reusable tissue phantoms. Scenarios that are often simulated are insertions of needles into the liver [1, 2, 3] and the contained vessels, into blood vessels for anesthetization or catheter placement [4, 5] or prostate brachytherapy [6, 7].

To provide such a simulation, different components are needed. The core problem is to provide a realistic model of a patient and display this model in a convincing and immersive virtual environment. For this, methods for visual rendering as well as methods for the interaction with the virtual patient model are needed. The latter generally is carried out using a haptic input device that enables the user to steer virtual tools and receive realistic force-feedback simulated by a haptic algorithm.

The behavior of needles inserted in the abdominal region can be highly influenced by respiration-induced organ motion. For instance, breathing influences and displaces especially the shape of parts of the liver that are close to the diaphragm. The displacement of the diaphragm close to the liver can reach up to 5 cm between full inspiration and full expiration [8]. Other organs as for instance the gall bladder or intestines are affected in the same way. For some needle intervention techniques, flexible needles are used that bend under the influence of the deformed surrounding tissue. In contrast, stiff needles influence the deformation of surrounding tissues and the breathing causes tilting of the needle outside of the patient's body. Both effects have to be included in a realistic simulation of needle insertion.

Real-time simulation of breathing motion for the lung has been performed by [9] for visualization purposes in an augmented reality framework. A model for the motion of abdominal organs is presented in [10], which is fast to compute for organ surfaces and was suggested to support radiotherapy by providing a real-time capable prediction of tumor motion based on depth imaging of the patients skin. In [1, 11], visuo-haptic simulation of respiratory motion of a virtual patient model was presented for liver biopsy and methods for parameter estimation for this simulation are given in [12, 13]. Another visuo-haptic simulation approach is proposed in [2], where the motion of the liver was integrated in an ultrasound simulation. Both approaches are limited to a simplified model of respiratory motion based on a sinusoidal displacement and do not incorporate breathing effects in the modeling of haptic forces. Similarly, [14] presents a simplified breathing model based on a sinusoidal geometric transformations in a virtual reality application for the visual simulation of angiography without haptic interaction.

Visualization of medical imaging data in visuo-haptic environments is typically performed by indirect volume rendering, i.e. classical rasterization of polygonal surface models of isosurfaces extracted from 3D image data. Another option is direct volume rendering, for which a thorough overview of methods and implementation is given in [15]. This method is especially suited for static volume data as for example used in [2]. To introduce deformations of the rendered volume images, methods for direct rendering using unstructured meshes have been given by [16, 17] and more recently by [18] and [19]. As for computation of soft tissue behavior, mesh based approaches come with different advantages as reduced computational load and drawbacks as a complicated mesh generation procedure. Instead of using a mesh based approach, in this work, we adapt the basic idea to use deformed rays during ray casting [20], and use respiratory motion models to visualize a globally deformed 3D CT image under breathing motion.

A central part of this work is about the insertion of needles into soft tissue. Using the finite element method, resulting deformations of tissue and interacting needle have been presented i.a. in [6, 21, 22, 23] and [24]. Also, haptic simulation of bending needles using the angular spring method was used in [25, 26], which is supposed to be an accurate simplification and is fast to compute. Alternatives to this concept are elastic rod methods [27, 28], as for instance used in [6].

Nowadays, spatio-temporal 4D CT image data acquired during free breathing [29] can be used to analyze the patient-specific motion of internal structures caused by respiration to improve radiation therapy of tumors in the thorax and abdomen. Recently in this context, a lot of effort has been put into the development of non-linear image registration techniques that enable a precise estimation of respiratory motion based on 4D image data. Furthermore, the development of subsequent respiratory motion analysis and modeling approaches [30] have been adressed. In this work, those techniques are employed to enable highly realistic rendering of virtual patient models under respiratory motion.

This work builds on a visuo-haptic framework [3] and methods from image registration and modeling of respiratory motion [31, 32]. It contributes a novel real-time capable method to display a virtual patient model under the influence of breathing motion and integrates the breathing motion into haptic algorithms. It introduces realistic models that include natural variations of the breathing motion. The key idea is to use a time varying displacement field describing the breathing motion to modify the sampling positions during ray casting for direct volume rendering and use the displacement field to translate the haptic device position into a reference space. In comparison to existing methods, our visuo-haptic rendering approach enables direct volume rendering, haptics, realistic models of complex local breathing and models based on actual patient data in a single framework. The article is divided into three main parts: First, methods for interactive visual and haptic rendering of a breathing patient are introduced. These are based on a model of respiration that is represented by a displacement field function, which is detailed in the second section. In the third part, the methods are demonstrated and evaluated based on an prototypical implementation of a needle insertion intervention.

2 Visuo-haptic Rendering

A 4D CT data set usually consists of a sequence of 3D CT images, which represent the patient's anatomy at different phases of a single breathing cycle. Therefore, a direct approach of using a 4D CT data set for a visuo-haptic simulation would be to periodically step through the sequence of CT images. However, this has major drawbacks: When only rendering a single cycle of images (a single 4D CT data set), no inter-cycle variations of the breathing motion (e.g., breathing depth) can be represented. Additionally, since the number of images is usually very low (usually 7-14 phases are reconstructed) compared to the length of a breathing cycle (~2-7s), it is not possible to provide a frame rate of at least 24 Hz for the visualization as needed by a human observer to get the impression of a fluid animation. The situation is even more delicate for haptic rendering, where an update rate of at least 1000 Hz is required. These requirements motivate new methods that can quickly compute a visual and haptic representation for any given time point in between the time points of the acquired image sequence.

The utilized simulation framework is based on direct visuo-haptic rendering, i.e. a volumetric voxel image is used for visual and haptic rendering of a virtual patient. Without a motion model, the virtual patient model is static. In the following, the associated space to this state will be called the reference space. Using a motion model and the voxel image associated to the reference space for rendering is a key idea of our methods. In this chapter, a function $u(\mathbf{X}, t) : \Omega \rightarrow \mathbb{R}^3 (\Omega \subset \mathbb{R}^3)$ that yields a displacement for any given point $\mathbf{X} \in \Omega$ in the image domain and for any simulation time point $t \in \mathbb{R}$ is used. This represents a mapping of each position $\mathbf{X}$ in the reference space to the corresponding point $\mathbf{x}$ in space and time of the virtual world space as shown in Fig. 1. In general, this function is required to be bijective, i.e. an inverse function $u^{-1}(\mathbf{x}, t)$ exists. A simple approxiation of this function to represent breathing motion would be a sinusoidal displacement $u(\mathbf{X}, t) = (0, a \cdot \sin(t), 0)^\top$, where a is the maximal amplitude in mm. This of course does not suffice to represent the complex local motion of organs under respiratory breathing in detail. An in-depth presentation of other possible motion models follows in section 3.

2.1 Visual Rendering using Motion Fields

Visual rendering of the patient image data deformed by breathing motion is based on a ray casting volume rendering method [15] with non-linear rays, for example used in [20] where ray deflectors are used to locally bend the rendering space. We build on this basic

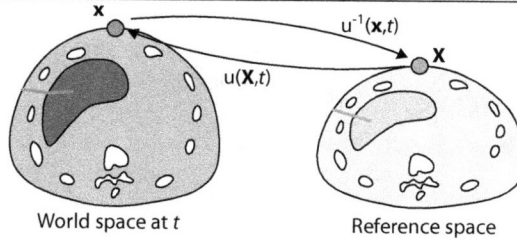

Figure 1: Schematic axial slice of a virtual patient model. For each point in the world space, positions $\mathbf{x}$ can be mapped to $\mathbf{X}$ in the static reference space and vice versa. Here, this is demonstrated for a point on the surface of the breathing patient and points along a needle path.

idea and adapt it so each ray that is cast through the image volume can be considered to be warped by a function representing the breathing motion. Here, we perform the warping as follows. For each sample position $\mathbf{x}$ on a viewing ray, the position $\mathbf{X} = \mathbf{x} + u^{-1}(\mathbf{x}, t)$ in reference space could be computed directly with the inverse displacement $u^{-1}(\mathbf{x}, t)$, which is not available for the motion models used. To solve this problem, we combine ray casting and computation of the inverse displacement on the fly: Starting from the camera position, the sample position $\mathbf{x}$ in the world space and the corresponding position along the warped viewing ray $\mathbf{X}$ are iteratively updated as

$$\mathbf{x}^+ = \mathbf{x} + \mathbf{d} \tag{1}$$
$$\mathbf{X}^+ = \mathbf{x}^+ - u(\mathbf{X} + \mathbf{d}, t) \tag{2}$$

while sampling along the viewing ray with ray direction vector $\mathbf{d}$ and sample distance $\|\mathbf{d}\|$. This is inspired by the fixed-point inversion approach from [33] and needs further explanation. In [33], it is shown that for an invertible displacement field, it is possible to compute the inverse by applying an iterative algorithm for each element of the field. In practice, we use Eq. (6) from [33] and substitute the deformation fields by the corresponding terms including the displacements, giving the sequence $\mathbf{X}_n = \mathbf{x} - u(\mathbf{X}_{n-1})$. This corresponds to our Eq. 2 for a given and fixed location $\mathbf{x}^+$. Instead of applying this algorithm several times for the same position (the authors state that normally a number smaller ten is sufficient), it is evaluated once for each sampling position and the value from the previous sampling point is used as an initial solution.

After trilinear interpolation of the volumetric reference image data at $\mathbf{x}^+$, application of a transfer function follows for each sampling step. Label data defined in the reference space are used for tagged volume rendering of a deformed volume in the same fashion by using nearest neighbor interpolation. In the same way, ray casting based X-ray simulation and ultrasound imaging simulation is performed. Multiplanar reformations (MPRs) are generated by applying the fixed-point algorithm with several iterations per point to compute the inverse at each sampling position without ray traversal.

In our framework, it is possible to only use direct volume rendering, but nevertheless the methods are applicable to surface based rendering as well and thus also interesting for fully surface based simulation frameworks. Using the function $u(\mathbf{X}, t)$, vertices of polygonal surface models can be displaced and used to render surface models of organs.

2.2 Haptic Rendering for Virtual Palpation and Ultrasound Probing

Haptic rendering of virtual palpation and ultrasound probing is similar to our previous approaches [34]: Multiple virtual contact nodes are placed on the surface of the virtual

Figure 2: Left: Needle path discretized by nodes $\mathbf{p}_i$, only the tip node is adjusted during insertion. Right: Nodes $\mathbf{n}_j$ representing the discretized needle are connected to proxies (red) by springs. These proxies are displaced by the breathing motion (blue).

tools and each of the positions $\mathbf{x}$ representing a node is connected to a virtual proxy position $\mathbf{p}$ by a spring to calculate friction forces. Structure repulsion forces are calculated by non-linear functions relating palpation depth to forces. To introduce breathing motion into the haptics computation, the device position is transformed from the world space to the reference space by the motion model.

To achieve this, again the inversion scheme of [33] is applied iteratively on the haptic device position $\mathbf{x}$, giving the position in reference space as $\mathbf{X}^+ = \mathbf{x} - u(\mathbf{X}, t)$ in each haptic rendering frame. Haptic force and torque computation then takes place in the reference space. Computing the absolute orientation [35] for the set of proxy positions and the set of proxy positions displaced by $u(\mathbf{x}, t)$ gives a rotational transformation that can be used to translate the resulting force back to the world space. In practice, we found the angle of the rotation to be less than $5°$ and thus it might be neglected.

To visualize local deformations at the palpation site, the methods presented in [3] resp. [36] for the needle are applied. Notice, that the resulting deformations and their visualization do not affect the force output of the haptic algorithms.

2.3 Haptic Rendering of Needle Insertion

For the modeling of needle insertion into soft tissue, several methods exist. Here, we build on the needle insertion algorithm presented in [3] and adapt it to enable curved insertion paths. In this method, the soft tissue behavior is modeled by linear springs, so no tetrahedral mesh is needed as for example in [24].

During needle insertion, the needle algorithm uses two sets of nodes to compute haptic forces based on breathing motion (Fig. 2) and provide a visualization of the bended needle:

- $P = \{\mathbf{p}_i \in \mathbb{R}^3\}_{1 \le i \le l}$: nodes representing the path of the needle during insertion
- $N = \{\mathbf{n}_j \in \mathbb{R}^3\}_{1 \le j \le m}$: nodes representing the complete discretized needle

New path nodes are placed along the insertion path in the reference space. Thus, the number of these nodes varies:

- $|P| = 0$: needle is outside the body,
- $|P| = 1$: needle tip is on the skin surface of the patient,
- $|P| \ge 2$: needle is inside the patient.

The nodes are equidistantly distributed along the insertion path and their position does not change during insertion except for the tip node, which is explained later. In Alg. 1, an overview of the haptic algorithm is given.

At first, the direction of the needle tip $\mathbf{d}_l$ in the reference space is computed (`getTipOrientInRefSpace` by

$$\mathbf{R} = \begin{bmatrix} u(\mathbf{p}_l + (1,0,0)^\top, t)^\top - u(\mathbf{p}_l, t)^\top \\ u(\mathbf{p}_l + (0,1,0)^\top, t)^\top - u(\mathbf{p}_l, t)^\top \\ u(\mathbf{p}_l + (0,0,1)^\top, t)^\top - u(\mathbf{p}_l, t)^\top \end{bmatrix}^\top + \mathbf{I} \qquad (3)$$

Alg. 1 In each iteration of the haptic loop, the algorithm computes new node positions P^+ and N^+ as well as the haptic force $\mathbf{f}$ and torque $\mathbf{t}$.

1: **input:** $\mathbf{x} \leftarrow$ haptic device position
2: **input:** $\mathbf{X} \leftarrow$ old device position in reference space
3: **input:** $\mathbf{q} \leftarrow$ haptic device orientation
4: **input:** $P \leftarrow$ set of path nodes from prev. step
5: **input:** $N \leftarrow$ set of needle nodes from prev. step
6:    $\mathbf{d}_l \leftarrow$ `getTipOrientInRefSpace`(P, N)
7:    $\mathbf{X}^+ \leftarrow \mathbf{x} + u(\mathbf{X}, \mathrm{t})$
8:    $P^+ \leftarrow$ `updatePathNodes`$(P, \mathbf{X}^+, \mathbf{d}_l)$
9: **if** ($|P^+| = 0$) **then**
10:      $N^+ \leftarrow$ `simpleNNodePlacement`$(\mathbf{x}, \mathbf{q})$
11:      $\mathbf{f} \leftarrow 0$, $\mathbf{t} \leftarrow 0$
12: **else**
13:      $N^+ \leftarrow$ `updateNNodes`$(P^+, N, \mathbf{x}, \mathbf{q})$
14:      $\mathbf{f} \leftarrow$ `computeForces`$(P^+, N^+, \mathbf{x}, \mathbf{X}^+)$
15:      $\mathbf{t} \leftarrow$ `computeTorque`$(P^+, N^+, \mathbf{x}, \mathbf{X}^+)$
16: **end if**
17: **return** $\{N^+, P^+, \mathbf{X}^+, \mathbf{f}, \mathbf{t}\}$

---

and then $\mathbf{d}_l = \mathbf{R}^{-1}\mathbf{r}_m / \|\mathbf{R}^{-1}\mathbf{r}_m\|$ with $\mathbf{r}_m$ being the needle tip node's direction vector. Together with the position of the haptic device tip in the reference space $\mathbf{X}$, this is used to update the set of path nodes (`updatePathNodes`). In case the needle is outside the patient's body, P remains empty. On first contact with skin, a node is placed at the contact position. In case the needle has entered the patient's body, a chain of nodes is placed as follows: The tip node $\mathbf{p}_l$ moves in direction $\mathbf{d}_l$ in case $\mathbf{X}$ moves forward relatively to its position from the previous iteration of the algorithm or otherwise towards the node behind the tip. If the distance $\Delta l = \|\mathbf{p}_{l-1} - \mathbf{p}_l\|$ becomes smaller than $0.5 \cdot \Delta p$ with Δp being the fixed spacing between path nodes, $\mathbf{p}_{l-1}$ is removed from the set. In case $\Delta l > 1.5 \cdot \Delta p$, a new node is placed on the line between the nodes in a way that its distance to $\mathbf{p}_{l-1}$ is Δp. For the tip node and newly placed nodes, the material properties stiffness k_j, cutting stiffness coefficients $a_{1,j}$ and $a_{2,j}$, cutting force f_j^{cut} and maximal friction force R_j are obtained for the position of the node via transfer functions relating CT image data to material properties or, if available, by using a labeling mask. To simulate a cutting force, forward movement of the path tip node is prohibited as long as the spring force connecting device position and the path tip node in direction of the needle is below the cutting force threshold:

$$a_{2,l}\Delta d^2 + a_{1,l}\Delta d < f_l^{\mathrm{cut}} \tag{4}$$

with $\Delta d = (\mathbf{X} - \mathbf{p}_l) \cdot \mathbf{d}_l$ being the distance between device position and path tip node. For $a_{2,l} \neq 0$, non-linear cutting forces as measured for example in [37] can be produced. Given these considerations, thus the path tip node is updated by

$$\mathbf{p}_l^+ = \mathbf{p}_l + \mathbf{d}_l \cdot \begin{cases} \Delta d & \text{if } \Delta d \leq 0 \\ 0 & \text{else if Eq. 4 holds} \\ \Delta d + \gamma_1 - \sqrt{\gamma_1^2 + \gamma_2} & \text{else if } a_{2,l} > 0 \\ \Delta d - \gamma_2 & \text{else} \end{cases}$$

with $\gamma_1 = \frac{1}{2}\frac{a_{1,l}}{a_{2,l}}$ and $\gamma_2 = \frac{f_l^{\mathrm{cut}}}{a_{2,l}}$.

No. Nodes	Force [N]	Deflec. [mm]	Diff. [mm]
15	0.5	8.6	-3.8
	1.0	17.1	-8.8
25	0.5	13.2	0.7
	1.0	25.8	-0.2
50	0.5	29.2	16.7
	1.0	53.2	27.2

Table 1: Simulated deflection of the needle tip and difference to measurements for a 16 gauge needle. The stiffness parameter has been tuned for 25 nodes.

As long as the needle is not in contact with the skin, no forces have to be computed and no physical needle model has to be employed to determine the needle node positions. Instead, in this case these are placed along the ray defined by haptic device position $\mathbf{x}$ and orientation quaternion $\mathbf{q}$ (simpleNNodePlacement).

Otherwise, the positions of the needle nodes N are computed by a discretized needle model implemented using the Bullet Physics library [38], which uses a Projected Gauss-Seidel solver. Each needle node is represented by a single rigid body and connected to its successor by a ball and socket joint and a rotational spring. The needle is forced to comply to the insertion path in the following way. Each pair of path and needle nodes representing a part of the needle that is inside the tissue is connected by a spring using the material stiffness k_j of the path node. Except for the tip node, the spring force is projected onto the plane perpendicular to the needle tangent at the node.

The needle is discretized by 25 elements, which is a trade-off between computation time and accuracy. Furthermore, the Bullet based physics simulation of the needle is not run only once per haptic simulation frame, but several times with a fixed time step of 1 ms to faster reach a static state. The actual number of iterations depends on the remaining available processing time of the haptic frame.

We calibrated the stiffness for a 16 gauge needle with a length of 150 mm: To this aim, we first measured the deflection caused by a lateral force at the tip of a needle fixed at the base for 0.5 N and 1.0 N resp., which we found to be 12.5 mm resp. 26.0 mm. Then the stiffness parameter for the rotational spring were adjusted to match this measurements in the simulation using 25 nodes. For a different number of elements, the resulting simulated deflection differ, see Tab. 1. In terms of convergence, we found that in the calibration setup, the mean node movement converges to a value below 10^{-5} mm after roughly 1200 iterations.

An additional spring is used to connect the base node position $\mathbf{n}_1$ of the needle with a position $\mathbf{v}$ to induce bending to the needle in case the user angulates the haptic device handle. This position is depending on the insertion point of the needle in world space, which is $\mathbf{s} = \mathbf{p}_1 + u(\mathbf{p}_1)$. Given this surface point, the position that is used for the spring is $\mathbf{v} = \mathbf{s} - \tilde{l}\mathbf{q}_z$. Here, $\tilde{l}$ is the length of the needle part that is still outside the tissue. The direction vector of the haptic device $\mathbf{q}_z$ is computed from the haptic device orientation quaternion $\mathbf{q}$ by using the quaternion rotation operator applied to the pure quaternion pointing in z direction $\mathbf{q}_z = \mathbf{q} \cdot (0, 0, 1)^\top \cdot \mathbf{q}^{-1}$.

Now, with a new needle path $\mathbf{P}$ and needle configuration, the forces and torques that will be displayed by the haptic device are computed. The force is the sum of:

1. A resistance force to cutting in needle direction at the tip

$$\mathbf{f}_{\text{cut}} = -(a_{2,l}\Delta d^2 + a_{1,l}\Delta d)\mathbf{d}_l \tag{5}$$

2. Friction force along the needle shaft. For each path node, an offset $\Delta x_i \in \mathbb{R}$ is updated in each iteration:

$$\Delta x_i^+ = \begin{cases} \Delta x_i + \Delta x & \text{if } |\Delta x_i + \Delta x| < \frac{R_i}{k_i} \\ \frac{R_i}{k_i}\text{sgn}(\Delta x_i + \Delta x) \end{cases} \quad (6)$$

with Δx being the relative movement of the haptic device in insertion direction. From these offsets, the total friction force is computed as

$$\mathbf{f}_{\text{fric}} = \sum_{2 \leq i \leq l} k_i \frac{\|\mathbf{p}_i - \mathbf{p}_{i-1}\|}{\Delta p} \Delta x_i \quad (7)$$

For larger numbers of path nodes n and high values of k_i this can act like a very stiff spring. To prevent unstabilities, i.e. overshooting associated to mass-spring systems with large stiffness, the change of the friction force is limited in each haptic frame by a fixed value.

3. A base force that results from the offset of haptic device position and the computed needle base projection onto the plane perpendicular to the insertion vector at the beginning of the needle path:

$$\mathbf{f}_{\text{base}} = \kappa \cdot [(\mathbf{n}_1 - \mathbf{x}) - (\mathbf{n}_1 - \mathbf{x}) \cdot \mathbf{d}_1] \quad (8)$$

with κ being the stiffness of a spring, which couples the virtual needle base and device position.

Torque is computed by using a rotational spring between the haptic device orientation and the tangential direction of the simulated needle at the air and tissue interface. Rotational forces around the needle z-axis are set to zero.

3 4D Motion Models

The motion model function $u(\mathbf{X}, t)$ was described as being a time varying function without further specification. This section will present different approaches to model and implement respiratory motion. We utilize existing methods from image registration and motion modeling of the lung (mainly [31, 32]) and introduce how these can be used in a real-time visuo-haptic liver puncture simulation with varying breathing cycles.

Our visuo-haptic simulation of a breathing virtual patient is based on displacement fields estimated from a 4D CT data set. This data set consists of a sequence of n 3D CT images $I_{j \in \{1,...,n\}} : \Omega \to \mathbb{R}$ and represents a single respiratory cycle from maximum inspiration over expiration back to total inspiration. In the following, the states of this cycle are labeled as end inspiration (EI), mid inspiration (MI), end expiration (EE) and mid expiration (ME). For each phase j from the sequence, a non-linear transformation $\varphi_j : \Omega \to \Omega$ exists, which describes the respiratory motion between an arbitrary reference phase and phase j. Here, this phase corresponds to the static state of the virtual patient. These transformations can be represented by $\varphi_j = id + u_j$ with displacement fields $u_j : \Omega \to \mathbb{R}^3$ that assign a displacement vector to each voxel. Estimation of respiratory motion based on 4D CT image data by non-linear image registration techniques has been a very active area of research in recent years. However, most publications on this topic deal with the special case of lung motion estimation [39, 40, 41]. In contrast, the realistic visuo-haptic simulation of a breathing patient requires an estimation of breathing-induced motion of all thoracic and abdominal structures displayed to the user. Estimating the motion of multiple structures is a challenging problem, as most registration approaches inherently assume the underlying

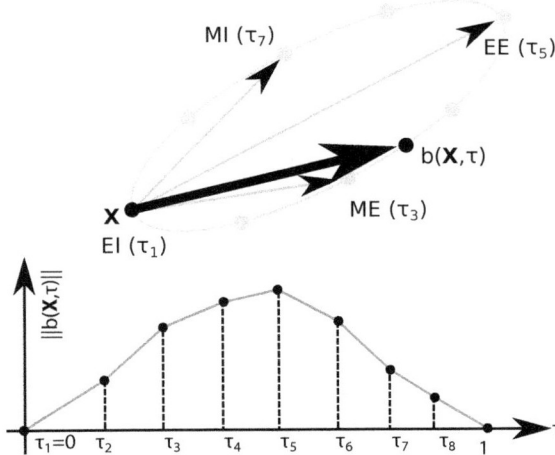

Figure 3: Upper: Plot of displacement for a fixed $\mathbf{x}$ during the cycle. Lower: Magnitude of the displacement $\|b(\mathbf{X}, \tau)\|$ for normalized cycle time τ. Here, $n = 8$ key frames placed at $\tau_{i=1..8}$ are used. Between two displacements given by adjacent key frames, interpolation takes place.

motion to be smooth. This assumption is obviously wrong at interfaces of structures sliding along each other (e.g., lung/liver and its surrounding tissue [31]). We, therefore, employ the registration approach proposed by Schmidt-Richberg et al. [31], which is able to handle those discontinuities.

As transformations between the reference image and each phase j are computed independently, noise or image artifacts can result in a temporally inconsistent motion estimation. Temporal inconsistencies can lead to visible motion artifacts during simulation and we, therefore, perform a PCA-based filtering of the estimated displacement fields to remove them, which is a common approach in respiratory motion modelling [42].

For the transformation from any phase j to the reference phase, the inverse of u_j is needed, which we prevent by inversion during run-time. Also, it is necessary to provide a transformation between the phases for each point in time. Modeling and a memory conserving implementation of this function $u(\mathbf{X}, t)$ is crucial. Theoretically, using inversion of the displacement fields or diffeomorphic registration, inverse displacement fields are available, but no satisfying inverse motion model could be build based on the inverse fields directly. In the following, different approaches for modeling the function are represented: The first one is a key frame based approach, in which all u_j are considered to be key frames in a sequence; in between two key frames, $u(\mathbf{X}, t)$ is computed by linear interpolation of adjacent u_j and u_{j+1}. The second approach is similar to the first, but also introduces extrapolation of out-of-sample predictions, i.e. states that are not captured in the 4D data. A third approach relies on the modeling of the breathing motion driven by a so-called surrogate signal.

3.1 Full Cycle Key Frame Approach

Similar to computer animation methods, each displacement field u_j in the sequence of images I_j is considered to be a key frame, and in between key frames, interpolation of the displacement fields takes place. All key frames are placed on a normalized motion cycle time line at $\tau_j \in [0, 1)$, as shown in Fig. 3. This yields a displacement $u(\mathbf{X}, t) = b(\mathbf{X}, \tau)$ at position $\mathbf{X}$ in reference space and the current normalized time $\tau \in [0, 1)$ using adjacent u_i and u_{i+1}, which are interpolated linearly based on adjacent τ_i and τ_{i+1}:

(a) Using the full breathing cycle (EI->EE->EI)

(b) Using only one half cycle (EI->EE)

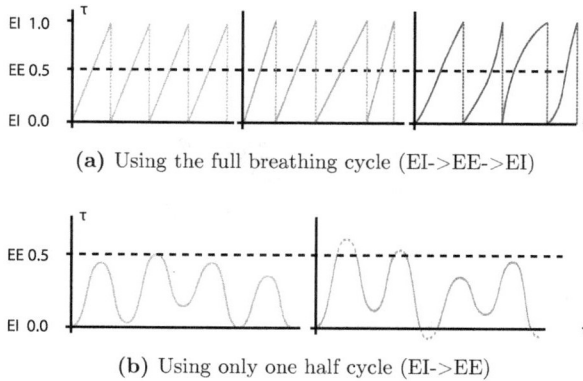

Figure 4: Functions for cycling through the image sequence (EI = end of inspiration, EE = end of expiration).

$$b(\mathbf{X}, \tau) = (1 - \alpha(\tau))u_i(\mathbf{X}) + \alpha(\tau)u_{i+1}(\mathbf{X}) \tag{9}$$

with $\alpha(\tau) = \frac{\tau - \tau_i}{\tau_{i+1} - \tau_i}$.

During the simulation, the value of τ is changed to run through the sequence. As depicted in Fig. 4a, several functions $\tau = f(t) : \mathbb{R} \to [0, 1)$ could be applied: (1) The obvious choice is to cycle through the sequence by a sawtooth shaped function with fixed period. (2) This can be augmented by introducing randomness to change the length of each period, but keeping $f'(t) = \alpha$ constant. (3) Furthermore, randomness can be introduced by varying $f'(t)$ during the cycle. This randomness introduces variations of the breathing to represent the natural variation of breathing.

The used number of key frames should reflect the variations and non-linearities in the breathing motion of the patient. At least, four key frames that correspond EI, ME, EE and MI are needed for a full cycle including hysteresis. The maximum number is limited by the available memory of the graphics hardware and the resolution of the displacement fields. We found that with high resolution displacement fields, the resulting amount of memory easily exceeds the available space when using the full sequence of available phases.

3.2 Half Cycle Key Frame Approach

The major disadvantage of the full cycle model is that only a single breathing cycle can be looped. The cycle length and the temporal distance between adjacent key frames can be varied, but maximum inspiration and expiration is fixed to the available maximum and minimum state captured in the 4D CT image sequence, limiting the approach to in-sample predictions. Since maximum inspiration and expiration varies naturally with each cycle, it is desirable to model this aspect.

To also include out-of-sample predictions, only half of the phases (e.g. only EI->ME->EE) can be used, which we call a half cycle approach. Oscillating between maximum expiration and maximum inspiration from the full cycle is used and beyond EI or EE, extrapolation takes place. Extrapolation is not possible with the full cycle approach, since all the key frames form a closed loop. The upper part of Fig. 4b visualizes a function that oscillates τ to produce an oscillation between EI and EE. The lower part represents a function that includes values of τ that do not fit into the range of maximal and minimal inspiration. Using extrapolation, the displacement fields for states beyond maximal and minimal inspiration can be approximated. We do not use adjacent key frames for the extrapolation using Eq. 9, but the key frames associated to maximum and minimum expiration. This gives the following extrapolation expressions for out-of-sample (OOS) predictions:

$$b_{\text{oos}}(\mathbf{X}, \tau) = (1 - \alpha_{\text{oos}}(\tau))u_{\text{EI}}(\mathbf{X}) + \alpha_{\text{oos}}(\tau)u_{\text{EE}}(\mathbf{X}) \tag{10}$$

with $\alpha_{\text{oos}}(\tau) = \frac{\tau - \tau_{\text{EI}}}{\tau_{\text{EE}} - \tau_{\text{EI}}}$.

As drawback of this method, hysteresis, i.e. different paths between EE->EI and EI->EE, is not included in this model.

3.3 Surrogate Signal-based Motion Model

The conceptual limitation of the previous two approaches is that either states beyond minimal and maximal inspiration from the sequence (full cycle approach) or hysteresis cannot be represented (half cycle approach). To overcome these limitation, real surrogate signals are used. These represent patient-specific variations of the breathing, which we consider a valuable contribution to realistic visuo-haptic simulation of respiration. Basically, a surrogate signal can be a 1D signal of the patient's breathing measured by a surrogate, for example a spirometry device or an abdominal belt. It is assumed that a linear correspondence exists between the measured surrogate signal and the actual motion of internal organs of the patient. For 4D CT imaging, surrogate signals are recorded for reconstruction and do not have to be acquired in an extra step.

Here, our surrogate signal-based motion model is used, which has been evaluated for diffeomorphic motion modeling of the lung [32]. Generally, a surrogate signal can be a signal of higher dimension; the aim is to increase accuracy of the resulting model. For instance, a depth image acquired by a time-of-flight camera could be used. We use a dimensionality of $n_{\text{sur}} = 2$ by combining a spirometry signal and its time derivative and denote it by $\hat{\mathbf{z}}(t) = (g(t), g'(t))^T : \mathbb{R} \rightarrow \mathbb{R}^{n_{\text{sur}}}$. This is done to combine the measured value of the spirometry signal with information indicating expiration resp. inspiration and thus enabling modeling of hysteresis.

Using surrogate signals $\mathbf{z}_j$ associated to the sequence of non-linear transformations φ_j, a linear motion model can be learned by multivariate regression under the assumption of a linear correspondence between surrogate signal and respiratory motion. First, the transformations φ_j are reformulated as column vectors $\mathbf{b}_j \in \mathbb{R}^{3m}$ with m being the number of image voxels of I_j. The model then relies on the mean motion vector $\bar{\mathbf{b}}$, a learned system matrix $\mathbf{B} \in \mathbb{R}^{3m \times 2}$ and the surrogate signal $\hat{\mathbf{z}}(t)$:

$$\mathbf{m} = \bar{\mathbf{b}} + \mathbf{B}\hat{\mathbf{z}}(t) \tag{11}$$

for which $\mathbf{B}$ can be estimated by multivariate regression.

With given $\mathbf{B}$, Eq. 11 can be rewritten as the linear combination of three column vectors $\mathbf{a}_{1..3} \in \mathbb{R}^{3m}$

$$\mathbf{m} = \mathbf{a}_1 g(t) + \mathbf{a}_2 g'(t) + \mathbf{a}_3 \tag{12}$$

Reinterpreting the column vectors as functions $a_{1..3} : \mathbb{R}^3 \rightarrow \mathbb{R}^3$ by rearranging the elements into a 3D image structure and using linear interpolation, computation of a single displacement now is defined as

$$u(\mathbf{X}, t) = a_1(\mathbf{X})g(t) + a_2(\mathbf{X})g'(t) + a_3(\mathbf{X}) \tag{13}$$

and can be used in the algorithms for visual and haptic rendering.

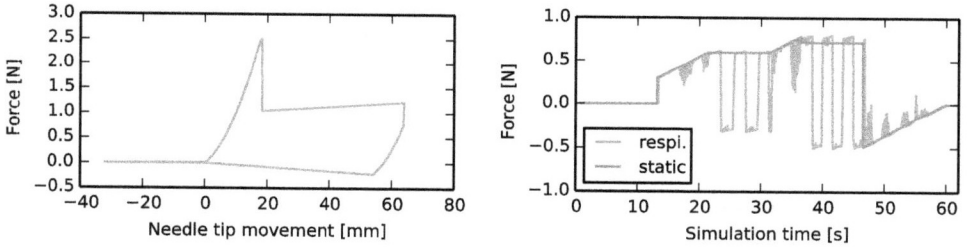

Figure 5: Forces acting on the haptic device in insertion direction for needle insertion along predefined insertion paths: (left) Modeling of measurements given in [37] (right) needle insertion into a virtual patient with and without simulation of respiratory movements.

4 Evaluation & Results

To support the applicability of the proposed methods, we first demonstrate forces computed by the needle insertion algorithm for given parameters. Then, we present the implementation of a demonstration system and give results of the visualization[1]. In the end, a performance analysis of the needle algorithm and the ray casting is presented.

4.1 Needle Force and Parameter Evaluation

Our needle insertion algorithm can model the measurements presented in [37] for ex-vivo needle insertion into bovine liver, see Fig. 5. To achieve this behavior, the parameters $a_1 = 0.048 \frac{N}{mm}$ and $a_2 = 0.0052 \frac{N}{mm^2}$ have been set according to [37] and $f^{cut} = 2.5N$ for the capsule of a virtual liver tissue phantom. Inside the liver, the cutting force has been set to $f^{cut} = 1N$ and friction parameters to $R = 0.025N$ and $k = 0.5 \frac{N}{mm}$.

To reflect our experience with liver puncture in PTCD simulation [3], the parameters were set to $a_1 = 1.2 \frac{N}{mm}$, $a_2 = 0$, $f^{cut} = 0.3N$ and the friction parameters as above. A resulting force plot is given in Fig. 5, for which the needle was steered along a predefined path into the liver of the virtual patient in caudal-crandial direction one time with respiratory motion enabled and one time without it. First, the needle was inserted into the liver over 10 seconds, then it was stopped, followed by an additional insertion further into the liver tissue. After an additional pause, the needle was retracted.

4.2 Demonstration System

In this section, the capabilities of our 4D visuo-haptic rendering framework are demonstrated for a liver puncture scenario[2]. For this purpose, a low-dose 4D CT data set (14 phases, $512 \times 512 \times 460$ voxels) was used to generate a sequence of displacement fields as described in section 3. As the reference phase, maximum inspiration was selected. Surrogate signal data of a spirometry device acquired for 4D reconstruction was available. Using this data, the motion models with different resolutions were created (64^3, 128^3 and 256^3 voxels). Additionally, the reference phase image data was resampled with a resolution of 256^3 voxels. Since this data set is based on low-dose CT data, the contrast of structures inside the liver is very low. For providing a training scenario of liver puncture, we artificially

---

[1]A video sequence is available in the supplementary material.
[2]Remarks on implementation are given in the appendix

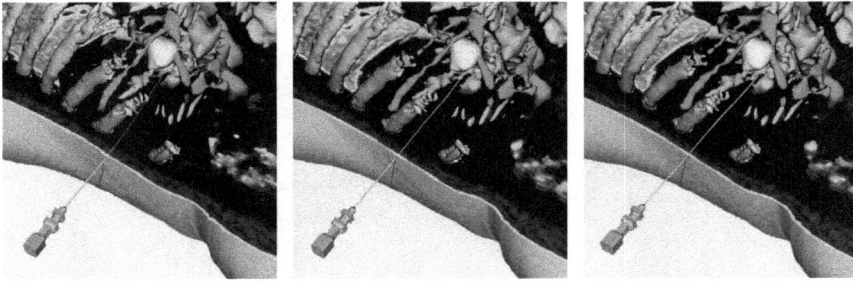

Figure 6: Sequence of mixed surface and volume rendering with surface model of a lesion (yellow), bile ducts (green), liver blood vessels (red) and bony ribs (white).

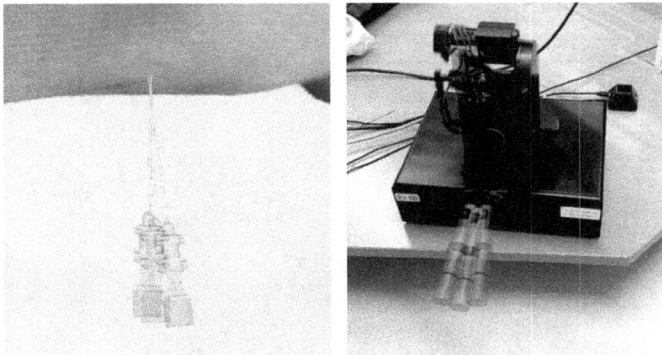

Figure 7: Overlayed image and photo sequence of virtual needle and haptic device handle with movement and rotation induced by breathing motion.

added the structures liver blood vessels, bile ducts and lesion. First, segmentation masks of the three structures were created by a rough registration of a segmentation of a similar patient image with label data and manual refinement of the result. Then, image values in the CT data where adjusted using the masks to represent typical values. Additionally, using the segmentation masks, surface models have been created using the Marching Cubes algorithm [43] followed by surface smoothing and decimation. This was also performed for threshold based segmentations of the patient's skin surface and bone structures. By this means, we are able to analyze the behavior of both ray casting based visualization and surface based visualization and show that our method is also well suited for surface based rendering.

4.3 Visual Results of the Motion Modeling

Fig. 6 shows a combined volume and surface rendering with a needle inserted towards a mock up tumor model. The breathing induced motion of the lung, liver and inside-liver structures can clearly be seen. Bending of the needle is also well visible. Forces resulting from the lever-like behavior of the needle can be clearly perceived at the haptic device handle. Fig. 7 shows the movement of the haptic device handle under free movement in the same scenario.

In Fig. 8, the effect of needle angulation by the user and breathing motion on the needle path is demonstrated. For the first case, the needle was inserted perpendicular to the surface for ca. 10 mm into a virtual tissue phantom without breathing motion. Afterwards the needle was hold, angulated and further insertion took place. This results in a slightly

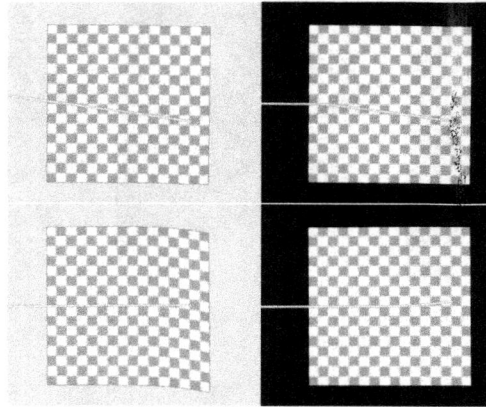

Figure 8: Clipped tissue phantom with effect of needle angulation during needle insertion (upper) and effect of breathing induced deformation of tissue at the needle tip on the needle path (lower). Left side: world space. Right side: reference space.

Figure 9: Visualization of the influence of a palpating finger with fixed position on the breathing patient model.

bended needle. For the second case, the needle has been inserted into the phantom under displacement of parts of the phantom. The needle remains nearly without bending, but a non-linear needle path in reference space can be perceived.

To demonstrate the rendering of local deformations combined with the breathing induced global displacement, Fig. 9 shows a sequence with a virtual finger that is fixed to a position close to the patient model's skin surface.

Resulting displacement fields are visualized using color coding of the projected direction in Fig. 10. Also, Fig. 11 presents different settings of the inversion scheme for a fixed breathing phase. For ray casting, it can be seen that using only a single iteration and not including the result from previous sampling points does not create a smooth rendering. With it, a smooth rendering is created and with twice the number of sampling points, only interpolation rendering artifacts vanish without affecting the overall result in a noticeable way. For the computation of a slice using the fixed point scheme, it is shown that a single iteration does not suffice, but 5 iterations is visually nearly indistinguishable from the result given by 50 iterations.

Fig. 12 shows the drawback of using low resolution displacement fields; in regions where discontinuities in the displacement fields are present, i.e. at the sliding lung boundary, smearing artifacts arise. The artifacts are present between lung and ribs, which is not a punctured region, making them not relevant for the haptic simulation.

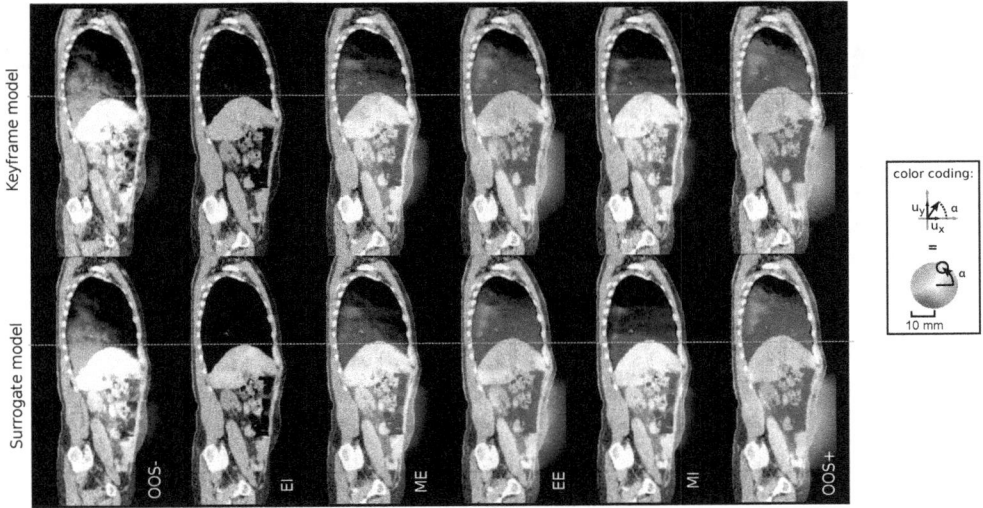

Figure 10: Resampled sagittal slices of the virtual patient CT data during the breathing sequence EI->ME->EE->MI and out-of-sample (OOS) predictions for both the key frame and the surrogate model. The direction of the displacements projected onto the slice are color code by the HSV color wheel, amplitude is indicated by opacity of the overlay (total opaqueness corresponds to 10 mm).

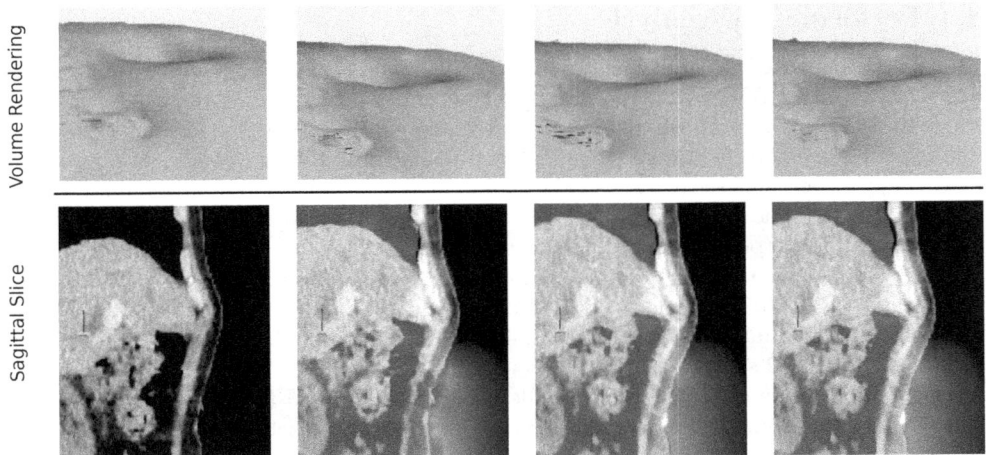

Figure 11: Effects of different settings of the inversion scheme. Upper row (left to right): Volume rendering of the navel without inversion, without incorporation of the result of previous samples, the scheme as described in the article and with doubled number of samples. Lower row: Sagittal slice with 0, 1, 5 and 50 iterations of the inversion scheme.

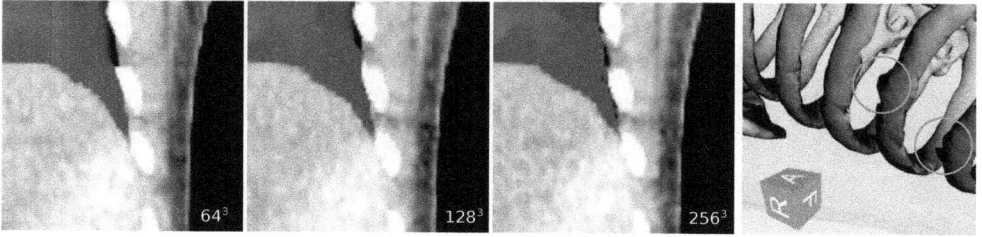

Figure 12: Left: Low resolutions of the displacement field lead to smearing artifacts at sliding interfaces. Right: Surface model of ribs are affected by this at a resolution the displacement field of 64^3 elements.

Model	Image size Voxel	Mb	Field size Voxel	Mb	N	Mem Mb	Rendering mean	stdev
none	small	151	0	0	0	151	16.36	0.10
none	large	1,085	0	0	0	1,085	15.99	0.12
key frame	small	151	64^3	4	14	210	35.74	0.16
key frame	small	151	128^3	34	14	621	36.83	0.22
key frame	small	151	256^3	268	6	1,762	37.52	0.33
key frame	large	1,085	64^3	4	14	1,144	35.90	0.16
key frame	large	1,085	128^3	34	14	1,555	36.05	0.15
key frame	large	1,085	256^3	268	4	2,159	36.21	0.32
surrogate	small	151	64^3	4	3	164	27.08	0.13
surrogate	small	151	128^3	34	3	252	27.48	0.90
surrogate	small	151	256^3	268	3	956	27.63	0.95
surrogate	large	1,085	64^3	4	3	1,098	26.32	0.13
surrogate	large	1,085	128^3	34	3	1,186	26.53	0.13
surrogate	large	1,085	256^3	268	3	1,891	26.55	0.20

Table 2: Ray casting rendering times in ms for the different motion models with a low (256^3 voxels) and high ($512 \times 512 \times 460$ voxels) resolution of the image data.

4.4 Performance Analysis

Run time behavior of the implementation in Nvidia Cuda is analyzed using a Nvidia GTX 680 with 3Gb of RAM. First, we analyzed the processing times for the rendering of a single frame by ray casting while using the presented methods for different image sizes and different displacement field sizes. The results are shown in Tab. 2. The resolution of the rendering viewport was set to 1224×1014 pixels. Note that both key frame approaches can rely on the same code for rendering and only differ in the determination of the interpolation parameter and interpolated key frames, which takes place before the ray casting.

Updating the position of vertices of surface models using Cuda is very fast: For surface models of bone (430,578 vertices), skin (145,648 vertices) and liver blood vessels (12,026 vertices), update times of 770.5±40.7 μs, 418.1±16.8 μs and 141.1±20.6 μs, resp. have been measured (252 samples).

Also, a performance analysis of the needle insertion algorithm for different numbers of needle nodes (15, 25 and 50) was performed on a PC with an Intel i7 CPU 970 @ 3.20GHz and 24 Gb of RAM. Fig. 13 shows box-plotted rendering times of the parts of Alg. 1 grouped into (1) update of displacements, (2) time stepping the physics simulation (3) total computation time. Furthermore, for a number of 25 needle nodes, the mean processing time for one step of the physics simulation has been measured, which is 14.5±15.7 μs, giving a mean number of 15.1±6.7 iterations of the physics simulation in each haptic simulation frame.

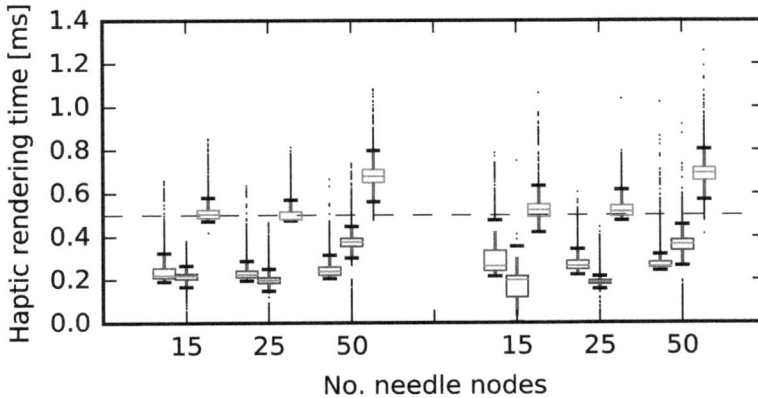

Figure 13: Box-plotted rendering timings of needle algorithm for the key frame based approach (left), and the surrogate signal based approach (right). Each pair of three contains of update of displacements (blue), physic simulation (red) and total computation time (green).

5 Discussion

The previous chapters of this article showed the general applicability of our presented methods and the performance of our implementation. It was shown that the influence of breathing motion modeled by the given approaches can be used for visuo-haptic interaction and creates realistic bending of a flexible needle. Besides this, bending and breathing motion influence the path taken by the needle through the virtual patient's tissue. Regarding haptic force feedback, the resulting forces can be perceived distinctively. For the palpation simulation, the angle of rotational back transformation of the resulting palpation force was small for the patient model under consideration. Probably, this is caused by the fact, that nearly no rotation is present in $u(\mathbf{x}, t)$ near the skin surface. The computed force and torque could directly be displayed to the user without the transformation. In general, this assumption might not be true for every patient model. Nevertheless it might be interesting to investigate if the effect of small changes of force direction can be perceived significantly and in which extent the type of haptic device has influence on this.

For the estimation of haptic parameters, we adjusted the parameters to reflect the behavior to be similar to previous versions of the simulation framework (e.g., [26, 3]) that did not include breathing simulation. We showed that the needle insertion algorithm is capable of simulating forces as measured in [37]. Also, we demonstrated that the stiffness parameters of the needle can be adjusted to resemble behavior of a 16 gauge needle. Further parameter estimation and evaluation should be performed in future work in case the framework is applied to a full feature training simulator and should include the assessment of face and construct validity.

The presented demonstration scenario uses a virtual patient with an artificially introduced lesion. Thus, the used surrogate signal and computed displacement function might not fully reflect reality. For patient data including a real lesion, the methods will incorporate the small changes in tissue behavior. Generally, the motion methods are from the domain of radiation therapy of lesions under respiratory motion, where an accurate prediction of the movement of the lesion is desired.

For the visualization, regions, in which large discontinuities of the resulting displacement field are present, smearing artifacts arise. These are especially visible at locations where a high gradient of image values exists. An example for this are the regions between ribs (high image values) and lungs (very low image values). For the puncture scenarios simulated by our framework, the lungs or structures inside of it are not relevant for haptic simulation and thus these artifacts only remain as an visualization issue. We consider the interpolation between voxels along the discontinuities at the interfaces of sliding structures as the source for this. By using displacement fields with a larger resolution, this will be mitigated in the future.

Concerning rendering performance, it was shown that, as expected, the introduction of motion models increases the time needed for volume rendering, but interactive frame rates are still easily achievable. Remarkably, the resolution of the displacement field does influence the performance only very little. Updating the positions of the vertices for surface rendering is negligible. For haptic rendering, we found that 25 nodes gave us the best results as a trade-of between plausible visualization of the discretized needle and a stable simulation.

For our method to work, we only need a simple displacement function and perform its inversion on-the-fly and only for needed elements. This is advantageous since it is straightforward to implement such a function. Also, the iterative fixed point inversion is always computed only once per sampling point and relies on accurate results from previous sampling steps. This applies for both the haptic rendering as well as the visual rendering by ray casting. For haptic rendering, the accuracy of the inversion method depends on two factors: First, the temporal sampling rate, i.e. the haptic update rate, which is very high. Second, the change of sampling location, which depends on the movement of the haptic device. For ray casting, the sampling rate, i.e. the spatial distance between sampling points on a ray influences the accuracy of the computed inverse displacement. Also, it depends on the rate of change of the displacement function, which is also dependent on the smoothness of the displacement field.

A central concern of our simulation framework is the goal of avoiding unstructured mesh models for haptic and visual rendering for the purpose of being able to omit the mesh generation process for new patients. Nevertheless, the motion models presented here could be integrated into coarse grid or mesh based frameworks by applying the displacement function to mesh nodes. For FEM based methods, it might be reasonable to apply it to static or boundary nodes.

Overall, we consider the introduction of the presented methods a very valuable contribution to visuo-haptic simulation of needle puncture interventions. The methods enable for the first time realistic visuo-haptic needle insertion simulation into a virtual breathing patient model based on a patient specific 4D image data set and real breathing signals. Especially the transfer of methods from image registration to visuo-haptic rendering enables a highly realistic model of respiratory motion.

6 Conclusion and Future Work

A visuo-haptic simulation framework for needle insertion capable of rendering virtual patients under the influence of breathing motion was presented. The motion models are fast to compute, making them suitable for visual rendering using ray casting or surface rendering, and can be used for haptic interaction with the virtual patient model under respiratory motion.

Here, we used a recorded spirometry surrogate signal. In the future, the source of the signal could be based on surrogate data recorded at run-time of the simulator. This way, training of an intervention could be augmented by having a training partner control the breathing of the virtual patient model. Alternatively, a realistic synthetic surrogate signal could be simulated during run-time [44].

Future work will include the investigation of methods for estimation of breathing motion for patients for which only 3D images are available. This way, motion models could be generated for the simulation without having to obtain a full 4D CT.

Additionally, the framework could be applied to other needle insertion interventions. If necessary, bevel-tip needle behavior could be easily integrated. Furthermore, the application of the presented respiratory models is not limited to (multi-)proxy based haptic algorithms and needle insertion and could be integrated in surgery simulation frameworks that rely on mesh based methods.

Appendix

Implementation of our 4D framework is split into a CPU component that deals with the haptic computations and a GPU component that is responsible for visualization. The ray casting based visual volume rendering of the breathing patient is implemented entirely using Nvidia Cuda. The rendering process writes to a pixel buffer object shared with the OpenGl environment of a VTK based rendering pipeline. Deformable triangular surfaces are also stored in shared pixel buffer objects. Additionally, VTK is used for the visualization of tools in the scene. Compared to the main memory of a modern workstation, the amount of available GPU memory is limited. Medical images and especially displacement fields are relatively large. In our Cuda-based GPU implementation, we store each image voxel by 9 bytes (4 bytes gray value, 4 bytes for a second channel, 1 bytes for the label set). To use fast texture interpolation, it was necessary to use single precision floats (4 bytes). Each element of the displacement field is stored by 16 bytes (4 bytes for x-, y- and z-component, 4 unused bytes). This way, a single image with a resolution of $512 \times 512 \times 460$ voxels and four displacement fields used for the key frame method at a resolution of 256^3 voxels already accounts for approx. 2 Gb of memory, which already fills a huge part of the available GPU memory on our reference hardware (Nvidia GTX 680 with 3Gb of RAM). Concerning the CPU based implementation of the haptic algorithms, it is worth mentioning that instead of performing look up and interpolation in the displacement fields just-in-time, all needed values are fetched all at once before performing Alg. 1 to save time. Also, the needle haptic algorithm was designed in a way that reduces random access to elements of the available image data; during insertion, only values resulting from the gray value and labeling image at the needle path tip are updated.

References

[1] P. F. Villard, F. P. Vidal, L. Ap Cenydd, R. Holbrey, S. Pisharody, S. Johnson, A. Bulpitt, N. W. John, F. Bello, and D. Gould, "Interventional Radiology Virtual Simulator for Liver Biopsy," *International Journal of Computer Assisted Radiology and Surgery*, pp. 1–13, 2013.

[2] N. Dong, Y. Wing, and Q. Jing, "A Virtual Reality Simulator for Ultrasound-guided Biopsy Training," *IEEE Computer Graphics and Applications*, vol. 31, no. 2, pp. 36–48, 2010.

[3] D. Fortmeier, A. Mastmeyer, J. Schröder, and H. Handels, "A Virtual Reality System for PTCD Simulation using Direct Visuo-haptic Rendering of Partially Segmented Image Data," *IEEE Journal of Biomedical and Health Informatics*, 2015.

[4] S. Ullrich, IEEE, and T. Kuhlen, "Haptic Palpation for Medical Simulation in Virtual Environments," *IEEE Transactions on Visualization and Computer Graphics*, vol. 18, no. 4, pp. 617–620, 2012.

[5] T. T. R. Coles, N. N. W. John, D. A. Gould, and D. D. G. Caldwell, "Integrating Haptics with Augmented Reality in a Femoral Palpation and Needle Insertion Training Simulation," *IEEE Transactions on Haptics*, vol. 4, no. 3, pp. 199–209, 2011.

[6] N. Chentanez, R. Alterovitz, D. Ritchie, L. Cho, K. K. Hauser, K. Goldberg, J. R. Shewchuk, and J. F. O'Brien, "Interactive Simulation of Surgical Needle Insertion and Steering," *ACM Transactions on Graphics*, vol. 28, no. 3, pp. 1–10, 2009.

[7] O. Goksel, K. Sapchuk, W. J. Morris, and S. E. Salcudean, "Prostate Brachytherapy Training with Simulated Ultrasound and Fluoroscopy Images," *IEEE Transactions on Biomedical Engineering*, vol. 60, no. 4, pp. 1002–12, 2013.

[8] P. Keall, T. Yamamoto, and Y. Suh, "Introduction to 4D Motion Modeling and 4D Radiotherapy," in *4D Modeling and Estimation of Respiratory Motion for Radiation Therapy* (C. Ehrhardt, Jan and Lorenz, ed.), Biological and Medical Physics, Biomedical Engineering, pp. 1–21, 2013.

[9] A. P. Santhanam, C. Imielinska, P. Davenport, P. Kupelian, and J. P. Rolland, "Modeling Real-time 3-d Lung Deformations for Medical Visualization," *IEEE Transactions on Information Technology in Biomedicine*, vol. 12, no. 2, pp. 257–70, 2008.

[10] A. Hostettler, S. A. Nicolau, Y. Rémond, J. Marescaux, and L. Soler, "A Real-time Predictive Simulation of Abdominal Viscera Positions during Quiet Free Breathing," *Progress in Biophysics and Molecular Biology*, vol. 103, no. 2-3, pp. 169–84, 2010.

[11] P. F. Villard, P. Boshier, F. Bello, and D. Gould, "Virtual Reality Simulation of Liver Biopsy with a Respiratory Component," in *Liver Biopsy* (H. Takahashi, ed.), ch. 20, InTech, 2011.

[12] F. Vidal, P. Villard, and E. Lutton, "Automatic Tuning of Respiratory Model for Patient-based Simulation," in *International Conference on Medical Imaging Using Bio-Inspired and Soft Computing (MIBISOC)*, pp. 225–231, 2013.

[13] P. F. Villard, F. P. Vidal, F. Bello, and N. W. John, "A Method to Compute Respiration Parameters for Patient-based Simulators," *Studies in Health Technology and Informatics*, vol. 173, pp. 529–533, 2012.

[14] X. Wu, J. Allard, and S. Cotin, "Real-time Modeling of Vascular Flow for Angiography Simulation," *International Conference on Medical Image Computing and Computer-Assisted Intervention (MICCAI)*, vol. 10, pp. 557–65, Jan. 2007.

[15] K. Engel, M. Hadwiger, J. Kniss, C. Rezk-Salama, and D. Weiskopf, *Real-time Volume Graphics*. AK Peters, Ltd., 2006.

[16] C. T. Silva and F. F. Bernardon, "A Survey of GPU-Based Volume Rendering of Unstructured Grids," pp. 1–22.

[17] J. Georgii, "A Generic and Scalable Pipeline for GPU Tetrahedral Grid Rendering,"

[18] J. Gascon, J. M. Espadero, A. G. Perez, and M. A. Otaduy, "Fast Deformation of Volume Data Using Tetrahedral Mesh Rasterization," vol. D, 2013.

[19] R. Torres, J. M. Espadero, F. A. Calvo, M. A. Otaduy, and H. G. U. G. Mara, "Interactive Deformation of Heterogeneous Volume Data," vol. D.

[20] Y. Kurzion and R. Yagel, "Space Deformation using Ray Deflectors," *Rendering Techniques' 95*, 1995.

[21] S. P. DiMaio and S. E. Salcudean, "Interactive Simulation of Needle Insertion Models," *IEEE Transactions on Biomedical Engineering*, vol. 52, no. 7, pp. 1167–79, 2005.

[22] C. Duriez, C. Guébert, M. Marchal, S. Cotin, and L. Grisoni, "Interactive Simulation of Flexible Needle Insertions based on Constraint Models," *International Conference on Medical Image Computing and Computer-Assisted Intervention (MICCAI)*, vol. 12, no. Pt 2, pp. 291–9, 2009.

[23] O. Goksel, K. Sapchuk, and S. E. S. Salcudean, "Haptic Simulator for Prostate Brachytherapy with Simulated Needle and Probe Interaction," *IEEE Transactions on Haptics*, vol. 4, no. 3, pp. 188–198, 2011.

[24] I. Peterlik, M. Nouicer, C. Duriez, S. Cotin, and A. Kheddar, "Constraint-Based Haptic Rendering of Multirate Compliant Mechanisms," *IEEE Transactions on Haptics*, vol. 4, no. 3, pp. 175–187, 2011.

[25] O. Goksel, E. Dehghan, and S. E. Salcudean, "Modeling and Simulation of Flexible Needles," *Medical Engineering and Physics*, vol. 31, no. 9, pp. 1069–78, 2009.

[26] M. Färber, T. Dahmke, C. Bohn, and H. Handels, "Needle Bending in a VR-Puncture Training System using a 6DOF Haptic Device," in *Proceedings of MMVR 17*, vol. 142, p. 91, Jan. 2009.

[27] M. Bergou, M. Wardetzky, S. Robinson, B. Audoly, and E. Grinspun, "Discrete Elastic Rods," *ACM Transactions on Graphics*, vol. 27, no. 3, p. 1, 2008.

[28] J. Spillmann and M. Teschner, "CORDE: Cosserat Rod Elements for the Dynamic Simulation of One-Dimensional Elastic Objects," *ACM SIGGRAPH 2007 Symposium on Computer Animation*, vol. 1, 2007.

[29] J. Ehrhardt, R. Werner, D. Säring, T. Frenzel, W. Lu, D. Low, and H. Handels, "An Optical Flow based Method for Improved Reconstruction of 4D CT Data Sets Acquired during Free Breathing," *Medical Physics*, vol. 34, no. 2, pp. 711–721, 2007.

[30] J. Ehrhardt and C. Lorenz, eds., *4D Modeling and Estimation of Respiratory Motion for Radiation Therapy*. Springer Berlin Heidelberg, 2013.

[31] A. Schmidt-Richberg, R. Werner, H. Handels, and J. Ehrhardt, "Estimation of Slipping Organ Motion by Registration with Direction-dependent Regularization," *Medical Image Analysis*, vol. 16, no. 1, pp. 150–159, 2012.

[32] M. Wilms, R. Werner, J. Ehrhardt, A. Schmidt-Richberg, H.-P. Schlemmer, and H. Handels, "Multivariate Regression Approaches for Surrogate-based Diffeomorphic Estimation of Respiratory Motion in Radiation Therapy," *Physics in Medicine and Biology*, vol. 59, no. 5, pp. 1147–64, 2014.

[33] M. Chen, W. Lu, Q. Chen, K. J. Ruchala, and G. H. Olivera, "A Simple Fixed-point Approach to Invert a Deformation Field," *Medical Physics*, vol. 35, no. 1, p. 81, 2008.

[34] D. Fortmeier, A. Mastmeyer, and H. Handels, "An Image-Based Multiproxy Palpation Algorithm for Patient-Specific VR-Simulation," in *Medicine Meets Virtual Reality 21, MMVR 2014*, vol. 196 of *Stud. Health Technol. Inform.*, pp. 107–113, IOS Press, 2014.

[35] B. K. P. Horn, "Closed-form Solution of Absolute Orientation using Unit Quaternions," *Journal of the Optical Society of America*, vol. 4, no. 4, p. 629, 1987.

[36] D. Fortmeier, A. Mastmeyer, and H. Handels, "Image-based Soft Tissue Deformation Algorithms for Real-time Simulation of Liver Puncture," *Current Medical Imaging Reviews*, vol. 9, no. 2, pp. 154–165, 2013.

[37] A. M. Okamura, C. Simone, and M. D. O'Leary, "Force modeling for needle insertion into soft tissue.," *IEEE transactions on bio-medical engineering*, vol. 51, pp. 1707–16, Oct. 2004.

[38] E. Coumans, "Bullet Physics Library."

[39] D. Sarrut, J. Vandemeulebroucke, and S. Rit, "Intensity-Based Deformable Registration: Introduction and Overview," in *4D Modeling and Estimation of Respiratory Motion for Radiation Therapy* (J. Ehrhardt and C. Lorenz, eds.), Biological and Medical Physics, Biomedical Engineering, pp. 103–124, Springer Berlin Heidelberg, 2013.

[40] R. Werner, A. Schmidt-Richberg, H. Handels, and J. Ehrhardt, "Estimation of Lung Motion Fields in 4D CT data by Variational Non-linear Intensity-based Registration: A Comparison and Evaluation Study," *Physics in Medicine and Biology*, vol. 59, no. 15, pp. 4247–60, 2014.

[41] K. Murphy, B. Van Ginneken, J. M. Reinhardt, S. Kabus, K. Ding, X. Deng, K. Cao, K. Du, G. E. Christensen, V. Garcia, T. Vercauteren, N. Ayache, O. Commowick, G. Malandain, B. Glocker, N. Paragios, N. Navab, V. Gorbunova, J. Sporring, M. De Bruijne, X. Han, M. P. Heinrich, J. A. Schnabel, M. Jenkinson, C. Lorenz, M. Modat, J. R. McClelland, S. Ourselin, S. E. A. Muenzing, M. A. Viergever, D. De Nigris, D. L. Collins, T. Arbel, M. Peroni, R. Li, G. C. Sharp, A. Schmidt-Richberg, J. Ehrhardt, R. Werner, D. Smeets, D. Loeckx, G. Song, N. Tustison, B. Avants, J. C. Gee, M. Staring, S. Klein, B. C. Stoel, M. Urschler, M. Werlberger, J. Vandemeulebroucke, S. Rit, D. Sarrut, and J. P. W. Pluim, "Evaluation of Registration Methods on Thoracic CT: The EMPIRE10 Challenge," *IEEE Transactions on Medical Imaging*, vol. 30, no. 11, pp. 1901–1920, 2011.

[42] J. McClelland, "Estimating Internal Respiratory Motion from Respiratory Surrogate Signals Using Correspondence Models," in *4D Modeling and Estimation of Respiratory Motion for Radiation Therapy* (J. Ehrhardt and C. Lorenz, eds.), Biological and Medical Physics, Biomedical Engineering, pp. 187–213, Springer Berlin Heidelberg, 2013.

[43] W. E. Lorensen and H. E. Cline, "Marching Cubes: A High Resolution 3D Surface Construction Algorithm," in *ACM SIGGRAPH Computer Graphics*, vol. 21, pp. 163–169, 1987.

[44] M. Wilms, J. Ehrhardt, R. Werner, M. Marx, and H. Handels, "Statistical Analysis of Surrogate Signals to Incorporate Respiratory Motion Variability into Radiotherapy Treatment Planning," in *SPIE Medical Imaging 2014, Image-Guided Procedures, Robotic Interventions, and Modeling* (Z. R. Yaniv and D. R. Holmes, eds.), no. 1, p. 90360J, 2014.

Ray-casting Based Evaluation Framework for Haptic Force Feedback during Percutaneous Transhepatic Catheter Drainage Punctures

Andre Mastmeyer, Tobias Hecht, Dirk Fortmeier, Heinz Handels

Abstract

Purpose. Development of new needle insertion force feedback algorithms requires comparison with a gold standard method. A new evaluation framework was formulated and tested on needle punctures for Percutaneous Transhepatic Catheter Drainage (PTCD).
Method. Needle insertion is an established procedure for minimally invasive interventions in the liver. Up-to-date, needle insertions are precisely planned using 2D axial CT slices from 3D data sets. To provide a 3D virtual reality (VR) and haptic training and planning environment, the full segmentation of patient data is often a mandatory step. To lessen the time required for manual segmentation, we propose direct haptic volume rendering based on CT gray values and partially segmented patient data. The core contribution is a new force output evaluation method driven by a ray-casting technique that defines paths from the skin to target structures, i.e. the right hepatic duct (RHD) near the juncture with the common hepatic duct (CHD). A ray-casting method computes insertion trajectories from the skin to the duct considering no-go structures and plausibility criteria. A rating system scores each trajectory. Finally, the best insertion trajectories are selected that reach the target. Along the selected paths, force output comparison between a reference system and the new haptic force output algorithm is carried out, quantified and visualized.
Results. The evaluation framework is presented along with an exemplary study of the liver using the atlas data set from a reference patient. In a comparison of our reference method to a newer algorithm, force outputs are found to be similar in 99% of the paths.
Conclusion. The proposed evaluation framework allows reliable detection of problematic PTCD trajectories and provides valuable hints to improve force feedback algorithm development.

1 Introduction

Surgical training systems let surgeons improve skills effectively without any risk [1]. Among others, preoperative planning, anatomic education and training of surgical procedures are the focus of these systems. Technically, the real-time performance for volume visualization, tissue deformation and haptic feedback are of major interest. Regarding the necessary virtual patients, the manual preparation mainly comprises the tedious contouring of all organs and structures in CT patient data. Here, our target organ, the liver and its vessels still have to be segmented at least semi-automatically to provide for accurate training and planning.

Whenever possible minimal-invasive interventions should be preferred, i.e. laparoscopy or needle insertions. In [2], needle insertion simulation is presented as a challenging field of research with many aspects ranging from mimicking stiffness, cutting and friction forces at the needle tip and shaft to needle bending in real-time.

Previously from our group, AcusVR [3, 4] (lat. acus=needle) has been published being a realistic and valuable tool for the simulation of needle punctures using a Sensable Phantom 6DOF (see Fig. 1, left). Its major bottleneck is the complete expert segmentation of patient image data without any gap. Alternatively, we propose direct haptic volume rendering using partially segmented data [5, 6]. Haptic transfer functions and the segmentation of only a few structures aim to provide a mock-up of a complete segmentation, where voxel classification based on a heuristical transfer function set-up fills the gaps between the explicitly delineated structures.

The workflow adressed in our project is (1) acquiring new patient data, (2) fast modelling of the virtual patient data set, (3) planning and training of the actual US-guided needle intervention by inspecting the patient with a virtual US simulation. The US simulation (not covered in this paper) features a needle guiding rail and realistic visualization of the US image and needle position.

From the physicians point of view, the liver is quite a common place for needle insertion procedures, e.g. in case of metastatic diseases. In 80% of cases, surgical resection of metastases cannot be carried out and the lesion must be accessed by alternative methods [7]. Preparation of CyberKnife image-guided radiosurgery comprises the insertion of gold threads into the lesion to enable real-time tracking of the target structure during radiation therapy [8]. The needle insertions have to be planned accurately for a resulting low number of needle repositionings. This results in a positive effect w.r.t. the healing process [9].

In the PTCD procedure adressed in this paper, a needle of 12-15 cm in length and 1.4 mm diameter and a catherizing filament of 45-100 cm length is inserted into the patient lying in supine position. Nowadays, the procedure is ultrasound guided and the targeted right biliary duct (RHD) should be dilated approximately to 1 cm diameter. In a sterile setting a small incision is made at the planned insertion point between the 6th and 7th intercostal space near the junction of the costocartilage. Then the needle is directed to the right hepatic duct (RHD) nearby the juncture with the common hepatic duct (CHD) [10]. For computer assisted planning systems, Baegert et al. [11] presented a concept in which the computation of optimal insertion trajectories is divided into two phases. In a first step, insertion trajectories are discarded when (1) they run through critical structures or (2) when the target is not reached within needle length. Afterwards, the remaining trajectories are scored using plausibility rating criteria.

Seitel et al. [12] revised this concept and present an implementation that selects an optimal trajectory using the Pareto principle. A trajectory is considered to be Pareto optimal if it cannot be improved in a criterion without being worsened in another. In a retrospective evaluation, test data were used where a needle insertion by a physician caused a complication. In four of the ten patients, the trajectory chosen by the doctor should not have lead to any complication.

The presented concepts can be unified in our new evaluation framework: haptic feedback in virtual environments has been qualitatively evaluated by [13], the techniques presented there are of key importance for regional anesthesia simulation [14]. However quantitative evaluation of the proposed algorithms still remains a gap to be filled. In this paper, we focus on the thorough evaluation of new force feedback algorithms by automatically generating a large number of plausible puncture paths. In our scenario, the dilated ducts in the right liver segment are the target structure. Force comparison is then carried out along the paths. Moreover, this paper customizes the 3D path planning for hepatic duct

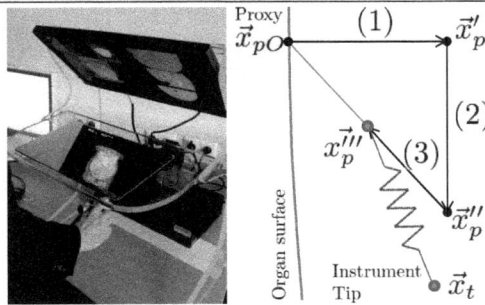

Figure 1: (Left) The haptic device and workbench. The user wears shutter-glasses for 3D immersion and watches the virtual patient in the mirror. He steers the virtual instruments with the haptic device below the mirror and gets force feedback when touching tissue. (Right) Proxy-based force calculation recapitulated. The proxy is held at the surface, the recalculated proxy position's distance to the tip defines the exerted force.

puncture adding a new criterion. The main purposes of trajectory planning in our project are:

1. Automatic generation of a high number of plausible paths to evaluate force output.
2. Generation of a few best paths for a patient to be proposed to the user as training reference paths.

A very important method used in this paper is the Ray-Casting technique, which is customized to the needs of needle trajectory planning. In a nutshell, the intensity of a pixel is determined by occlusion and quality criteria subject to surgery planning aspects. The paper is organized as follows: First, we describe the data used. Force calculation is briefly reviewed as presented in [6] and [15]. The virtual patient modeling heuristics for the PTCD scenario are summarized. Afterwards, we expound the ray-casting high quality path generation method used to evaluate force outputs. Finally, assessment is done quantitatively by comparing force calculations from the reference system AcusVR and the new approach [6].

2 Methods

One standard abdominal CT patient scan with voxel size $1.552 \times 1.552 \times 2$ mm^3, 256^2 pixels in-plane and 234 slices is used (see Fig. 0.2(a)). Dimension reduction from 512^2 to 256^2 pixels is obtained by resampling and necessary for the visualization algorithms to run performant and within the memory constraints of the graphics hardware (NVIDIA Quadro 4000). The complete segmentation of the virtual patient including among others bone, fat, muscle, skin and liver and liver vessels is available and used for haptic rendering [3, 4]. This data set and the AcusVR algorithm [4] is our gold standard to which we compare force output. In contrast, the newer system AcusVR2 only needs a subset of the segmentations for force output (see Fig. 0.2(b)).

As systems overview, in Tab. 1 we compare the reference system to AcusVR2 feature-wise. The preparation time of virtual patients is shortened significantly, only some structures are segmented manually. We provide an US-guided puncture simulation that reflects the current state-of-the art puncture method. The direct volume rendering technique is carried out on graphics hardware, no polygon models are necessary. Real-time deformation of CT data using different instruments such as a palpation finger, needle and US-device is implemented. Contrast agent injected inside the bile ducts is visualized using an X-Ray

Feature \ System	AcusVR	AcusVR2
Haptic Device* / max. Force [N]	1.5 6DOF / 8.5	1.5 High Force 6DOF / 37.5
Segmentation Workload [h] / Model	40 / full segmentation	8 / partial segmentations
US-guided Puncture Simulation	No	Yes
Volume Rendering Technique	Polygon Models	+Direct Volume Rendering
Visualization of Tissue Deformation	No	Yes
Use of Partially Segmented Data	No	Yes
Fast X-Ray Simulation	No	Yes
User Scoring System (Ref. Paths)	Yes	Yes
Force Evaluation Framework	No	Yes
Path Planning Concept	No	Yes

Table 1: Comparison of AcusVR vs. AcusVR2. Bold typesetting indicates topics adressed in this paper. *We use Geomagic Phantom Premium devices (TM).

simulation. For the education of medical students, experienced physicians can define reference paths, which the trainee can use to compare his planning to. The trials of the student can be scored to document the learning effect over several runs. The force feedback evaluation component combined with path planning described in this paper enables the development of new accurate force feedback algorithms.

2.1 Direct Haptic Volume Rendering

As shown in the right part of Fig. 1, in proxy based haptic rendering [16, 6, 15], the device tip $\vec{x}_t$ is attached to a virtual spring with stiffness parameter k. The organ surface proxy $\vec{x}_{pO}$ sticks to an organ surface and is the origin of a triangle of forces. On the other end, the spring is held back by a calculated proxy $\vec{x}'''_p$. The force between tip and proxy is depended on their Euclidean distance and is given by Hookes law. More specific, the force calculation is dependent on the haptic parameters T_N, R and k, which denote surface penetration force [N], viscosity [m²/s] and stiffness [N/m] respectively and are material dependant (see Fig. 2.2.1). T_N describes the maximum force exerted until an organ capsule is penetrated, k is the spring constant used in Hookes law for the virtual spring between tip and proxy and R describes how viscous a material is. The calculation is carried out in three steps (see Fig. 1 right): (1) The proxy position $\vec{x}'_p$ for the surface penetrability along the normal vector of a virtual surface is determined. (2) The position $\vec{x}''_p$ tangentially to the organ surface is calculated. (3) A viscosity term retracts the proxy to the final position $\vec{x}'''_p$. Now the spring is virtually set inbetween $\vec{x}_t$ and $\vec{x}'''_p$ and the emitted force is calculated. The calculation for haptic feedback runs in real-time at 2000 Hz.

2.2 Virtual Patient Modeling

In the new force rendering method proposed in [6], partially segmented patient data is used. Transfer functions are used to obtain the haptic parameters if missing a segmented structure at the needle tip. An axial slice (see Fig. 0.2(c)) shows plausible tissue classifications between large volume structure such as skin (orange), fat (yellow) and bone (white). In these classes, different haptic parameters are valid. However, parts of the liver, the fascia, the small volume and key structures blood vessels and bile ducts fall falsely into the domain of the large volume structures fat and bone. Consequently, semi-automatic segmentations or surface models are still provided for these structures. For instance, the haptically very salient structure "fascia" in the intercostal spaces is modeled as a cylindrical spline surface fitted through the rib cage (see Chap. 2.2.2). Manual modelling of the tissues in the intercostal spaces have taken 15h in AcusVR, now we end up with 20 minutes semi-automatic spline-modelling.

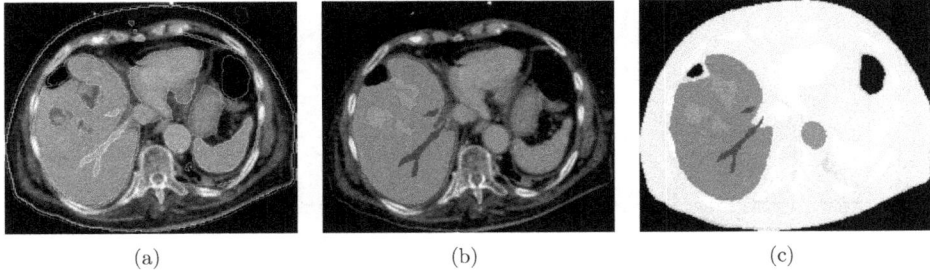

(a)   (b)   (c)

Figure 2: An axial slice of the reference data: (a) original gray values with complete segmentation, (b) set of partial segmentations used: liver (brown), ducts (green), arteries (red), veins (blue), (c) visual transfer function applied with tissue classes air (black), skin (orange), fat (yellow), bone (white) and partial segmentations.

2.2.1 Transfer-Function-Setup for a Reference Patient

In a first step, we calculate label statistics to estimate the normal distribution parameters of the underlying grey values from our reference patient's segmentations. Then, we determine the intersections of the distributions of a few adjacent tissues and have coined the term "transition thresholds" [6]. Exemplary determination of such Bayesian transition thresholds can be seen in Fig. 3. The Bayesian thresholds minimize the classification errors in terms of false positives and negatives between two adjacent tissue classes. The resulting bayesian thresholds are listed in Fig. 2. Note, that a slight tuning of the found values to the right or left can offer better haptic experience. At this juncture, visual inspection using color coding with a visual transfer function (see Figs. 4 and 0.2(c)) corresponding to the intervals is a useful tool to check plausibility. The tuning of the thresholds is about three times the standard deviation of the noise present in the data set. Preferably the noise in the data w.r.t. the scan protocol can be measured in the center of a water phantom. If such a pre-scan is not available, we locate the aorta near the spinal column, define a small circular measurement ROI of 1-1.5 cm diameter in three adjacent central slices with a small amount of surrounding bony structures to determine mean and standard deviation. More specific, we choose the slices nearby the lower end of the kidneys, where the vertebral disk is in parallel to the image plane. This is usually the upper or lower disk of the vertebra L3. The standard deviation then serves as a rough noise estimate. In our reference patient we measured 14 HU standard deviation. For bone, we chose to shift the threshold to the right by three standard deviations (42 HU) for a slightly more conservative setting. By this means, we decrease the misclassification of fat while still keeping the correct classification of the cortical bone shells, especially for the frontal rib parts, which consist of softer tissue such as costal cartilage. The justification here is that in the haptic simulation the bones are rendered as risk structure that shall not be penetrated, so misclassified marrow or spongy bone is irrelevant in this context.

In comparison to our lumbar puncture set-up [6], for the PTCD liver puncture we define the transfer function in a simplified way. We reduce the set of classes to air and three tissues: skin, fat, bone (see Fig. 0.2(c)). The only muscular structure encountered on typical needle paths in our scenario are the fascia for which a special model in Chap. 2.2.2 is proposed.

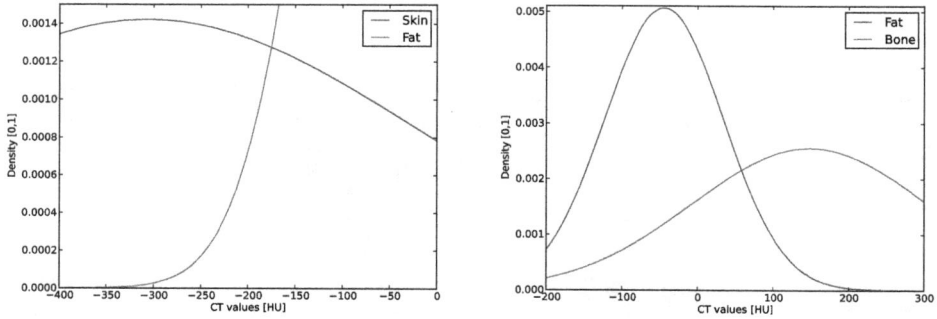

Figure 3: Determination of a bayesian optimal threshold for the transitions. (Left) skin (blue line) to fat (red line) normal distributions with cross-over at -173 HU. (Right) fat (blue line) to bone (red line) normal distributions with cross-over at 58 HU.

Transition	Thresholds [HU]
Air - Skin	-800*
Skin - Fat	-173
Fat - Bone	100 (58+42)

Table 2: Bayesian "transition thresholds" for the reference patient. A '*' indicates statistical significance ($p < 0.05$). For fat-bone, a slightly more conservative setting of 100 HU performs favorable over the threshold found by the bayesian approach.

For a new patient, the thresholds in Fig. 2 have to be carefully tuned manually resp. automatically adapted, which is beyond the scope of this paper. The goal is to achieve plausible and homogeneous large volume material regions, which can be checked using the proposed color-coding of the CT data (see Figs. 0.2(c), 4). More specifically, the intercostal spaces and rib shells should be clearly fall into the fat (yellow) and bone (white) classes (see Fig. 0.2(c)).

The resulting haptic transfer functions for our reference patient are shown in Fig. 2.2.1. Note, the transfer function concept supports any function different from the simple constant segments used here. In intervals with a mix-up of many different materials, non-constant transfer functions can be used. For example, in the lumbar simulator [6] we proposed such

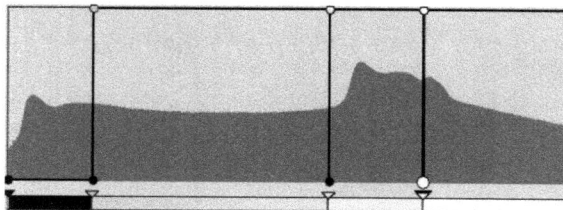

Figure 4: Transfer function intervals used for color coded rendering. The black interval represents air [-1024, -800], skin is orange [-801, -173], fat is yellow [-174, 99] and bone is encoded in white color [101, 3072] on the HU scale.

an interval and two of the haptic parameters ascend linearly from one material to the other (muscle to bone).

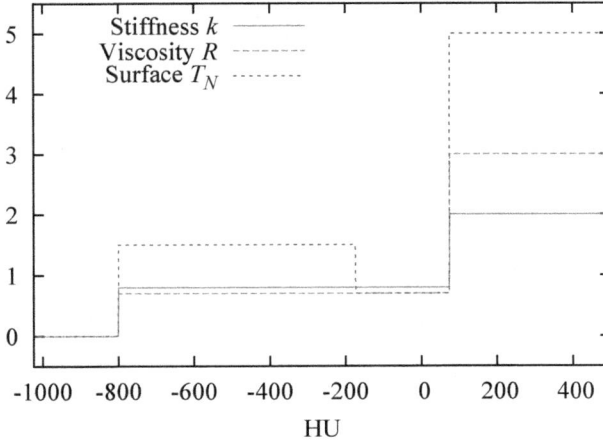

Figure 5: Transfer functions for haptic parameters: Corresponding to the color coding visual transfer function we define the haptic parameters spanning over the same material intervals. For a material, the parameter values are the same as in the full segmentation approach, where each label has attributed a tuple of (k, R, T_N).

2.2.2 Partial Use of Segmentation Models

A structure that is haptically very important are the fascia. They are located in the spaces between the ribs and provide a significant cut-through feeling when penetrated. To save time on the segmentation of the intercostal layers of fascias and muscles and to provide a good haptical experience a single mathematical surface is used. As shown in Fig. 6, the fascia are modeled as a cylindrical spline surface $s(\phi, h)$ that is fitted through the rib cage [17]:

$$s(\phi, h) = \begin{pmatrix} s_x(\phi, h) \\ s_y(\phi, h) \\ s_z(\phi, h) \end{pmatrix}, \ 0 \leq \phi \leq 2\pi, \ h_0 \leq h \leq h_1 \tag{1}$$

where angle ϕ and height h are cylinder coordinates. The functions s_x, s_y and s_y define the coordinates of the surface, and we can rewrite Eq. 1 more specific as:

$$s(\phi, h) = \begin{pmatrix} x_0 + R(\phi, h) \cdot cos(\phi) \\ y_0 + R(\phi, h) \cdot sin(\phi) \\ H(\phi, h) \end{pmatrix}, \tag{2}$$

where (x_0, y_0) is the center of the cylindrical coordinate system and the radius $R(\phi, h)$ and height $H(\phi, h)$ are B-spline surfaces defined over the rectilinear (ϕ, h)-domain:

$$B(\phi, h) = \sum_{n=0}^{N} \sum_{m=0}^{M} c_{n,m} \cdot N_{n,k+1}(\phi) \cdot N_{m,l+1}(h) \tag{3}$$

where $N = 14$ und $M = 4$ denote the number of knots, $c_{n,m}$ are the control coefficients, $k = 3$ and $l = 3$ are the degrees of the B-Spline base functions $N_{n,k+1}(\phi)$ and $N_{m,l+1}(h)$. The date line (where the corresponding ends of the surface meet) of the spline curve is put into the spinal column. We have to take care about a smooth transition from $\phi = 0$ to $\phi = 2\pi$ and claim periodicity:

$$\frac{\partial^n B(\phi = 0, h)}{\partial^n \phi} = \frac{\partial^n B(\phi = 2\pi, h)}{\partial^n \phi}, \ n = 0, 1, 2, 3 \tag{4}$$

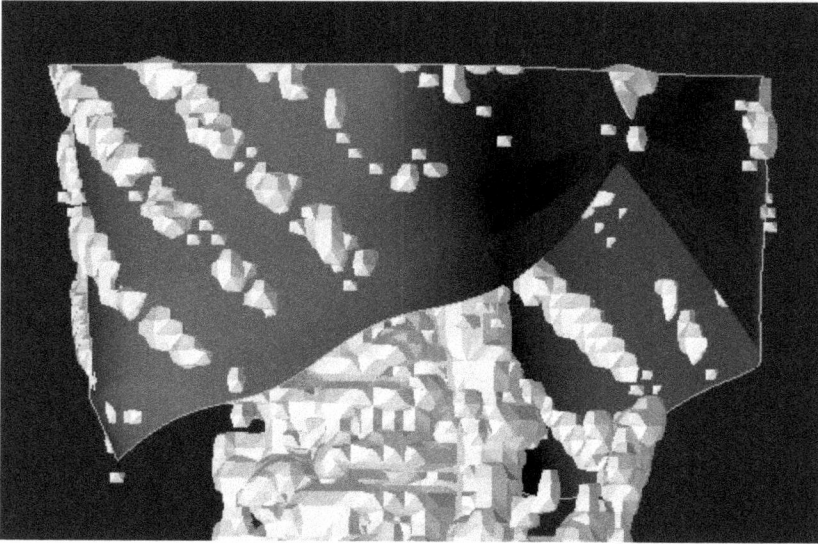

Figure 6: The B-Spline surface fitted through the rib cage models the fascia. The rib cage points are extracted from the CT data using a conservative threshold of 200 HU.

For the liver numerous semi-automatic segmentation methods are available, which reach DICE coefficients up to 95 % on average [18, 19, 20, 21]. For the necessary accuracy in planning and training systems, the results still might have to be manually inspected and corrected even if the methods claim to be fully automatic and high quality.

Other very important structures such as blood vessels (risk), bile ducts (target) and gallbladder are segmented manually at the current state of the project. Optionally for better targeting, the bile ducts segmentation can be broken down to its branches, and the small area of the RHD/CHD juncture can be marked as target. This combined approach guarantees high accuracy and training effect in important areas and good quality fast heuristic segmentation in other regions.

The risk structures intestines and lungs including the pleural recesses can be segmented as air holes inside the body (cf. Fig. 0.2(c), black surrounded by yellow/orange areas). Special care is necessary for filled intestines and the pleural space to be included in the lungs segmentation as pneumothorax must be avoided.

For lower time effort of the patient modelling process, we skip the segmentation of the peritoneum and fine tissue layers of the intercostal spaces. For now we also do not segment the fine nerves and blood vessels along the lower parts of the ribs, which also in high resolution data is a difficult task.

In summary, the virtual patient has to be carefully reviewed by the modeller for correct applicability of the heuristics and risk or target structures to be represented accurately.

2.3 Customized Ray-Casting

In our new evaluation framework, we calculate a large number of plausible puncture paths automatically, which are used to steer the needle tip in and out ("reference paths") assuming constant velocity (see Fig. 7 left). Hence, absolutely reproducible force outputs are obtained for comparing different haptic force calculation algorithms. Finally, a high number of paths consisting of two points are automatically defined hitting the target without obstacles.

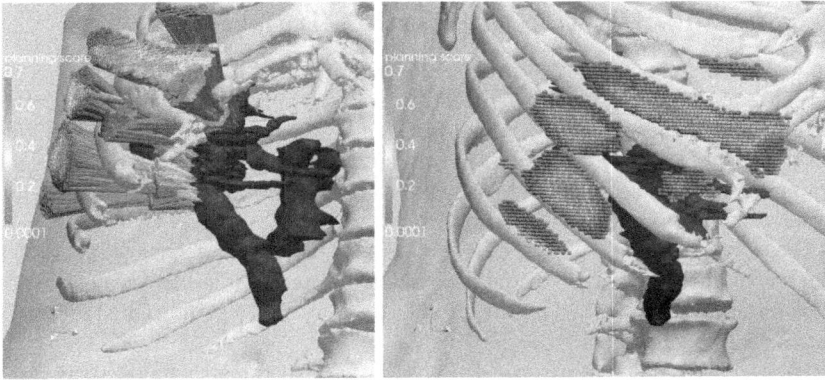

Figure 7: Reference paths (colored), skin (tan) and bone (white). (Left) path starting points on the skin. (Right) paths targeting the ducts. Coloring corresponds to the quality of the path deduced from the soft constraints.

Technically, ray-casting is part of the ray tracing technique used for photo realistic rendering of virtual scenes. Ray casting does not include reflection and optical refraction. The volume-rendering integral models absorption and emission of light and is evaluated along rays emitted from an imaging device, typically a camera screen. In the commonly known algorithm, the screen is implemented as an image plane from where the rays are cast into the scene [22]. We customize ray-casting in two aspects to our needs: (1) the image plane is replaced by the skin voxels of the patient, (2) the intensity is determined by visibility and quality aspects (planning score). For our needs, the simplified discretized volume rendering integral without emission term is:

$$I\left(v_{skin}\right) = max_{v_{targ}}\left\{Q\left(v_{skin}, v_{targ}\right) \cdot \prod_{v \in Br(v_{skin}, v_{targ})} V\left(v\right)\right\} \tag{5}$$

where $I\left(v_{skin}\right)$ denotes the intensity of a skin voxel, v_{targ} is the voxel of the target structure, Q is the quality function, Br is the Bresenham-line algorithm and visibility V is a binary function, which becomes zero when a risk structure is hurt (occlusion) or needle length is exceeded.

Thus ray-casting is used to determine the visibility of the biliary vessel from the perspective of the source structure, i.e. the skin. The algorithm checks whether a direct line to the target duct can be drawn without violating the hard constraints. Our ray-casting technique is driven by the fast 3D-Bresenham algorithm [23], which determines the set of ray voxels $Br\left(v_{skin}, v_{targ}\right)$ from the skin to the target structure. The Bresenham algorithm uses integer arithmetic operations only to draw a line from source to target voxels. In our implementation, line-of-sight connections from each skin voxel line to each target voxel are drawn. For all rays starting from a skin voxel, the best scored path is selected as a "reference path". In the evaluation process, using automatic needle steering (see Chap. 2.5), taking into account not only one path outgoing from a source voxel would drastically increase the computational burden with little added insight gain in the evaluation study. The ray-casting algorithm is implemented in CUDA and runs in parallel on NVIDIA graphics hardware.

2.4 Scoring and Selection of Insertion Trajectories

In our path scoring functions Q and V, the concept of Baegert et al. [11] is used. Hard constraints - contained in V - strictly limit the set of possible trajectories. Any trajectory affected by at least one of these hard constraints ($V = 0$) is removed from the set of candidate trajectories. For example, by this means, puncturing of bone is avoided. All other trajectories are rated using soft constraints encoded in Q. In the following paragraphs, three constraints are presented as examples.

The occlusion constraint (Fig. 0.8(a)) excludes all trajectories that are blocked on their way from the skin to the target through a risk structure (gallbladder, bone, blood vessels, lungs and pleura, intestines). The target is clearly covered by the risk structure on this trajectory.

The distance to critical structures constraint (Fig. 0.8(b)) rates the trajectory P using the smallest distance to a risk structure as a function of the minimum $d_{r,min}$ and $d_{r,max}$ the maximum of all trajectories:

$$d(P) = \frac{d_r(P) - d_{r,min}}{d_{r,max} - d_{r,min}} \tag{6}$$

Finally, the angle criterion from Fig. 0.8(c) counts the voxels along the needle shaft inside a cut bile vessel and tests for a certain number of voxels being visited. With our data the chosen voxel number of five corresponds to 7.76 to 10 mm. Consequently, the angle between needle and vessel is small as the paths are selected that tend to go in parallel to thin vessels. This is motivated by the insertion of a catheter filament after the puncture, which can be moved forward more easily in the direction of the vessel.

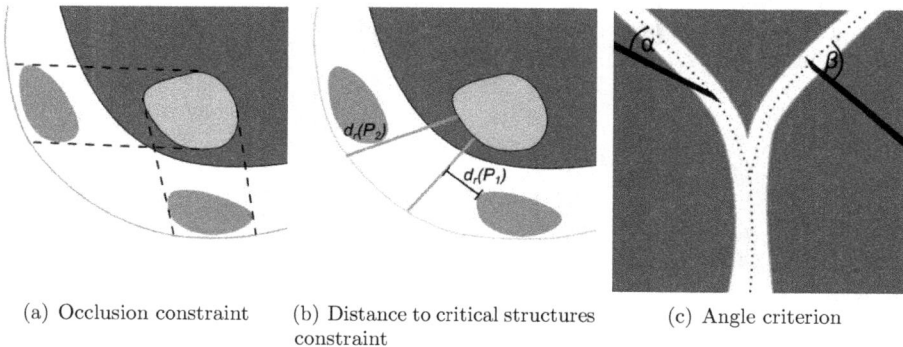

(a) Occlusion constraint (b) Distance to critical structures constraint   (c) Angle criterion

Figure 8: Schematic representation of selected constraints for determining the optimal trajectories. (a) The target is in pink, the liver in dark red, the risk structures in gray and the skin is in orange. In (b), the occluded skin is shown in red and a good trajectory (P_1) is opposed to a bad trajectory (P_2). In (c), the angle criterion is schematically depicted.

The final score Q is a normalized average of the criterion scores. The criterion scores are normalized to the interval from 0 (min.) to 1 (max.) by linear scaling (see Eq. 6). Conceptually, weights could be used to steer the influence of the criteria at this point. In our current set-up, the criterions are all equally weighted.

For AcusVR2, false positive bone voxel detection errors are expected in the peripherial puncture zones (colored reddish in Fig. 7) nearby the ribs. This is exactly the area from where paths can slide along the rib bone fringes (see Fig. 7). Medically, it is also justified not to puncture very closely below the rib bones, where nerves and vessels can be located. Thus, these nearby bone paths are removed from the candidate set by increasing the

Worst Paths			Best Paths		
Rank in MSE	MSE↓ [N²]	MAE [N]	Rank in MSE	MSE↓ [N²]	MAE [N]
3508	0.13871*+	2.6407	20	0.000519602	0.7
3507	0.134711+	1.2	19	0.000495456	0.7
3506	0.131929+	3	18	0.000480816	0.7
3505	0.130984+	3	17	0.000477881	0.609207
3504	0.128317+	1.45791	16	0.000280114	0.600661
3503	0.124766+	1.2	15	9.8E-06	0.14
3502	0.119085+	2.86975	...	0	0
3501	0.108103*+	2.88296	1	0	0

Table 3: Comparison of force output values calculated by AcusVR to new algorithm variant. Asterisks indicate significantly different force feedback ($p < 0.01$). Plus signs mark paths where air holes are present in the segmentation. MSE means "mean squared error", MAE denotes the "maximum absolute error". The errors are sorted descending by MSE.

quality threshold in the trajectory planning procedure. We end up with 3508 paths out of 4437 (see Fig. 7).

The selected paths reflect successful trainee experience with the system, i.e. starting from the skin they reach the RHD/CHD target within needle insertion length (12-15 cm) and do not violate the hard constraints. Paths clearly hitting bone, lungs/pleural space, intestine and blood vessels are dismissed by these constraints (occlusion). Paths nearby a risk structure get a lower score by the soft constraints. In practical training experience the trainee gets a feedback (red light) and diminished score from the system when such a structure is hurt. With our new Geomagic 6DOF High Force device used in AcusVR2, much higher forces can be exerted as in the original AcusVR set-up (37.5 N vs. 8.5 N). Force rendering of bone has been changed in the newer haptic algorithm, thus comparison results would systematically be biased on bone touching paths. Hence, also from this technical perspective dismissing the bone touching paths is justified. The change of the bones force rendering does not affect the other tissues.

2.5 Force Comparison and Metrics

At every position of the reference path at the needle tip two force outputs are calculated: (1) by the algorithm used in AcusVR using the full segmentation and (2) by the method using a partial segmentation and gray values based transfer functions.

Generous oversampling of the voxel values is used to satisfy the sampling theorem. We acquire 2000 equally spaced sampling force tuples (duples) per insertion distributed over 12-15 cm needle length at maximum.

As measures to compare the force output values we show the "mean of squared errors" (MSE) and "maximum absolute error" (MAE). The duples define a natural relation between the force values: at the same place the same forces are expected. So for statistical assessment of the errors found, the p-value from paired two-sided t-tests is used.

3 Results

In Tab. 3 the errors for the force ouputs along the paths are shown for the two error measures, MSE and MAE. Due to the large amount of data, we only show tail and head of a sorted error list. In the left resp. right half of the table, the worst resp. best case paths of this study are given in the MSE metric.

We encounter a small number of significantly different force feedback from the reference system AcusVR (see Fig. 0.9(c)). In these cases for AcusVR, closer investigation shows air gaps in the series of labels encountered along the needle path (see Fig. 3). For MSE the vast majority of errors is nearby 0 (see Fig. 0.9(a)).

Many of the worst maximum absolute errors are not significant (also cf. Figs. 3, 0.9(b), 0.9(c)), so this kind of error has an outlier, peak-like characteristic (see Fig. 3).

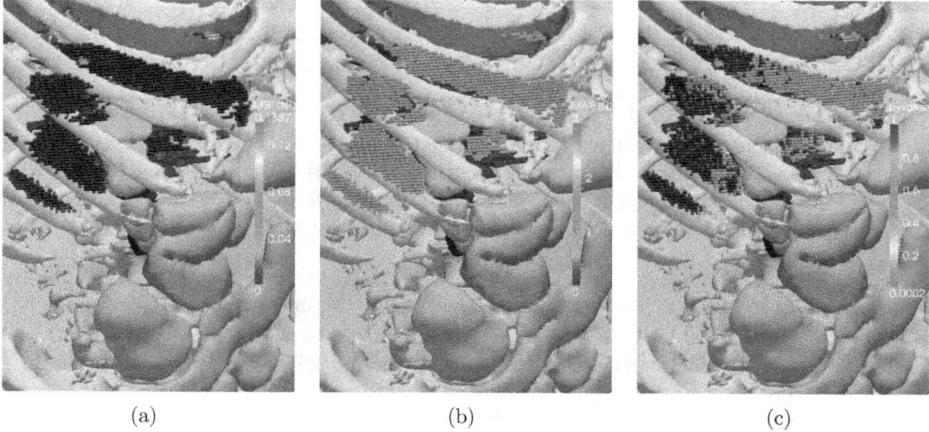

(a)   (b)   (c)

Figure 9: Color coded errors of reference paths: (a) MSE, blue coloring denotes very low errors (b) MAE, light blue coloring indicates a systematic error of 0.7 N and (c) p-value, red coloring shows very little significant errors. Here, lungs and intestines are rendered to show that our planning dismisses paths hitting these risk structures.

Figure 10: Force curves for a typical path (rank 683) with a maximum absolute error of 0.7 N: AcusVR calculated force (blue) vs. newer algorithm (magenta): The force outputs for the paths are very similar despite of errors caused at the skin. The reason here is that skin detection is performed heuristically by AcusVR2 while AcusVR uses the manual segmentation.

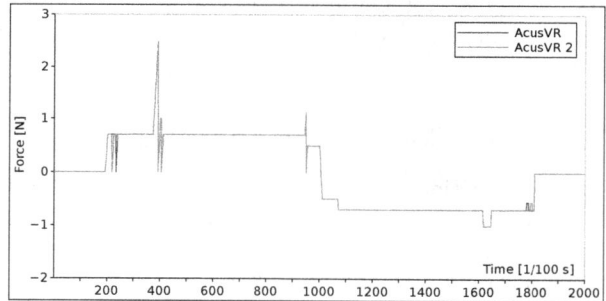

Using CUDA for path planning calculations takes only 3 minutes of time instead of over 15 minutes in a CPU implementation. The simulation of needle steering takes about 20 minutes, the evaluation of the results finishes after 30 minutes for 3508 paths.

On average we found MSE resp. MAE to be 0.0056 ± 0.0097 N^2 resp. 0.73 ± 0.15 N. A systematic bias of 0.7 N in terms of MAE can be observed in Figs. 0.9(b) and 3. Statistically significant errors are present in only 0.8 % of all paths ($p < 0.05$). The maximum absolute error observed overall is 3 N.

4 Discussion

In [6], a new concept for virtual patient modeling has been presented that considerably reduces the segmentation preparation workload from days to hours.

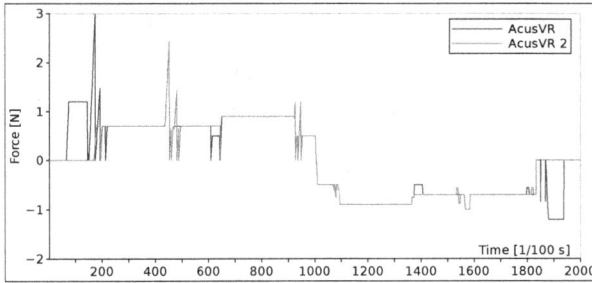

Figure 11: Force curves for worst case paths (rank 3508) with significant errors: AcusVR (blue) vs. AcusVR2 (magenta): Errors caused by ECG cables occur just before the skin. Here, only AcusVR is affected. On the other hand, the heuristic in AcusVR2 could misclassify metallic cables as thin bony structure.

There we evaluated the system using 12 manually defined paths only. In [24], lumbar puncture is adressed and our framework has been introduced. In this paper, we focus on the PTCD puncture procedure and its special requirements. The evaluation and planning framework produces a large number (3508) of automatically generated, densely packed quality paths for PTCD. The path generation considers the special requirements of the PTCD procedure, such as insertion angle into a bile vessel. For instance, the criteria could easily be customized to exclude nearby below rib paths but include just-above rib trajectories. The intercostal artery and nerves, following the lower border of the rib, motivates to go through the intercostal space above the rib. The price for this enhanced level of detail in the patient model would be segmentation time for this fine structure, which is difficult, but of course the system can be flexibly enhanced along this line. Another argument is, that using the US-proble with some pressure aligns the probe in parallel to the ribs. The needle guiding rail at the end of the long side of the probe favors an insertion position in the middle between the ribs, which corresponds to our current quality criteria. However, going through the intercostal space just above a rib could be more safe than penetrating just below, where the intercostal artery and nerves are located. This could be reflected in the segmentation, but would cause much more time effort in virtual patient preparation. A heuristic detecting a nearby lower rib part and using a safety margin could help here, we postpone this to future work.

To our satisfaction the errors are very small and underline the new system to be very similar to the gold standard system. The used heuristics are simple and easily adapted to a new patient and reduce manual preparation time from 40 to 8 hours.

The systematic bias of 0.7 N for the MAE metric can be explained by slightly different time points in which organ borders are detected. While both algorithms do structurally the same, the detection instants can differ slightly (see Fig. 3). For the haptic experience of the user, this is not a crucial point as long as the emitted forces are equivalent and the distance between the detections are not too large.

The analysis of the worst case paths very well exposes flaws in the system or virtual patient modeling, which can be improved. In our exemplary study, we discovered peripheral structures in the pathway of the needle that are treated differently by the reference and the new system. In our experiment, closer investigation revealed ECG cables in the way of the needle paths (see Fig. 3). These flaws can be easily corrected by changing the system to recognize the cables accordingly or dismiss the faulty trajectories in the planning procedure as in reality cables would not be punctured. Generally, at the skin outside the patient clothing, tubes or cables are typical sources of the force differences encountered.

A few best paths from the planning procedure with small force errors can be used in the virtual patient model to serve as reference training paths for the students. Of course, a physician should review the paths.

To sum up, our new evaluation framework underlines direct haptic rendering with partially segmented structures to be a valuable method. In terms of haptic experience, important structures such as the fascia are clearly reproduced by the simulation and for unsegmented structures errors are small. As shown, the high number of test paths helps to further prove the validity in comparison to the reference system AcusVR. Generally speaking, the proposed evaluation framework is a good concept for the development of haptic algorithms and error analysis in this field. However, a reference patient and a validated system such as AcusVR is needed in this approach. But emerging from this reference data and system, patient-specific training and planning at reduced manual preparation work-load is only a few steps ahead.

In future, we will use the proposed evaluation methodology to further improve the algorithms for the PTCD site, develop a heuristic for real-time liver and risk structure voxel classification and test for inter-patient applicability of the used heuristics. We also aim at automatizing the segmentation of internal liver structures, i.e. its vessels and bile ducts. For the project in general, we intend to consider respiratory movement using 4D CT data resp. simulation of breathing by a model. Another interesting aspect would be the simulation of punctures also from inside the patient, i.e. an invasive surgery is involved. We plan to evaluate AcusVR2 with the proposed framework on 10 reference patients with cholestasis to provide an elaborate proof of concept of the new system.

The concept presented enables starting from an evaluated system to develop a new force feedback method with less burden of manual segmentation preparation time. At this juncture we aim at the educational, training and planning field and ideally envision to transfer the results later into clinical use (CAS).

Acknowledgement

This work is supported by the German Research Foundation (DFG, HA 2355/10-1).

Conflict of Interest

Andre Mastmeyer has no conflict of interest. Tobias Hecht has no conflict of interest. Dirk Fortmeier has no conflict of interest. Heinz Handels has no conflict of interest.

Informed Consent

Informed consent was obtained from all patients for being included in the study. The identity of the subjects under study is not revealed.

References

[1] C. Basdogan, M. Sedef, M. Harders, and S. Wesarg, "VR-based simulators for training in minimally invasive surgery," *IEEE Comput Graph Appl*, vol. 27, no. 2, pp. 54–66, 2007.

[2] N. Abolhassani, R. Patel, and M. Moallem, "Needle insertion into soft tissue: a survey.," *Medical engineering & physics*, vol. 29, no. 4, pp. 413–31, 2007.

[3] M. Färber, E. Hoeborn, D. Dalek, F. Hummel, C. Gerloff, C. A. Bohn, and H. Handels, "Training and evaluation of lumbar punctures in a VR-environment using a 6DOF haptic device," *MMVR16/Stud Health Technol Inform*, vol. 132, pp. 112–114, 2008.

[4] M. Färber, F. Hummel, C. Gerloff, and H. Handels, "Virtual reality simulator for the training of lumbar punctures," *Methods Inf Med*, vol. 48, no. 5, pp. 493–501, 2009.

[5] A. Mastmeyer, D. Fortmeier, and H. Handels, "Anisotropic Diffusion for Direct Haptic Volume Rendering in Lumbar Puncture Simulation," *Tolxdorff T., Deserno, T.M., Handels*

H., Meinzer H.P. (Hrsg.), Bildverarbeitung für die Medizin 2012, Informatik aktuell, Springer Verlag, Berlin, pp. 286–291, 2012.

[6] A. Mastmeyer, D. Fortmeier, and H. Handels, "Direct Haptic Volume Rendering in Lumbar Puncture Simulation," Stud Health Technol Inform, 173, pp. 280–286, 2012.

[7] P. L. Pereira, "Actual role of radiofrequency ablation of liver metastases," Eur Radiol, vol. 17, no. 8, pp. 2062–70, 2007.

[8] M. J. Murphy, "Tracking moving organs in real time," Seminars in Radiation Oncology, vol. 14, no. 1, pp. 91 – 100, 2004. High-Precision Radiation Therapy of Moving Targets.

[9] S. Nath, Z. Chen, N. Yue, S. Trumpore, and R. Peschel, "Dosimetric effects of needle divergence in prostate seed implant using 125l and 103pd radioactive seeds," Med Phys, vol. 27, no. 5, pp. 1058–66, 2000.

[10] L. Liwu, Practical Clinical Ultrasound Diagnosis. World Scientific Publishing Company, 1997.

[11] C. Baegert, C. Villard, P. Schreck, and L. Soler, "Multi-criteria trajectory planning for hepatic radiofrequency ablation," pp. 676–84, 2007.

[12] A. Seitel, M. Engel, C. M. Sommer, B. A. Radeleff, E.-V. Caroline, C. Baegert, M. Fangerau, K. H. Fritzsche, K. Yung, H.-P. Meinzer, and L. Maier-Hein, "Computer-assisted trajectory planning for percutaneous needle insertions," Med Phys, vol. 38, no. 6, pp. 3246–59, 2011.

[13] S. Ullrich and T. Kuhlen, "Haptic palpation for medical simulation in virtual environments.," IEEE transactions on visualization and computer graphics, vol. 18, pp. 617–25, Apr. 2012.

[14] S. Ullrich, O. Grottke, E. Fried, T. Frommen, W. Liao, R. Rossaint, T. Kuhlen, and T. M. Deserno, "An intersubject variable regional anesthesia simulator with a virtual patient architecture.," International journal of computer assisted radiology and surgery, vol. 4, pp. 561–70, Nov. 2009.

[15] K. Lundin, A. Ynnerman, and B. Gudmundsson, "Proxy-based haptic feedback from volumetric density data," Eurohaptics Conference, pp. 104–109, 2002.

[16] D. C. Ruspini, K. Kolarov, and O. Khatib, "The haptic display of complex graphical environments," Proceedings of the 24th annual conference on Computer graphics and interactive techniques SIGGRAPH 97, vol. vol, pp. 345–352, 1997.

[17] P. Dierckx, P. Suetens, and D. Vandermeulen, "An algorithm for surface reconstruction from planar contours using smoothing splines," Journal of Computational and Applied Mathematics, vol. 23, pp. 367–388, Sept. 1988.

[18] P. Campadelli, E. Casiraghi, and A. Esposito, "Liver segmentation from computed tomography scans: a survey and a new algorithm.," Artificial intelligence in medicine, vol. 45, no. 2-3, pp. 185–96, 2009.

[19] A. Mastmeyer, D. Fortmeier, E. Maghsoudi, M. Simon, and H. Handels, "Patch-based Label Fusion using Local Confidence-measures and Weak Segmentations," SPIE Medical Imaging 2013, pp. 86691N–1–86691N–11, 2013.

[20] A. M. Mharib, A. R. Ramli, S. Mashohor, and R. B. Mahmood, "Survey on liver CT image segmentation methods," Artificial Intelligence Review, vol. 37, no. 2, pp. 83–95, 2011.

[21] T. Heimann, B. van Ginneken, M. Styner, Y. Arzhaeva, V. Aurich, C. Bauer, A. Beck, C. Becker, R. Beichel, G. Bekes, F. Bello, G. Binnig, H. Bischof, A. Bornik, P. Cashman, Y. Chi, A. Cordova, B. Dawant, M. Fidrich, J. Furst, D. Furukawa, L. Grenacher, J. Hornegger, D. Kainmuller, R. Kitney, H. Kobatake, H. Lamecker, T. Lange, J. Lee, B. Lennon, R. Li, S. Li, H. P. Meinzer, G. Nemeth, D. Raicu, A. M. Rau, E. van Rikxoort, M. Rousson, L. Rusko, K. Saddi, G. Schmidt, D. Seghers, A. Shimizu, P. Slagmolen, E. Sorantin, G. Soza, R. Susomboon, J. Waite, A. Wimmer, and I. Wolf, "Comparison and evaluation of methods for liver segmentation from CT datasets," IEEE Trans Med Imaging, 2009.

[22] K. Engel, Real-time Volume Graphics. Ak Peters Series, A K Peters, Limited, 2006.

[23] J. E. Bresenham, "Algorithm for computer control of a digital plotter.," IBM Systems Journal, vol. 4(1), pp. 25–30, 1965.

[24] A. Mastmeyer, T. Hecht, D. Fortmeier, and H. Handels, "Raycasting based Evaluation Framework for Needle Insertion Force Feedback Algorithms," Tolxdorff T., Deserno, T.M., Handels H., Meinzer H.P. (Hrsg.), Bildverarbeitung für die Medizin 2013, Informatik aktuell, Springer Verlag, Berlin, pp. 3–8, 2013.

Real-Time Ultrasound Simulation for Training of US-Guided Needle Insertion in Breathing Virtual Patients

Andre Mastmeyer[a,1], Matthias Wilms[a], Dirk Fortmeier[a], Julian Schröder[a], Heinz Handels[a]
[a] Institute of Medical Informatics, University of Lübeck, Lübeck, Germany
[1] Corresponding author
This work is supported by DFG HA 2355/11-2

Abstract

One draw-back of most existing VR ultrasound training simulators is the use of static 3D patient models neglecting physiological changes induced e.g. by respiration or heart motion. In this paper to the aim of more realistic Ultrasound simulation, breathing motion extracted from 4D CT image data is integrated into our visuo-haptic simulation framework. The simulated ultrasound images are used for the training of US-guided needle insertion procedures in liver surgery. The methodology developed enables US simulation, 3D visualization and haptic steering of the ultrasound probe and the needle in real-time in breathing virtual bodies. Keywords: Ultrasound simulation, realistic breathing modeling, needle puncture.

1 Introduction

In this article, ultrasound (US) simulation is presented within a simulator animating a breathing virtual patient based on 3D CT data and a motion model steered by a realistic breathing pattern signal. US imaging in general or lesion puncture can be trained and planned with our simulation. Generally, virtual reality simulators offer physicians a virtual training environment, low cost for the interventions training and planning to be favored over potentially harming real patients. One focus of the development of virtual reality (VR) simulators in recent years lies on the simulation of US imaging for diagnosis and interventions such as needle punctures [1, 2, 3, 4]. From our group, systems and methods for simulating the puncture workflow in the liver area [5] and the spinal canal [6] have been published. In order to enable a realistic work-flow training, besides visual rendering of the patient, techniques for virtual haptic interaction are currently under development. We use special haptic I/O devices to offer the possibility to navigate the US probe and the needle. A restriction of most of the existing VR training simulators is the use of static patient images disregarding the motion of the anatomy in the area of interest. This can be a viable assumption e.g. for simulating lumbar punctures [6]. However, with puncture interventions in the abdomen near the diaphragm (liver) or lower thorax (thoracentesis) it is a huge simplification, since these structures can move to a large extent (5 cm) under the influence of respiratory motion [7]. They are affected by strong deformations that should be taken into account for realistic puncture simulations. Previously published approaches try to incorporate breathing by simple parametric, regular, periodic linear shear models. For example in [8], a sine-shaped regular movement field is proposed, which only is a rough approximation of realistic respiratory motion. The realistic modeling, simulation and estimation of respiratory motion is subject of current research in the field of radiation therapy of abdominal and thoracic tumors [9]. In our paper, this is integrated with the GPU-enhanced real-time simulation of US-images based on CT patient image data. The success of ultrasound-guided needle punctures is highly dependent on the skills of the user. Possibilities of training and planning successful puncture procedures in clinical environments are hardly available to the medical student. Just in time planning and training of US-guided interventions are frequently performed on real patients and under supervision of experienced physicians, which is not a harm- and stress-free environment for both medical apprentices and patients. Alternatively, doll models can be used for training, which are not specific to an actual clinical case. To remedy this situation, we propose the training and planning of ultrasound examinations and needle puncture interventions with a 4D VR simulator. The advantage of a simulator is that the ultrasound imaging of disease patterns can learned patient-specifically without endangering or molesting the living patient. In such a "serious computer game" setting, the automatic evaluation of the diagnosis and the puncture try made by the trainee is an attractive option. Furthermore as preparation, trained and planned upcoming real interventions should benefit in terms of quality and time-effort achieved in the actual procedure conduct.

This paper describes the implementation of an US simulation on Graphics hardware (CUDA). The simulator uses 4D CT (3D+t) data prepared in a modeling step to simulate the ultrasound imaging under realistic patient motion. Only certain key structures such as bile ducts, blood vessels and other key structures need to be segmented for an accurate localization and visualization. In addition, an ultrasound Doppler simulation is optionally available to display the flow in blood vessels. The US simulation is based on the methods of Reichl et al. [10], Wein et al. [11] and Karamalis [12].

The paper is organized as follows: First the used 4D data sets are briefly described. Then we summarize the estimation and use of a breathing motion model for US simulation on static 3D patient data. Imaging simulation at the US probe is then elaborated. The results are presented as images and additional video material.

2 Methods and Materials

The starting point for this work is a VR training simulator (Figures 1, 2) for various puncture procedures (e.g. liver biopsies) developed by our group [5, 6, 13, 14]. The simulation of the virtual patient is based on a static 3D and a dynamic 4D CT data set (14 phases) from which a motion model is pre-generated. We use a voxel size of 2x2x2.7 mm after resampling to a 256^3 grid to cope with the memory limits of our NVIDIA Quadro 4000 graphics card. In the visualization part, a direct volume rendering method based on ray-casting is used [14].

2.1 Respiratory Motion Models

In recent years, the field of radiotherapy for lung and liver tumors is augmented by new imaging techniques, such as spatio-temporal 4D imaging (CT and MRI). 4D CT and MRI image data can be used to improve treatment by the analysis of individual patient respiratory motion patterns. A 4D CT data sets consist of a sequence of n 3D CT images $I_{j\in 1,...,n} : \Omega \to \mathbb{R} \, (\Omega \subset \mathbb{R}^3)$, which represent the patient's anatomy in different phases of

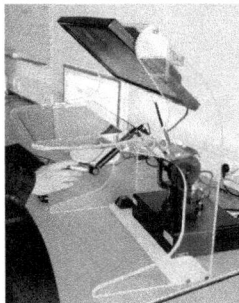

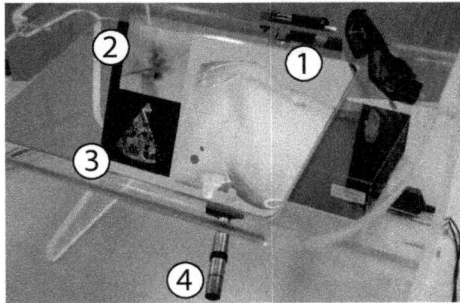

Figure 1: The workbench for eye-hand coordination: Wearing stereoscopic shutter glasses the user looks at the scene reflected by a semi-transparent mirror.

Figure 2: UI of our simulator with: (a) (1) Main rendering window, (2) X-ray rendering window, (3) ultrasound rendering window and (4) haptic device handle. The system uses a Geomagic Phantom Premium 1.5 6DOF (HighForce) as haptic I/O device and a combination of shutter glasses and a stereoscopic monitor for visuo-haptic immersion.

a single respiratory cycle. Non-linear deformations $\varphi_j : \Omega \to \Omega$ between the phases I_j and a selected reference phase I_{ref} are estimated by image registration [15] to establish voxel-wise correspondences.

Next, we briefly describe our model for realistic breathing motion [9]. In our method using the spirometry signal $s(t)$ from image acquisition, breathing motion is parametrized based on a 2D spirometry signal $\hat{\mathbf{z}}(t) = (s(t), s'(t))$ using the time derivative $s'(t)$. It can represent different depths of breathing (inter-cycle variability) and distinguish inhalation and exhalation phase. Assuming that a linear relationship between the respiratory signal and the internal movement is valid, the previously determined n transformations φ_j with respiratory signal states $\hat{\mathbf{z}}(t_j)$ are used for the interpolation of the 4D data from a multivariate linear motion model:

$$\hat{\varphi}(\mathbf{x}, t) = \bar{a}_1(\mathbf{x}) \cdot s(t) + \bar{a}_2(\mathbf{x}) \cdot s'(t) + \bar{a}_3(\mathbf{x}), \ \mathbf{x} \subset \Omega, \tag{1}$$

the coefficients $\bar{a}_{1..3}$ (vector fields) of which have been determined by linear regression. Applied to the image data I_{ref}, the trained motion field function $\hat{\varphi}(\mathbf{x}, t)$ provides the associated reference image under motion for continuous time t [13]:

$$I_t(\mathbf{x}) = I_{ref}(\mathbf{x}) \circ \hat{\varphi}(\mathbf{x}, t). \tag{2}$$

2.2 Ultrasound Simulation

The ultrasound simulation working on I_t can be divided into six steps. They are visualized in Figure 3 and described in the following paragraphs.

1. Sampling of the 4D CT Data: In the first step, a 2D image depending on the orientation and position of the US probe is generated from the 3D+t data $I_t(\mathbf{x})$ sampled on A-mode beam fan points x_i starting with x_0 near the transducer. In advance, also the direction vectors $\mathbf{d}$ of the individual beams are calculated on the graphics card in parallel. Per beam one CUDA block and one thread per sampled point is used.

2. Calculation of the Acoustic Impedance: On a ray fan beam, once individual points x_i and the HU intensities $I_t(x_i)$ have been sampled, the corresponding acoustic impedance Z_i can be estimated:

$$Z_i = 349.281 \cdot \rho(x_i) - 0.151261 \cdot \rho(x_i)^2 + 0.00117651 \cdot \rho(x_i)^3 \tag{3}$$

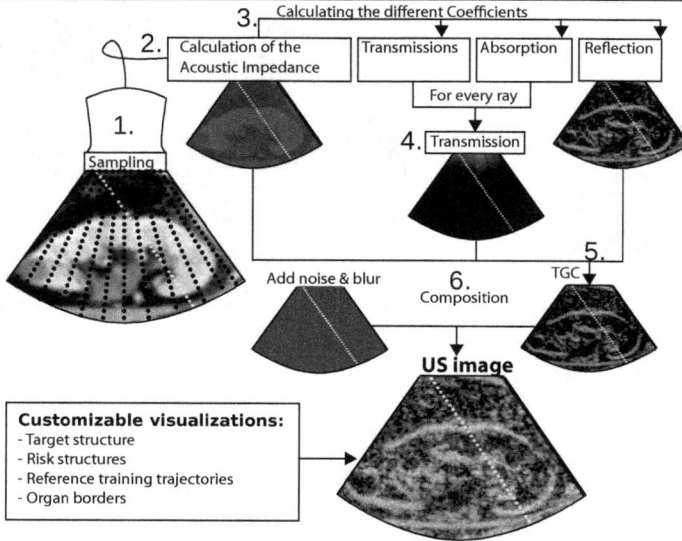

Figure 3: Scheme of the individual US simulation steps, starting with the sampling of the CT image towards the simulated US image. The yellow dotted line shows the target path of the needle in a US-guided puncture using the rail guidance. The numbers comply with the paragraphs in the text.

The conversion from HU intensities to densities ρ is based on Schneider et al. [16], see Table 1. Since the propagation velocity c of ultrasound is dependent on the tissue, the acoustic impedance $Z = \rho \cdot c$ is interpolated between air, water and bone as proposed by e.g. Reichl et al. [10]. For lung, bone and vessels, segmentation masks are used to provide correct values [17]. Due to the deviation of the estimated values from standard values found in the literature [17], at this point selected segmentation masks are used to correct for lung, bone and vessels as the estimate from Eq. 3 is inaccurate for them.

In the preparation of the latter structures, the segmentation of vessels is the most challenging, while bone and lungs can be segmented by standard methods sufficiently. For educational purposes, the targeted lesion should be segmented also.

3. Calculating the Coefficients: Using the same CUDA kernel layout, the transmission and reflection coefficients are calculated from the acoustic impedance Z and the direction vectors $\mathbf{d}$ of the beam ray [12]. The transmission T_i and reflection R_i can be estimated as [10, 17]:

$$T_i = \frac{4 \cdot Z_i \cdot Z_{i+1}}{Z_{i+1} + Z_i}, \; R_i = \left(\frac{Z_{i+1} - Z_i}{Z_{i+1} + Z_i}\right)^2 \tag{4}$$

The angle of incidence of a ray on a border of an anatomical structure can be calculated with estimated surface normals (image gradient). Finally, the absorption coefficient μ_i at position x_i can be determined by the combination of HU values and those proposed by the labeled data from the literature [17] for special structures. For unsegmented soft tissue (common structures), an average absorption coefficient of $0,55dB/cm$ is used [17].

4. Calculation of Transmission and Reflection: The incoming intensity at a pixel can not be individually, independently and in parallel be calculated for all pixels, as it depends on the tissue properties of the previously traversed media. This motivates a changed CUDA kernel layout: a CUDA block is called per transducer iterating over all sampled points on the respective beams and calculates the remaining intensity for each point. The emitted intensity from the probe continuously converts into heat, absorption and reflection. In the simulation, a normal intensity $I_0^{US} = 1$ is emitted from the probe. Absorption and transmission factors decrease it with increasing distance from the probe:

$$I_{in}^{US}(x_i) = I_{in}^{US}(x_{i-1}) \cdot T_i \cdot \exp(-\mu_i \cdot s \cdot f/10) \tag{5}$$

with s the sample spacing and f the sound frequency. On its way inside the body, the stepwise calculated intensity $I_{in}^{US}(x_i)$ equals the proportion, which still is present at a certain depth in the tissue and is available for reflection. For efficiency reasons neglecting dispersion, we assume that the reflected intensity with reflection angle ϕ_i and reflection coefficient R_i:

$$I_{ref}^{US}(x_i) = I_{in}^{US}(x_i) \cdot \cos(\phi_i)^2 \cdot R_i \tag{6}$$

travels on the same way back to the transducer where it came from. We use $cos(\phi_i) = (\mathbf{d} \cdot \nabla Z_i) / (\|\mathbf{d}\| \cdot \|\nabla Z_i\|)$ in a quadratic Lambert's cosine law accentuating specular reflection [10]. Backward, the finally received intensity $I_{fin}^{US}(x_i) = I_{ref}^{US}(x_i) \cdot I_{in}^{US}(x_i)$ again has been decreased stepwise caused by the tissue properties cumulated in $I_{in}^{US}(x_i)$.

5. *Post-Processing of Data - Time Gain Control (TGC):* With the returned signals received at the probe, a post-processing takes place. Usually, the larger the distances of the reflections from the probe, the stronger signals are attenuated by the tissue. Now, a depth compensation step can assure the same reflections rendered for the same intensities. We compensate for the attenuation by the tissue through a depth d dependent TGC gain, which is also present in commercial US devices. Returned signals are amplified depending on their reflection distance resp. time. The TGC gain used is based on the attenuation of the selected frequency in a fabric with a constant attenuation coefficient of $0,55dB/cm$, which is the average value for soft tissue equivalent [17]. By Eq. 7, the attenuation for a used frequency of 3 MHz and depth d can be calculated:

$$f(d) = \exp(-0.55 \cdot d \cdot 3/10.0)^2. \tag{7}$$

To amplify a signal intensity $I_{fin}^{US}(x_i)$ from a certain depth the round trip attenuation has to be considered, hence the exponential is squared. With this attenuation gain, the amplified signal is calculated:

$$I_{amp}^{US}(x_i) = \frac{I_{fin}^{US}(x_i)}{f(d)} \cdot I_0^{US}. \tag{8}$$

Due to the assumed constant attenuation in the tissue, behind weakly absorbent tissue brightening can occur. This happens, e.g. behind a filled urine bladder, due to a low attenuation coefficient of about $< 0.02dB/cm$ (of water) [17].

6. *B-mode Composition of the US Image:* At the different points in time, the composition of the beam fan image is based on the weighted image sum from Karamalis [12]. Finally besides assisting overlay visualizations, an artificial Perlin noise is added to the image and it is folded with a Gaussian mask, so that the typical ultrasound image appearance is mimicked. More visualizations can be added for training purposes: outlines or transparent overlays of the targets of the puncture, risk structures, other optionally segmented objects and a Doppler simulation by color modulation, so that even small blood vessels become visible. The puncture needle is shown in gray in the ultrasound image, the projected target trajectory of the needle subject to the needle guide rail mounted at the side of the US probe is yellow-dashed.

3 Results

Figure 4 compares a real and simulated US image of a kidney.

HU range	Equation for $\rho =$
HU > 100	$1.017 + 0.592 \cdot 0.001 \cdot HU$
$100 \leq HU > 22$	$1.003 + 1.169 \cdot 0.001 \cdot HU$
$22 \leq HU > 14$	1.03
$14 \leq HU > -99$	$1.018 + 0.893 \cdot 0.001 \cdot HU$
$-99 \leq HU$	$1.03091 + 0.0010297 \cdot HU$

Table 1: Case-based calculation of density from HU values [16].

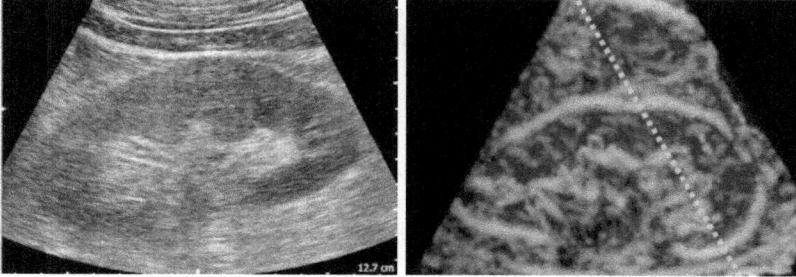

Figure 4: Example of a real (left) and a simulated (right) US image of the kidney.

The shape of the kidney is clearly visible in both images, but the real image has softer edges and a radial blur. Furthermore, the kidneys show their typical local US-noise. This was not considered in our current simulation. Figure 5 and the supplied video material[1] illustrate simulated US images and renderings of the liver during breathing with various auxiliary visualizations present, so vessels and target lesion can be clearly differentiated. The simulated breathing deformations to the tissue and needle in Figure 5 are clearly visible. Dark areas without sound reflection in the lower left of the simulated US image correspond to the lungs, a risk structure not to be punctured.

The non-linear deformations due to respiratory motion are also shown explicitly in the supplied video material[2]. For an US image of output size 256x256 pixels, 256 beams in parallel CUDA-blocks are calculated with 512 beam points in CUDA-threads. The calculation of the US simulation on its own requires 8.017 ms with a NVIDIA Quadro 4000 and achieves a maximum of 124 frames per second.

4 Conclusions

In this paper, the real-time simulation of ultrasound images under realistic breathing motion was presented based on 4D CT images and some key structure segmentations. The typical US shading in tissue by reflection and absorption can be successfully simulated. In addition, auxiliary visualizations, such as simulated Doppler US, can be added to the US image. A Doppler US replica is needed, since a Doppler US simulation is not possible due to lack of blood flow information with the available 3D data sets. The training and planning of needle puncture interventions under realistic breathing motion is successfully enabled using our software. In the future, we intend to implement enhanced Doppler simulation using simulated blood flow information, the use of two haptic devices for better eye-hand coordination and improve on typical US imaging artifact such as a radial blur and noise pattern, that can be slightly observed in Figure 4. To not require 4D CT scans for every patient we plan to deform existing motion models to new 3D patient data.

---

[1]https://goo.gl/AvXjQd

Figure 5: Time sequence of liver puncture during exhalation: ribs (gray), bile ducts (left: green, right: pale red), a simulated lesion (yellow). and Doppler simulation for blood vessels (red-yellow) as optional assisting visualizations. Dark areas on the lower left of the US image correspond to the lungs, where sound is not reflected. A full movie with similar content can be found on the web: https://goo.gl/AvXjQd

References

[1] L. Ap Cynydd, N. W. John, F. P. Vidal, D. A. Gould, E. Joekes, and P. Littler, "Cost effective ultrasound imaging training mentor for use in developing countries," *Stud Health Technol Inform*, vol. 142, pp. 49–54, 2009.

[2] F. P. Vidal, N. W. John, A. E. Healey, and D. A. Gould, "Simulation of ultrasound guided needle puncture using patient specific data with 3d textures and volume haptics," *Computer Animation and Virtual Worlds*, vol. 19, no. 2, pp. 111–127, 2008.

[3] D. Magee, Y. Zhu, R. Ratnalingam, P. Gardner, and D. Kessel, "An augmented reality simulator for ultrasound guided needle placement training," *Medical & biological engineering & computing*, vol. 45, no. 10, pp. 957–967, 2007.

[4] C. Forest, O. Comas, C. Vaysière, L. Soler, and J. Marescaux, "Ultrasound and needle insertion simulators built on real patient-based data," *Stud Health Technol Inform*, vol. 125, p. 136, 2006.

[5] D. Fortmeier, A. Mastmeyer, and H. Handels, "Image-based soft tissue deformation algorithms for real-time simulation of liver puncture," *Curr Med Imaging Rev*, vol. 9, pp. 154–165, 2013.

[6] M. Färber, F. Hummel, C. Gerloff, and H. Handels, "Virtual reality simulator for the training of lumbar punctures," *Method Inform Med*, vol. 48, pp. 493–501, 2009 2009.

[7] P. Keall, T. Yamamoto, and Y. Suh, "Introduction to 4d motion modeling and 4d radiotherapy," in *4D Modeling and Estimation of Respiratory Motion for Radiation Therapy* (J. Ehrhardt and C. Lorenz, eds.), Biological and Medical Physics, Biomedical Engineering, pp. 1–21, Springer Berlin Heidelberg, 2013.

[8] P. Villard, F. Vidal, L. Cenydd, R. Holbrey, S. Pisharody, S. Johnson, A. Bulpitt, N. John, F. Bello, and D. Gould, "Interventional radiology virtual simulator for liver biopsy," *Int J Comput Assist Radiol Surg*, vol. 9, no. 2, pp. 255–267, 2014.

[9] M. Wilms, R. Werner, J. Ehrhardt, A. Schmidt-Richberg, H.-P. Schlemmer, and H. Handels, "Multivariate regression approaches for surrogate-based diffeomorphic estimation of respiratory motion in radiation therapy," *Phys Med Biol*, vol. 59, p. 1147–1164, 2014.

[10] T. Reichl, J. Passenger, O. Acosta, and O. Salvado, "Real-time ultrasound simulation on GPU," in *Proc CSIRO ICT Centre Conference*, Nov. 2008.

[11] W. Wein, S. Brunke, A. Khamene, M. Callstrom, and N. Navab, "Automatic ct-ultrasound registration for diagnostic imaging and image-guided intervention," *Med Image Anal*, vol. 12, no. 5, pp. 577 – 585, 2008.

[12] A. Karamalis, *GPU Ultrasound Simulation and Volume Reconstruction*. Master Thesis, Faculty of Computer Science at Technical University of Munich, 2009.

[13] D. Fortmeier, M. Wilms, A. Mastmeyer, and H. Handels, "Direct visuo-haptic 4d volume rendering using respiratory motion models," *IEEE Trans Haptics*, vol. PP, no. 99, pp. 1–1, 2015.

[14] D. Fortmeier, A. Mastmeyer, J. Schroder, and H. Handels, "A virtual reality system for ptcd simulation using direct visuo-haptic rendering of partially segmented image data," *IEEE J Biomed Health Inform*, vol. PP, no. 99, pp. 1–1, 2015.

[15] A. Schmidt-Richberg, R. Werner, H. Handels, and J. Ehrhardt, "Estimation of slipping organ motion by registration with direction-dependent regularization," *Med Image Anal*, vol. 16, pp. 150 – 159, 1/2012 2012.

[16] U. Schneider, E. Pedroni, and A. Lomax, "The calibration of ct hounsfield units for radiotherapy treatment planning," *Phys Med Biol*, vol. 41, no. 1, p. 111, 1996.

[17] J. Bushberg, J. Seibert, E. Leidholdt, and J. Boone, *The Essential Physics of Medical Imaging*. Wolters Kluwer Health, 2011.

Random Forest Classification of Large Volume Structures for Visuo-Haptic Rendering in CT Images

Andre Mastmeyer, Dirk Fortmeier, Heinz Handels
Institute of Medical Informatics, University of Lübeck, Lübeck, Germany

Abstract

For patient-specific voxel-based visuo-haptic rendering of CT scans of the liver area, the fully automatic segmentation of large volume structures such as skin, soft tissue, lungs and intestine (risk structures) is important. Using a machine learning based approach, several existing segmentations from 10 segmented gold-standard patients are learned by random decision forests individually and collectively. The core of this paper is feature selection and the application of the learned classifiers to a new patient data set. In a leave-some-out cross-validation, the obtained full volume segmentations are compared to the gold-standard segmentations of the untrained patients. The proposed classifiers use a multi-dimensional feature space to estimate the hidden truth, instead of relying on clinical standard threshold and connectivity based methods. The result of our efficient whole-body section classification are multi-label maps with the considered tissues. For visuo-haptic simulation, other small volume structures would have to be segmented additionally. We also take a look into these structures (liver vessels). For an experimental leave-some-out study consisting of 10 patients, the proposed method performs much more efficiently compared to state of the art methods. In two variants of leave-some-out experiments we obtain best mean DICE ratios of 0.79, 0.97, 0.63 and 0.83 for skin, soft tissue, hard bone and risk structures. Liver structures are segmented with DICE 0.93 for the liver, 0.43 for blood vessels and 0.39 for bile vessels.
Keywords: Classifier based segmentation, large volume, liver structures, multi-dimensional feature space, leave-some-out cross-validation, voxel-based visuo-haptic direct volume rendering, CT post-processing, patient-specific virtual reality simulation.

1 Introduction

The efficient segmentation of abdominal structures in the liver area is important for patient-specific visuo-haptic rendering in virtual reality (VR) needle insertion simulation [1]. Large volume structures are usually segmented either by full manual contouring or semi-automatically with threshold and connectivity based approaches [2]. The latter approach still requires manual seed point and threshold selections as well as morphological post-processing[3] which is time-consuming. Here we propose a quick random forest classification (RFC) of large volume structures to help on-time hepatic surgery and radiation treatment training and planning [4]. After our classification, patient preparation potentially is reduced to segmentation editing of the remaining key liver structures such as hepatic vessels or tumors. With GPU-based massive parallel approaches currently proposed for random forest classification [5], efficient RFC is a matter of seconds. In the abdominal area, large inter-patient shape variations and pathologies can occur. Our method consists of two steps after general label and feature selection: classifier training using a reference patient or group and application to a new patient. In the preparation phase the selected features and labels are key factors and determine the accuracy of the results when applied to new patients.

The clinical state of the art for our focused tissue classes is defined by: manual contouring [6] which can take up to 40 h depending on the level of detail of segmentation. Seeded region growing [2] requiring manual thresholds and seed points selection. Structure-wise morphological post-processing [3] and manual segmentation review and editing[1] still are often mandatory.

In this contribution we present a new efficient whole-body classification of selected key tissues. We use a RFC framework and define multi-dimensional label transfer functions that make the labeling of large-volume structures in the targeted unseen patient a snap and available on-line during direct visuo-haptic volume rendering driven by voxel-classification.

2 Methods

2.1 Data and Preprocessing

The data used consists of 10 patient data sets from clinical routine CT scans with 512x512 pixels and 1-3 mm slice distance. The number of slices taken from the full liver area ranges from 50 to 140; pixel sizes are limited from 0.637 to 0.835 mm. All addressed structures for this study were manually segmented by three medical experts. The patients were mainly of similar body fat distribution and acquisition was carried out in portal-venous phase. Patient data preprocessing comprises z field of view cutting to the liver-area, removal of structures outside the body, e.g. table, cables and devices, by auto-seeded volume growing and morphological hole filling.

Before the training phase, a histogram matching [7] to a chosen representative reference patient is carried out to normalize the image intensities of the data sets. We use five equidistant volume percentages as match points for piece-wise linear intensity interval scaling. By this means the patient-specific intensity variations are reduced which can be caused e.g. by different contrast agent perfusion states in the patients. For the RFC learning phase, the intensity data is augmented by additional feature maps described in the next section, which improves the discrimination of the structures in a higher dimensional feature space.

2.2 Random Forest Classification

Highly efficient random forest classification has been described in depth by other authors [4, 8, 9]. It is very appealing to be integrated into our direct visuo-haptic volume rendering approach described in [1].

Generally, we start with a training sample set S that contains individual pre-classified samples:

$s_i = (l^i, f_0^i, f_1^i, ..., f_n^i)$. Regarding one training image I with N voxels, a sample corresponds

---

[1]http://www.slicer.org/ and http://www.itksnap.org/

to a voxel at position index i $(i \leq N)$. The label map l^i as class identifier and $n + 1$ selected derived feature maps $f_{0..n}$ gives the sample set S:

$$S = \left\{ \left(l^0, f_0^0, f_1^0, ..., f_n^0 \right), ..., \left(l^i, f_0^i, f_1^i, ..., f_n^i \right), ..., \left(l^N, f_0^N, f_1^N, ..., f_n^N \right) \right\}.$$

These features used in the learning stage of the random forest classifier R and facing new patient images, we can obtain a label estimate $\hat{l}^j$ for a feature sample $f^j = \left(f_0^j, f_1^j, ..., f_n^j \right)$ from R for new patient data voxels at positions j:

$$\hat{l}^j = R\left(f^j \right).$$

For the accuracy of the voxel classification result (ideally $\hat{l}^j = l^j$ if the gold-standard l^j is known) it is important to select label and feature maps that allow the RFC to discriminate well.

For our experiments in this study, we have chosen the following intensity and spatial features:

(1) The basic feature naturally is the image intensity: $f_0^i = I\left(i \right)$.

(2) The second (spatial) feature is the distance from the skin. It is derived from the image intensities as signed Euclidean distance D [mm] of the voxel world position $\vec{x}_i$ from the skin surface:

$$f_1^i = D_{skin}\left(\vec{x}_i \right). \tag{1}$$

The skin surface is obtained by thresholding the intensity data by 200 HU. Being inside the body box is indicated by convention as a positive sign of the Euclidean distance.

(3) The third feature investigated is the gradient magnitude of the image:

$$f_2^i = \left| \nabla I\left(\vec{x}_i \right) \right|. \tag{2}$$

The features are easily calculated for training and classification of new patient images.

2.3 Implementation Details and Study Set-up

The described method efficiently computes voxel classifications based on random forest classification. For only two features, the classifier can be stored and displayed as a 2D transfer function image. Yet another feature yields a 3D volume transfer function image and so on. RFCs can be easily sub-sampled to GPU compatible transfer functions images to serve as n dimensional lookup tables that can be used effectively and efficiently for direct volume rendering as proposed in [1].

In this paper, we define two gapless label maps offering supposedly high discriminative power for classification. This way, we generate two specialized RF classifiers for different sets of target structures:

1. Large volume structures with labels for skin, soft tissue (muscles/fascia, bile/blood vessels, heart, kidneys, splen, liver, stomach, pancreas), compact bone and risk structures (lungs, intestine). We ignore the gall bladder and cables, the former can contain pathologic stones; both are of atypical appearance (Fig. 1a).

2. Liver structures with labels for liver, bile ducts and hepatic blood vessels. We aggregate all other structures in a container label similar to the soft tissue label from set 1 (Fig. 1b).

There is always a background label for air outside the body (Fig. 1).

In this study, we train the feature combinations (f_0, f_1), (f_0, f_2), (f_1, f_2) and (f_0, f_1, f_2) for each label map. On completion of the preprocessing steps, the two structure specific RFCs are trained in two opposed leave-some-out experiments using an open source RFC framework [10]:

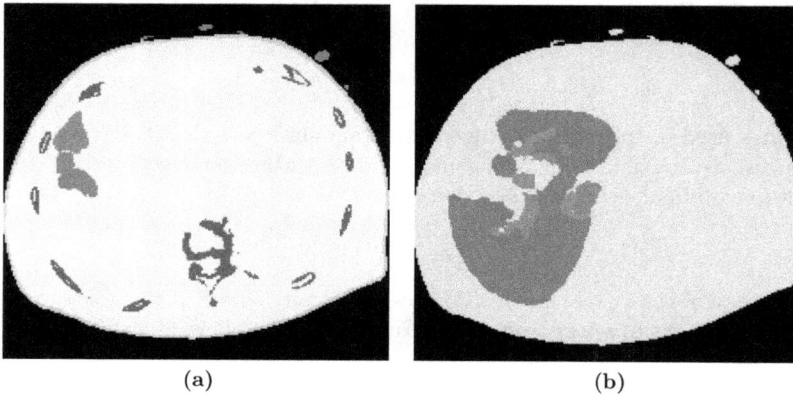

(a)   (b)

Figure 1: Label maps for two RFCs with air outside the body in black: (a) Large volume structures (orange=skin, yellow=soft tissue, purple=bone, red=risk structure, grey=ignored structures), (b) liver structures (brown=liver, green=bile ducts, red=hepatic blood vessels, orange=other objects).

Leave-90%-out: For each feature map tuple from one patient a RFC is trained. Nine test patients are left out from training, one patient serves for training. This is the fastest way to generate RF classifiers. $\binom{10}{9} = 10$ very time efficient classifiers are built.

Leave-30%-out: Classifiers are built from training groups of 7 patients. Three test patients are left out from training, seven patients serve for training. Significantly more time is used for training and to conduct the experiment, but over-fitting RFCs to one patient is expected to be mitigated. In total $\binom{10}{7} = 120$ classifiers are built, i.e. $\binom{9}{7} = 36$ classifiers are available to one test patient.

Subject to the chosen feature combination and specialization w.r.t. structures, the classifiers are then ready to be applied in 10 leave-9-out and $3 \cdot \binom{10}{3} = 360$ leave-3-out test patient classifications. They are applied to the intensity image data of the patients left-out from training. The evaluation metric chosen is the DICE similarity coefficient (DSC) against reference segmentations. Time measurements are carried out on a Dell Precision T3500 workstation for the more complex leave-3-out variant.

3 Results

The structure-specific RFCs show very promising results for some feature combinations. The final multi-label segmentations were generated by applying a classifier R to each voxel of a targeted test patients.

Fig. 2 shows qualitative results for the large volume structure for patient 5 classified by a RFCs trained with patients 1, 2, 4, 6, 7, 8, 10 and feature set (f_0, f_1). Complete quantitative results are shown in Tabs. 1 and 2 and Figs. 4 and 5.

As can be seen, the best average DICE coefficients for the tissues can be found in bold and underlined font in Tabs. 1 to 2 on the right. In terms of large volume structures, we achieve best mean (median) DSC values of 0.79 (0.84) for skin, 0.97 (0.97) for soft tissue, 0.63 (0.62) for bone and 0.83 (0.92) for risk structures. Overall, the classifiers trained with 7 patients and three features perform favorable. Regarding liver structures, we can achieve 0.93 (0.95) for the liver, 0.43 (0.44) for blood vessels and 0.39 (0.35) for the difficult bile ducts. Qualitative results are shown in Fig. 3.

(a) 2D transfer function with (f_0, f_1): intensity (x) and skin distance (y)   **(b)** Classification result

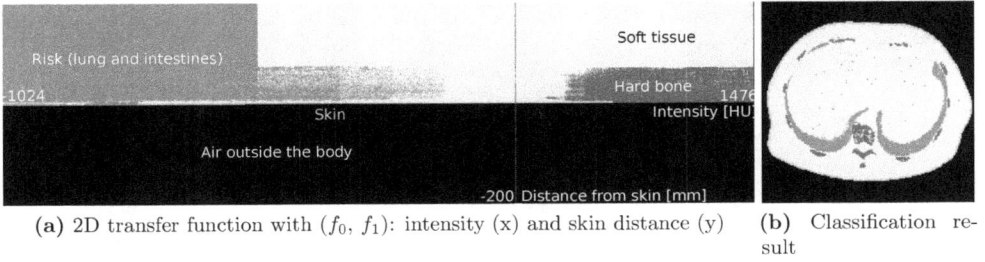

Figure 2: Large volume structures multi-label segmentation results: (a) The 2D transfer function image generated from a classifier from Tab. 2a. (b) Axial slice of a segmentation: Skin, soft tissue, bone and risk structures (lungs) are clearly differentiable despite some speckles.

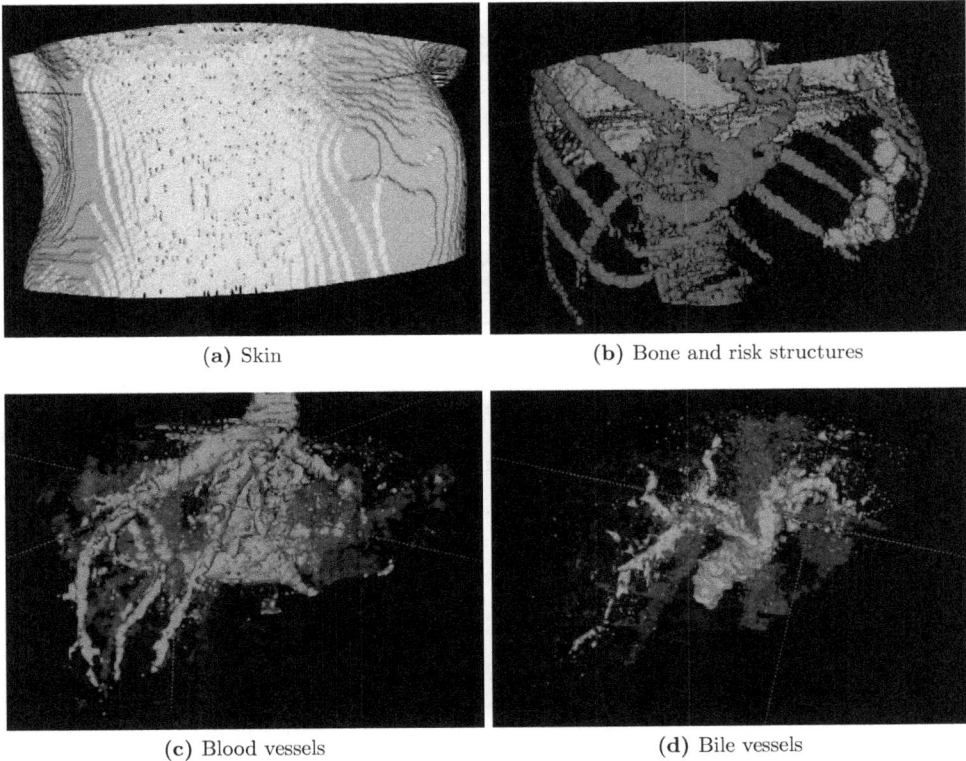

(a) Skin

(b) Bone and risk structures

(c) Blood vessels

(d) Bile vessels

Figure 3: Multi-label segmentation results in right-anterior view: (a) Skin, (b) bone and risk structures (despeckled), cf. Fig. 2. (c) The rendered result from an optimal blood vessel 3D transfer function, cf. Tab 1d. (d) The result from an optimal bile vessel 3D transfer function, cf. Tab. 2d. The despeckled liver mask with its apexes is shown as a frame of reference in transparent brown.

Tiss. \ Tar.pat. [DSC±Std.]	1	2	3	4	5	6	7+	8	9	10	Mean±Std.	Median
Skin	0.67±0.09	0.77±0.18	0.74±0.13	0.69±0.11	0.76±0.14	0.74±0.16	0.58±0.08	0.64±0.18	0.77±0.17	0.80±0.12	0.72±0.07	0.74
Soft t.	0.94±0.01	0.97±0.01	0.97±0.01	0.97±0.01	0.98±0.00	0.95±0.01	0.94±0.02	0.97±0.00	0.97±0.01	0.97±0.01	0.96±0.01	0.97
Bone	0.56±0.10	0.59±0.07	0.56±0.04	0.56±0.08	0.75±0.04	0.52±0.07	0.39±0.14	0.48±0.04	0.56±0.06	0.67±0.10	0.56±0.09	0.56
Risk*	0.78±0.04	0.92±0.02	0.90±0.03	0.93±0.04	0.93±0.02	0.86±0.08	0.14±0.03	0.82±0.07	0.88±0.05	0.92±0.07	0.81±0.23	0.89
Mean±Std.	0.74±0.14	0.81±0.15	0.79±0.16	0.79±0.17	0.86±0.10	0.77±0.16	0.51±0.29	0.73±0.18	0.79±0.15	0.84±0.12	0.76±0.19	0.79
Liver	0.92±0.02	0.87±0.17	0.88±0.19	0.88±0.17	0.90±0.15	0.73±0.18	0.82±0.13	0.85±0.21	0.85±0.21	0.78±0.24	0.85±0.05	0.86
-Blood	0.01±0.01	0.40±0.20	0.53±0.19	0.47±0.21	0.52±0.18	0.29±0.12	0.37±0.12	0.46±0.21	0.45±0.17	0.39±0.18	0.39±0.14	0.43
-Bile	0.22±0.17	0.13±0.10	0.19±0.10	0.14±0.07	0.11±0.06	0.07±0.05	0.20±0.12	0.24±0.15	0.17±0.12	0.18±0.08	0.16±0.05	0.17
Mean±Std.	0.38±0.39	0.47±0.31	0.53±0.30	0.50±0.30	0.51±0.32	0.36±0.27	0.46±0.26	0.52±0.25	0.49±0.28	0.45±0.25	0.47±0.30	0.48

(a) 2D feature set (f_0, f_1)

Tiss. \ Tar.pat. [DSC±Std.]	1	2	3	4	5	6	7+	8	9	10	Mean±Std.	Median
Skin	0.29±0.12	0.53±0.26	0.45±0.23	0.43±0.26	0.50±0.21	0.43±0.21	0.37±0.18	0.39±0.30	0.53±0.20	0.30±0.21	0.42±0.08	0.43
Soft t.	0.93±0.02	0.97±0.01	0.96±0.01	0.96±0.01	0.98±0.00	0.96±0.01	0.95±0.01	0.96±0.01	0.97±0.01	0.97±0.01	0.96±0.01	0.96
Bone	0.54±0.14	0.57±0.08	0.56±0.04	0.52±0.06	0.73±0.03	0.53±0.07	0.53±0.13	0.48±0.04	0.52±0.06	0.64±0.09	0.56±0.07	0.54
Risk*	0.69±0.08	0.82±0.08	0.82±0.06	0.85±0.07	0.78±0.10	0.77±0.06	0.55±0.30	0.77±0.09	0.78±0.05	0.86±0.05	0.77±0.09	0.78
Mean±Std.	0.61±0.23	0.72±0.18	0.70±0.20	0.69±0.22	0.75±0.17	0.67±0.21	0.60±0.21	0.65±0.23	0.70±0.19	0.69±0.26	0.68±0.22	0.69
Liver	0.37±0.18	0.91±0.06	0.91±0.03	0.91±0.04	0.91±0.07	0.91±0.05	0.62±0.21	0.89±0.07	0.90±0.05	0.94±0.02	0.83±0.18	0.91
-Blood	0.06±0.01	0.45±0.20	0.19±0.09	0.39±0.18	0.31±0.16	0.45±0.19	0.29±0.08	0.46±0.20	0.53±0.23	0.16±0.08	0.33±0.15	0.35
-Bile	0.39±0.11	0.19±0.05	0.19±0.08	0.25±0.08	0.20±0.08	0.08±0.05	0.41±0.09	0.51±0.07	0.41±0.08	0.27±0.13	0.29±0.13	0.26
Mean±Std.	0.27±0.15	0.52±0.30	0.43±0.34	0.52±0.28	0.47±0.31	0.48±0.34	0.44±0.14	0.62±0.19	0.61±0.21	0.46±0.34	0.48±0.29	0.47

(b) 2D feature set (f_0, f_2)

Tiss. \ Tar.pat. [DSC±Std.]	1	2	3	4	5	6	7+	8	9	10	Mean±Std.	Median
Skin	0.60±0.10	0.84±0.09	0.88±0.07	0.89±0.05	0.87±0.07	0.83±0.10	0.43±0.07	0.82±0.05	0.84±0.09	0.78±0.07	0.78±0.14	0.83
Soft t.	0.89±0.02	0.90±0.01	0.88±0.01	0.88±0.01	0.92±0.01	0.89±0.01	0.94±0.01	0.91±0.01	0.90±0.01	0.89±0.01	0.90±0.02	0.90
Bone	0.08±0.02	0.10±0.02	0.10±0.02	0.09±0.02	0.11±0.02	0.07±0.02	0.07±0.04	0.07±0.02	0.08±0.02	0.09±0.01	0.09±0.01	0.09
Risk*	0.21±0.03	0.27±0.07	0.26±0.07	0.29±0.07	0.24±0.04	0.31±0.08	0.07±0.01	0.26±0.06	0.28±0.06	0.28±0.09	0.25±0.06	0.27
Mean±Std.	0.45±0.32	0.53±0.35	0.53±0.35	0.54±0.35	0.53±0.36	0.53±0.35	0.38±0.35	0.52±0.36	0.53±0.35	0.51±0.33	0.50±0.35	0.53
Liver	0.83±0.09	0.93±0.02	0.93±0.03	0.92±0.03	0.94±0.03	0.93±0.03	0.92±0.03	0.92±0.02	0.90±0.02	0.94±0.02	**0.92±0.03**	**0.93**
-Blood	0.11±0.06	0.26±0.13	0.37±0.16	0.28±0.11	0.30±0.11	0.24±0.14	0.09±0.06	0.27±0.11	0.33±0.13	0.36±0.16	0.26±0.09	0.28
-Bile	0.04±0.03	0.05±0.02	0.05±0.03	0.05±0.02	0.03±0.02	0.02±0.01	0.05±0.03	0.06±0.03	0.06±0.03	0.05±0.03	0.05±0.01	0.05
Mean±Std.	0.33±0.36	0.41±0.38	0.45±0.36	0.42±0.37	0.42±0.38	0.40±0.39	0.35±0.40	0.42±0.37	0.43±0.35	0.45±0.37	0.41±0.37	0.42

(c) 2D feature set (f_1, f_2)

Tiss. \ Tar.pat. [DSC±Std.]	1	2	3	4	5	6	7+	8	9	10	Mean±Std.	Median
Skin	0.57±0.11	0.86±0.10	0.86±0.09	0.85±0.09	0.86±0.08	0.83±0.11	0.56±0.06	0.77±0.08	0.86±0.09	0.76±0.07	**0.78±0.11**	<u>0.84</u>
Soft t.	0.95±0.01	0.97±0.01	0.97±0.01	0.97±0.01	0.98±0.00	0.96±0.01	0.95±0.02	0.97±0.00	0.97±0.01	0.97±0.01	**0.97±0.01**	<u>0.97</u>
Bone	0.62±0.10	0.65±0.08	0.59±0.06	0.59±0.09	0.78±0.05	0.55±0.07	0.42±0.15	0.52±0.05	0.59±0.07	0.70±0.11	**0.60±0.09**	0.59
Risk*	0.78±0.04	0.92±0.02	0.90±0.02	0.94±0.03	0.94±0.02	0.88±0.04	0.15±0.02	0.83±0.06	0.89±0.03	0.93±0.05	**0.82±0.23**	0.90
Mean±Std.	0.73±0.15	0.85±0.12	0.83±0.14	0.84±0.15	0.89±0.08	0.80±0.15	0.52±0.29	0.77±0.16	0.83±0.14	0.84±0.11	**0.79±0.19**	0.83
Liver	0.36±0.11	0.93±0.06	0.92±0.04	0.92±0.05	0.92±0.08	0.94±0.03	0.82±0.11	0.91±0.08	0.92±0.05	0.96±0.02	0.86±0.17	0.92
-Blood	0.06±0.01	0.54±0.24	0.37±0.15	0.47±0.21	0.42±0.21	0.54±0.19	0.32±0.16	0.53±0.25	0.62±0.26	0.39±0.17	**0.43±0.15**	<u>0.44</u>
-Bile	0.26±0.19	0.26±0.08	0.25±0.08	0.28±0.09	0.20±0.09	0.10±0.06	0.51±0.14	0.45±0.13	0.43±0.08	0.34±0.10	**0.31±0.12**	0.27
Mean±Std.	0.23±0.12	0.58±0.27	0.51±0.29	0.56±0.27	0.51±0.30	0.53±0.34	0.55±0.21	0.63±0.20	0.66±0.20	0.56±0.28	**0.53±0.28**	0.56

(d) 3D feature set (f_0, f_1, f_2)

Table 1: 2D/3D feature groups from a leave-90%-out experiment (a-d): Each cell of the sub-tables shows mean DSCs for the considered tissues with a targeted patient classified by 9 RFCs individually trained with one of the training patients. * Risk structures comprise lung and intestines not to be cut by a puncture needle. + obese patient. Best average values from sub-tables in bold font, best values from this table and Tab. 2 underlined on the right.

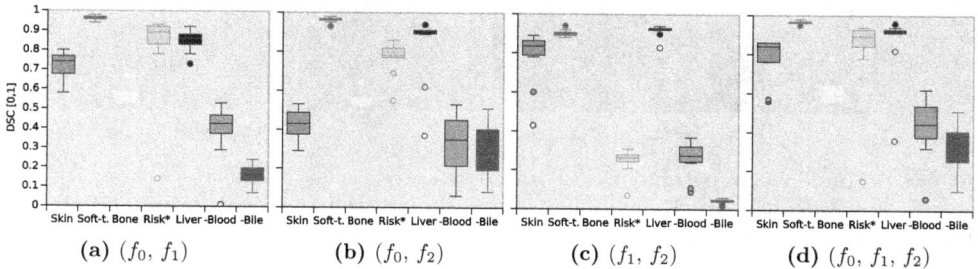

(a) (f_0, f_1) **(b)** (f_0, f_2) **(c)** (f_1, f_2) **(d)** (f_0, f_1, f_2)

Figure 4: Boxplots from leave-90%-out experiments and feature combinations, cf. Tab. 1.

Tiss. \ Tar.pat. [DSC±Std.]	1	2	3	4	5	6	7+	8	9	10	Mean±Std.	Median
Skin	0.71±0.02	0.84±0.04	0.85±0.14	0.84±0.03	0.88±0.01	0.84±0.04	0.46±0.10	0.64±0.12	0.83±0.03	0.91±0.04	0.78±0.13	0.84
Soft t.	0.95±0.00	0.97±0.00	0.94±0.16	0.97±0.00	0.98±0.00	0.96±0.01	0.92±0.16	0.94±0.16	0.97±0.00	0.98±0.00	0.96±0.02	0.96
Bone	0.60±0.03	0.65±0.02	0.57±0.10	0.58±0.02	0.76±0.01	0.56±0.03	0.35±0.06	0.47±0.08	0.57±0.02	0.69±0.03	0.58±0.11	0.57
Risk*	0.76±0.01	0.92±0.00	0.89±0.15	0.94±0.00	0.93±0.00	0.91±0.02	0.14±0.03	0.80±0.14	0.89±0.01	0.94±0.01	0.81±0.23	0.90
Mean±Std.	0.76±0.13	0.84±0.12	0.81±0.14	0.83±0.15	0.89±0.08	0.82±0.15	0.47±0.29	0.71±0.18	0.81±0.15	0.88±0.11	0.78±0.20	0.81
Liver	0.50±0.04	0.95±0.01	0.95±0.00	0.94±0.00	0.95±0.00	0.94±0.01	0.89±0.02	0.93±0.01	0.93±0.01	0.96±0.00	0.89±0.13	0.94
-Blood	0.06±0.01	0.38±0.14	0.33±0.07	0.36±0.10	0.35±0.08	0.34±0.10	0.14±0.09	0.35±0.13	0.45±0.16	0.35±0.08	0.31±0.11	0.35
-Bile	0.19±0.03	0.17±0.01	0.19±0.02	0.18±0.01	0.04±0.00	0.04±0.00	0.44±0.03	0.36±0.05	0.35±0.02	0.22±0.02	0.23±0.11	0.19
Mean±Std.	0.25±0.18	0.50±0.33	0.49±0.33	0.49±0.32	0.48±0.35	0.44±0.37	0.49±0.31	0.55±0.27	0.58±0.25	0.51±0.32	0.48±0.32	0.49

(a) 2D feature group (f_0, f_1)

Tiss. \ Tar.pat. [DSC±Std.]	1	2	3	4	5	6	7+	8	9	10	Mean±Std.	Median
Skin	0.41±0.04	0.72±0.02	0.75±0.03	0.74±0.04	0.80±0.03	0.62±0.04	0.55±0.04	0.65±0.02	0.69±0.02	0.44±0.05	0.64±0.13	0.67
Soft t.	0.95±0.00	0.97±0.00	0.97±0.00	0.97±0.00	0.98±0.00	0.96±0.00	0.95±0.01	0.97±0.00	0.97±0.00	0.97±0.00	**0.97±0.01**	**0.97**
Bone	0.60±0.03	0.60±0.01	0.56±0.01	0.52±0.01	0.74±0.01	0.55±0.01	0.60±0.04	0.50±0.01	0.53±0.01	0.62±0.01	0.58±0.06	0.58
Risk*	0.71±0.01	0.88±0.01	0.87±0.01	0.90±0.01	0.88±0.01	0.81±0.02	0.13±0.11	0.81±0.02	0.83±0.01	0.88±0.00	0.77±0.22	0.85
Mean±Std.	0.67±0.20	0.79±0.14	0.79±0.15	0.78±0.17	0.85±0.09	0.73±0.16	0.56±0.29	0.73±0.18	0.76±0.16	0.73±0.21	0.74±0.20	0.74
Liver	0.59±0.12	0.93±0.01	0.94±0.00	0.93±0.00	0.95±0.00	0.93±0.01	0.83±0.07	0.92±0.01	0.91±0.01	0.95±0.00	0.89±0.10	0.93
-Blood	0.07±0.01	0.29±0.10	0.12±0.02	0.23±0.07	0.20±0.06	0.25±0.08	0.24±0.06	0.30±0.10	0.30±0.11	0.10±0.01	0.21±0.08	0.23
-Bile	0.36±0.03	0.18±0.01	0.24±0.02	0.29±0.02	0.19±0.01	0.08±0.01	0.34±0.04	0.51±0.02	0.42±0.02	0.30±0.03	0.29±0.12	0.29
Mean±Std.	0.34±0.21	0.47±0.33	0.43±0.36	0.48±0.32	0.45±0.36	0.42±0.37	0.47±0.26	0.58±0.26	0.54±0.26	0.45±0.36	0.46±0.32	0.46

(b) 2D feature group (f_0, f_2)

Tiss. \ Tar.pat. [DSC±Std.]	1	2	3	4	5	6	7+	8	9	10	Mean±Std.	Median
Skin	0.59±0.02	0.85±0.02	0.87±0.02	0.89±0.01	0.87±0.01	0.83±0.02	0.41±0.04	0.79±0.02	0.84±0.02	0.78±0.01	0.77±0.15	0.83
Soft t.	0.88±0.02	0.90±0.00	0.88±0.00	0.88±0.00	0.92±0.00	0.89±0.00	0.95±0.00	0.92±0.00	0.91±0.00	0.89±0.00	0.90±0.02	0.90
Bone	0.08±0.00	0.10±0.00	0.10±0.01	0.10±0.00	0.11±0.01	0.08±0.01	0.09±0.01	0.07±0.00	0.08±0.00	0.10±0.00	0.09±0.01	0.10
Risk*	0.22±0.00	0.29±0.01	0.29±0.01	0.31±0.01	0.26±0.01	0.35±0.02	0.08±0.00	0.28±0.01	0.30±0.01	0.31±0.01	0.27±0.07	0.29
Mean±Std.	0.44±0.31	0.54±0.35	0.54±0.35	0.54±0.35	0.54±0.36	0.54±0.34	0.38±0.35	0.52±0.35	0.53±0.35	0.52±0.33	0.51±0.35	0.54
Liver	0.86±0.01	0.94±0.00	0.95±0.00	0.94±0.00	0.96±0.00	0.94±0.00	0.94±0.00	0.93±0.00	0.92±0.00	0.96±0.00	**0.93±0.03**	0.94
-Blood	0.17±0.02	0.25±0.03	0.36±0.06	0.28±0.03	0.29±0.04	0.20±0.03	0.08±0.01	0.27±0.04	0.30±0.04	0.33±0.06	0.25±0.08	0.28
-Bile	0.05±0.01	0.05±0.00	0.06±0.01	0.05±0.01	0.03±0.00	0.02±0.00	0.06±0.01	0.07±0.01	0.07±0.01	0.07±0.01	0.05±0.02	0.06
Mean±Std.	0.36±0.36	0.41±0.38	0.46±0.37	0.42±0.38	0.43±0.39	0.39±0.40	0.36±0.41	0.42±0.37	0.43±0.36	0.45±0.37	0.41±0.38	0.42

(c) 2D feature group (f_1, f_2)

Tiss. \ Tar.pat. [DSC±Std.]	1	2	3	4	5	6	7+	8	9	10	Mean±Std.	Median
Skin	0.59±0.05	0.87±0.02	0.90±0.02	0.90±0.03	0.90±0.01	0.81±0.04	0.46±0.04	0.78±0.02	0.88±0.01	0.79±0.02	**0.79±0.14**	**0.84**
Soft t.	0.96±0.00	0.98±0.00	0.97±0.00	0.97±0.00	0.99±0.00	0.97±0.01	0.95±0.00	0.97±0.00	0.98±0.00	0.98±0.00	**0.97±0.01**	**0.97**
Bone	0.74±0.02	0.69±0.02	0.62±0.01	0.60±0.03	0.80±0.01	0.62±0.02	0.38±0.02	0.55±0.01	0.63±0.02	0.71±0.03	**0.63±0.11**	**0.62**
Risk*	0.77±0.01	0.94±0.00	0.92±0.00	0.92±0.00	0.95±0.01	0.95±0.00	0.92±0.02	0.15±0.01	0.86±0.02	0.90±0.00	**0.83±0.23**	**0.92**
Mean±Std.	0.76±0.13	0.87±0.11	0.85±0.14	0.86±0.15	0.91±0.07	0.83±0.13	0.48±0.29	0.79±0.15	0.85±0.13	0.86±0.11	**0.81±0.19**	**0.85**
Liver	0.49±0.06	0.96±0.01	0.96±0.00	0.95±0.00	0.97±0.00	0.95±0.00	0.90±0.02	0.95±0.00	0.94±0.01	0.97±0.00	**0.90±0.14**	**0.95**
-Blood	0.07±0.01	0.47±0.14	0.39±0.09	0.42±0.11	0.44±0.10	0.37±0.11	0.17±0.10	0.49±0.12	0.51±0.16	0.38±0.10	**0.37±0.13**	**0.41**
-Bile	0.28±0.04	0.29±0.02	0.37±0.04	0.34±0.02	0.31±0.02	0.16±0.01	0.61±0.03	0.59±0.05	0.49±0.02	0.50±0.03	**0.39±0.14**	**0.35**
Mean±Std.	0.28±0.17	0.57±0.28	0.57±0.27	0.57±0.27	0.57±0.29	0.49±0.33	0.56±0.30	0.68±0.20	0.65±0.21	0.62±0.25	**0.56±0.28**	**0.57**

(d) 3D feature group (f_0, f_1, f_2)

Table 2: 2D/3D feature groups from a leave-30%-out experiment (a-d): Each cell of the sub-tables shows mean DSCs for the considered tissues with a targeted patients classified by 36 RFCs each trained with seven training patients. * Risk structures comprise lung and intestines not to be cut by a puncture needle. + obese patient. Best average values from sub-tables in bold font, best values from this table and Tab. 1 underlined on the right.

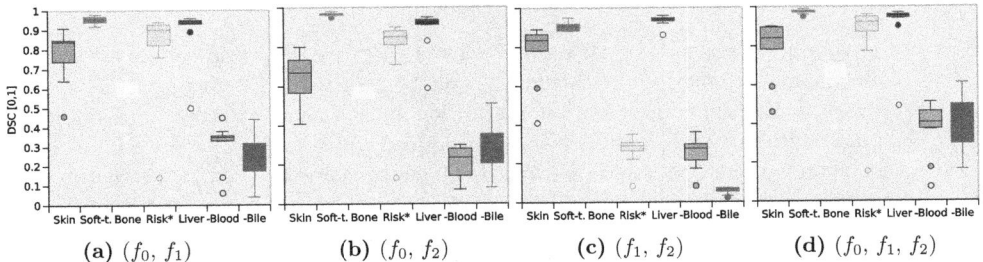

(a) (f_0, f_1)   **(b)** (f_0, f_2)   **(c)** (f_1, f_2)   **(d)** (f_0, f_1, f_2)

Figure 5: Boxplots from leave-30%-out experiments and feature combinations, cf. Tab. 2.

Average training time for each RFC with seven patients and three feature dimensions is 10 seconds on an Intel Xeon W3530@2.8 Ghz processor with 8 cores (ht) and 24 Gb main memory which is used at a level of 50%. Mean classification timing measurements indicate 1.6E-06 seconds per sampled voxel (625000 Hz), which translates to 3.7 seconds per dataset. Single voxel classification fits well into our haptic volume-rendering loop detecting voxel labels at the needle tip and running at 2000 Hz [1].

4 Discussion

In this work, we present a new concept for highly efficient single and whole-body voxel classification ready to be applied in the context of direct visuo-haptic volume rendering. Another important aspect of this work is enabling patient-specific VR simulation availablity. Typically in a clinical setting, there is no time available for tedious manual segmentation of unseen patient data from acute cases. Our results prove high quality segmentation of large volume and liver structures for single voxels and complete volume datasets is possible in a very timely manner. The results shown are very promising regarding the two factors of quality and time effort for individual samples as well as whole volumes. The ratio of quality and segmentation speed is unprecedented. The DSC values shown in this work are normally obtained using much more time consuming methods, which partially involve manual user interaction.

Large volume structure segmentation is very good from our point of view w.r.t. to our patient-specific virtual reality simulator. The achievable DSCs for the hepatic vessels are good. However despite the fast automatic segmentation, liver vessel structures still need visual inspection and manual correction to connect some isolated branches to the main tree, especially when it comes to the most difficult structure, i.e. bile ducts imaged without special contrast agent.

The proposed features for a targeted structure are easily identified from our result tables. Skin is obviouly segmented best including the spatial feature f_1 among others, i.e. the skin distance, in the feature set: Feature set (f_0, f_2) delivers worst results for the skin. The recommendation generally is to use the 3D feature set with 7 individuals trained. It is the most robust and generalizable choice.

However, the results for the liver could point to a special feature group (f_1, f_2) (skin distance vs. gradient magnitude) to be researched more thoroughly. The training of such a 2D RFC is much faster and high-frequency sample classification of course also profits. Postprocessing of the achieved segmentations to remove small isolated voxel groups (despeckling) would further improve the evaluation results [3].

5 Conclusion

The use of random forest classification and selected feature dimensions opens up a new perspective to clinically relevant near-time CT volume processing for various tasks, such as just-in-time patient-specific intervention 4D VR simulation using direct volume rendering [11]. Instead of just discrete labels, also visuo-haptic characteristics from a continuous domain for volume rendering could be learned. Of course some low-contrast structures are not segmented consistently well, such as fine vessel trees or pathologies as their appearance is very heterogeneous. From the perspective of a first study, with a few features, we show very promising results which surely can be further optimized, also for other structures.

Acknowledgements

This work is supported by the German Research Foundation (DFG HA2355/11-2).

References

[1] D. Fortmeier, A. Mastmeyer, J. Schroder, and H. Handels, "A virtual reality system for ptcd simulation using direct visuo-haptic rendering of partially segmented image data," *Biomedical and Health Informatics, IEEE Journal of*, vol. 20, pp. 355–366, Jan 2016.

[2] R. Adams and L. Bischof, "Seeded Region Growing," *IEEE Trans. Pattern Anal. Mach. Intell.*, vol. 16, no. 6, pp. 641–647, 1994.

[3] J. Serra, *Image analysis and mathematical morphology*. London New York: Academic Press, 1982.

[4] A. Criminisi, J. Shotton, D. Robertson, and E. Konukoglu, "Regression forests for efficient anatomy detection and localization in ct studies," in *Medical Computer Vision. Recognition Techniques and Applications in Medical Imaging*, pp. 106–117, Springer, 2011.

[5] H. Grahn, N. Lavesson, M. Lapajne, and D. Slat, "Cudarf: A cuda-based implementation of random forests," in *Computer Systems and Applications (AICCSA), 2011 9th IEEE/ACS International Conference on*, pp. 95–101, Dec 2011.

[6] Y. Wu and L. Yencharis, "Commercial 3d imaging software migrates to pc medical diagnostics," *Adv. Imag. Mag.*, pp. 16–21, 1998.

[7] L. Nyúl, J. K. Udupa, and X. Zhang, "New variants of a method of mri scale standardization," *IEEE Trans. Med. Imag.*, vol. 19, no. 2, pp. 143–150, 2000.

[8] L. Breiman, "Random forests," *Machine Learning*, vol. 45, no. 1, pp. 5–32, 2001.

[9] T. Hastie, R. Tibshirani, J. Friedman, and J. Franklin, *The elements of statistical learning: data mining, inference and prediction*, vol. 27. Springer, 2005.

[10] F. Pedregosa, G. Varoquaux, A. Gramfort, V. Michel, B. Thirion, O. Grisel, M. Blondel, P. Prettenhofer, R. Weiss, V. Dubourg, J. Vanderplas, A. Passos, D. Cournapeau, M. Brucher, M. Perrot, and E. Duchesnay, "Scikit-learn: machine learning in python," *Journal of Machine Learning Research*, vol. 12, pp. 2825–2830, 2011.

[11] D. Fortmeier, M. Wilms, A. Mastmeyer, and H. Handels, "Direct visuo-haptic 4d volume rendering using respiratory motion models," *Haptics, IEEE Transactions on*, vol. 8, pp. 371–383, Oct 2015.

Patch-based Label Fusion using Local Confidence Measures and Weak Segmentations

Andre Mastmeyer[a], Dirk Fortmeier[a,c], Ehsan Maghsoudi[a], Martin Simon[b], Heinz Handels[a]

[a] Institute of Medical Informatics, University of Lübeck, Lübeck, Germany
[b] Clinic for Radiology and Nuclear Medicine, University Medical Center Schleswig-Holstein, Lübeck, Germany
[c] Graduate School for Computing in Medicine and Life Sciences, University of Lübeck, Germany

Abstract

A system for the fully automatic segmentation of the liver and spleen is presented. In a multi-atlas based segmentation framework, several existing segmentations are deformed in parallel to image intensity based registrations targeting the unseen patient. A new locally adaptive label fusion method is presented as the core of this paper. In a patch comparison approach, the transformed segmentations are compared to a weak segmentation of the target organ in the unseen patient. The weak segmentation roughly estimates the hidden truth. Traditional fusion approaches just rely on the deformed expert segmentations only. The result of patch comparison is a confidence weight for a neighboring voxel-label in the atlas label images to contribute to the voxel under study. Fusion is finally carried out in a weighted averaging scheme. The new contribution is the incorporation of locally determined confidence features of the unseen patient into the fusion process. For a small experimental set-up consisting of 12 patients, the proposed method performs favorable to standard classifier label fusion methods. In leave-one-out experiments, we obtain a mean Dice ratio of 0.92 for the liver and 0.82 for the spleen.
Keywords: Multi-atlas based segmentation, label fusion, patch-based, local confidence, weak segmenter.

1 Introduction

Multi-atlas based segmentation of abdominal organs has gained considerable attention in the last years [1, 2, 3]. Clinical applications comprise hepatic surgery and radiation treatment planning. The bottle-neck task for the planning phase is the manual expert delineation of the target organs in the patient data. In the abdominal area, the challenge lies in coping with the very large inter-patient shape and structure variations and dealing with pathological cases. Three steps usually define a multi-atlas segmentation: registration, label map warping and label fusion. While in the first step the accurate registration is very important, another research focus lies on the final classifier label fusion of the segmentation candidates.

Several new strategies have been published recently: On a global scale, Asman [4] proposed the combination of benefits from multi-atlas approaches and dedicated segmentation methods. Agarwal [5] proposed local confidence measures to extend the previously developed SIMPLE algorithm. Hao [6] uses local texture features to train a support vector machine for local fusion. Chen [7] learns several weak segmentations to build a strong one. Non-local STAPLE is a reformulation of the original STAPLE algorithm in a non-local means framework incorporating image intensities into the process [8].

Preprocessing of our data consists of manually cropping the z-range of the data, thresholding and affine followed by non-linear registration. In this paper we use a diffeomorphic demons based registration approach [9]. After these preprocessing steps we obtain several candidate segmentations which fit the unseen patient more or less accurately. To unify the candidate segmentations, we present a new local label fusion technique using adaptive weights in a patch-based framework that takes gray value features of the targeted unseen patient data into account.

2 Methods

2.1 Data and Preprocessing

The data used consists of 12 clinical routine scans with 512x512 pixels and 5 mm slice distance. The number of slices ranges from 126 to 157; pixel sizes are limited from 0.637 to 0.835 mm. Livers and spleens were manually segmented by our clinical partners.

To normalize data sets w.r.t. the contained structures a manual z-cropping procedure takes place. The region selected covers the cranial beginning of the iliac crest to the caudal slices of the heart. By this means, the number of slices used in the following steps is reduced to 50 on average and the abdominal organs are included in the remaining data. The next step consists of the removal of structures outside the body box, which could hinder the image registration process. Patient table, cables and spurious artifacts from the table are removed this way. Mainly, volume growing and morphological operations are used here. For the affine registration step, the data is thresholded by 0 HU to highlight important structures (bones, inner organs), which help the affine registration to converge fast and provide a coarse overlap of the structures. The thresholding step is motivated by the below zero Hounsfield values of fatty connective tissue embedding the inner organs. The distance measure chosen is the sum of squared differences (SSD). The result of the coarse registration step is an affine transformation matrix, which is co-applied to the label data.

On completion of these steps, the 11 target data sets are registered to the reference data using a non-linear registration approach with diffeomorphic demons [9, 10]. In sum, 132 non-linear diffeomorphic registrations are carried out, 11 for each of the 12 leave-one-out experiments. The registrations are conducted on the cropped image data using a four resolution pyramiding scheme. The result of this phase are smooth deformation fields between the 11 target and the left-out reference image, which can be used to co-align the associated 11 segmentations to the unseen reference image.

The intersection and union (see fig. 1a, b) of the individual segmentations are calculated as assisting organ masks to estimate the organ gray value distribution in the reference image resulting in the mean μ_{org} and standard deviation σ_{org} (see section 2.3). Another purpose of the masks is to reduce the search space for the proposed algorithm, see section 2.2.1.

On grounds of the rather anisotropic data all results from the previous steps are used in the resolution with:

- original 5 mm slices and
- 1 mm slices by resampling.

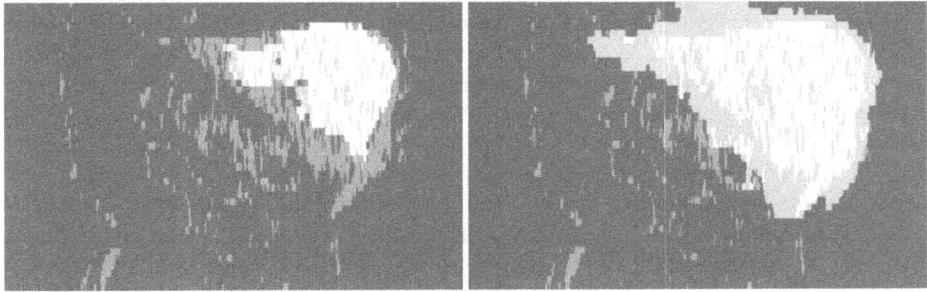

(a) Intersection (white) vs. weak segmentation (gray)

(b) Union (light gray) vs. included weak segmentation (white)

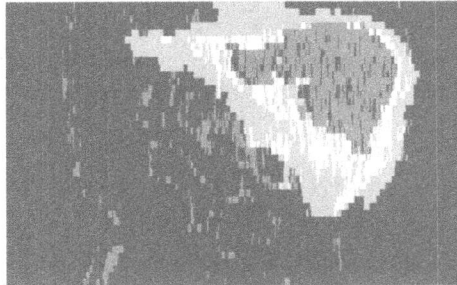

(c) Band (light gray and white) vs. weak segmentation (gray)

Figure 1: Union, intersection and unsure candidate band: The union of all segmentations around the weak segmentation of one subject (a). The intersection of the segmentations (b). The resulting banded region of interest for the calculations (c).

Resampling uses linear interpolation for gray value CT data and nearest neighbor interpolation for the segmentations.

2.2 Neighborhoods and Performance Cues

Majority Voting (MV) and Sum Rule (SR) fusion [11, 12] are by far the fastest fusion methods and deliver very good results. The bottleneck of many new fusion algorithms is computation time. To speed up the computations, we define sparse neighborhoods. Moreover, computation takes place in a band near the supposed organ border only.

2.2.1 Banded Calculation

For this means, the previously calculated organ masks are interpreted as (1) surely included voxels as seen in fig. 1a (intersection of the segmentations) and (2) candidate voxels for the voxels inside the union of all individual segmentations and outside the surely included voxels (see fig. 1c). Thus, subsequent calculations only take place in the band of candidate voxels, i.e. the result of an XOR between union and intersection of the segmentations.

2.2.2 Sparse Neighborhoods

The core of patch based label fusion is to compare a center patch in the unseen reference patient at a current voxel x_i to other patches in their neighborhood. These neighboring patches are extracted from the target subjects which are aligned via registration methods to the unseen patient.

Typically, the patch size is smaller than the neighborhood size, see fig. 2a. The definition of the neighborhood radius N_{rad} and patch radius P_{rad} strongly affects the performance of the algorithm. Smaller patch and neighborhood sizes boost the performance of the algorithm while the accuracy of the results may decrease.

Basically, the neighborhood of a voxel consists of adjacent voxels contained in a certain shape. In this work we restrict ourselves to cubical neighborhood and patch geometry. The full neighborhood simply consists of all voxels around a center voxel contained in the neighborhood shape, see fig. 2a. In terms of offset vectors (m, n, o) given in image coordinates, the neighborhood set $N(i)$ of a voxel x_i can be defined as follows:

$$N(i) = \bigcup_{m,n,o=-N_{rad}}^{N_{rad}} (m, n, o) \tag{1}$$

A sparse neighborhood only considers a smaller number of voxels compared to the full neighborhood. The first sparse neighborhood proposed here only takes into account every 2nd voxel (see fig. 2b):

$$N(i) = \bigcup_{m,n,o=-N_{rad}}^{N_{rad}} \begin{cases} (m, n, o), & m, n, o \, are \, all \, even \, numbers \\ \emptyset, & otherwise \end{cases} \tag{2}$$

The second "very sparse" neighborhood only takes into account voxels at the outer edges and corners, see fig. 2c. In terms of offsets, the sparsest neighborhood can be defined as:

$$N(i) = \bigcup_{m,n,o=-1}^{1} \begin{cases} (2 \cdot m \cdot P_{rad} + 1, \, 2 \cdot n \cdot P_{rad} + 1, \, 2 \cdot o \cdot P_{rad} + 1), & (m, n, o \, all \neq 0) \\ & \vee \, (((i \oplus j) \oplus k) \\ \emptyset, & otherwise \end{cases} \tag{3}$$

where $\oplus$ denotes the XOR operator. In this neighborhood the patches compared do not overlap but are still connected at a face or corner.

To account for anisotropic voxels as present in our data, calculations can be additionally restricted to the current slice that contains the voxel studied. The reason for this constraint is that with anistropic voxels (5mm slices) the geometry of the neighborhood can span much more space in z-direction than in x- and y-directions. Therefore, a metrically more isotropic neighborhood can be achieved using this restriction. A significant computational performance boost is another benefit of it. The different neighborhood sizes are shown in tab. 1.

2.2.3 Selected algorithms

Based on the previous reasoning the following variations of the proposed method resp. input data are studied:

Our algorithm in tab. 2 is denoted by the short-cut PBLC for "Patch Based Local Confidence". Furthermore we use the algorithms "Simultaneous Truth and Performance Estimation" (STAPLE) [13], "Selective and Iterative Method for Performance Level Estimation" (SIMPLE) [14], "Majority Voting" (MV) and "Sum Rule" (SR) [11, 12].

2.3 Patch-based Label Fusion

Patch-based label fusion for hippocampus and ventricle segmentation was introduced by Coupe [15]: A voxel x_i is set to be the center of a cubical (1) neighborhood and (2) patch. Neighborhood size and patch size may differ to adapt the algorithm to structure sizes and

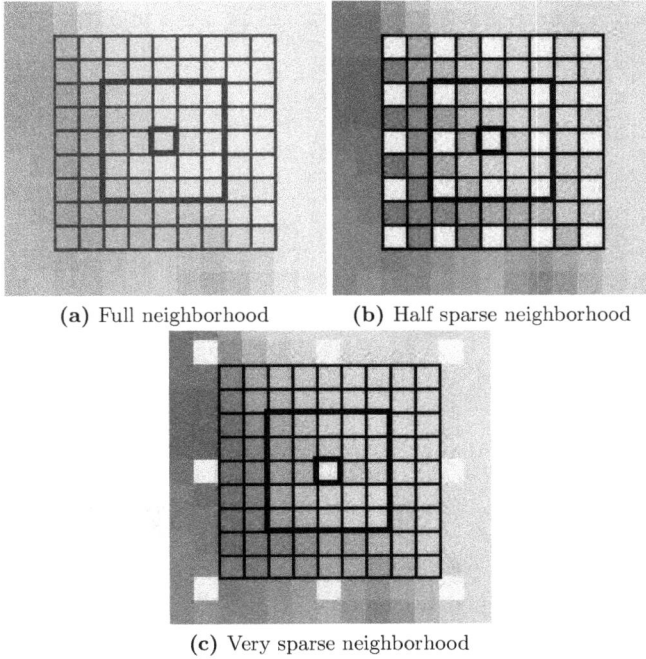

(a) Full neighborhood (b) Half sparse neighborhood

(c) Very sparse neighborhood

Figure 2: Center voxel (thick small square), neighborhood definition (grid with thin lines) and patch (thick square): Every voxel in the neighborhood region of a center voxel is visited (a). Only every second voxel (yellow small squares) is used for patch comparison (b). Only voxels at the corners and face centers are visited for comparison (c). The patch radius P_{rad} is set to a value of 2 and the neighborhood radius N_{rad} equals 4.

Neighborhood	$2 \cdot N_{rad} + 1 = 9$ Slices	Single Slice
Full	$9^3 = 729$	$9^2 = 81$
Sparse	$5^3 = 125$	$5^2 = 25$
Very Sparse	14	9

Table 1: Neighborhood sizes for $N_{rad} = 4$ and $P_{rad} = 2$.

Alg.-Acronym	Neigborhood Density	In-Plane Restriction	Resampling to 1 mm Slices
PBLC 1	full	no	no
PBLC 2	full	yes	no
PBLC 3	sparse	yes	no
PBLC 4	very sparse	yes	no
PBLC 5	very sparse	no	yes
PBLC 6	sparse	no	yes
PBLC 7	full	no	yes

Table 2: Algorithms variants used and their acronyms.

spatial mismatches from the registrations. Image traversal visits all voxels, compares the patch under study with patches in the neighborhood and computes a weighted average label guess by:

$$L_{est}(x_i) = \frac{\sum_{s=1}^{N} \sum_{j \epsilon N(i)} w(x_i, x_{s,j}) \cdot L(x_{s,j})}{\sum_{s=1}^{N} \sum_{j \epsilon N(i)} w(x_i, x_{s,j})} \tag{4}$$

where L_{est} is the continuous label estimate for a voxel, N is the number of atlases, $N(i)$ refers to the set of neighborhood voxels for i, w are the weights dependent on the reference data voxel under study x_i and the voxel $x_{s,j}$ in subject s at neighbor j. Finally, $L(x_{s,j})$ represents the label in the atlas of subject s at position j. The label estimate L_{est} is a fuzzy estimate, i.e. with binary label data it ranges from 0 to 1, and the label guess is defined by thresholding with e.g. 0.5. In the weight w the comparison of the reference patient gray value patch $P(x_i)$ centered at x_i and the target patient patch with center $x_{s,j}$ takes place as $w(x_i, x_{s,j}) = exp\left(-\frac{\|P(x_i), P(x_{s,j})\|_{L_2}}{h}\right)$. Here, the negative normalized L_2-norm divided by a decay parameter h is used as a patch distance measure, embedded in an exponential term. Consequently, the weight values lie in the continuum from 0 to 1 and low differences are preferred. The decay parameter h is recommended to be the minimal gray value patch distance in the L_2-norm.

In our proposed method, we use a weak segmentation as additional prior to the deformed atlas label data sets. Thus, we set the weights introducing local confidence measuring as follows:

$$w(x_i, x_{s,j}) = exp\left(-\frac{1 - J(P_{wSeg}(x_i), P_{seg}(x_{s,j}))}{h}\right) \tag{5}$$

where $P_{wSeg}(x_i)$ describes the label patch originating from the unseen reference image gray values that underwent some weak segmentation; and $P_{seg}(x_{s,j})$ is the label patch from the target subject atlas data. Lastly, J calculates the Jaccard coefficient and h is the decay parameter. These weights correlate the deformed atlas segmentations to the hidden truth guessed by a thresholding criterion, our weak segmenter:

$$\forall x \epsilon P_{wSeg}(x_i): \quad L(x) = \begin{cases} 1, & if \quad \mu_{org} - l \cdot \sigma_{org} < G(x) < \mu_{org} + l \cdot \sigma_{org} \\ 0, & otherwise \end{cases} \tag{6}$$

Here, L is the label at voxel x from the label patch, G describes the gray value in the reference image data, μ_{org} and σ_{org} are the organ normal distribution parameters estimated in the intersection of the candidate segmentations (see fig. 1c). The standard deviation factor l is dependent upon the organ under study. The intersection voxels used to estimate μ_{org} and σ_{org} are supposedly surely contained inside the liver resp. spleen of the reference patient.

On whole image scale, the results of the weak segmentation can look like point clouds where many positively labeled voxels concentrate in the area of the organ (see fig. 3a).

In summary, the described fusion method computes local similarity resp. confidence measures in the neighborhood of the studied voxel as weights for the neighboring labels to be averaged.

2.4 Study Set-Up

In a leave-one-out scheme we conduct 12 experiments: per experiment a multi-atlas segmentation is carried out (see section 2.1) for liver and spleen. It consists of an affine and variational registration of the image intensity data while co-warping the associated

(a) Typical weak segmentation　　　　　　　(b) Fusion image

(c) Resulting (blue overlay) vs. reference (yellow contour) segmentation

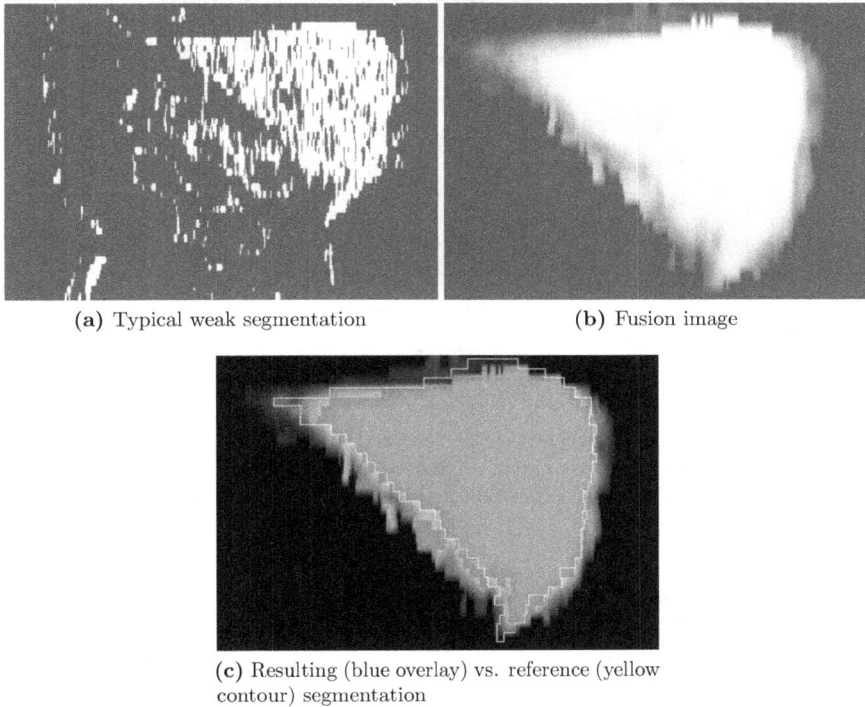

Figure 3: Intermediate and final results: The weak segmentation roughly indicates the organ borders and its inside by positive label concentration (a). The fusion image shows the fuzzy labeling (b). The expert segmentation is compared to the guessed segmentation (c).

label maps. Afterwards the label maps are fused with the proposed seven method variants and compared to four standard algorithms.

The proposed method is sensitive to the decay parameter h, for which we found a reasonable setting is 0.1. This way, very similar patches in the weak segmentation and the warped atlas label data contribute over-proportionally to the averaging. The final segmentation is generated by thresholding the resulting fusion weight map with 0.618. The patch radius P_{rad} is set to a value of 2 and neighborhood radius N_{rad} is chosen as 4. The organ dependent standard deviation factor l for our weak segmenter is chosen as 1 resp. 3 for the liver resp. spleen.

3 Results

Figs. 3 and 5 show qualitative results for reference patient 1. Quantitative results for the liver and spleen are shown in tab. 3 and fig. 4.

Overall, consistent advantages in comparison to the standard methods can be observed. PBLC4-5 mainly are the overall winners of the contest, which holds true for all evaluation metrics used.

The Dice coefficients are generally higher for the liver. The Mean Surface Distance globally is lower than the slice distance of the original data and on average is lower for the larger organ, i.e. the liver, while the Hausdorff distances are smaller for the spleen.

We take a closer look at the surface distances for one patient to inspect the location of the main errors in this metric. In fig. 5a the medial area of the liver is shown, here we typically

Organ	Liver			Spleen		
Alg. \ Metric	Dice	MSD [mm]	HD [mm]	Dice	MSD [mm]	HD [mm]
SIMPLE	0.88±0.06	3.30±1.47	31.48±9.30	0.78±0.12	3.49±1.93	27.90±13.04
VoteRule	0.90±0.04	2.99±1.17	29.81±12.99	0.79±0.15	3.33±2.23	24.85±12.03
SumRule	0.90±0.04	3.07±1.18	30.00±12.97	0.79±0.15	3.38±2.26	23.51±11.83
STAPLE	0.88±0.04	3.99±1.49	33.32±14.73	0.71±0.17	5.19±3.44	34.49±16.31
PBLC1	0.91±0.03	2.85±1.06	29.45±11.25	0.79±0.15	3.50±2.47	25.47±10.50
PBLC2	0.91±0.04	2.73±1.05	28.53±11.50	0.79±0.14	3.31±2.10	23.08±12.62
PBLC3	0.91±0.04	2.71±1.03	28.45±11.48	0.79±0.14	3.27±2.08	22.87±12.71
PBLC4	0.91±0.03	2.65±0.95	28.19±11.34	0.80±0.14	3.15±2.04	23.13±12.25
PBLC5	0.92±0.02	2.57±0.83	27.51±11.18	0.82±0.14	3.15±2.39	22.48±11.99
PBLC6	0.91±0.03	2.75±0.93	28.03±10.87	0.80±0.14	3.35±2.28	22.67±12.08
PBLC7	0.91±0.03	2.78±0.94	28.26±10.84	0.80±0.14	3.39±2.26	22.69±12.21
Winner	PBLC5	PBLC5	PBLC5	PBLC5	PBLC4	PBLC5
Winner w/o Resampling	PBLC4	PBLC4	PBLC4	PBLC4	PBLC4	PBLC3

Table 3: The table shows Dice coefficients, Mean Surface Distance (MSD) and Hausdorff Distance (HD) for four standard algorithms and seven variations of the proposed algorithm in our leave-one-out experiments. PBLC wins the competition with the fastest variant of the proposed algorithm (bottom rows).

observe a higher distribution of errors than on the periphery. This is also indicated in fig. 3c where the segmentation in blue leaks out of the yellow contour which depicts the aimed reference segmentation. The same observation is true for the spleen, the medial area is depicted in fig. 5b. The organ ensemble is shown finally in fig. 5c, where we also note that surface errors are smaller for the spleen than for the liver. In fig. 5c some higher errors can also be noticed on some peripheral spots of the liver.

Computation times for a single unseen patient on a Intel Xeon W3530 2.8 GHz workstation using 6 parallel threads are around one hour for PBLC1 and 2.5 minutes for PBLC4, which is the fastest variant of the algorithm w.r.t. the used data, see tab. 4.

Organ \ Alg. [min:sec]	PBLC1	PBLC2	PBLC3	PBLC4	PBLC5	PBLC6	PBLC7
Liver	50:16	6:38	2:25	1:28	12:52	44:58	242:19
Spleen	14:44	2:32	1:02	0:56	6:34	16:16	79:13

Table 4: Computation times for a label fusion targeting one patient on a Intel Xeon W3530 (6 threads) workstation in minutes:seconds.

Statistical testing of all results using one-way ANOVA showed no significant differences, but there is a clear tendency to favor the proposed method and thin slice CT data.

4 Conclusion

The overall results for the new method underline to follow the proposed direction of research. We can also posit the benefit of thin slice CT data for label fusion algorithms in general, which we only have simulated in our experiment. Of course resampling can not provide the missing details present in fine resolution data sets.

The most accelerated variant PBLC4 (approximately more than 20 times faster compared to PBLC1) while supposedly more inaccurate due to using a sparse neighborhood is not inferior to the other competitors. In fact this algorithm only performs calculations in a slice-wise manner, which is appropriate for highly anisotropic data. While very sparse, the spatial extension of the neighborhood is highest for this algorithm variant.

Regarding geometry and volume, the size and shape of an organ are important factors for the outcome of the algorithms. Larger organs tend to have higher Dice coefficients and lower Mean Surface Distances. The Hausdorff Distance characterizes outliers which are more likely to occur in complex shaped organs such as the liver with its lobes, fissures and apexes.

A closer inspection reveals that high surface distances occur in the fissures between the lobes of the liver which are not visible in the rendering and which are generally very difficult to segment resp. register. Thus organs with complicated geometric features such as fissures and lobes are prone to higher Hausdorff distances while compact organs such as the spleen are typically easier to tackle. The higher errors on the periphery of the liver might be due to some difficulties the registration algorithms face with aligning the rib cage correctly. We can see the mark of blurred rib lines in fig. 5c.

Summarizing, we present a new concept for a local patch-based confidence measure capable to combine dedicated strong or weak segmentation algorithms with multi-atlas label fusion. The incorporation of reference gray value image features opens up a new perspective of connecting the worlds of dedicated segmentation algorithms and multi-atlas based label fusion [4]. From the perspective of a first study, here a very weak segmenter is used for reference image feature generation, but in sum with the local confidence based fusion approach shows quite promising results in this small scale study with 12 patients.

In future new weak segmentation algorithms could be used. The threshold based weak segmenter used here could also be easily replaced (1) by stronger segmentation methods or (2) can incorporate more sophisticated preprocessing algorithms, such as (1) Level-Sets [16] or Graph-Cuts [17] on one hand and (2) image region homogenizers (e.g. Anisotropic Diffusion [18]) on the other hand. Another line to follow would be the enlargement of the study to 20-30 patients to provide more shape variability to the system which should further improve the performance. Post-processing of the segmentations might also be of value, registration and fusion artifacts which occur as spurious voxel groups and spikes could be favorably smoothed out. This might be achieved by a dedicated segmentation algorithm such as Graph-Cuts [17] which could be fed with the obtained results to improve just the fringe of the segmentation. Because of the averaging nature of the fusion algorithms the major bottleneck is to capture the finer shape details as present in the medial and lower apex of the liver, while artifacts from the registration algorithms such as spikes need to be smoothed away.

For the proposed method, the trade-off of the influence between the weak segmenter and the warped expert segmentations is a delicate question. In this implementation the correlation of the experts takes place after the correlation of one expert with the weak segmentation is done. Finally, they are averaged with the same weight. In the averaging scheme the system could try to weight the individual correlation results using a performance measure to give better correlations a higher influence in the average (weighted averaging) or automatically sort out outliers as presented in the SIMPLE method [14].

The main problem for the overall system remains the time complexity and quality of the non-linear registrations. For patient individual surgery planning, a system should be capable of delivering a segmentation result over night. With upcoming GPU-based massive parallel approaches [19] accurate pairwise non-linear registration will soon be a matter of less than ten minutes for a pair of data sets.

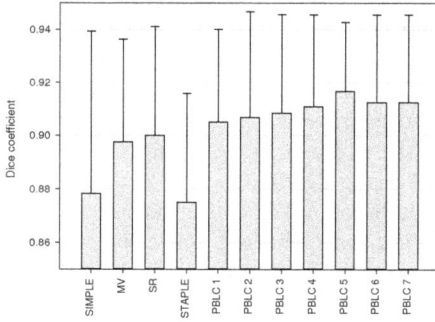

(a) Liver: Dice coefficients

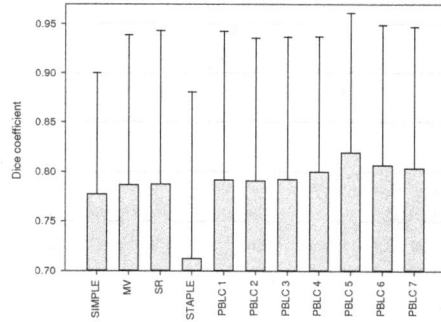

(b) Spleen: Dice coefficients

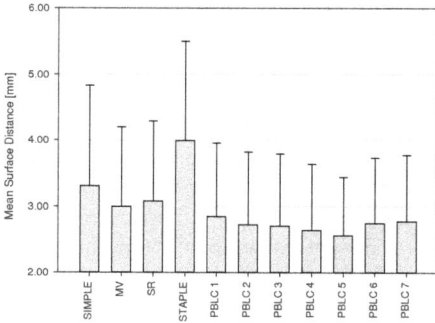

(c) Liver: Mean Surface Distances

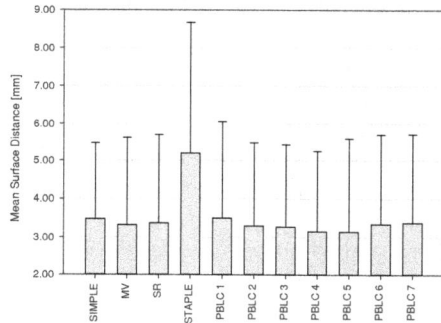

(d) Spleen: Mean Surface Distances

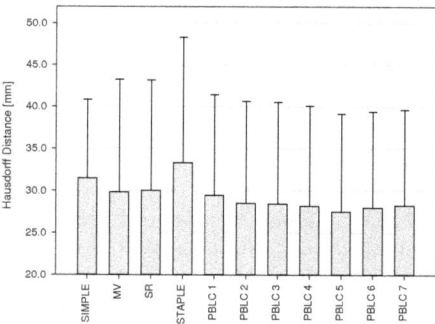

(e) Liver: Hausdorff Distances

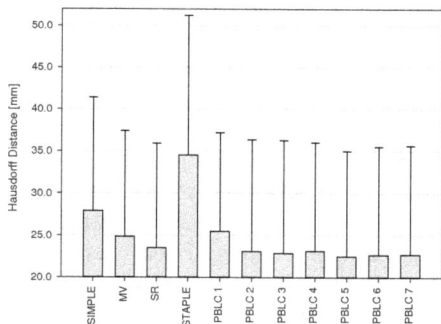

(f) Spleen: Hausdorff Distances

Figure 4: Bar charts with mean and standard deviation of the evaluation metrics.

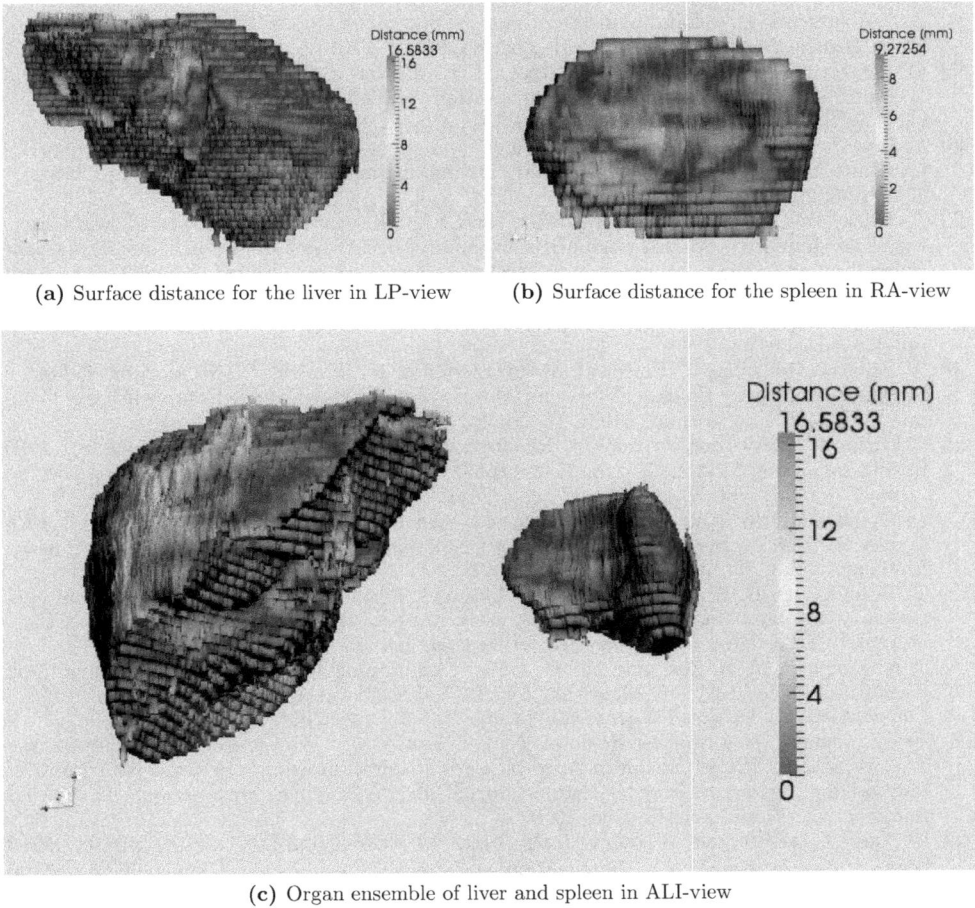

(a) Surface distance for the liver in LP-view

(b) Surface distance for the spleen in RA-view

(c) Organ ensemble of liver and spleen in ALI-view

Figure 5: Surface distances for the different organs under study of a patient.

Acknowledgements

This work is supported by the German Research Foundation (DFG-HA2355/10-1).

References

[1] M. Oda, T. Nakaoka, and T. Kitasaka, "Organ Segmentation from 3D Abdominal CT Images Based on Atlas Selection and Graph Cut," *Abdominal Imaging*, vol. 7029, pp. 181–188, 2011.

[2] R. Wolz, C. Chu, K. Misawa, K. Mori, and D. Rueckert, "Multi-organ abdominal ct segmentation using hierarchically weighted subject-specific atlases," *Medical Image Computing and Computer-Assisted Intervention: MICCAI*, vol. 7510, pp. 10–17, 2012.

[3] M. Suzuki, M. Linguraru, and K. Okada, "Multi-organ segmentation with missing organs in abdominal ct images," *Medical Image Computing and Computer-Assisted Intervention: MICCAI*, vol. 7512, pp. 418–425, 2012.

[4] A. J. Asman and B. a. Landman, "Simultaneous Segmentation and Statistical Label Fusion," *SPIE Medical Imaging 2012*, vol. 8314, pp. 83140Y–83140Y–8, 2012.

[5] M. Agarwal, E. a. Hendriks, B. C. Stoel, M. E. Bakker, J. H. C. Reiber, and M. Staring, "Local SIMPLE Multi-Atlas-based Segmentation Applied to Lung Lobe Detection on Chest CT," *SPIE Medical Imaging 2012*, vol. 8314, pp. 831410–831410–7, 2012.

[6] Y. Hao, J. Liu, Y. Duan, X. Zhang, C. Yu, T. Jiang, and Y. Fan, "Local Label Learning (L3) for Multi-Atlas based Segmentation," *SPIE Medical Imaging 2012*, vol. 8314, pp. 83142E–83142E–8, 2012.

[7] T. Chen, B. C. Vemuri, A. Rangarajan, and S. J. Eisenschenk, "Mixture of Segmenters with Discriminative Spatial Regularization and Sparse Weight Selection.," *Medical Image Computing and Computer-Assisted Intervention: MICCAI*, vol. 14, pp. 595–602, Jan. 2011.

[8] A. J. Asman and B. A. Landman, "Non-local STAPLE : An Intensity-Driven Multi-atlas Rater Model," *Medical Image Computing and Computer-Assisted Intervention: MICCAI*, pp. 426–434, 2012.

[9] A. Schmidt-Richberg, J. Ehrhardt, R. Werner, and H. Handels, "Diffeomorphic Diffusion Registration of Lung Images," Workshop Proceedings, Medical Image Computing and Computer Assisted Intervention: MICCAI, (Bejing, China), pp. 55–62, Sept. 2010.

[10] J. Ehrhardt, R. Werner, A. Schmidt-Richberg, and H. Handels, "Statistical Modeling of 4D Respiratory Lung Motion Using Diffeomorphic Image Registration.," *IEEE Transactions on Medical Imaging*, vol. 30, pp. 251–65, Feb. 2011.

[11] J. Kittler and F.M. Alkoot, "Sum versus Vote Fusion in Multiple Classifier Systems," *IEEE Transactions on Pattern Analysis and Machine Intelligence on Pattern Analysis and Machine Intelligence*, vol. 25, no. 1, pp. 110–115, 2003.

[12] T. Rohlfing, D. B. Russakoff, and C. R. Maurer, "Performance-based Classifier Combination in Atlas-based Image Segmentation using Expectation-Maximization Parameter Estimation.," *IEEE Transactions on Medical Imaging*, vol. 23, pp. 983–94, Aug. 2004.

[13] S. K. Warfield, K. H. Zou, and W. M. Wells, "Simultaneous Truth and Performance Level Estimation (STAPLE): an Algorithm for the Validation of Image Segmentation.," *IEEE Transactions on Medical Imaging*, vol. 23, pp. 903–21, July 2004.

[14] T. R. Langerak, U. a. van der Heide, A. N. T. J. Kotte, M. a. Viergever, M. van Vulpen, and J. P. W. Pluim, "Label Fusion in Atlas-based Segmentation using a Selective and Iterative Method for Performance Level Estimation (SIMPLE).," *IEEE Transactions on Medical Imaging*, vol. 29, pp. 2000–8, Dec. 2010.

[15] P. Coupé, J. V. Manjón, V. Fonov, J. Pruessner, M. Robles, and D. L. Collins, "Patch-based Segmentation using Expert Priors: Application to Hippocampus and Ventricle Segmentation.," *NeuroImage*, vol. 54, pp. 940–54, Jan. 2011.

[16] S. Osher and J. A. Sethian, "Fronts propagating with curvature-dependent speed: Algorithms based on hamilton-jacobi formulations," *Journal of Computational Physics*, vol. 79, no. 1, pp. 12–49, 1988.

[17] Y. Boykov and V. Kolmogorov, "An Experimental Comparison of Min-cut/Max-flow Algorithms for Energy Minimization in Vision.," *IEEE Transactions on Pattern Analysis and Machine Intelligence*, vol. 26, pp. 1124–37, Sept. 2004.

[18] P. Perona and J. Malik, "Scale-space and edge detection using anisotropic diffusion," *IEEE Transactions on Pattern Analysis and Machine Intelligence*, vol. 12, no. 7, pp. 629–639, 1990.

[19] M. Modat, G. R. Ridgway, Z. a. Taylor, M. Lehmann, J. Barnes, D. J. Hawkes, N. C. Fox, and S. Ourselin, "Fast Free-form Deformation using Graphics Processing Units.," *Computer Methods and Programs in Biomedicine*, vol. 98, pp. 278–84, June 2010.

Direct Haptic Volume Rendering in Lumbar Puncture Simulation

Andre Mastmeyer[a], Dirk Fortmeier[a,b], Heinz Handels[a]
[a] Institute of Medical Informatics, University of Lübeck, Lübeck, Germany
[b] Graduate School for Computing in Medicine and Life Sciences, University of Lübeck

Abstract

The preparation phase for surgical simulations often comprises the segmentation of patient data, which is needed for realistic visual and haptic rendering. Expert segmentation of 3D patient data sets can last from several hours to days. In this paper we introduce a direct haptic volume rendering approach for lumbar punctures. Preparation time spent for segmentation is much shorter and compared to our reference system nearly identical force output at the needle tip can be observed. The number of structures to be completely segmented by an expert is reduced from 11 to 3 tissues in abdominal data sets with 300 slices.

1 Introduction

Using computer-based surgical simulators surgeons can develop and refine skills harmlessly. Surgical simulators cover platforms used for preoperative planning, anatomic education and training of surgical procedures. The main components of such simulation systems, i.e volume visualization, elastic tissue deformation and haptic feedback are challenging tasks for real-time performance. Additionally, in the preparation phase the segmentation of patient data has to be carried out, which is then used for realistic rendering. Manual segmentation of 3D patient data sets can last from several hours to days depending on the necessary anatomical parts and structures.

In [1] a comprehensive survey is given about the field of "needle insertion". Needle insertion procedure simulations must mimic stiffness, cutting and friction force at the needle tip and shaft. Phases during needle insertion are: Pre-puncture pull-back, puncture incident and penetration phase. Needle deflection (bending) and tissue deformation are major problems for realistic real-time simulations.

Our reference system AcusVR delivers highly realistic haptic rendering via a force feedback device (Sensable Phantom 6DOF HF, see fig. 1) and 3D stereoscopic indirect volume rendering [2, 3]. In [3] the use of our system for lumbar punctures is evaluated by medical experts. It is pointed out that puncture simulation is a valuable tool for the training of medical students.

However, in this setup the expert segmentation of patient image data is a challenge and takes away up to 40 hours of work time per patient. To relieve this bottleneck, here a direct haptic volume rendering with partially segmented data is chosen. We analyze gray value distributions of certain tissues in a preparation step and propose to perform force feedback computation directly on the image intensity data. This is supplemented with segmentations of a few certain key structures. Transfer functions are modeled in terms of haptic parameters such as surface, stiffness and friction parameters. The method follows the same approach as commonly used in visual direct volume rendering where color and transparency transfer functions are modeled.

In case of lumbar punctures the relevant tissues present are just a few, especially the large structures "skin" and "bone" can be modeled without expert segmentation.

The paper is organized as follows: First the used data sets are described. Force calculation is briefly described as an update to the method of Lundin et al. [4]. Then we analyze the gray values of the organs and define non-overlapping tissue class intervals. These results are used to define a transfer function with haptic parameter tuples as function values. Evaluation is done qualitatively by user test and quantitatively by comparing force output from the reference system and the new approach.

2 Methods and Materials

From our previous work we use three standard abdominal CT patient data sets with pixel size 0.42, 0.77 and 1.0 mm and voxel height of 1.0 mm each. The number of slices are 240, 409 and 300. Bone, ligaments, spinal canal, intervertebral disks, fat, muscle, skin and liver are manually segmented by experts and used for haptic rendering in the setups described in our former work. The organ gray value distributions in our three patient are very similar. Thus, in the remainder of this paper the patient with the smallest field of view (see fig. 4a) shall serve as a reference patient.

Force Calculation: In proxy based haptic rendering the device tip $\vec{x}_t$ is connected via a virtual spring with stiffness constant k to a proxy $\vec{x}_p$. The algorithm controls force output by manipulation of the proxy position and spring constant. The proxy position in our simulator are calculated similar to Lundin et al. [4] in three steps (see fig. 3): First the proxy position $\vec{x}_p'$ for the surface penetrability along the normal vector of a virtual surface is determined. Then the position $\vec{x}_p''$ tangentially to the surface is calculated. Finally, a viscosity term retracts the proxy to the position $\vec{x}_p'''$. Each movement is influenced by the haptic parameters "surface" T_N, "stiffness" k and "viscosity" R. For example, surface penetration, i.e. the new proxy position $\vec{x}_p'$, is defined as follows where $\hat{N}$ is the surface normal and $\vec{d} = \vec{x}_t - \vec{x}_p$:

$$\vec{x}_p' = \begin{cases} \vec{x}_p + \hat{N}\left(\vec{d}\cdot\hat{N} - T_N/k\right) & \text{if } T_N < k\left(\vec{d}\cdot\hat{N}\right) \\ \vec{x}_p & \text{otherwise} \end{cases} \tag{1}$$

We adopted this strategy in [5] for needle insertion and used fully segmented CT image data. Here we use partially segmented CT image data and redefine the haptic parameters as follows:

$$\begin{bmatrix} T_N \\ R \\ k \end{bmatrix} = \begin{cases} (T_N^{sg}, R^{sg}, k^{sg})^T, \\ \quad \text{if material segmented} \\ (\infty, R^{bone}, k^{bone})^T, \\ \quad \text{if } I_{CT}(\vec{x}_t) > 176HU \\ \quad \text{and } |\nabla I_{CT}(\vec{x}_t)| > 30 \\ (T_N(I_{CT}(\vec{x}_t)), R(I_{CT}(\vec{x}_t)), k(I_{CT}(\vec{x}_t)))^T, \\ \quad \text{otherwise} \end{cases} \tag{2}$$

If the needle tip enters a segmented structure the constants for the corresponding material are used. Bone is detected by a combined threshold criterion using the gray values $I_{CT}(\vec{x}_t)$ and the image gradient of the Gaussian smoothed image data $|\nabla I_{CT}(\vec{x}_t)|$ with $\sigma = 2$. In case of the needle tip located in unsegmented structures, the haptic parameters are obtained from a transfer function we define in the following paragraphs.

Transfer Function Design: In a first step, based on the full segmentations of the structures, normal distributions are fitted to their gray value histograms. Bayes optimal thresholds between two adjacent tissues are then determined as intersection of the tissue distributions (see table 1a). They are termed "transition thresholds" in the following. The needle tip encounters these tissue borders modeled as thresholds while traversing the body towards the spinal canal.

During visual inspection of the gray value distribution pairs, significant overlaps in gray value distributions can be observed. In fact, only the transition from air to skin can be modeled very accurate by a simple threshold (-524 HU) as the separation of their normal distributions is highly significant with $p<0.002$. For the other transition thresholds the errors are at least minimized by the Bayesian threshold approach.

In contrast to the reference system AcusVR only the key structures flavum ligaments, intervertebral disks and spinal canal are segmented by an expert. These are small structures not well discriminable from the large structures or important key structures, i.e. the spinal canal as the target.

The transition thresholds determine intervals for certain parameter tuples. The interval sequence builds up a transfer function, which can hold color (see fig. 4c) or haptic (see fig. 4d) parameter tuples as function values. The transition thresholds actually used in the new approach are marked with plus signs in table 1a.

A visual volume rendering is carried out to confirm the adequacy of the transfer function intervals to separate tissues (see axial slice in fig. 4b). As can be seen the separation of skin (orange), fat (yellow), muscle (red), bone (white) and mixed material (blue) is plausible. The spinal canal and intervertebral disk as well as the flavum ligaments are often misclassified as muscle or mixed materials. For these important parts, expert segmentations are still used to ensure realistic haptic rendering and training effect.

Spongy bone and other soft tissues often fall into the muscle and mixed material interval from 76 to 176 HU where many gray value distributions overlap. In this area a linear function for stiffness and viscosity parameters, and a step function for surface force is used (see fig. 4d). On the right end of the gray value scale cortical bone is the tissue with the highest gray values. Finally, a conservative threshold for cortical bone of 176 HU is used in our method which allows detecting the bone shells.

In summary, a combined heuristic approach is set up. First, there is the use of the partially segmented patient data (ligaments, spinal canal, disks) to correctly reflect the location of these important structures. For the other tissues haptic transfer functions are defined. A special treatment is used for the soft tissue to cortical bone transition (see eq. 2). A simple gray value and smoothed image gradient magnitude threshold are combined to render bone boundaries more reliably. This minimizes the effect of isolated bony voxels that can occur spuriously distributed over the image apart from real bone.

Evaluation: Qualitative user testing is carried out on the three patients. The reference system AcusVR we compare our algorithm to is described in previous work from our group [2, 3]. For the automatic quantitative evaluation we implement a path steering along predefined vectors (reference paths). The virtual needle moves back and forth along the various reference paths assuming a constant velocity (see fig. 2). Following this approach we are able to obtain reproducible and comparable results for testing different haptic rendering algorithms. Moreover, force output generated this way can be compared to data from real needle insertion tests as described in [1] where the needle is moved by a robot with constant velocity.

As measures to compare the reference implementation force output and our new direct haptic rendering the sum of squared differences, maximum absolute error and p-value from paired t-tests are used.

Statistical Tests: We use two-tailed t-tests for pairwise mean comparison (see table 1a), paired t-test for force output comparison (see table 1b) and one-way ANOVA to compare more than two mean values (three patient gray value comparisons).

3 Results

We evaluated the direct haptic volume rendering with a set of 12 manually defined paths (see fig. 2) that reflect trainee experience with the system. The valid paths $v_{1,0}$ to $v_{2,4}$ reach the spinal canal target (10 paths) respectively collide with bony risk structures in case of b_0 and b_1 (2 paths).

In table 1b the errors for the manually defined paths in comparison to the reference algorithm are shown. Regarding the valid paths only the force output of path $v_{1,0}$ is significantly different from the reference path. In this case clothing is recognized by our algorithm and thus surface force is generated for this structure. A valid path very close to the reference implementations force output is depicted in fig. 5a. The differences between the forces generated by the former and new algorithm are small as pointed out in fig. 5b. On the other hand, the bone paths b_0 and b_1 show significantly different force feedbacks from the reference system as the new method generates higher forces for bone. The new algorithm presented in this paper detects cortical bone with the combined threshold criterion quite reliably and sets the surface threshold T_N to infinity. Our current setup uses a "Sensable 6DOF HF (High Force)" device which can produce higher forces effectively.

To sum up, to a certain degree the algorithm is prone to misclassification of gray values as there are always gray values from the tails of the class gray value distributions. Structures not segmented (clothing) in the reference system can lead to force output in the new approach.

One-way ANOVA comparing the gray value distributions of the same segmented organs in our three patient shows no statistical differences. This is true both in full organ segmentations, segmented single slices as well as between slices and volumetric segmentations. Regarding this, to start from scratch with new patients there are two time-saving possibilities: (1) The expert segmentation of skin, fat, muscle can be carried out in selected slices nearby the vertebrae L1, L2 and L3 to determine patient specific transition thresholds. There the disks in-between the vertebrae are aligned nearly parallel to the image axial slice. The individual tuning of the transition thresholds for every new patient is the better but more time consuming option. (2) For new patients data with similar characteristics to our cohort, haptic rendering using the provided transition thresholds will yield similar quality. Full expert segmentation of spinal, canal, intervertebral disks and ligaments is still needed in both cases.

4 Conclusions

We have presented a new approach that reduces the patient data preparation workload from 11 structures to three structures to be segmented completely. Haptic rendering performance is assessed quantitatively on one reference patient and qualitatively on three patients by user experience. Resistance of important organ borders such as bone and ligaments can be clearly perceived. However, the segmentation of some risk, target and haptical important structures still cannot be avoided as errors are not tolerable here to keep the training effect realistic.

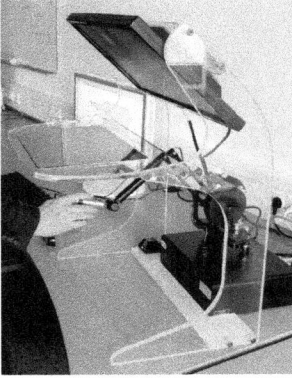

Figure 1: The haptic device and workbench.

Figure 2: Valid reference paths (green) and paths puncturing bone (red).

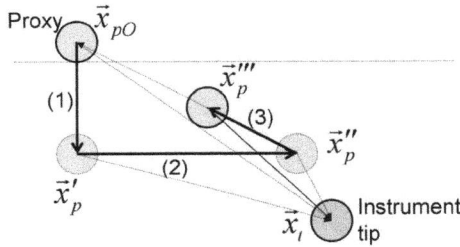

Figure 3: Proxy recalculation starting from the old position $\vec{x}_{pO}$ as defined by Lundin et al. [4].

Transition	Thresh. [HU]	$p<$
Air vs Skin	-524$^+$	0.008
Skin vs Fat	-134$^+$	0.24
Fat vs Muscle	-59$^+$, 101	0.6
Fat vs Ligament	76$^+$	0.4
Muscle vs Ligament	-94, 96	0.5
Muscle vs Bone	-104, 106	0.24
Fat vs Bone	116	0.17

(a) Bayesian "transition thresholds" for reference patient, p-values indicate tissue class separation. Plus signs indicate gray values used in the definition of the transfer functions.

Path	Sq. Err. sums [N^2]	Max. error [N]	$p<$
$v_{1,0}$	8.4107	1.98612	0.033*
$v_{1,1}$	0.0312021	0.164136	0.423
$v_{1,2}$	6.76678	1.50206	0.085
$v_{1,3}$	0.507304	0.441025	0.452
$v_{1,4}$	1.72941	0.5	0.395
$v_{2,0}$	8.14373	1.6514	0.196
$v_{2,1}$	2.51276	0.5	0.897
$v_{2,2}$	2.98023	0.5	0.650
$v_{2,3}$	3.63139	0.5	0.896
$v_{2,4}$	2.62	0.5	0.195
b_0	74.501	3.16717	0.003*
b_1	33.1852	2.74801	0.044*

(b) Comparison to reference algorithm for user relevant paths. Asterisks indicate significantly different force feedback.

Table 1: Tables contain (a) the threshold analysis and (b) evaluation of reference paths.

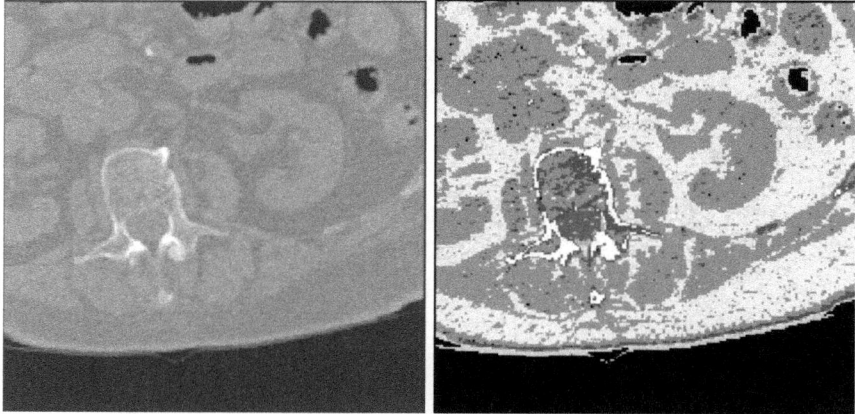

(a) An axial slice of the reference data .

(b) Transfer function applied to the axial slice from the left. The target "spinal canal" is marked as overlay (green).

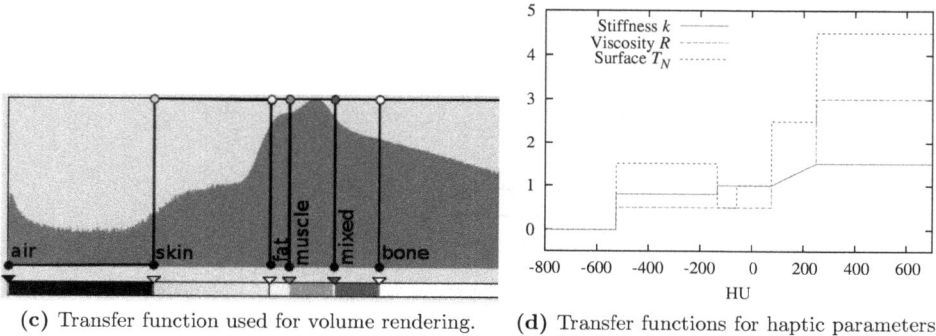

(c) Transfer function used for volume rendering.

(d) Transfer functions for haptic parameters.

Figure 4: From graphic to haptic volume rendering.

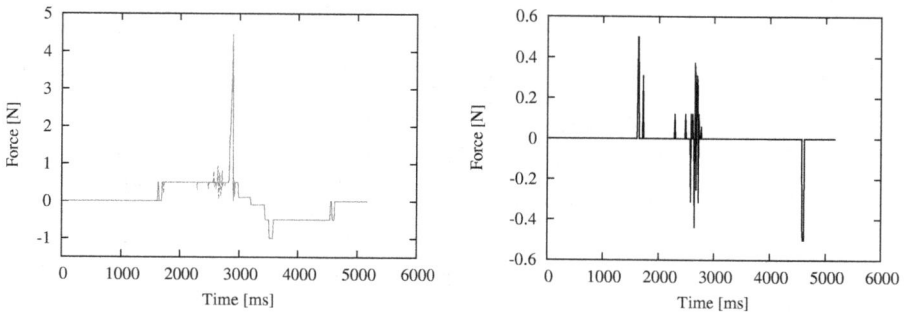

(a) Force outputs on valid path force curve $(v_{2,1})$. The transfer function based haptic rendering (red) and reference implementation (green) behave nearly identical.

(b) Difference force curve.

Figure 5: Force output and difference.

Acknowledgement

This work is supported by the German Research Foundation (DFG, HA 2355/10-1).

References

[1] N. Abolhassani, R. Patel, and M. Moallem, "Needle insertion into soft tissue: a survey.," *Medical engineering & physics*, vol. 29, no. 4, pp. 413–31, 2007.

[2] M. Färber, E. Hoeborn, D. Dalek, F. Hummel, C. Gerloff, C. A. Bohn, and H. Handels, "Training and evaluation of lumbar punctures in a VR-environment using a 6DOF haptic device," *MMVR16/Stud Health Technol Inform*, vol. 132, pp. 112–114, 2008.

[3] M. Färber, F. Hummel, C. Gerloff, and H. Handels, "Virtual reality simulator for the training of lumbar punctures," *Methods Inf Med*, vol. 48, no. 5, pp. 493–501, 2009.

[4] K. Lundin, A. Ynnerman, and B. Gudmundsson, "Proxy-based haptic feedback from volumetric density data," *Eurohaptics Conference*, pp. 104–109, 2002.

[5] M. Färber, J. Heller, and H. Handels, "Simulation and training of lumbar punctures using haptic volume rendering and a 6DOF haptic device," *Proc. of SPIE Medical Imaging*, vol. 6509, pp. 0F1–0F8, 2007.

Infinite Science
Publishing

www.ingramcontent.com/pod-product-compliance
Lightning Source LLC
Chambersburg PA
CBHW061928190326
41458CB00009B/2685